A Sparrowhawk's Lament

How British Breeding Birds of Prey are Faring

David Cobham

with illustrations by Bruce Pearson

DEDICATION

To my wife Liza, my best friend and the love of my life.

Published by Princeton University Press,
41 William Street, Princeton, New Jersey 08540
In the United Kingdom: Princeton University Press, 6 Oxford Street,
Woodstock, Oxfordshire OX20 1TW
nathist.press.princeton.edu

Requests for permission to reproduce material from this work should be sent to
Permissions, Princeton University Press

British Library Cataloging-in-Publication Data is available

Library of Congress Control Number 2014932451
ISBN 978-0-691-15764-1

Production and design by **WILD**Guides Ltd., Old Basing, Hampshire UK.
Printed in Malaysia

10 9 8 7 6 5 4 3 2 1

CONTENTS

FOREWORD

All birds are equal, but some are more equal than others. It's a simple truth that as a group our raptors command more attention than the majority of our other bird fauna, and always have done. I'm often asked by young and old which is my favourite bird. It's a very difficult question but only because I struggle to separate Sparrowhawk and Kestrel. And when I bounce the question back, Peregrine, Golden Eagle and Osprey frequently betray a similar passion for birds of prey.

I spent the summer of '76 returning a brood of Barn Owls to the wild in Hampshire. It was a magical task and certainly a formative influence on my early fascination with both predators and their conservation. They had come indirectly from David Cobham but it was many years before we met and our mutual obsession for British raptors properly realized. Thus, when I heard he was writing this book it was eagerly anticipated.

This book has many strengths: it is not only crammed with ornithological references but also cultural, historical, sociological, military, literary and artistic, making it a fascinating and refreshing read. And it is also deliberately contemporary, a detailed 'snapshot' of these birds right now, in terms of numbers, population trends and a wide range of attitudes. But for me its real strengths are its very personal reflections on a lifetime of interest and concern, an intimate exposition of boundless curiosity and a rare but essential pragmatic modesty when it comes to fact and expertise. At no point does the author pose as the authority; he meets and learns from those at the very top of their fields or those properly qualified to comment on everything from issues of persecution to secretive aspects of the birds' behaviour. And as he has not shied from those issues, this is also a frank exposé of a guild of birds struggling to survive in the twenty-first century. It outlines conservation successes but equally highlights the abject plight of species such as the Hen Harrier, Golden Eagle and Goshawk, all birds still burdened by deliberate, brutal and illegal persecution.

I read this book, enjoyed it, learned a lot and ultimately, through its infectious enthusiasm, I felt inspired to work harder myself when it comes to finding solutions to ensure the future survival of this unique and very special group of birds. It does British birds of prey a great service, and boy do they need it – so I hope that you will read it and be suitably inspired too.

Chris Packham

INTRODUCTION

In what state that ever I be,
Timor mortis conturbat me.

As I me walkëd one morning,
I heard a bird both weep and sing,
This was the tenor of his talking:
Timor mortis conturbat me.

I asked this birdë what he meant;
He said, 'I am a musket gent;
For dread of death I am nigh shent,
Timor mortis conturbat me.

'Jesus Christ, when he should die,
To his Father loud gan he cry,
"Father," he said, "in Trinity,
Timor mortis conturbat me."

'When I shall die, know I no day;
In what place or country, can I not say;
Therefore this songë sing I may:
Timor mortis conturbat me.'

I was in hospital waiting for an operation for colon cancer when I first read this anonymous fifteenth-century poem, which I have called *A Sparrowhawk's Lament*. It set me thinking. In 15 minutes they would be coming to wheel me down to the theatre. Times like these concentrate the mind wonderfully. Why, in this poem, is a male Sparrowhawk worrying about the fear of dying? Then the bond between man and hawk or falcon was iron-clad. For over 3,000 years man had depended on their hunting skills for his next meal. Was the Sparrowhawk able to look into a crystal ball and foresee the future of his species – an echo of Leonard Cohen growling "*the future it is murder*:" persecution and pesticides?

This thought passed through my mind as I was wheeled down to the theatre. The surgeon popped in to say hello as the canula was fitted. The anaesthetist offered comfort as the anaesthetic swelled in my veins. The clock at the end of the room blurred and as an icy black curtain swooshed up my arm, I am sure I heard a bell ring followed by a chorister singing *Timor mortis conturbat me*.

The next thing I remember was a disembodied voice saying, "David, come on, David." A face swam into focus. It was a nurse in the high-dependency unit checking that I was all right. I had shared the male Sparrowhawk's fear of death. There was now an indefinable bond between us.

As I convalesced I began to wonder if all our British breeding birds of prey shared the Sparrowhawk's same anxiety of the fear of death? At the beginning of the nineteenth century game preservationists embarked on a reign of systematic and vicious persecution,

---

Timor mortis conturbat me is a Latin phrase commonly found in late medieval Scottish and English poetry that translates as 'fear of death worries me.'

ensuring that the Goshawk was extinct by 1889, the Marsh Harrier by 1898, the Osprey by 1908, the Honey Buzzard by 1911 and the White-tailed Eagle by 1916. Thankfully, since 1981 all birds of prey have been fully protected by law. I decided on a plan of action. I would go on a quest to find out how each of these species was faring. As a wildlife filmmaker and conservationist of birds of prey over the last 40 years, I wanted to share my memories of encounters with these thrilling predators. Foremost among those accompanying me on my travels would be the world-famous wildlife artist Bruce Pearson, whom I first met, in Antarctica, in 1976.

There are 15 species of birds of prey breeding in the British Isles: Osprey, Honey Buzzard, Red Kite, White-tailed Eagle, Marsh Harrier, Hen Harrier, Montagu's Harrier, Goshawk, Sparrowhawk, Common Buzzard, Golden Eagle, Kestrel, Merlin, Hobby and Peregrine Falcon. At the beginning of each chapter I will detail the population of that particular bird of prey in the British Isles. These figures have been extracted from *Population Estimates of Birds In Great Britain and the United Kingdom*, a survey carried out by The Royal Society for the Protection of Birds and published in *British Birds* magazine in 2013. It shows whether a bird's population is increasing, declining or remaining stable, and when the survey was carried out.

I will set out to meet the writers, artists, poets, wildlife filmmakers and television presenters who have done so much to rehabilitate birds of prey in the public's mind. I will also talk with a wide cross-section of scientists, conservationists and all those, who strive to safeguard our precious raptors. I want to carry out a detailed appraisal across the British Isles to discover the true state of our relationship with our British birds of prey and how they are faring, and how many still share the Sparrowhawk's fear of death implied in the phrase *Timor mortis conturbat me*.

THE SPARROWHAWK

British Isles population (2006–10): 35,000 pairs (declining)

Before starting on our quest, Bruce asked me about the incident that had sparked my interest in the Sparrowhawk. I told him that my Damascene moment with a Sparrowhawk was not on the road to Damascus but on the road to Docking in Norfolk. It was midsummer and I was following another car. There were woods on either side of the road. The car in front of me swerved slightly. I slowed down and saw the reason why. A bird lay twitching on the side of the road.

It was a male Sparrowhawk, not much bigger than a Mistle Thrush. I picked it up. Its orange-red eye was still open. Its beak opened and a dribble of bloody mucous eased out. I felt a shudder pass through the bird's body. Its eye lost its fiery brilliance and the lid sealed over. The Sparrowhawk was dead.

I went into the wood a short way and laid the corpse down amongst the brambles and bracken. As I looked down I felt there was now an indefinable bond between us. This was going to be a detective story. I had to find out about the living bird, its place in our history and culture and why the male Sparrowhawk featured in the poem *A Sparrowhawk's Lament* had this fear of death.

My first port of call was Professor Ian Newton, a highly respected scientist who had spent over 27 years studying Sparrowhawks in Dumfriesshire. It is probably the most detailed and longest-running study undertaken of any bird of prey population. He replied, "Sparrowhawks are not the easiest birds to watch, and are rather unpredictable in their appearance. As a result most of one's sightings occur by chance. The small birds which gather at garden feeders are, of course, well known to attract Sparrowhawks. The problem is one can sit for hours before a Sparrowhawk appears, and then get only a split-second view of it."

He made an excellent suggestion. In the breeding season Sparrowhawk watching is much easier. In early spring they can be seen displaying over the wood in which they intend to nest. Once the eggs have been laid the birds can be watched from a hide in a nearby tree as they raise their young. He went on to suggest, however, that "for seeing large numbers of flying Sparrowhawks, there is nothing better than sitting at a migration watchpoint, such as Falsterbo in southern Sweden, where hundreds of Sparrowhawks can fly over each day in the autumn migration season."

There was one other person whose opinion I valued, Dave Culley. He has created a unique website called *Sparrowhawk Island*. It involves no fewer than 16 cameras set up around a copse on the island where he lives in Cheshire, all of which record a pair of Sparrowhawks throughout the breeding season. He gets 39,000 hits a week. Dave has been recording Sparrowhawk behaviour for ten years, observing three different pairs during that time. He has recently edited the best material from the cameras into a fantastic DVD, *The Secret Life of the Sparrowhawk*.

I had held the dead Sparrowhawk in my hands and had tantalizing glimpses of Sparrowhawks from time to time. I needed a reference point if I was going to describe the bird in detail. I explained my problem to Dave and in a couple of days he emailed me a stunning, pin-sharp portrait, beautifully lit, of his wild adult male. I gazed in awe at the photograph. How could anyone contemplate killing such a handsome bird? The wildlife author and journalist, Mark Cocker, has called it 'arguably our most beautiful raptor.'

In his book *The Hill of Summer*, J.A. Baker writes of the Sparrowhawk 'The male Sparrowhawk lives very close to the edge of things. He is a primitive, an aboriginal among birds, savage in killing because his power is small. His long legs look thin and fragile, like stems of amber.'

The Sparrowhawk has developed some interesting adaptations in its role as a deadly hunter of small birds. It has a bony ridge immediately above the eye, below its white eye-stripe, which protects the bird's eyes when it plunges into thick foliage after prey. The Sparrowhawk's eyes change colour as it matures: they are greenish-yellow when it fledges and a month later are lemon-yellow. From then on they become darker and in males change to orange and may even become blood-red in older birds. The bill is black at the tip shading to blue where the bill meets the waxy, yellow cere. The yellow legs of the Sparrowhawk are very long, useful for grabbing prey from a dense hedge. Its feet are also specially adapted with fleshy protrusions so that it can close them tightly without injuring itself. The female after landing on the nest during the incubation period walks in on her knuckles so as not to puncture the eggs. The middle toe is longer than the rest and its talons, like an assassin's dagger, are needle sharp.

Like many birds of prey the female Sparrowhawk is larger than the male; in fact she is almost twice his size. She is also a much plainer bird lacking the handsome blue back or chestnut breast feathers of the male. She is much bulkier and sometimes mistaken for a male Goshawk.

In flight one notices that the Sparrowhawk's wings are short and rounded and the tail is long and barred underneath. It is this long tail that enables the bird to brake to a dead halt in the air.

Years ago, for the first time, I saw a Sparrowhawk do just that. It was the end of February, a beautiful day, and my wife Liza and I were walking in the pine woods bordering the sand dunes at Holkham in Norfolk. Suddenly there was a commotion as a panic-stricken, shrieking Redwing flew towards us with a male Sparrowhawk zigzagging through the tree trunks in hot pursuit. For an instant, I registered a frozen frame of the Sparrowhawk; hooked beak, eyes blazing, long legs with black, scimitar talons spread reaching forward ready to grab. At the last moment it saw us, flared its tail, turned through ninety degrees and disappeared towards the sand dunes and the sea.

I watched the Redwing as it flew off, still swearing vigorously, to the safety of a hedge at the edge of the woods. We continued on our walk and, almost immediately, bumped into our great friend the wildlife artist, Bruce Pearson, easel set up, painting away. As if on cue, we all said "Did you see the Sparrowhawk?" That painting is now in our living room and not long afterwards my brother Richard sent me a single tail feather from a male Sparrowhawk, with four dark bars top and underside. It is Sellotaped to the frame.

Sparrowhawks do not hunt all the time – they spend most of their day perched within the canopy of a tree, just watching. The cryptic markings on their breast feathers break up their outline, making them very difficult to spot. They will move from tree to tree watching for the right opportunity. They then make a short, silent dash and snatch the unsuspecting prey from its perch by a single taloned foot, with the dexterity of one of Fagin's pickpockets. Their other hunting method, to which their short, rounded wings and long tail are supremely adapted, is low-level hedgerow hopping.

When I was driving home from King's Lynn in Norfolk, there was one long hedgerow along a minor road where almost invariably I used to see a female Sparrowhawk. This was *her* hunting flight. Flap, flap, flap, glide. This is seat-of-the-pants flying, inches from the ground, and then a quick flick upwards and a barrel roll over the hedge onto unsuspecting prey on the other side. To travel at such speed, so close to the ground and with the ability to pass through the smallest gap in a hedge, Sparrowhawks must have the equivalent of the head-up display in a ground attack fighter. They are flying by wire, their reflexes making life or death decisions based on memories programmed into hunting skills.

In general, during the breeding season, male Sparrowhawks hunt for small birds within their woodland territory while the females, once the young are old enough, will range much farther afield in the open countryside hunting for anything up to the size of a Wood Pigeon.

The decisions on where to hunt are probably based on experience. One Sparrowhawk will have made a successful kill on sparrows after passing through a particular gap in a hedge, another knows that flicking over a garden wall will line it up for a strike on Collared Doves feeding on a bird table.

The Sparrowhawk's kill does not employ the finesse of the Peregrine, which administers a *coup de grâce* by breaking its prey's neck. The Sparrowhawk simply seizes its prey and squeezes it to death with its needle-sharp talons. This may take some time and quite often the hawk will pluck and break into its prey while it is still alive.

Chris Packham talking about a Sparrowhawk kill: "If the death of a Greenfinch on your patio as the Sparrowhawk crouches over it plucking its feathers, throwing them to

the breeze, is too grisly for you, you are shutting your mind to what is just a moment in the beautiful complexity of the ecosystem to which the Sparrowhawk belongs."

Ian Newton had written 'don't waste time watching for kills.' Nevertheless I thought I would have a go. Our kitchen window looks out onto the lawn and across the chicken run to the water meadows beyond. Just by the gate into the chicken run we have put up a trough bird feeder. Running alongside it is a privet hedge which continues on to border the right-hand side of the chicken run. Nearer to the house is an ornamental pear tree under which we have hung a vertical feeder.

This is an extract from my journal for 7th January 2010, my best day's watching:

> 'Heavy snow, four inches at least. -2°C at night. As I'm washing up after breakfast I see the trough feeder is filled with Chaffinches, House Sparrows and two or three Reed Buntings. Wood Pigeons, Stock Doves and Collared Doves barge in and push the smaller birds out. Suddenly all the birds take flight, disappearing into the privet hedge. A female Sparrowhawk flashes through left to right dashing for the upright feeder, stands on its tail, having missed its target, and flies straight back past the kitchen window to its willow tree lookout next door. About ten minutes later all the small birds again scatter for cover except for two Blue Tits and a Great Tit feeding on the upright feeder. A gun metal blue streak flashes left to right across the lawn, does a 45 degree barrel roll revealing a burnt sienna and yellow flash as the musket makes a grab by the feeder. Then there were two. It's so quick, it almost deceives the eye.'

Sparrowhawks have probably been killing in this opportunistic way since Mesolithic times, ten thousand years ago, when they were first identified accurately through archaeological remains. The late Derek Yalden and Umberto Albarella in their book *The History of British Birds*, published in 2009, used the Białowieza National Park on the Polish–Belorussian border as an example of the wide range of habitats that would have existed in Mesolithic Britain. The bird life there had been very accurately surveyed enabling Yalden and Albarella to extrapolate the likely population of individual species during Mesolithic times. They estimated that the population of Sparrowhawks in Britain would then have been about 22,000 pairs.

The first writer to mention the Sparrowhawk was Aristotle (384–322 BC) in his *Historia Animalium* '… all the kinds of eagle, and the kites and both hawks – both the pigeon-hawk and the sparrow-hawk (these differ greatly in size from one another) …'

The Sparrowhawk is mentioned in the first book in English to deal with falconry. *The Boke of St Albans* was supposedly written by Dame Juliana Berners and published in 1496. It dealt specifically with the laws of ownership of different birds of prey in Tudor England and what rank of person should be allowed to fly them.

> An eagle for an Emperor
> A gyrfalcon for a King
> A falcon and a tiercel for a Prince
> A falcon of the rock for a Duke
> A falcon peregrine for an Earl
> A bastard for a Lord
> A saker and a sakeret for a Knight
> A lanner for a Squire

A merlin for a Lady
A hobby for a young Squire
A sparrowhawk for a Priest
A musket for an Holy-water Clerk
A kestrel for a Knave.

Some of the terms used need clarifying. 'A falcon of the rock' probably meant a red-plumaged falcon, a first year bird. The most confusing reference is to a 'bastard.' There are two possibilities either a buzzard – not a great bird for a Lord to fly – or, as some have suggested, a bastard bird, a Saker × Lanner cross.

Near the bottom of the list we find 'A musket for an Holy-water Clerk.' Johnson's dictionary defines the word musket as being fly-sized, derived either from the French *mousquet* or the Italian *mosquetto.* It has also been defined as the name for a male hawk of a small kind, for example the Sparrowhawk.

Each parish had a Holy-water Clerk who was responsible for distributing the Holy Water, which was sacramental, but not capable of absolving sins. Holy-water Clerks should preferably be unmarried. They led a pretty austere life. But they were allowed to fly a male Sparrowhawk, a tricky bird to train. Ecclesiastics were as devoted to falconry as their lords and masters.

Such a man was Thomas Weelkes, organist and instructor of the choristers at Chichester Cathedral between 1602–23. He was renowned for his church music and his madrigals. Unfortunately he fell out with the Cathedral authorities on account of his heavy drinking and immoderate behaviour. He was dismissed and then reinstated. He was obviously interested in hawks for he wrote the music for a madrigal dedicated to a *Sparrowhawk Proud.*

A Sparrowhawk proud did hold in wicked jail
Music's sweet chorister, the Nightingale,
To whom with sighs she said: "O set me free!
And in my song I'll praise no bird but thee."
The hawk replied, "I will not lose my diet
To let a thousand such enjoy their quiet."

The first bird book, *Avium Praecipuarum,* was published in 1544. William Turner, who wrote it, has been called the Father of British Ornithology. In it Turner commented on the natural history writings of Aristotle and Pliny but it also contained first hand observations of birds that he had identified. He named 120 birds, including the *sparhauc,* the Sparrowhawk.

In 1538 Henry VIII decreed that each head of family acquire a surname for himself and his family. *Sparhauc* was how William Turner spelled Sparrowhawk. So, just under 500 years ago, an Englishman called Sparhauc handed his name down to his sons. Over the years, to make it easier to pronounce, the *hauc* was eliminated. The addition of the letter *s* to denote Spark's son came later and so the family name of Sparks was established.

John Ray's *Ornithologia* published in 1676, first in Latin and then in English, was written with Francis Willughby. It mentioned the Sparrowhawk among its 190 descriptions of British birds. It is a very significant book because it tried to bring a sense of order to a hitherto random assembly of notes and observations, in an attempt at classification.

It was not until 1735 that Carl Linnaeus, from Uppsala in Sweden, provided a simple solution with his *Systema Naturae*. Each living thing was given a name, usually in Latin, and placed in a four-tier system – class, order, genus and species. Twenty-three years later Linnaeus added a refinement that was to remain the benchmark in classification for many years to come. Each species was to be given a double name: a combination of the genus and the species names. The Sparrowhawk became *Accipiter nisus*.

The legend of Nisos, which gives the Sparrowhawk its second name, is descended from Greek mythology. Nisos was King of Megara. Minos harboured a grudge against Nisos so he attacked Megara and put it under siege. Nisos had a special purple lock of hair, which kept him safe from harm. He also had a beautiful daughter, Scylla. She looked down from the battlements, saw Minos and fell in love with him. While Nisos was asleep she snipped off the special lock of hair, so delivering the town into the hands of Minos.

As he died, Nisos changed into a Sparrowhawk. Scylla was snubbed by Minos. He thought she had behaved appallingly. Heartbroken, she threw herself into the sea and was drowned. As a punishment she was turned into a small bird. Thereafter Nisos, the Sparrowhawk, continually chased Scylla, the small bird, ensuring that she suffered in perpetuity for her treachery. It is a beautiful legend but it didn't get me any closer to understanding the Sparrowhawk's fear of death.

At the end of the eighteenth century the systematists were still arguing about classification when ornithology took a new turn. Ecology's founding father was a Hampshire parson, the Reverend Gilbert White. He kept a detailed diary of everything he saw in the natural world. His book *The Natural History of Selborne* has probably been reprinted more times than any other book. Swallows and House Martins were his particular favourites. 'As soon as an hawk appears he (a swallow) calls all the swallows and martins about him; who pursue in a body, and buffet and strike their enemy till they have driven him back from the village, darting down from above on his back, and rising in a perpendicular line in perfect security.'

The next subject on Ian Newton's list of Sparrowhawk behaviour, which he suggested I should study, was their courtship and, in particular, their aerial display.

There was generally a pair of Sparrowhawks that nested on the Sculthorpe Moor Reserve in Norfolk and I rang Nigel Middleton, the Hawk and Owl Trust reserve warden, to ask if they had started displaying yet. In the middle of April it was still incredibly cold. "It'll have to warm up a lot before the birds will even think of it," Nigel said.

I spent several days watching a section of wood in which the Sparrowhawks had nested the previous year. There was no displaying but plenty of activity. Several times I saw the female slip out of the corner of the wood and return with an item of prey towards where they had nested before. It was getting very frustrating. This is an extract from my journal:

'17/5/10. At about 13.00 two Sparrowhawks appeared over the Sladden woods, above the reddish-leaved poplars. They were at a good height just in vision to the naked eye. They began what I'd been so anxious to see, their courtship display. The male climbed quickly above the female, ringing up, then dived vertically passing the female. He threw up at the end of his dive to grapple with her, talon to talon, beak to beak. Too far away to hear screaming. The two birds kept on soaring drifting out over the reserve, repeating their display routine 10 or 15 times. Very exciting. At last I've seen it.'

A few days later I had a phone call from Dave Culley. "I'm sending you a clip of the male Sparrowhawk displaying; it's quite unique, I learn something new every day." He was quite right: the male, all fluffed up, was on a branch above the female which was out of sight. He was working himself into a frenzy, bobbing up and down and nibbling his taloned feet. This continued for about a minute before he suddenly turned round and showed his vent, again all fluffed up, to the female before flying off. Quite simply, he was demonstrating what an attractive mate he was; that he had big talons and was an exceptional hunter.

The threat of birds of prey to the rearing of game for shooting was quickly recognized by landowners and in 1831 the Game Act was passed, legalizing the role of gamekeepers. A.E. Knox, writing in 1854 and then living near Petworth in Sussex, had been trying to increase the number of Pheasants in the wild on his estate. An extract from his diary reads: 'June 23rd, 1854. Denyer the keeper has just come up to the house, to tell me that during the last two days he has missed several of the young Pheasants. He had the mortification of seeing a hawk, out of shot, carrying off one of the young Pheasants in its claws.'

Three days later, on returning home, Knox noted 'The first object that met my eyes on driving up to the hall door was a row of dead Sparrowhawks, seven in number, which D. had impaled, each upon its own peculiar stick, with its wings spread and tail expanded, as if to make the most of it: there were the Patagonian old female, and the little cock, with his blue back and red breast, and five immature birds, some of them larger than the latter.' The term *Patagonian* seems rather obscure but the Oxford English Dictionary describes it as meaning huge, large, immense: a reference to the tall inhabitants of that region. It was therefore quite applicable to the larger hen Sparrowhawk.

That the Sparrowhawk was not persecuted into extinction must have been largely due its natural behaviour of keeping to the woods. Nevertheless determined efforts to exterminate them were widespread. Two factors helped the Sparrowhawk. First, Gilbert White's *The Natural History of Selborne* stimulated a burgeoning enthusiasm for natural history throughout the middle years of the nineteenth century. Secondly, the horrors of the First World War gave a reprieve to Sparrowhawks as gamekeepers joined up and were drafted into the trenches.

By the 1920s bird enthusiasts had forsaken the gun for a pair of binoculars or telescope. The *British Birds* journal during this period published more and more detailed studies of birds and their behaviour, including the Sparrowhawk. J.H. Owen, published five detailed reports between 1926–36. The first study was on the eggs of the Sparrowhawk. Towards the end of his study, he notes: 'In 1925 the keepers seemed to be more thoroughly at work in this neighbourhood and I found hawks hanging in woods where they had not been molested, except by myself, for years.'

Perhaps this was because the First World War was over and keepers, who had joined up, were returning to their former occupation with renewed zeal. Over the next 20 years, Owen continued studying Sparrowhawks, with undiminished energy, and contributed papers to *British Birds* on their diet and hunting habits.

In 1937 the first monograph on the Sparrowhawk was published. *The Sparrowhawk's Eyrie* is quite a short book, but a remarkable achievement as the author, W.W. Nicholas, was an engineer with a full-time job. Bird-watching and photography were his hobbies. Brian Vesey-Fitzgerald in his foreword says 'Mr Nicholas puts forward much – and strong – evidence in favour of the Sparrowhawk at least so far as game is concerned. You may

even think it is conclusive evidence. And he has many interesting things to say about small birds and Sparrowhawk.'

It is a charming book written by a very enthusiastic amateur. Here he describes a fascinating passage of behaviour: 'The cock bird swooped up with food and startled both hen and young. The former turned round and snapped at him. He immediately took wing with a loud scream, dropping the food to earth as he did so, to be followed by the hen.'

For a moment I thought I had stumbled upon what had made the male Sparrowhawk fearful of dying. The author calls this a family quarrel but I think the cock had not called on approaching the nest as he should have done. It may be some comfort to the male Sparrowhawk to know that Professor Ian Newton, during 27 years of research on Sparrowhawks, only found six males killed during the breeding season in this way.

It was reading this excellent book that reminded me that the third aspect of a Sparrowhawk's year that Ian Newton suggested I should concentrate on was their breeding season. 'With a hide in a nearby tree,' he wrote, 'the nest can, of course, be watched at close quarters, and the feeding of the young and other parental behaviour be seen in detail.'

At the time in question I had just recovered from an operation to repair a hernia and was also coping with a leaking mitral valve in my heart which, now and then, left me very short of breath. The prospect of climbing ladders to a hide up in a tree was a bit daunting. I would have to rely on Dave Culley again. Here are some notes I made while watching video footage on his *Sparrowhawk Island* website.

'10/3/08. 08.25. The nest is in a hawthorn tree. An inverted 'crown of thorns.' Female, walking round, fussily arranging sticks into a bowl shape. Stamps sticks into place with her feet. Pauses, inspects her handy work. She pushes a recalcitrant stick with beak quite violently. Settles down into nest, waggles about to make it more bowl-shaped.'

It is increasing day-length, the photoperiod, that kick-starts the Sparrowhawk's breeding season. I marvel that the first six weeks, when the male feeds the incubating female and the newly hatched young, are programmed to coincide with the fledging of the tit family – their main prey item. The tits are, in turn, tied to the emergence of Winter Moth caterpillars, which feed on the foliage of trees.

'14/4/08. 07.25. The plucking post, a broken branch of willow tree lying horizontally. The female is very relaxed, puffed up, foot up. She starts to preen her breast feathers. Male enters from right, lands on her back and copulates. It is over in an instant. Male exits. Female rouses and preens.'

'13/6/08. 09.15. The female is on the edge of the nest watching first egg hatch. There are 5 eggs altogether. Chick struggling out of egg: enormous head, very thin neck and almost naked body, last to emerge. Chick struggles right out, clear of the egg and collapses. Female inches forward and inspects the chick. Now she waddles forward, settles down to brood chick and remaining eggs.'

'24/6/08. 19.30. The female is feeding the chicks. Their eyes are button-black. She seems to dish out food equally – quite large gobbets of meat now. All stuffed with food, crops bulging, trying to stay awake. One gives in, its head falling down to lie on the side of the nest. Soon all of them crash out. Female stands on guard, one leg up, relaxed.'

The male chicks develop faster than the female chicks so that all of them get a fair share of the food brought in.

> '8/7/08. 07.35. Chicks are now looking like Sparrowhawks. The female arrives with food. Her beak rips through prey. She is an elegant butcher. It is delicately served up. She leaves. The chicks eyes now green-grey. They start wing flapping. No lift off. They face outwards unlike eyass Peregrines that face inwards to avoid falling from the nest ledge.'

> '14/7/08. 08.35. Good weather. One chick left in nest, lying down. Others perched on branches nearby. One of them is preening, chin scratching, wing stretching. There is still some down at base of its tail. Nest flattened, flies everywhere.'

> '15/7/08. 08.45. An empty nest. Two chicks perched on a branch nearby. The others are out of sight. The male dashes in with food, exits at speed. All the young appear and take it in turns to feed. There are four females, one male. When feeding they are up to 45 pulls a minute.'

> '20/7/08. 07.55. The empty nest with relics of kills. It's like a battlefield, bones picked clean, bleaching in the sun. Dave Culley tells me that one of the young Sparrowhawks has made its first kill down on the spinney floor, a Collared Dove.'

Many juvenile Sparrowhawks die in the first months after they leave the nest. They fly into windows, are hit by cars, and have accidents in all sorts of other ways. More die during the hard weather of January, February and March. Research also shows that juveniles take time to hone their hunting skills.

> '29/3/11. 14.15. A juvenile hen Sparrowhawk plunged into the bottom of the privet hedge after finches feeding at bird station. Then took stand on the gate into the chicken run. It looked around, plunged in again. No luck. Then back up on feeding trough. Another dive into the hedge. Nothing. It was doing what Richard Mabey calls 'chasing shadows.'

> '2/4/11. 12.15. From the kitchen window saw the juvenile female Sparrowhawk perched on the bird feeding trough, looking very disconsolate. It had probably just missed a strike. A cock Pheasant strolled beneath her, she took no notice. A Magpie flew from the chicken run and perched on the far end of the trough. The Sparrowhawk suddenly became alert, eyeing it up and down. Was she going to make a grab for it? The Magpie started sidling down the trough. The Sparrowhawk suddenly roused itself, fluffed up its feathers to increase its size. The Magpie got bolder, took another hop forward and made a slashing motion at the Sparrowhawk with its bill. The Sparrowhawk flew off.'

As I riffled through the pages of last year's notebook two feathers fluttered out, the tail feathers of a male Sparrowhawk. I had picked them up under a particular tree in a nearby wood, where a Sparrowhawk sometimes roosted. All birds moult regularly and Sparrowhawks have a tough life. They depend on their feathers being in tip-top condition if they are going to be successful hunters. They moult in summer because there is plenty of food about, vital for growing good new feathers. They do not lose all their feathers at once. If that was the case the bird would be unable to fly and would starve to death. Twelve feathers make up the Sparrowhawk's tail. If you split them up into left and right you would perhaps get the centre two feathers dropped first, then the outermost ones. This is to ensure that the growing feathers, which are very fragile, have always got the support of the old feathers. The wing feathers are moulted in the same way so that the bird can always hunt successfully.

The impact of Sparrowhawks on small bird populations was studied by one of the greatest post-war professional ecologists, David Lack. In 1954 he had written *The Natural Regulation of Animal Numbers*, in which he commented on research carried out by Luuk Tinbergen in 1946 on the impact of the Sparrowhawk on small bird populations. This was very valuable research, the first of its kind. Tinbergen had chosen four birds to study in detail: House Sparrow, Great Tit, Chaffinch and Coal Tit. There is a charming set of drawings of a Sparrowhawk as it approaches, lifts over a fence, grabs its prey, turns and climbs rapidly away. Many of Tinbergen's figures were based on assumptions. Lack challenged Tinbergen's research. He wrote: 'While Sparrowhawks killed a high proportion of the available House Sparrows and some other species, it does not necessarily follow that, if Sparrowhawks were removed, House Sparrows and other birds would increase.'

Lack claimed that when Sparrowhawk numbers were drastically reduced by gamekeepers during the latter half of the nineteenth century and the beginning of the twentieth century there did not appear to have been a corresponding increase in songbirds, habitually the Sparrowhawk's main prey. There was another major limiting factor at work, the availability of food. By killing some of the songbird population in autumn and early winter, Sparrowhawks might reduce competition for food during the winter, allowing more small birds to survive.

The Protection of Birds Act 1954 gave full legal protection to all birds of prey except the Sparrowhawk. During the war years, gamekeepers had been conscripted and Sparrowhawks were not persecuted. They were not protected because the population had quadrupled by the end of the war and may have reached the highest figure since the early 1800s.

Gilbertson and Page, proprietors of *The Gamekeeper and the Countryside*, published a booklet on the control of vermin. Editions came out in 1938, 1945 and 1952. The Sparrowhawk was rated one of the worst offenders: 'the most destructive of our common winged vermin.' Various traps and nets were illustrated in which they could be caught. There were instructions on shooting them. Keepers were advised to wait until the hen bird was sitting 'Always shoot the cock bird first; the hen can be got at almost anytime.'

In the 1940s and 1950s, the first organochlorine pesticides were introduced and almost simultaneously the Sparrowhawk population crashed. What the gamekeeper had been trying to do for over a hundred years these pesticides accomplished almost overnight.

The Sparrowhawk became extinct in East Anglia but at that time no one perceived the link. On 17 December 1962 it was, at last, given the same protection as all other birds of prey. Gilbertson and Page had to add an insert to their 1962 edition of their *Control of Vermin* book adding 'as Sparrowhawks are now protected under The Protection of Birds Act 1954, all references in this book to the taking of the eggs and the capturing and killing of these birds are null and void.'

I wondered what I could do to help Sparrowhawks. Much sooner than I anticipated, a telephone call told me that a friend had something that might interest me. He arrived carrying a cardboard box. Inside were six Sparrowhawk chicks, still in down but with their primaries, secondaries and tail feathers showing well. Paul, a forester, had been thinning out a wood at Holkham. He had felled a pine tree and when he went to cut off the top and side branches, found an old crows' nest with the six chicks scattered about. Could I save them? Luckily I thought I could.

Nearby, there were some empty pig sheds in a quiet location where there would be no disturbance. I made a frame covered in hessian to cover the window. The walls were covered in hessian too. I placed branches as perches throughout the shed and re-created their nest in a corner near the window. Finally, I fixed a plastic drainpipe so that I could deliver food to the nest without being seen.

I placed the Sparrowhawk chicks in their 'nest' and left them to it. The next morning I crept up and looked through the peep-hole. They were all there, some standing up, heads flicking round, big black pupils in their green-grey eyes, checking on everything that moved around them. The others were lying down. The smallest one looked a bit under the weather. I dropped their food, day-old chicks and small bits of Rabbit with fur still attached, down the drain-pipe. It made them jump. Soon they were pulling at the food, although the runt didn't join in. I left them to it. On my next visit I could see that the runt had not made it but fortunately the others were fine.

Over the next three weeks I was able to watch them discreetly through my peep-hole and assess how they were developing. They had already started wing-flapping and their baby down was disappearing as the covert feathers emerged. There was a lot of scratching to get rid of down on their heads. Gradually, the difference in size between the males and females became apparent – the three females were appreciably bigger than the two males. Blue-bottles buzzing around, attracted by decaying old food, were being watched intently. Finally, the young hawks started to leave the nest – hopping onto the perch I had attached to their nest and from there, with short flaps, negotiating their way to other perches. As they became more adventurous they flew the full length of the shed. Initially their landings were a bit 'hit and miss', involving a lot of wing-flapping and over-balancing. They spent most of the day perched on the branches, flapping and scratching to get rid of the last remnants of down. Then they would draw up one leg and doze off.

The young Sparrowhawks were now over six weeks old and I thought they were well enough developed to be released. One evening, a friend and I quietly approached the 'hawk house' and gently released the hessian frame covering the window. We retreated and watched. For a moment nothing happened and then suddenly, like partridges topping a hedge, they 'bomb burst' out into the open and disappeared in all directions.

I kept on putting out food for them. Some of them did return from time to time but soon their sporadic appearances dried up. How many of them would have survived their first winter – two out of the five, I reckoned.

In 1986 *The Sparrowhawk*, the definitive monograph, was written by Professor Ian Newton. He was only a boy when he found his first Sparrowhawk nest and this led to a life-long fascination with the bird. For 27 years Ian Newton studied the Sparrowhawk in Dumfriesshire. Everything that you would want to know about the bird is there in the book in great detail. Nobody has studied the Sparrowhawk, or probably any other raptor, quite so painstakingly as Ian Newton. It is a monumental work that may never be surpassed. Ian Newton adds a note of caution: 'No one who is interested solely in bird population problems would choose to study Sparrowhawks. Compared to many other birds, Sparrowhawks are scarce and highly secretive, spending most of their time in cover. They are thus impossible to count directly or to observe in the field for any length of time. Finding nests in numbers entails endless hours of searching, and inspecting nest-contents requires many difficult climbs. For me, however, it was the challenge of getting to grips with these elusive birds which gave them their appeal.'

While reading this I suddenly remembered Ian Newton's last piece of advice if I was going to study Sparrowhawks: 'However, for seeing large numbers of Sparrowhawks, there is nothing better than sitting at a migration site, such as Falsterbo in south Sweden, when hundreds of Sparrowhawks can fly over each day in the autumn migration season.

Falsterbo – where exactly was it? I pulled down my *Times Concise Atlas of the World* and checked the map of Sweden. There it was right at the tip, seemingly only a stone's throw from Denmark. I needed another pair of eyes with me, sharp ones, and I immediately thought of Eddie Anderson – ex-gamekeeper and highly acclaimed TV producer, whom I had known for years. The flight was routine, we picked up our car and in no time at all we were crossing the 16 kilometre long Øresund Bridge linking Denmark to Sweden.

There was a gale howling in from the south as we left our hotel in the morning. Thirty minutes later we were in Falsterbo. It was a ghost town. Most of the villas, more expensive as we got closer to the sea, had been closed up for the winter. Suddenly, Eddie yelled "Sparrowhawk!" There were Sparrowhawks galore. We saw six in about 15 minutes. I saw one female land on a garden fence, shake herself and then look purposefully around before taking off again.

Eventually we landed up at the golf club car park. In front of us was the lighthouse, now the Falsterbo Bird Observatory. This was definitely the right spot – there were birders everywhere crouching in the dunes, buffeted by the wind, anxiously scanning the sky. Every now and then someone would shout "Sparrowhawk!"

The Sparrowhawks were flying in from the north against the wind in threes and fours, rather like Wood Pigeons coming in to roost. They appeared out of the trees, hit the wind, were blown upwards and then dived down to ground level to escape the full force of the

gale before disappearing out of sight. Frequently, after reaching the sand dunes at the edge of the sea, they would be blown back to where we were watching. By now we had seen 15 Sparrowhawks in 15 minutes and it seemed as though they were raining down on us like arrows. 'A quiver of Sparrowhawks' was the collective noun later coined by Eddie for such a gathering of hawks.

We left the car park and drove out beyond the lighthouse to a spot that commanded a good view over the dunes to the sea. Leaning into the wind, we fought our way through the dunes towards the sea. A wavering wedge of Cormorants beat their way along the shore. Then a flock of Brent Geese and, best of all, seven Barnacle Geese, a family group, headed south. Turning inland another Sparrowhawk executed a roller coaster ride in and out of the pines – and a Merlin – or was it?

We got back to the car park where someone confirmed Eddie's Merlin. I decided to stay put while Eddie, head down, staggered off into the teeth of the gale. Now I understood what the Sparrowhawks had to contend with. On his return, he told me he had pressed on and, right at the tip of the peninsular, met the two official counters gazing out over the Øresund Straight, checking migrants flying south.

We were up early the next morning as we knew that we had to be on the Øresund Bridge to Copenhagen before 07.30. President Obama was flying in and the bridge would be shut for an hour. Our return flight was scheduled for a ten o'clock take-off. It could be a bit tight. Under pressure my navigating went to pot. Then a miracle occurred. We saw a tiercel Peregrine flying left to right. "It's showing us the way – take the next turn off." Now we were on the right road. As the toll by the bridge came into view I thought we had made it in time. But no, it was not to be. As we drove up police cars pulled out and sealed off the road. Fortunately we were not delayed long and were soon being escorted across the bridge to the airport. We dropped off the hire car and checked in for our flight home.

A few days later I checked the migration counts for Sparrowhawks during the three days we had been in Sweden. On the day we had arrived 641 had been counted, 48 the next day (the day we were at Falsterbo) and 334 on the day we left. It was a wonderful experience but what a difference a gale makes!

There is no doubt that the great majority of people that I meet are bird of prey enthusiasts. Some of them, however, may have reservations about Sparrowhawks. Very soon I was to have first hand experience of the anger this bird creates.

At the Royal Norfolk Show a member of SongBird Survival had a go at Nigel Middleton, the Sculthorpe Moor Reserve warden, about Sparrowhawks, stabbing him repeatedly on the chest with his index finger, telling him that they should be culled. I was watching this from about 30 metres away. For 20 minutes this person harangued Nigel without drawing breath. Eventually Nigel was able to tear himself away and rejoin me. He was wiping his face, which was covered in spittle. "David, we've got to do something about this."

Mark Cocker put his finger on the problem right away: 'A group like SongBird Survival is fascinating not for what it tells us about the true state of affairs with our birds, but for what it says about us. Blaming the Sparrowhawk is a classic example of creating a scapegoat – that poor reviled bird that serves as a lightning conductor for our feelings of disappointment, frustration and anger when things aren't as they should be.' Sparrowhawks have been persecuted by gamekeepers, poisoned by pesticides and now vilified by SongBird Survival. Perhaps there was an echo of truth in the last line of that poem about the Sparrowhawk – *Timor mortis conturbat me.*

There have been several surveys carried out that demonstrate that Sparrowhawks have no impact on songbird populations. The most important is the Common Bird Census of 13 species in the centre of an oak wood, Eastern Wood, which was carried out at Bookham Common near Leatherhead in Surrey from 1949 to 1979 by members of the London Natural History Society. Professor Ian Newton was particularly interested in this survey as all the species studied feature in a Sparrowhawk's diet. Seven species increased in numbers over the 31-year period and two declined. None of the 13 species was more numerous during the 1960s and 1970s when Sparrowhawks were absent due to pesticides. The survey showed, without doubt, that Sparrowhawks do not reduce populations of woodland songbirds. The survey initiated by Dr Geoffrey Beven still continues and is the longest-running natural history survey undertaken in Europe.

It is intensive farming, not Sparrowhawks, that has had such a devastating effect on some farmland birds. During the 40-year period from 1967–2010 the Skylark was down by 64%, the Linnet by 74%, the Yellowhammer by 56%, and the Corn Bunting by 88%. Worst of all, the Grey Partridge was reduced by a frightening 91%. Hedgerows have been grubbed out, insecticides have wiped out the insects upon which partridge chicks and other young farmland birds depend, herbicide sprays have removed all the seed-bearing weeds, and there has been a switch from spring-sown to autumn-sown cereals, with a consequent loss of winter stubbles and seed to be gleaned from them during the winter months.

In 2005 Defra, the Department for Environment, Food and Rural Affairs, launched two schemes to ameliorate this situation. Entry Level Stewardship (ELS) is open to all farmers if they can raise the requisite number of points per hectare for the options they have chosen. Field margins, grassland management and hedgerow management are some of the options that can be taken up. Agreements last five years and are paid at a flat rate of £30 per hectare. Higher Level Stewardship (HLS) is more specific than ELS, being aimed at practices that are more environmentally beneficial, and agreements last for ten years.

It is no surprise then that Sparrowhawks have deserted the countryside for better opportunities in the suburban garden. This is where the Sparrowhawks versus songbirds conflict has reached its peak. Since 1987 the amount of food fed to garden birds has increased seven fold. Over the same period, the majority of garden birds have been on the increase – Blackbird up by 90–103%, Wood Pigeon by 64–98%, Great Tit by 60–102%, Robin by 65–103%, Collared Dove by 60–100%, Greenfinch by 67–99% and Goldfinch by 50–93%. Over the same period the Sparrowhawk population has risen by 70–97%, although between 1995 and 2008 it had decreased by 7% to 40,000 pairs. The latest survey in 2010 shows a further reduction to 35,000 pairs. In addition, the very cold winter of 2010–11 is likely to have reduced the population even further.

The tiny male Sparrowhawk struggles to survive for more than two days without food. The following is an extract from my journal:

'21/1/12. 15.45. At the Sculthorpe Moor Reserve. Cold grey day, some bright intervals. Very windy. In the Whitley hide at the reserve watching a male Sparrowhawk hunting. He was 'still'-hunting from one of two dead birch trees out on the reedbed. Nearby, on one of the feeders, a flock of Long-tailed Tits were taking a last snack before roosting. One of

them was obviously on lookout. As soon as the Sparrowhawk swooped in they scattered into the willow undergrowth. He made several lightning dashes to the edge of the wood and into reedbed – all unsuccessful. He went to roost hungry. The Long-tailed Tits survived to fascinate us another day.'

Recently there has been a major breakthrough. SongBird Survival funded a joint research project run by the British Trust for Ornithology and the Game and Wildlife Conservation Trust that analysed the latest data on songbirds and predators. To quote from their joint report, 'This is a high quality study based on unique long-term and large-scale data sets. For the majority of songbird species examined, there is no evidence that increases in common avian predators are associated with large-scale depression of prey abundance or population declines.' A question mark remained over three species: Tree Sparrow, Bullfinch and Reed Bunting. Further research was required on them. By and large, though, the Sparrowhawk has been exonerated.

This, then, is the roller-coaster ride of the Sparrowhawk since the fifteenth century. For 400 years it was revered and protected. Then, at the click of a trigger, for the next 200 years it was mercilessly persecuted by gamekeepers because it interfered with the popular sport of game shooting. But the musket, the male Sparrowhawk, had no crystal ball to foresee this. What was it that generated such a morbid fear of death in the fifteenth century?

I thought long and hard about this and could come to no conclusion until I chanced upon the final sentence in one of Derwent May's columns in *The Times* 'The Sparrowhawks themselves have to be on the alert for they in turn are persecuted by the much more powerful Goshawks.'

The population of Goshawks in the fifteenth century would have been extensive before the forests were cut down for boat building, housing and fuel. I think it is the ever-present threat of the silent killer, the Phantom of the Forest, that put the fear of death into our musket. The Medici assassin armed with a thin razor sharp stiletto versus the much stronger Samurai warrior with a Damask toughened katana sword. No contest.

Research by Luuk Tinbergen in Holland, before the Second World War, noted that many Sparrowhawks were brought to Goshawk nests in his study area and that eventually this might well be a controlling factor in Sparrowhawk populations. Today the Goshawk population in the British Isles is estimated at 400 pairs and rising.

Spare a thought then for the musket, the male Sparrowhawk, this beautiful, spectacular bird. Because they are at the top of the food chain Sparrowhawks are always living on the edge. When dusk falls is when they are particularly at risk. It is dusk now and I am out in the garden, under one of the big Sycamore trees, watching the Barn Owls hunting over the water meadows. They have had a good year and have raised three young.

Ever since I picked up that dying bird all those years ago, Sparrowhawks have lurked in my subconscious. They appear at the strangest times and that is what happened now. There was the flicker of a wing and there, not three metres away, the unmistakable silhouette of a male Sparrowhawk perched on a branch above and beyond me. He was leaning forward, shoulders hunched, tight feathered. Gradually he relaxed, then roused with a crisp rustle of his feathers. He was ready for sleep. As I watched, the orange-red of his eyes sealed over and the black cloak of darkness wrapped around him. I knew that he was safe.

THE OSPREY

British Isles population (2006–10): 250 pairs (increasing)

The first rare British bird of prey that I saw was an Osprey. It was 26 April 1946 and my brother Richard and I were walking across a meadow towards the large lake at Castle Howard in Yorkshire. Our long-suffering mother had just dropped us off while she went to visit her mother, Granny Strickland, at nearby Huttons Ambo. During the school holidays we often came here to check out the duck population. During the autumn and winter there were always plenty of Mallard, Teal and Wigeon accompanied by Tufted Duck and Pochard. We had once been lucky enough, during a particularly hard winter, to see a drake Smew, white with a dramatic black blob around its eye followed by pen strokes of black at its crest and from its breast leading along the back to its tail. It was a fabulous bird.

But this was spring and would be our last visit before we went back to school. As we neared the lake we noticed a commotion caused by Black-headed Gulls mobbing a biggish bird perched high up in a dead tree on the island. My first thought was that it was a Cormorant. But through our battered binoculars we could make out chocolate-coloured upperparts, primaries and tail and, when it ducked to avoid the strafing attacks of the gulls, we could see that the chocolate colour passed up the bird's neck and continued as a dark streak though the eye. It had a hooked beak and the crest feathers on its head were the same dark brown edged with white. Its legs were grey-green. It was definitely an Osprey. We looked at each other and grinned. This was a red-letter day and we could not wait to tell our mother about it. We kept on watching and then, irritated by the cacophony of the

gull's frustrated calls, the Osprey with great dignity slipped off its perch and wafted off down the lake before disappearing from sight.

Mother urged us to write to *British Birds* magazine about it and in the next issue there was a mention of David and Richard Cobham seeing an Osprey at Castle Howard lake in April, one of several reports of Ospreys migrating through England from their wintering grounds in West Africa to Norway and Sweden where they breed.

Sixty years later I was on a train with my friends Eddie and Tina Anderson on our way up to Aviemore in the Highlands of Scotland. We were going to meet Roy Dennis, one of the world's authorities on this fascinating bird and largely responsible for its remarkable resurgence. I had known Roy since 1974, when as Highland Officer for the Royal Society for the Protection of Birds he had been my mentor while I was making the first full length-film for the BBC Natural History Unit on the Peregrine Falcon in Scotland.

During our journey to Scotland we talked about the Osprey and its place in ornithological history. The Greek playwright Aristophanes (450–388 BC) mentions it in his play *The Birds*. The Osprey is part of the chorus along with kestrels, falcons, goshawks and eagles in this play about Cloudcuckooland. Aristotle (384–322 BC), a disciple of Plato, was probably describing the Osprey when he wrote in his *Historia Animalium* 'Another kind of eagles is the so-called sea eagles or Ospreys. Their neck is large and thick, feathers curved, rump broad. They dwell by the sea and by coastal headlands; when seizing prey and unable to carry it they are often borne down into the deep water.' To add to the confusion, the Greek word *haliaietos* is used for describing both the Osprey and the Sea Eagle.

William Turner mentioned the Osprey in his *Avium Praecipuarum*, published in 1544 'A bird much better known today to Englishmen than many who keep fish in stews would wish; for within a short time it bears off every fish.' John Caius, in 1570, gives a very accurate description of an Osprey that he kept 'It is the size of a kite, having the head marked with white and dusky lines, as in a badger; an eagle's beak; eyes black in the middle, golden in the outer circle.' He pays particular attention to the Osprey's feet 'the legs thick and scaly; the foot with curved claws and blue; four toes scaly above for quite half their length, fissured for the rest, rough on the lower half and sharp for a firm hold.'

The Osprey was believed by the *hoi polloi* to have magical properties and was certainly considered as vermin because it was the custom, as it still is, to eat fish on Fridays. William Harrison, a canon of Windsor, wrote in 1577 'We have also Ospraies, which breed with us in parks and woods, whereby the keepers reap in breeding no small commodity; for so soon almost as the young are hatched, they tie them to the butt end of trees, where the old ones finding them, do never cease to bring fish unto them, which the keepers take.'

There were various attempts at naming the Osprey: Gesner (1555) *Falco cyanopoda*, Aldrovandus (1599) *Haliaetus*, Willughby (1676) *Balbusardus*, and Ray (1678) *Osprey*.

Carl Linnaeus (1707–78) was the first to classify the Osprey. For some reason he made a mistake and classified it as belonging to the falcon family, as *Falco haliaetus*. It was not until 1809 that the mistake was realized and the Osprey was more appropriately named *Pandion haliaetus*. By then the Osprey had become a rare breeding bird in England.

Earlier in this chapter I gave a rather superficial description of the Osprey I saw at Castle Howard all those years ago. This is a more accurate one. The markings on the head of an Osprey compel attention. They are very graphic. The feathers on the head are white but there is a dark slash of brown running from its beak across the eye to the bird's nape.

This may help reduce glare to the eyes, which are a vivid yellow. It has a crest which is dark in the middle with brown flecks in the white areas above the eye-stripe. Its beak is blue-black and the cere above blue-grey. Its nostrils, situated in the cere, are adapted to close as it dives into water. The Osprey's back and upperwings are chocolate brown. The tail feathers are buff-coloured with dark brown barring. The under-wings, apart from the dark primaries, are white, as are its breast feathers. There is a halter of brown breast feathers just below the crop. The feathers on the upper part of the legs are white. The pale grey, scaly lower legs lead to powerful taloned feet, well adapted for catching fish. The feet have two interesting features: the outer toe is reversible, meaning that a fish can be firmly held by two taloned toes in front and two behind; and to enhance this adaptation and maintain a hold on a slimy, wet, wriggling fish the skin of the undersides of the toes is as abrasive as coarse sandpaper.

It was the Osprey's taste for fish that originally caused its demise in England. Later, the rearing of game for shooting and the Game Act of 1831 sealed the fate of any bird with a hooked beak.

Nowhere was the persecution more intense than in Scotland. In his book *Silent Fields*, published in 2007, Roger Lovegrove gives a chilling account of Charles St John's part in bringing the Osprey to extinction 'Three miles from Scourie in Sutherland he shot a female off her nest and took the two eggs. He then lamented the evident distress of the male, saying he was remorseful that he had shot its mate. At another Sutherland site he failed to shoot the adults but took the young and then shot the male at a further nest, missed the female, but took the three eggs.'

By 1908 the Osprey was extinct as a breeding bird in the British Isles. When we met Roy Dennis at his home one of the first questions I asked him was whether he thought that the Osprey had ever been extinct in Scotland? Roy was quite emphatic, "No, I'm quite sure that it was never extinct. The true meaning of extinction is that there are none around at all. There have always been Ospreys every year on migration. And at the Loch Arkaig nest where they attempted to nest in 1908 a solitary male returned each year to rebuild the nest until 1913."

"These accounts do not appear in the books. Then there was a pair at Loch Loyne that reared young in 1916. My firm belief is that from then on occasional breeding took place in Scotland. One of the young might come back or a bird lost on migration and you'd get breeding for a year or two years. Then there'd be a bird by itself for a few years and then another pair, and so on."

"There was definitely a pair at Loch Garten in the mid-1930s. During the war Loch Garten was a restricted military area and no one was allowed in. What happened then nobody knows. Then I met someone who told me he saw a nest with young at Loch Garten after the war. Relying on my present knowledge of Ospreys, I believe the eyrie tree at Loch Garten was in use from the early 1930s, probably with some absences, through to 1954 with young raised in some of those years. The site remained a secret."

The history of the Loch Garten site, which was the lift-off point for the recovery of the Osprey population in Scotland, is well documented in Roy Dennis's book *A Life of Ospreys* published in 2008. In 1955 the Ospreys returned and laid in the same Scots Pine tree, but the secret got out and the eggs were stolen. In 1956 the eggs were stolen from an eyrie in the nearby Rothiemurchus Forest.

George Waterston, the director of the RSPB in Scotland, realized that a determined effort was needed to protect the nest at Loch Garten. In 1957 a team of dedicated wardens were rostered in to guard the nest. Unfortunately only one Osprey returned to breed.

The following year, 1958, started well. A pair of Ospreys returned to breed in the eyrie, which was situated in the flat canopy at the top of an old Scots Pine. It is what Roy calls a 'Granny Pine', maybe as much as 300 years old. 'Operation Osprey' was launched by George Waterston with round-the-clock surveillance by a team of wardens and volunteers. An egg was laid and that same night a known egg collector was seen lurking about and chased off. Despite the 24-hour surveillance, three weeks later an egg collector sneaked in and managed to rob the eyrie. The two eggs were smashed. In Roy's words, "it was a total disaster."

In 1959 important decisions were made which were to influence the future of the Loch Garten Ospreys. The owner of Abernethy Forest, in which Loch Garten was situated, allowed it to be turned into a protected bird sanctuary. Now no one could enter the area without prior permission and for the first time, in advance of the arrival of the Ospreys, a full complement of wardens and volunteers was in position to protect the site. The male and female arrived in the third week of April, the first egg was laid a week later and by the end of the first week in June there were three newly hatched young in the nest.

George Waterston then did something quite remarkable. Instead of trying to keep it a secret, he invited the public to come and watch the Osprey's home life. It was a turning point in nature conservation. That year 14,000 people came to see the birds. Watching through binoculars and telescopes from a special vantage point, they were able to share the private life of the Ospreys until the young flew.

The rest, as they say, is history. 'Operation Osprey' was a huge success. In 1960, the year Roy started work as an Osprey warden, there was a proper observation hut from which the public could view the nest. Closer to the tree was a carefully concealed and camouflaged hut from which the wardens and volunteers could watch and guard the nest. The trunk of the eyrie tree was wrapped round with barbed wire to deter any tree climbers and electronic warning devices were installed to detect anyone trying to climb the tree.

The success of 'Operation Osprey' was one of the top stories of that time. News of it reached Edgar Anstey at British Transport Films in London, where they were in the middle of making a film promoting the West Highland Railway. As Ospreys were topical so they must be included. When it was pointed out to him that the Ospreys were on the east coast he over-rode their objections. So it was that John Buxton, a friend of mine, was despatched to Aviemore to get a footage of the famous Ospreys catching fish.

This is John's story: "I went to Loch Garten and contacted Roy Dennis who was the warden there. He was very helpful and suggested I try a certain loch. I went there and had a look around. There was a promontory with a solitary pine tree at the end of it. That looked a likely spot to me. I noticed a family camping nearby and went over and asked if they'd seen an Osprey catching fish. Oh, yes, they said, there's a big black-and-white bird that comes here every evening about 7.30 and makes a big splash in the loch and carries away a fish. That's good enough for me, I thought. I thanked them, got my gear and set up my camera on the end of the promontory. As the film was for the cinemas I was using a wind-up 35 mm Newman-Sinclair camera. It took a 200-foot roll of Eastmancolor negative film. It was a very primitive system compared to today's sophisticated cameras. Anyhow, to cut a long story short, promptly at 7.30 the Osprey appeared above the loch, did a couple of circuits and then dived down and caught a fish. I got it all on film, I was very lucky. I think I was probably the first person to film the Ospreys after 'Operation Osprey' had been set up."

In 1960 two chicks were reared and fledged, in 1961 three got off, and in 1962 just one chick was fledged. In 1963 eggs were laid, but a storm damaged the nest and it was abandoned. Although vandals tried to cut the eyrie tree down in 1964, three young were raised. By 1970, despite the storms and criminal interference, 25 young had been reared and fledged.

But in 1971 there was another disaster, as Roy recounts, "The nest was raided during the night and, once again, the eggs were stolen. It was a terrible blow for all concerned. The egg thieves were caught as they left the forest but the eggs were never recovered." To prevent further robberies the eyrie tree's big side-branches were removed and the trunk was covered with anti-climb paint and swathed in even more barbed wire. In Roy's words, "The Osprey tree looked terrible." Nevertheless the Ospreys returned to breed and by 1976 a total of 36 young had been fledged at Loch Garten.

The success of 'Operation Osprey' prompted the RSPB, who had recently purchased the Loch Garten reserve, to make a full-length film on the Osprey. Hugh Miles, who was then head of the RSPB film unit, set off in the spring of 1977 for Scotland with his wife Sue and two small children in a camper van. I had first met Hugh in the early seventies when he had been filming Barn Owls on the Holkham estate in Norfolk. Roy Dennis had arranged for Hugh to film on a private estate in Moray where there were three Osprey eyries. Hugh told me that at that time that if he had failed as a natural history cameraman he would certainly have been able to get a job at SGB, the scaffolding company. To film at the Osprey eyries he had to erect scaffolding towers 20 metres high. The planks on which his hide rested were old, cracked and wobbly. There was no thought of Health and Safety.

The film, which was shot over two years, followed a pair of Ospreys from the time of their arrival in spring through the breeding season to their departure for their winter quarters in West Africa. It is a masterpiece. As a filmmaker myself I can appreciate the patience and cunning necessary to create such a superb portrait of the Osprey. Some sequences are outstanding: the mating sequence at the nest, both adults falling asleep during the lengthy incubation period, eyes sealing over and their heads collapsing as if pole-axed; the reptilian heads of the young chicks; the female Osprey mantling over the chicks to protect them from an intruder; the sequence in the rain when the male could not fish and the female was trying to cover the chicks to keep them dry; and finally the shots of the male catching fish. These caused a sensation when they were first shown. To get the shots the conditions had to be perfect: the water had to be backlit and the wind in the right direction so that the Osprey would fly towards camera. At the last moment Hugh used a catapult to flick a dollop of trout food in front of the hide to make sure that the Osprey plunged in at the right spot framed by the camera.

The shot of which Hugh was most proud was a reflection, filmed at sunset, of the male Osprey landing on the top of a branch. The extraordinary thing about this is that the shot entailed finding the right branch. The one that Hugh found was big and very heavy and had to be lashed to the roof of the camper van to be driven to the location. It then had to be planted in a spot where the male Osprey would recognize it as a useful perch and be reflected in the water as it flew in and landed on it. This was no simple feat!

The Osprey film had its premiere in 1980. It was so well received that the BBC acquired it and it was transmitted on BBC2 in *The World About Us* slot in 1981. The BBC set such store on it that it was given the front cover of the *Radio Times*. When it was shown it pulled in an audience of four million viewers. It was Hugh's stepping stone to becoming one of the world's foremost wildlife filmmakers.

At Loch Garten another pair of Ospreys had bred every year until 1985, by which time a total of 52 young had been fledged. In 1985 the male died and the following year the tree was vandalized again. From 1988 onwards the Ospreys reared young every year, reaching a cumulative total of 82 by 2001. By now the Ospreys at Loch Garten were internationally famous. Visitors poured in at a rate of 60,000 a year. In 2001 the present visitor centre was built. At last there was a big car park and access for all to the centre which was built of wood sourced from the surrounding forest and cunningly designed to blend into the countryside.

Inside there was a shop where books, binoculars, telescopes and everything a bird-watcher might need were on display. There was an area where hot drinks and snacks could be purchased and eaten. Volunteers were on hand to give out the latest information and show you to where you could sit comfortably and watch the nesting Ospreys through special viewing slits. For those visitors who wanted something extra special there were five screens onto which images from the Closed Circuit Television (CCTV) cameras mounted round the nest were projected. Big close-ups of the Ospreys, so close that the numbers on

their rings could be read, had never been seen before and also revealed interesting facets of Osprey behaviour – although none so riveting as the drama-riven relationship of the Ospreys known as Henry, the hero, and E.J., the heroine.

Henry was hatched at a nest on the Black Isle in 1998. He had a standard metal British Trust for Ornithology (BTO) ring on his left leg, plus a colour ring with the letters H.V. etched into it. He arrived at Loch Garten five years later. E.J. was ringed as a chick at a nest in Perthshire in 1997. In 2002 she briefly appeared at Loch Garten before being chased off by the resident female. Orange V.S., was caught and ringed by Roy at the Rothiemurchus fish farm in 1994. He had been responsible for rearing eight young, but his eggs were twice robbed and on two occasions predated by Pine Martens.

It was against this background that the melodrama of Henry and E.J. unfolded. In 2003 Henry appeared at Loch Garten and mated with Olive, whose mate had died over winter. Just before she was due to start laying another male appeared. Henry successfully drove him off but the next day yet another male appeared. There was a battle and Henry, who was exhausted from the previous day's challenge, was defeated.

Olive's new mate was a failure so she left. Shortly afterwards Henry re-appeared and chased off the male in residence and took back his territory. He played the field for a bit but could not find a soul mate. Then, on 16 June, E.J. flew into Loch Garten and the pair stayed there for the rest of the summer before travelling south to their winter quarters in Africa.

In the spring of 2004, E.J. returned to Loch Garten and mated with Orange V.S.. Henry arrived a few days later and quickly regained his territory. Then for the next fortnight E.J. was subjected every morning to sustained attacks from another female. The climax came on 17 April when E.J. beat off three ferocious attacks and won.

At last, Henry and E.J. were able to resume a normal life at the nest. E.J. was incubating three eggs; one of the clutch of four had been destroyed during the attacks. Henry was bringing in plenty of fish to their nest. As is quite normal, the three chicks squabbled amongst themselves. The youngest chick, a bit of a runt, was constantly picked on by the other two, so much so that all his head feathers were plucked out and he became bald. The volunteers named him 'Baldrick'. All the chicks fledged and the whole family departed on migration by the end of September.

In 2005 E.J. was back by the end of March and courted by several different males. There was no sign of Henry. A new male, red-white 8T, from a nearby nest became dominant, mated with E.J. and she started to lay a clutch of eggs. At the end of April a very bedraggled Henry appeared. He had probably been held up by storms when passing through Spain. He asserted his rights to E.J. and the nest site and drove off his rival. His late arrival meant there was no chance of his fathering any chicks. But he regained his strength and renewed his bond with E.J. by providing her with plenty of trout from the Rothiemurchus fish farm.

E.J. made her usual early touch-down at Loch Garten in 2006 and was immediately courted by Orange V.S. They refurbished the nest, mated and Orange V.S. regularly brought in fish. On 10 April Henry reappeared. He landed on the nest and then carried out a spectacular 'roller-coaster' display 300 metres above the nest. He dived on the nest and after a furious three-hour fight V.S. was seen off. The rest of summer passed off quietly. Three young were fledged and they all migrated south.

In 2007 E.J. returned to Loch Garten a bit later than usual. Quick as a flash V.S. was in there, refurbishing the nest and paying court to E.J. even though he had another female on

the go at a nearby nest. By 21 April E.J. had laid two eggs. In the middle of a storm the next day an Osprey was heard calling over the nest site. Henry was back! Henry cleared out the nest, kicking out two eggs and went about the business of being a model mate. E.J. laid two more eggs. Henry dispatched those as well. Would she lay another clutch?

The world held its breath – would she, wouldn't she? By 11 May a replacement clutch had been laid. The eggs started to hatch, heralding a saga of tragedy. The first chick may have died when Henry flew into the nest, entangled in fishing line, and accidentally stepped on the chick, killing it. The second was chilled in a day of heavy rain and died. And the third egg never hatched, the chick was dead in the shell. As before, Henry and E.J. stayed together for the rest of the summer and then went their separate ways south to spend the winter.

E.J. returned as usual in the spring of 2008 but Henry did not. So V.S. had his way with E.J. as well as looking after his other nest. Between 2002 and 2007 the Loch Garten Ospreys reared eight young, making a grand total of 90 since 1954.

In 2008 Simon King was the anchorman at Rothiemurchus in Scotland when the BBC's *Springwatch* started a new series based in Norfolk. Ospreys were to be the main recurring theme in the reports he was to send back to Bill Oddie and Kate Humble at the *Springwatch* base in Norfolk. In one of his first reports he said, "This in my opinion is one of the best places in the world to watch wild Ospreys hunting. It's super for fisherman – both the human kind and the feathered variety. You've got to think of these lakes as being a bird table for Ospreys, but instead of seed and peanuts it's fish – their exclusive food."

Having established the Osprey as a formidable hunter, Simon sets the scene on a pair of nesting Ospreys: "We've been staking out a nest which is in the most magnificent spot. Hopefully we can now go live to pictures of that nest – John Aitchison is in the hide. Can you hear me, John? That's a nod. Why have we chosen this spot? Well, just look at it, utterly stunning. One of the most beautiful settings for an Osprey nest I have ever encountered. Furthermore there's something special about this pair. Can we see the sitting bird there ... yes. That's the female, sitting on the nest, in this beautiful lemon light of the setting sun. There's something special about them because we know a great deal about them. I say 'we do' when in fact it has been watched and recorded over many years by Osprey expert Roy Dennis. He's been following their progress – that means he knows a tremendous amount about them, which means we've already got something of their character to talk about. This is the male bird which Roy ringed when it was a chick 14 years ago. We know a precise age on him. And he's looking a little tired, which is understandable. 14 years old. They can live to about 20, he's getting on a bit. This is the female bird. She doesn't have a ring so we know less about her. We think she's about ten years old. What we do know is that they've been together for seven years and in that time they've raised 18 chicks. This year they have three eggs, that's quite normal. The male bird brings in food while she's incubating. He's the one who does the hunting. She does the sitting, waiting for the chicks to hatch. There, she takes food from him and leaves him to get on with the business of incubating the eggs. And he's obviously a good father, an old hand at this. He settles down on the eggs, clearly pretty tired too, but with 18 chicks to his name you can hardly blame him. The female comes back to sit on the eggs. Is he going to budge? No. Eventually she just screams in his ear – come on, will you please move, your job is to get more fish, my job is to sit on the eggs. Eventually, wearily, he gets up – you can feel the ache in his legs. Okay, I will go hunting again. A great, great pair."

This is a masterclass in how a presenter sets the scene. We now know where we are, that it's a beautiful setting. Roy Dennis, the Osprey expert, has been introduced. Therefore the age of the birds and the number of chicks they've produced is official. And we have heard about their home life and begin to know them as characters. We empathize with them. This is what *Springwatch* does so well.

Back to Simon on Day 2 of *Springwatch*: "We know there are three eggs in the nest. Some of the views that you've been seeing into the nest are quite special. From John's point of view from the hide, he can't really see into the nest. But we have a remote camera like this one. Roy Dennis put the camera in the other day so that we can now get a good look into the nest. The eggs are expected to hatch about now so John has been staking this out. Very excited female, calling loudly, standing over the nest. This John's view from the hide, this is the remote camera. The male comes into the nest with food. Looks like the eggs have moved. Can't quite see what's happening now. But the moment that female starts tearing up that fish ... there, bottom left. A little chick, a shred of life, not much bigger than its mother's foot. Charming. It always amazes me that these great big powerful, predatory birds with weapons on their feet have the ability to be so sensitive."

What an evocative description. We are charmed by the arrival of the chick, a shred of life, and the innate skill of such powerful predators in dealing so sensitively with their newly hatched chick. Simon uses the views from the camera on the nest to reveal intimate moments in the relationship between the two parent birds. "There's a very marked change in attitude from the male bird. Brings food in the morning. Female nagging him a little bit. She says, 'I want a little bit more.' Bingo! He reacts with a great big fish, the second meal of the day. She keeps nagging him. Now he brings a third fish in. At this stage the youngsters don't have a big appetite. That's all going to change as they grow. It is his responsibility to feed the whole family –his mate, the chicks and himself. He's rising to the task beautifully. He comes back to the nest with a fourth fish and, unusually – I've never seen this before – the male starts feeding the chicks himself." Another important stage in the family life of the Ospreys. The arrival of the chicks has reinforced the bond between the parent birds and we are given a tantalizing, privileged glimpse of behaviour that Simon has never seen before.

In his next report on the nesting Ospreys Simon draws a parallel with clearing up at home after the children have had their evening meal: "At this stage the chicks are not very demanding as far as diet is concerned. There must be a surplus of fish which probably means it's a stinking place – just as well it's not 'smello-vision.' There's a lot of activity not only in bringing in fish but also in refurbishing. After the chicks have hatched she is off looking for new furniture for the nursery – bark and twigs. Often picked up off the forest floor but ... Wow! Look at that! Trying to snap it off the tree itself. Common behaviour for an Osprey. The male also wants to add to the nest – crack! He fumbled. But no, take another look. This for me is breathtaking. The precision of the bird. He turns his feet, snaps the twig, then loses it. But somehow – he's not missing a wing-beat – when he comes into view again – it's in his feet. That just goes to show the astonishing precision of these birds."

The home-life of Ospreys takes on a more sinister note, echoing newcomers trying to take over the 'home turf' in *Eastenders*. Simon again: "All looks calm at first, the male doing a bit of house-keeping, the female sitting on the nest. There! An intruding male, right over the top of the nest. Our fellow is galvanized into action. Takes off to gain height, while the female goes into a frenzy of display, calling, flapping – 'Keep out, sunshine – this nest is taken, thank you very much.' It's a sure sign of the solidarity of our pair who've been together for seven years and raised 18 young. A really strong, solid pair. Ah, here comes the intruder. And our fellow dive-bombs him, chases him away. And that's not all. Our female leaves the nest and dive-bombs another predator, a Buzzard. A small bird of prey compared to an Osprey, but nonetheless a danger to our chicks. A Buzzard, if he caught the nest unprotected, would definitely grab the chicks. Fortunately no damage. The female comes back to the nest to resume incubating the chicks."

And finally the *pièce de résistance*, the icing on the cake, Simon's description of the Osprey catching a fish: "Here's our high-octane bird in action. It's always surprising to me how high Ospreys fly when they're patrolling, looking for a fish. Also astonishing when you watch these birds scanning the lake. They have to deal with glare, with reflection and to make a decision on the size and position of the fish before committing to a plunge dive.

Nonetheless they are masters of the art. They get their sights set, feet forward. In they go. It really is an astonishing feat, particularly so because some of the fish are quite chunky. An Osprey weighs one-and-a-half kilos and the fish must be half a kilo – that's a third of its body weight. It's like me a 12-stone man trying to pull a 4-stone kid out of a swimming pool, flying! It's ridiculous. Let's look at it again. In he goes. That's such a spectacle. I love it. And then he lifts up to the surface, gets a better grip. Gives a shake to shed some of the water so that it's lighter still. And then, I love this, they always try to orientate the fish in their feet so that it points forward like a torpedo and creates the least wind drag. Lovely."

Over 12 days Simon has given us a privileged look at the private life of the Osprey and has shown us that they too have the same roller-coaster lives as we do. He has forged a bond between us and this particular bird of prey.

Back to Roy in Scotland. He readily acknowledges the beneficial effect of *Springwatch* on conserving birds of prey, and most particularly of Ospreys. Here is an extract from my journal at that time:

'5/6/12. *We've taken a break from interviewing and Roy is showing us some Osprey nests. The first one is quite near his house in a 130-foot-tall Douglas Fir. The top of the tree bends over and the nest has been built over a fork in the bough. The female can be seen sitting high in the nest brooding chicks. The second nest is in a dead larch, not high up at all and only 200 yards from a house. Again the female is sitting high on the nest brooding chicks. The male flies in with a large stick. The female stood up, flew off in disgust but probably for a bit of exercise. Did one circuit and returned. It's a beautiful site with a view of the Moray Firth in the background. The female is called Beatrice after an oilrig of that name out in the North Sea. The last site was the most interesting. It had history. We were looking at it through a screen of backlit Scots Pines. Beyond there was a recently seeded field in the middle of which were three trees.*'

Roy takes up the story: "If you look to the right of the two live trees there's a dead tree and the male bird is perched there. The original nest used to be in that tree from 1966 onwards. They stayed there for 15 years. Then they moved to the next tree. The nest kept on being robbed so I took branches off, more and more of them, and eventually the tree died. We rebuilt the nest at the top of the tree and that was successful for many years. Last winter it all got a bit shaky so we rebuilt the nest in the top of the next tree. When they returned they went straight to our nest, added to it so that it's nearly twice the size now. She's on chicks and, if you look carefully, you can see the radio tag on her back."

By 2008 the population of Ospreys in Scotland was nearing 200 pairs. Gradually they were spreading throughout Scotland and re-colonizing their ancestral eyries. More and more migrant Ospreys were being seen passing through England on migration. I went to Rutland Water in the Midlands to talk to Tim Mackrill, manager of the Osprey Reintroduction Project. Tim told me, "The key year was 1994. That year we had two Ospreys, a male and a female, that summered here at Rutland Water. So everyone got very excited – we've got a male, we've got a female. In 1995 when they return we'll have a breeding pair. Rutland Water was an absolutely ideal place. It was built in the 1970s to provide drinking water for the Midlands. The encouraging fact is that before it was built Anglian Water, which runs it, thought about conservation. Tim Appleton was appointed warden and the Leicestershire and Rutland Wildlife Trust were brought in to run it. It soon

developed into a very exciting place for birds and was declared as a Site of Special Scientific Interest, an SSSI. To get back to Ospreys, in 1995 we worked out that the 1994 birds were just young birds from Scotland doing a bit of exploring. They are incredibly faithful to their natal site and they'll generally migrate back there to breed."

That got the ball rolling for a translocation project. It had been done successfully with White-tailed Eagles in Scotland and with Red Kites in the Chilterns so there was plenty of knowledge on tap. Roy Dennis came down from Scotland, had a meeting with Tim Appleton and Stephen Bolt who worked for Anglian Water and it was decided that we would try to get a licence to translocate Osprey chicks from Scotland. It was a hefty process negotiating with Scottish Natural Heritage and Natural England, but finally in 1996 the licence was granted. The only stipulation was that only the smallest of the chicks in a nest was to be taken.

An extract from Roy Dennis' diary: '6 July 1996. To the first nest near Carrbridge where started the collection of young Ospreys for collection to Rutland Water. Three young in nest A11 – ringed all three and collected the smallest. Took youngster back home and placed it in special aviary – fed it on fresh rainbow trout. Set off for Morayshire to the high tree, nest KO6. Three chicks – collected the smallest chick. Then to Fochabers nest KO6. Both adults present, three big chicks and a big nest. Took smallest chick. Finally to large nest near Forres. Three chicks, all rather small, took smallest. Put all the chicks together in an artificial nest and fed them on trout. Helen from Rutland Water arrived.'

Helen Dixon had been appointed as the project officer. Three days later she and Roy transported the eight young Ospreys from Scotland to Rutland Water where special release pens on stilts had been built. The front and top of each pen were enclosed in plastic mesh. This allowed the young birds to become accustomed to their surroundings and imprinted on Rutland Water. The sides and back were solid. The birds were monitored with CCTV and food was delivered to them via a hatch so that they would not associate it with humans.

Three weeks later, on 30 July, the first release took place. With short flights at first the young Ospreys were soon flying farther and farther away from the release pens, familiarizing themselves with the land around Rutland Water and imprinting a map of it

on their memory. All the birds had been radio-tagged so that their daily flights could be monitored. Sadly, of the eight birds moved from Scotland in 1996 and released at Rutland Water, only four survived to migrate. In 1997 the licence for taking Ospreys from Scotland was changed so that the eldest or middle chick could be taken. From then on the survival rate improved immensely. Fifty-five out of 56 birds survived to migrate.

It was in 1997 that Tim Mackrill, then aged 15, started working as a volunteer: "In 1999 two young males released in 1997 returned to Rutland and stayed all summer, visiting the artificial pole-mounted nest sites we had built. In 1999 we satellite-tagged 14 of the 64 Ospreys released and one very telling statistic was that we found that 13 of the 14 birds flew south from Rutland and ended up on the south-west coast of England, following their ancestral memory as if they were migrating from Scotland. They're then faced with a daunting 1,000 kilometre flight across the sea, which some of them don't make. Then there's the Sahara to cross before they get to their winter quarters in Senegal and The Gambia. Only one of the satellite-tagged birds made it back but of the remainder ten returned to Rutland and established the possibility of a breeding population."

But it was not until 2001 that one of the Rutland returning males attracted a passing female on her way back to Scotland. He had already built a nest, and the staff and volunteers held their breath. The pair mated and three eggs were laid, only one of which hatched. The chick was ringed by Tim Appleton. On 30 July it fledged and flew off to migrate on 20 August. The translocation of the Ospreys from Scotland to Rutland Water was proved to be an unqualified success – the first breeding of Ospreys in England for 150 years.

Between 2001 and 2007 the original pair and another pair reared a cumulative total of 18 young. In 2006 Tim Mackrill took over the management of the project and two years later the Osprey-viewing centre at Lyndon was rebuilt. Two years after that a camera was installed so that the public could view images of the Osprey's behaviour at the nest. Tim said, "What I think is most significant is that these images were streamed to our web-site. Something like 5,000 people a day were watching key moments like hatching. They weren't just from this country but from Australia, Canada and even a lady in a caravan park in California watching them on her computer – that's halfway round the world. It's just amazing how Ospreys capture people's imagination. If you can get people watching Ospreys like that it can bridge the gap, encourage people to take more of an interest in the natural world."

I asked Tim about persecution. Had there been any? "Yes, in the last three years we've lost three males in the early part of the spring. They went off fishing and never came back. For three to disappear in thirteen months was very suspicious. The talk within the local community is that they were killed intentionally by someone who didn't like their fish being taken." I was staggered that a bird which the public had so obviously taken to its heart should be so wilfully destroyed.

I asked Roy what the present state of the Osprey was and he told me, "Here in Moray and the Dornoch Firth the population is no longer increasing, it has stabilized. But in the Borders and Dumfries and Galloway it's increased. And from just one or two pairs in England there are now three in the Lake District, three pairs at Kielder, five or six at Rutland and two or three in Wales. There must be 270-plus pairs. The big increases in the future will be in England and Wales. The outlook is good."

What was there still to be learnt about the Osprey? "We need to know much more about their migration south to their winter quarters in Africa and how they live there.

That's why satellite tagging is really significant. I'd been down to The Gambia with Hugh Miles in 1979 when the RSPB Osprey film had been made but learnt nothing more than that this is one of the places where Ospreys spend their winters. I was keen to embark on another fact-finding trip."

It was therefore no surprise to watch BBC TV's *Autumnwatch* in 2011 and follow Roy on his quest. The starting point was the Montgomery Wildlife Trust reserve on the Dyfi Estuary in Wales, where a pair of Ospreys had nested for the first time and reared three chicks. The project team and Roy arrived at the nest and the three chicks were brought down to be ringed and for satellite tags to be fitted. Roy is going to follow their progress during their autumn migration. The female parent bird, Nora, circles overhead, keeping an anxious eye on the proceedings below.

Roy notes, "The chicks are fully grown, but not yet ready to fly. That's perfect." There are two males, Einion and Dulas, and a female, Leri. Each chick is ringed to give it an individual identification and then fitted with a satellite tag held in place on the chick's back by a light nylon harness. The tag not only gives the bird's position but also speed, direction and altitude – a wealth of detail from a device that weighs the same as a packet of crisps and carries its own solar panel to provide power.

At the end of August Roy checks on the young Osprey's progress. They have all fledged successfully and the character of the birds have become evident. Leri was the last to fledge, Dulas the second and Einion, supremely confident and adventurous, the first. Now that they have left the nest, their mother Nora sets off on her migration, leaving them to the care of their father. His job is to feed them well and, over the next few weeks, make sure that they are self-reliant and able to tackle the nearly 5,000 kilometre trip to West Africa. Sadly, only half of all chicks survive their first migration.

Crossing the Bay of Biscay and then the Sahara are two of the biggest challenges the migrating Ospreys face. Information received from Einion's satellite tag indicated that he had flown in from the sea the previous evening and gone to roost in the wood where Roy was now standing. He also knew that Einion had left the wood at dawn and flown down the coast to an estuary where Ospreys are often seen on migration. There was an Osprey there but it wasn't Einion; it was bird ringed in Germany. Einion had rested and fed and flown on.

Following Einion's flight path from his satellite tag readings, Roy was positioned on the hills overlooking the Strait of Gibraltar. High up in the sky were clouds of raptors circling, using the up-draughts to gain height for the crossing to Morocco and Africa. But there was no sighting of Einion. He was ahead of Roy, making good time. He had passed Malaga at 2 p.m. and was strong enough to fly straight across to Africa. Dulas, the other male, had made it too. But Leri came to grief soon after reaching Africa.

Einion's satellite readings told Roy that for the last six weeks he had been at a big coastal lagoon near Dakar in Senegal. This was an area of mangrove swamp, tidal mud flats and open water with plenty of fish – perfect Osprey habitat. You can understand why Ospreys want to spend their winters here. All Roy and his helper, Solomon, have to do is find an Osprey with a blue ring on its leg and a satellite tag on its back. There are plenty of Ospreys to check. They are mostly adults and Einion will find it difficult fitting in with them. Time is running out, so Roy asks some men with a fishing boat to help them. At last they see a juvenile Osprey making itself inconspicuous, hiding behind the bushy branches in the mangrove swamp. But it is not Einion.

One of the fishermen points and calls "Osprey!" Roy scans through his binoculars. Is it really him? He studies the Osprey flying past them. It is! After a five-hour search Roy is relieved to have found Einion. His professional credibility was on the line. The shape of the satellite tag on its back is quite distinctive. There is no doubt about it and Roy and the local fisherman are equally excited. "Time for a hug," says one of the fishermen who had never believed that Ospreys came from Europe. The satellite tag convinced him.

"Satellite tracking really is wonderful," says Roy. "It links Wales with Senegal in Africa and northern Europe with The Gambia and Guinea-Bissau. This means that we are all working together for the conservation of Ospreys all over the whole of our world."

The fortunes of the Osprey have risen like the phoenix from the ashes of centuries of persecution. Conservationists like Roy Dennis have secured their future forever.

THE HONEY BUZZARD

British Isles population (2011): 44 pairs (increasing)

As I left Roy Dennis at the end of my trip to Scotland, thanking him for his help, he shook my hand and said, "Don't forget, David – a Honey Buzzard isn't a buzzard and it doesn't eat honey!"

There has always been a certain mystique about this bird and the confusion about its name has never been corrected. Carl Linnaeus in 1746 exacerbated the problem when he assigned to the Honey Buzzard the scientific name *Pernis apivorous* – *pernis* from the Greek for a type of hawk and *apivorous* from the Latin *apis,* a bee, and *vorus,* eating. I had never seen a Honey Buzzard but I did know some facts: I knew it was the second rarest British breeding bird of prey; it was a late summer migrant, breeding throughout Europe, principally in Scandinavia, Russia and Asia. Britain was on the western edge of its breeding range and it migrated mainly back to Africa during the winter

I recalled that in 2005, on the BBC Television programme *Springwatch,* they had shown a Honey Buzzard that had ditched into the sea off the Isle of Wight and was being cared for by the Hawk Conservancy in Hampshire. Wildlife cameraman Gordon Buchanan had interviewed the girl who was looking after the bird before it could be released. I noticed that it had a much longer neck than a Common Buzzard and that its head was more like that of a Cuckoo, not wedge-shaped as in a typical bird of prey. Its eyes were a glorious yellow. My immediate impression was that it was quite unlike any other British breeding bird of prey.

Some more facts: it is in the late spring, as it displays over its chosen nesting site or later in the summer when it starts feeding its young, that Honey Buzzards are most likely to be seen. When the eggs are being incubated, Honey Buzzards are very secretive, both adults staying mainly below the canopy even when off the nest. It is believed that the male uses this period to locate wasps' nests, making a mental map of their positions. He does this so that as soon as the eggs have hatched he is able to feed wasp grubs to the hungry chicks.

My research had already turned up other intriguing titbits that would readily have found favour in an Agatha Christie novel: the domestic bliss of Hubert and Maria, a mysterious can of film, unexploded bombs and a diplomat in Geneva. I also knew that those who studied the Honey Buzzard kept the whereabouts of the birds they were watching a closely guarded secret.

I knew there was a 'watchpoint' for Honey Buzzards near Scarborough in North Yorkshire and luckily had a friend who lived nearby. I had known Mick Carroll for the last ten years, ever since I had persuaded Natural England to let the Hawk and Owl Trust become its partner in the running of the Fylingdales Moor reserve. He was a member of the North of England Raptor Forum and he knew everyone who was studying raptors. As luck would have it he knew John Harwood who was studying Honey Buzzards in the wooded valleys west of Scarborough. I asked Mick if he thought John would talk to me. He was sure he would.

A few days later Mick rang and told me that John would be glad to meet us at the viewing point at Wykeham Forest at two o'clock on 17 July. My journal for that day reads:

'17/7/12. Left Pickering and drove to viewing point at Crosscliff Wood. Brilliant view across valley. A mix of conifers and deciduous trees. Two Common Buzzards – one executing a switchback flight in the sky, and the other poised against the breeze, hovering.'

When John Harwood arrived I asked him if he remembered seeing his first Honey Buzzard. He said, "My friend, David, rang and told me that he had just seen three Honey Buzzards. I told him I'd meet him the next day. I was driving the kids back from the supermarket and, perhaps over-excited about seeing the Honey Buzzards and crashed my car. The kids were a bit shaken up and the car was a write-off. The next day I rushed round to my parents, borrowed their old BSA bicycle, and biked all the way up here to Crosscliff Wood – quite a ride! I set up my 'scope and that's when I saw my first Honey Buzzard. It just lifted out of the forest right in front of me. No wing-clapping display just a straightforward wheeling, soaring flight. It was the next year that I first saw wing-clapping – I watched one that clapped a hundred sequences in an hour-and-a-half. We've had quite good breeding success – three, possibly four pairs breeding and raising young."

John produced a folder of photographs of individual Honey Buzzards in flight. They were very good quality and what was obvious to me was that there was no uniformity in the plumage, as in most other birds of prey. I asked him why he had taken them and he explained, "I looked in books but I couldn't marry up what I was seeing with their descriptions. They said that males had a broader tail-band and a broader trailing edge and the primaries were diffused – I was always struggling. By taking lots of photographs you get to know the birds as individuals and name them. Raggy, a male, for instance, has some of his secondaries missing. He's got a fault there and there'll always be a gap. Photographs are definitely the key."

There was little activity in front of us so John suggested we move downhill and watch the wooded valley where the River Derwent has its origin. We parked by a gate leading up to a farm. Mick set up his very expensive telescope and we all scanned the area ahead of us. Nothing much happened for about thirty minutes. Suddenly John said, "I'm sure that's a Honey Buzzard." We all had a look through Mick's telescope. John was quite emphatic, "Definite – flat wings, long tail and long neck." I watched it through my binoculars as it

slowly floated along the ridge, wheeling now and then. Suddenly, a Common Buzzard flew up out of the wooded hillside and challenged it. They squared up to each other for a moment. Then, honour satisfied, the Common Buzzard returned to its patch of wood and the Honey Buzzard continued on its way – a magic moment. All the way back to Pickering I mused over the diagnostic features that distinguish a Honey Buzzard from a Common Buzzard – flat wings, long tail, long neck and cuckoo-shaped head.

These diagnostic features are superbly depicted in Lars Jonsson's *Birds of Europe.* Jeremy Mynott in his book, *Birdscapes,* extols the virtues of this pocket-sized bird book. Lars Jonsson, he writes, '... has an astonishing virtuosity and a feel for life-like movement that have rarely been equalled. Most pages are enlivened with a little vignette showing a head from a different angle or the bird in some active pose.' Of particular interest to me was that Jeremy wrote 'a Honey Buzzard on straight wings glides over a Common Buzzard that has slightly bowed ones.'

Back home I consulted my copy of *Eagles, Hawks and Falcons of the World* by Leslie Brown and Dean Amadon, published in 1989. Jack Harrison's illustrations showed just two variations – adult light phase and dark phase. The illustrations were obviously drawn from skins because he had given the birds yellow ceres – a bit of a howler! J.A. Baker, who wrote that masterpiece *The Peregrine*, stated 'Pictures are waxworks beside the passionate mobility of the living bird.' He might have added that, in reality, they often bear no relation to the wide variety of plumage as the birds progress into adulthood.

Adult male and female Honey Buzzards are very similar. The tip of the bill is black and fades upwards to blue-grey. The cere is dark grey. Unlike other birds of prey there are no bristles around the eye, which is bright yellow and appears rounder because the eyelid is not so extensive, and it is not shielded as in other birds of prey by a prominent supra-orbital protective ridge. The cuckoo-like head and long neck are special adaptations for burrowing into wasps' nests. The head is covered by short, stiff, scale-like grey feathers, which may possibly protect the bird from being stung by wasps. In the female these feathers may be paler than in the male. The neck and upperparts are dark brown. The light brown tail has two broad, black bands at the base and another, broader one, at the tip, which has a white edge. The underparts are white with narrow brown streaks from the crop downwards, changing to broad, dark bars on the rest of the underside. The yellow legs are thick and scaly. The short black talons are straight and blunt, specially adapted for digging out wasps' nests. Honey Buzzards walk easily and can run as fast as a chicken.

What I have described here is what is known as the standard, text-book Honey Buzzard's plumage, but it is not necessarily the commonest. The breast colouring of Honey Buzzards varies tremendously and ranges from dark plum coloured to almost completely white and unmarked. The plumage of juveniles is equally variable, although most are dark brown and, having regular barring on their wings and tail, they are very like the Common Buzzard. However, their eyes are dark brown.

My next port of call was the bird of prey watchpoint at Swanton Novers in Norfolk. Honey Buzzards have been nesting there and at nearby Sennowe Park for the last 20 years. Here I met Robert Baker who has been the Honey Buzzard warden at Swanton Novers for the past 17 years. I asked him how long Honey Buzzards had been nesting in that area and he said, "I've talked to the old head keeper here and he reckoned, back in the '60s, they had Buzzards here. There were no Buzzards in Norfolk then, so they must have been Honey Buzzards."

I then asked Robert what attracted Honey Buzzards to Swanton Novers and was told, "They need good quality woodland with big trees to nest in, oaks for preference. And most importantly they want ponds with good amphibian populations. When they first arrive there are no wasps nests. So, from early May to the latter part of June, they're feeding on frogs and other amphibians. From the end of June they feed mainly on wasp grubs. To sum up, the Honey Buzzard's preferred breeding habitat is old woodland with big trees near a stately home with a lake."

I immediately realized that Holkham Hall in Norfolk, the Palladian-style ancestral home of the Coke family, the Earls of Leicester, of Holkham, absolutely fitted the bill. It had extensive grounds of 10,000 hectares, mature woodland and a lake, ideal habitat for a Honey Buzzard.

I knew just the man to talk to – Andy Bloomfield – who wrote the excellent *Birds of the Holkham Area* guide book. I asked him how he got interested in raptors and he explained, "A life-long obsession with birds of prey didn't emerge until my early teens. In the late '70s and '80s birds of prey were phenomenally rare in North Norfolk. I didn't see a Sparrowhawk 'till 1981 – it lay dead alongside a Fieldfare below a neighbour's shattered garage window. Hunter and hunted coming to the same abrupt end after the Fieldfare's dash for safety. It was two years later that I saw my first live one. Then, it was hard to believe that within ten years they would be relatively common, with seven pairs nesting within a three mile radius of my house. It's the same with other raptors. I saw four Rough-legged Buzzards before I saw a Common Buzzard. Now the Common Buzzard is the commonest bird of prey. There are 30 pairs of Marsh Harriers breeding on the estate or on the reserve. Red Kites are nesting here and so is that rarest of British birds of prey, the Montagu's Harrier. Gradually the countryside around me seems to be becoming a much more welcome place for raptors. Changing attitudes have helped Holkham, a large and active shooting estate, become one of the richest environments for raptors in the county."

Andy's book informed me that the Honey Buzzard had not nested at Holkham but that there had been 16 recorded sightings from 1854 to 1993. The most famous Honey Buzzard was in 1976, before Andy's time. It was present in the pine woods at nearby Wells for five days in October. Not only was it incredibly tame, allowing a close approach, but it was also seen excavating a wasps' nest. Bird-watchers and dog walkers were able to walk past within 20 metres of the bird, which was quite unconcerned and oblivious as it dug away, finally revealing the wasps' nest. During the time it was present the bird became quite a celebrity.

The first Honey Buzzard recorded at Holkham, described in Stevenson's *Birds of Norfolk,* was a female killed there in July 1854. This is now an exhibit in the Holkham collection. Stevenson notes: '… the grey head in this species denotes the adult state, all other peculiarities of plumage, from the deep brown of the earliest stage, being either gradual advances to maturity or more often accidental varieties.' Later, Stevenson writes: 'In September, 1854, a young male was captured at Holkham, and in this case the bird was observed by a keeper to rise from a bank near a wasps' nest, and was trapped soon afterwards on the same spot.'

I knew I must inspect the two specimens in the collection and, at the same time, I wanted to look at two books which might be in the Holkham library. The first was a translation into English of Ray and Willughby's *Ornithologia* published in 1678. In it I was sure there was the first description of a Honey Buzzard, and I was keen to confirm whether this was the case. The Holkham library might also contain a copy of Eleazar Albin's *A Natural History of Birds* published between 1731 and 1738, which contained the first illustration of a Honey Buzzard.

I contacted Dr Suzanne Reynolds, curator of the library, who confirmed the existence of those titles in the library and offered to arrange for me to see the bird collection at the same time. A few days later I drove over to Holkham and parked by the steps leading into the building. As I did so a side door opened and Suzanne Reynolds beckoned me over. Rather than making me trek up to the library she had brought the books I had requested to her office. I started with Ray and Willughby's *Ornithologia,* the first significant bird book in the world, bringing order out of a hitherto random assembly of names and observations.

John Ray was educated at Cambridge University, where he was elected Greek and Mathematical lecturer at Trinity College and was already interested in biology when he met Francis Willughby. Together they made three journeys through England and Wales and a fourth through Europe. They took every opportunity to obtain specimens from the market, dead and alive, making detailed drawings and descriptions. By 1 October 1663 they were in Venice and saw 'Ruffs, Avocets and Water Rails, besides a Little Egret and a Sea Eagle, and Brambling Finches in profusion.'

On their return, Willughby, who was not very strong, became ill and died. An annuity he bequeathed to Ray gave him the impetus and means to write the *Ornithologia.* When their book was published in 1676, Francis Willughby's name was at the head of the title page, although it is generally believed that the book was the work of John Ray.

The great strength of the *Ornithologia* was that it attempted a simple classification based on which were land and which were water birds. It went further than that in that it systematically classified those birds with similar characteristics into separate classes: Land birds 1 – those with crooked beaks and claws; and Land birds 2 – those with straight beaks. There were further sub-divisions, for example of Land birds 1 into diurnal birds of prey, nocturnal birds of prey and fruit-eaters. Altogether, some 230 birds were described.

There were very good illustrations, mainly from dead birds, and some interesting observations. For example: 'What becomes of the cuckoo in the wintertime, whether hiding herself in hollow trees or other holes and caverns she lies torpid, and at the return of spring revives again; or rather at the approach of winter, being impatient of the cold, shifts place and departs into hot countries, is not as yet to me certainly known.' It was, perhaps, the start of the enquiring mind into another aspect of the natural world – hibernation and migration.

The book I now held in my hand was the translation from the original Latin text into English and had been published in 1678. It was in three parts: *Of the Art of Fowling, Of the Ordering of Singing Birds* and finally *Of Falconry*. I flicked through the pages of the second part and there on page 72 was the description of the Honey Buzzard. The authors point out several important features: 'the cere is black with the nosthrils, which are not exactly round, but long and bending. The irides of the Eyes of a lovely bright yellow or Saffron colour.'

One of the authors must have climbed up to a Honey Buzzards' nest, for they note: 'We saw one that made use of an old Kites' nest to breed in, and that fed its Young with Nymphæ of Wasps: for in the nest we found the Combs of Wasps Nests, and in the stomachs of the Young the limbs and fragments of Wasp-Maggots.' They go on to observe 'This bird runs very swiftly like a Hen.' They would also have seen that its talons were short and stubby, all the better for digging out a wasps' nest. Then, to my amazement, they pin-point the diagnostic features which distinguish it from the Common Buzzard: '1. In having a longer tail. 2. An ash-coloured head. 3. The Irides of the Eyes yellow. 4. Thicker and shorter feet. 5. In the broad transverse dun beds (brownish-grey bars) or streaks in the wings and tail; which are about three inches broad.' They conclude by stating emphatically that 'It hath not as yet (that we know of) been described by any Writer, though it be frequent enough with us.' It was John Ray who coined the name Honey Buzzard which has confused us ever since. My friend Richard Fegen, a first class writer of television comedies, was intrigued and put pen to paper:

> *Consider this bird*
> *And logic gets fuzz-ed*
> *It doesn't eat honey*
> *And it isn't a buzzard.*

There was no illustration in the *Ornithologia* of a Honey Buzzard, so I turned to the three volumes of the *Natural History of Birds* by Eleazar Albin published between 1731 and 1738. He was an accomplished artist and in volume one there was a full page plate of a Honey Buzzard. It was the first time a likeness of this bird had been attempted. It was a little bit crude and the barring across the chest was more like that of a Goshawk rather than the bold splotches of a Honey Buzzard.

I was about to leave when Lord Coke came in. I congratulated him on the number of Marsh Harriers nesting on the estate: 30 pairs in 2012. He asked me what I was doing and I told him about my book and my current interest in Honey Buzzards. He wanted to know if they took game birds and I was able to assure him that they did not. They turned up at places like Holkham because of the parkland, old trees and the lake and fed on frogs from May until the end of June and thereafter mainly on wasps. I thanked him for letting me look at the bird books and was then handed over to Colin Shearer to look at the collection of stuffed birds that is housed in the old servants' hall.

There were 220 species in the collection. Lord Leicester had shot some of them and the head keeper, Sam Bone, accounted for most of the remainder. The main taxidermist employed was J.A. Cole of Norwich. Colin led me over to the case of Honey Buzzards. There on the left was the adult female killed in July 1854 and facing it was the young male trapped near a wasps' nest in September of the same year.

As I drove away from Holkham, satisfied and grateful for what I had seen, I could not help wondering what impact the craze for collections of stuffed birds had had on some of our rarer species. Had the Honey Buzzard once been more widespread than it is now? I needed to talk to an expert, and I knew just the man.

Steve Roberts has been studying Honey Buzzards for 25 years and he has done more than anyone to dispel the myths that surround this bird. He deals in facts: "When I started my work on Honey Buzzards there was a tiny crowd of people who said that Honey Buzzards should be left alone because they were too sensitive. So the first thing I've tried to do is to raise the profile of the Honey Buzzard, to give it better recognition. To show that you can do research work on them, that they are not that sensitive provided you're sensible. Increasingly, if people understand what you're doing and see the results you are achieving, it's very encouraging when they accept your point of view. Now there are groups of enthusiasts working in Wales, the New Forest, Surrey, Sussex and Kent, Hampshire, Nottinghamshire, Yorkshire and Scotland. The breeding population of Honey Buzzards in the British Isles, at the start of the 21st century, was given as 30 confirmed pairs plus a further possible 21 pairs. This is minuscule compared to a European population of 160,000 breeding pairs. Practically all the original observations on breeding populations have been confined to lowland woodland. Now, upland conifer plantations have been identified as breeding areas. We studied a 3,500 hectare block of upland conifer plantation and compared it with a 24,000 hectare lowland woodland in southern England. In the upland woodland three active nests were found. There was a fourth pair but their nesting attempt failed. Seven nests were located in the lowland wood, with another pair possibly breeding but not confirmed. This study shows that there is a far greater potential habitat in which Honey Buzzards can breed. Our current estimate is that the Honey Buzzard breeding population in the British Isles should be revised upwards to between 100–150 pairs."

On 17 February 2012, BBC Television showed an item on *The One Show* in which Mike Dilger interviewed Steve Roberts. They had a Closed Circuit Television (CCTV) camera sited by the Honey Buzzards' nest in which were two well-grown chicks. Mike and Steve are watching images relayed from the nest. At that moment the female arrived with a bit of wasp comb and set about feeding her chicks. Mike reminds us that although these images are captivating, the main purpose is to ring the two Honey Buzzard chicks. Steve climbs the tree and the two chicks are lowered in a canvas bag. While Mike holds the chick Steve fixes a coloured ring on the bird's leg. He explains that these coloured bands contain a unique letter code, revealing where and when the chicks hatched. The other chick is ringed and they are replaced in the nest. Mike wishes them well for their extraordinary non-stop flight to Africa that they will soon be undertaking.

I asked Steve what the exposure on *The One Show* had achieved? He replied, "Everything helps to raise the profile of the bird. Nest cameras and ringing have been a springboard to greater knowledge of their breeding behaviour. Previously, papers stated categorically that Honey Buzzards reared in England did not return there to breed. We have proved, through the use of nest cameras and ringing, that juveniles leave their natal site and migrate to Africa before returning to the British Isles, two years later, to breed. This is how we found out. In 2006 a pair of Honey Buzzards nested in South Wales. The female had been ringed as a chick in 2000 and the male in 2002. The female had first been seen in 2004 and in 2005 paired up with the male and they built a 'summer nest', a trial nest. The following year they bred and reared one chick. This was the first confirmed breeding in the UK of British-reared birds. We knew all this because we were able to put a camera on the nest and match up the black identifying letters and numbers etched into the white rings. Since then we've also had birds that returned to their natal area to breed. One even mated with its mother."

I knew that Steve had spent a season watching a Honey Buzzard nest in detail, checking on the food brought in. He said, "The Honey Buzzard feeds its young chicks the pupae and larvae that it digs out of wasps' nests. There are two species of wasps that nest underground – the Common Wasp and the German Wasp. These nests have to be dug out but as they are generally situated in the leaf-litter of the wood they are readily accessible. Other wasps, such as the Norwegian Wasp, build nests suspended from vegetation. But whatever the species there would be no point in harvesting them before they have properly developed. So the Honey Buzzard probably uses this period to map out the location of wasps' nests for future reference. In the meantime, the male parent bird hunts for amphibians, particularly frogs, and feeds them to the chicks. Frogs and wasp grubs make up the bulk of the young Honey Buzzard's diet. I hope that my work and that of my fellow enthusiasts will foster a better understanding of the Honey Buzzard, dispel the myths that have surrounded it and assist in the conservation of the species in the British Isles. It is not the hyper-sensitive bird of prey that some writers have dubbed it. It is no different from any other bird of prey and, as such, should be treated with the respect that it deserves. If anyone has concerns about the Honey Buzzard's tolerance to disturbance I urge them to read the chapter on Honey Buzzards in Major Anthony Buxton's book *Sporting Interludes at Geneva*."

The book *Sporting Interludes at Geneva* immediately rang a bell. I remembered that Major Anthony Buxton had been a diplomat at The League of Nations in Geneva from 1929. In his spare, time he and his companion, George Crees, used to go bird-watching in the wooded valleys that carried water into the river Rhone. This is Buxton's account of what happened on 23 May one year: '… and there I sat, when – swish, flop! And a whacking great hawk landed in a spruce just over my head. Little birds are very pleasant, but once in a way I do like something big, and here it was – and not only big but unknown. I put my telescope on him with that pleasant sensation which only a telescope gives, and gives to the full when the object is something really new. The bird was obliging enough to sit perfectly still for his examination, and I recognized him from his portrait in Dresser's *Birds of Europe* as a cock Honey Buzzard, lazily enjoying the morning sun and apparently in full possession of all he surveyed.'

Anthony Buxton then very cleverly introduces the male Honey Buzzard just as if he was a character in a play: 'If you think of an old gentleman with grey hair (parrot grey) and a brilliant yellow eye, dressed in a white tie, white shirt, white waistcoat, short white trousers and a grey-brown tail coat with dark bars across the tails, you will gain a very fair idea of his appearance. Was he expecting a lady, and, if so, what would she be like?'

We are now on tenterhooks wondering what his mate will be like: 'There was no long delay; two great birds glided past me – my new acquaintance following a forbidding-looking female the colour of a chocolate éclair fading to coffee on parts of the tail. This is not, I understand from the books, the correct dress for a hen Honey Buzzard, but I cannot help that, and in any case it was the dress she wore.'

Shortly afterwards the Honey Buzzards' nest was found: 'There, in an ivy-covered oak, was a large, untidy nest, and from it with a splutter of wings came the hen, knocking off as she rose a sprig of fresh oak leaves. Judging by the hawk standard they were not shy, and by the time I had finished with them their tameness, especially that of the hen, was quite absurd. It was impossible to go on calling them 'the cock' and 'the hen'; I shall always know them as "Hubert" and "Maria".

Anthony Buxton realized that there was a unique chance of photographing the Honey Buzzards at the nest. Help was needed. The Geneva Fire Brigade and telephone service both said no. Their ladders were for the benefit of the public and not for bird nesting. Eventually, a tree surgeon agreed to help and produced the very article. As Buxton explains: 'This absurd contraption, which could be raised, lowered and turned at any angle, was first dumped at about fifty metres from the nest.' Slowly, it was moved forward, day by day, until the hide on top of the ladder was only three metres from the nest, by which time the birds took no notice of it whatsoever. 'To go into details, and you can go into details when you watch from such a short distance, the babies were for the first fortnight delightful little balls of creamy cotton-wool, with black noses and black (not yellow) eyes, which played very like puppies that are just beginning to walk. What did they eat? Wasp grubs, of course, and wasps grubs galore.' Anthony Buxton worked out that the Honey Buzzards, Hubert and Maria and their two chicks, accounted for 90,000 wasp grubs during their three-month stay in the valley leading into the Rhone.

For three years running Buxton and Crees watched and photographed the family life of the pair of Honey Buzzards, Hubert and Maria. He ends with this plea: 'Will these pictures do what I should like them to do? Will they persuade those to whom the pheasant and the partridge are sacred birds to stay the hands of their keepers from destroying, as they have destroyed, everything with a hooked beak and a sharp claw, without bothering to find out how they gain a living? Surely a bird that comes all the way from Africa to eat ninety thousand of our wasps in a season is worth something better than a charge of powder and shot.'

I was checking the story again when I suddenly noticed this sentence: 'The film camera spring was pressed with the right hand the moment the parent passed a slit in the hide on its way to the nest, while the left hand felt for the camera release in the hope of a portrait as it lit.' Buxton had been filming as well as taking still photographs. But what had happened to the film?

I rang Eddie Anderson, who had travelled with me to Falsterbo in Sweden to watch the Sparrowhawk migration. He told me that when he was working for Anglia Television he had interviewed John Buxton, Anthony Buxton's son. John was an eminent wildlife cameraman and conservationist who, almost single-handed, had restored the fortunes of the Common Crane as a breeding bird in the British Isles. Eddie remembered that during the interview John, after he had reminisced about his grandfather, a big game hunter, went on to talk about his father, who was also a wildlife photographer and a passionate conservationist. The story of Hubert and Maria was discussed and John revealed that his father had filmed them and, moreover, that the cans of film were at his home in the gun room. This was very exciting news.

I immediately rang John and he confirmed that his father had filmed the Honey Buzzards and that indeed the cans of film were stacked up in the gun room. I asked him if we could try and restore the film with a view to looking at it. That was alright as far as he was concerned but he warned me that I must remember that it was silver nitrate film and might be unstable and combust spontaneously. This was very worrying.

I was cheered up later in the day when I spoke to Ian Newton. He said there was a Honey Buzzard researcher in the Netherlands that I ought to talk to – Rob Bijlsma. I emailed him and a week later we made contact. He immediately sent me a long email detailing his impressions of the Honey Buzzard: 'Originally the Honey Buzzard was a sort of enigma to me. It's a late arrival to the breeding grounds (from early May onwards), very secretive, not very vocal, the male and female both incubate which means that males don't bring food to the incubating female – they forage for themselves. Nests are often hidden and the birds keep quiet near the nest. Only when the eggs have hatched can you spot food being brought in. That's the time when you need to climb the highest trees in the forest and make a nest for yourself just below the tree top. I cut away all the obstructing branches and settle down to watch for 4–6 hours. By scanning the sky and horizon I try to spot food-carrying adults. Several flights in are enough to make a triangulation and pin-point the nest site. It works like a charm. Honey Buzzards are wonderful birds. They may seem weak and J.F. Naumann (1780–1857), the German naturalist, describes them as an ignoble, cowardly raptor. Obviously, he never saw one close to hand. They will remain on the nest as you climb up to it, and then strike you with powerful wing-beats. Or peck you on the nose! The stiff feathers on the neck can be raised when agitated and I never forget the first one I captured. An adult was digging up a large wasps' nest and I stalked and captured it by hand. How yellow the pupil was, how powerful the wing-beats, the audible panting, the bill dripping. The surprisingly powerful grip (not like the death grip of a Goshawk, but powerful nonetheless). The scaly feet and the strange feathers in the neck. The feathers look scaly, and according to the book they are stiff enough to shield against wasp stings.'

Rob went on to tell me that he had taken on several Honey Buzzards from rehabilitation centres and released them back into the wild: 'Several of these birds became very tame,

especially Warp (named after the warp speed of the Starship Enterprise). She was near death when found but recuperated unbelievably fast. And there was Burp (yes, he was burping a lot). These birds I could follow closely throughout the day for weeks, watching how they located and predated wasps' nests. It turned out that the stiff feathers are not so much used as a shield against stings, but can be rippled very fast. In this way, wasps cannot even land on the head, especially when done in combination with head shaking. The strangest thing happens when a Honey Buzzard attacks a wasps' nest. All flying workers attack, but these attacks die down after a couple of minutes until no further attacks take place. It is more likely that the wasps themselves produce a chemical signal. Interestingly, not only do the attacks stop, but all incoming workers with food stop arriving. Remember that Honey Buzzards do a lot of digging before they can even touch a wasp comb. It may take an hour to extricate it from the ground. Honey Buzzards do get stung. I have seen Burp, for example, fleeing a nest followed by a string of angry workers, and frantically starting to preen underneath his wings, taking out wasps. Another time, he jumped suddenly, followed by hectic preening. It was precisely the reaction you'd expect to being stung. In contrast to myself, though, he had his plumage in order and seemed relaxed again in no time. In an evolutionary way, it makes sense for Honey Buzzards to be more insensitive to stings than we are.'

I have always treated wasps with the greatest of respect. When I lived in London I had a small garden and in the left-hand corner was a rotten tree stump. It had been there for years. One summer wasps built their nest under it. They were a nuisance and I tried every way I could to get rid of them. I even poured petrol down into the nest. I tied a bit of rag to a bamboo cane, lit it and touched the petrol soaked entrance to the wasps' nest. There was a satisfactory *whump!* I congratulated myself, job done. Three months later in the autumn my black Labrador, Friday, and I were doing some tidying up in the garden. I saw the rotten tree stump and thought to myself, just put the garden fork under it and it'll come out like a rotten tooth. I did just that and in a fraction of a second my dog and I were covered in wasps. I do not think I actually screamed, but I do remember peeling off my poloneck sweater and throwing it as far away as possible. My poor dog could not get rid of them so easily and was miserable for days after. The memory of that wasps' nest haunts me still.

Digging up wasps' nests is second nature to Dr Manuel (Manny) Hinge. He had made films on wasps, on Honey Buzzards and all the birds of prey that inhabited the New Forest. I knew he had also made a great number of excellent films for the BBC Natural History Unit. In particular, he had worked with Hugh Miles on *The Phantom of the Forest*, the excellent film on the Goshawk. He worked very closely with Peter Dodson, who had developed high-definition mini-cameras for nest surveillance. I was anxious to meet them both but knew that I would not get anywhere unless I had Andy Page, the head keeper for the New Forest, on my side. Luckily, Eddie Anderson had directed a natural history series the year before, part of which had been shot in the New Forest. He and his wife, Tina, volunteered to come with me to pave the way.

There was also Chris Packham, who had lived in the New Forest nearly all his life. Years ago, his teacher, Mr Buckley, had contacted me and asked if I could help this very keen young lad get hold of a couple of Barn Owls. I had just finished my cinema film *Tarka the Otter* and had two captive-bred Barn Owls which needed a home and I was able to send them to Chris. I thought I would give him a ring before I went down there. I asked him about his memories of the New Forest and he said, "We lived on the east side of Southampton and I remember my father taking me on lizard-catching expeditions on the heathlands of the New Forest, coming back with jam jars full of lizards. And then our first batting evening. I wanted to see a bat. We went camping, pitched our tent and saw what was undoubtedly a Daubenton's Bat. I was over the moon. The north of the New Forest was very quiet then and you might only see three or four people in a morning. It's only in recent years that it has become more crowded. There is a deer problem. They graze away the understorey until it's as smooth as a billiard table. And, of course, there are the ponies and cattle too. Where I live, the guy who manages it has certainly done his bit. He's a good naturalist and it's brilliant for butterflies, good numbers of Silver-washed Fritillaries, White Admirals, Brimstones, the whole lot. Bluebells, Honeysuckle and all the things you don't see if you walk five hundred metres down the road because there it's massively overgrazed. The first Honey Buzzard I saw would have been in 1979. I was with a fellow called Dave Scott and we were driving along a road and a Buzzard flew over and he said "Honey Buzzard." We leapt out and it started spiralling around and it was a Honey Buzzard without a shadow of a doubt. In those days Honey Buzzards were incredibly well guarded. Had I heard what Colonel Richard Meinertzhagen had done. Honey Buzzards nested in the New Forest in 1957 and he was determined that they shouldn't be disturbed by egg collectors. So he put up notices at all the entrances to the wood: 'Unexploded Bombs – Keep Out.' It certainly kept people out but got Meinertzhagen into trouble from the War Office for 'alarming the public.'"

Chris finished by saying, "The New Forest is a place that's under tremendous pressure, but it's still aesthetically beautiful and it still holds some species of importance in the British Isles. You'll enjoy it."

Just before we left for the New Forest I heard from Jan Faull, Archive Production Curator at The British Film Institute. They would be interested in seeing if Anthony Buxton's film of the Geneva Honey Buzzards could be rescued. This was good news indeed.

I had arranged with Manny Hinge that we would meet him at our hotel on arrival and had asked whether he could take us on a trip around the New Forest – just to give us a flavour. I knew that the Forest had been established over 900 years ago as a hunting forest by William the Conqueror and that it was unique, covering nearly 15,000 hectares and consisting of woodland, heathland, grassland and marsh. An extract from my journal:

'14/8/12. 1430. Manny Hinge was waiting for us outside our hotel. He's a big man, very genial and highly intelligent. He has a PhD in deer management. Honey Buzzards are his obsession. He's been filming them since the early 1990s but has been plagued by changes in equipment and the switch from film to tape. As we skirted Minstead Woods, Manny told us that Hawfinches have done well this year. He stopped his car to point out one of his transmitters set up at the top of a conifer. They've been sited at the top of tall trees to transmit signals from a nest camera deep in the forest – it was too far to cable. Stopped to watch two newly fledged Hobbies. One parent bird swished past, very elegant, fast flight. The two young were fluttering, rather like Cuckoos, from branch to branch of a dead tree. A bit farther on we looked down on a herd of Fallow Deer. About a hundred of them, chestnut with white spots. One pale one, not albino. Nearby, a Common Buzzard sat in a dead tree overlooking the little sandy valley. Manny moved us on and we cut under the*

A31 – there's an underpass with CCTV to check on those who use it. We saw stampeding horses but couldn't see what caused it. At Cadnam's Pool we saw a hawker dragonfly darting about, skimming the water elegantly. Then through Fritham where we put up a juvenile hen Sparrowhawk. It flew ahead of us and then plunged into a ditch after a cock Chaffinch. Missed it. Wasn't at all fazed by our car, settled in tree, glared around, then flew off. From there we drove to Acres Down. Brilliant light. It's an excellent viewpoint looking over where Goshawks and Honey Buzzards nest. Wood Pigeons flying around but nothing else. Isle of Wight seen in the far distance. Stayed there about 30 minutes and then back to the hotel.'

As we thanked Manny for the guided tour, I told him that etiquette dictated that I ought to interview Andy Page first. Would it suit him if I met him at the hotel for a chat about 11 a.m.?

The next morning saw us sitting in Andy Page's office, facing him across his desk. Outside it was teeming down. I asked him to tell us about his job. He told us, "I've been head keeper here for sixteen years. Originally I only looked after half of the New Forest but about eighteen months ago I took over the whole forest. We've also amalgamated with the south-east district as well. That stretches as far up as Farnham and down to the South Downs. The New Forest is a mecca for bird-watchers. We have eight different birds of prey breeding here and there's another six species that can be seen hunting through the forest at various times of the year. My problem is that I have to balance caring for the wildlife with forestry work – work which can impact on the landscape and its wildlife. In the old days each tree was assessed individually and a nest could be spotted and that tree would be spared. Nowadays a tree is cut and processed in less than a minute. That's why one of my most important jobs is inspecting each section of wood before it is felled, checking for bird of prey nest sites. I do this with a small group of Forestry Commission keepers and a few dedicated enthusiasts. Birds of prey in the New Forest have been documented since Victorian times because of egg collectors and taxidermists. Over the last fifty years detailed observations have thrown light on the private lives of the New Forest's birds of prey. Unquestionably, the most elusive and mysterious of our birds of prey is the Honey Buzzard. Looking for nests can take forever. You go to the obvious places first, the trees you'd expect them to nest in and then work in from there. They are very secretive. They fly in and out of the wood not necessarily in relation to where the nest site is. They'll fly low along rides, take a right and come out on the other side of the wood. We searched one wood, checked every tree. Everyone ignored the *Liriodendron*, the tulip tree – that's where the nest was!"

It was still raining when we left Andy. Back at the hotel Manny was waiting for us. We found a quiet room, checked the tape recorder and asked him how he got started? "There were two people who influenced me. First, there was Eric Ashby. He made films in the New Forest and he used to give film shows at the community centre in the mid-1960s. My mother would take me there and I sat there taking it all in. That took me from stills to movies The second person that moulded my career was Hugh Miles. He actually concentrated on filming animals behaving naturally. I was following Hugh's standard when I started making a film about Honey Buzzards in 1997. Hugh always wanted to push the frontiers forward. I've never filmed things that were easy – I've always gone for the hard shoots, species that haven't been filmed before. My first attempt failed. I got a few shots of them flying away and that was that. If you fail at something it sort of eggs you on. Anyhow a little bit later I was making a film in France and was told that they'd got hundreds of Honey Buzzards there. The next year I went back with all my kit including a 25 metre scaffold tower. And the only things the owners of the land forbade me to do were: to set fire to it; pick any mushrooms; or shoot anything and eat it. Anything else, do what you like. I took a friend with me – he was the nest finder – so I could just get on with making the film. We had a bit of luck early on, almost tripped over a Honey Buzzard that was digging out a wasps' nest. It flew off and we waited for it to come back – because you know they're going to come back. We put a hide on the opposite side of the ride and waited. Nothing happened. So I parked the camper van in the middle of the wood and ran an audio cable from there to a microphone placed by the wasps' nest. As soon as I heard the wasps making a lot of noise I snuck into the hide and there was the Honey Buzzard digging out the nest. Brilliant!"

I asked Manny if the Honey Buzzards ever got stung? "I don't think anyone knows, to be really honest. Their heads are very well protected with short, stiff feathers. They probably also endow themselves with lots of wasp scent from digging into the nest. Therefore a wasp, after the immediate reaction, wouldn't necessarily sting its own kind. From my 25 metre tower in France I've spent a lot of time just watching them. They bring wasp comb in and they feed the young chicks wasp grubs out of the comb or just give them the comb depending on the age of the young. Afterwards the adults take the empty papier-mâché comb and force it down into the base of the nest. Why? Is it waterproofing? Is it to prevent predators finding the nest? Or could it be its antiseptic properties or a protective scent? It's a behaviour that needs studying more closely." I interrupted, "What about CCTV?" "That's Peter's department – talk to him," Manny replied.

So off we went to find Peter Dodson. On the way there I told Eddie and Tina that I remembered being at the BBC Natural History Unit in Bristol when Heinz Sielmann showed his Black Woodpecker film for the first time. He had, day by day, carefully cut away the back of the tree until there was a hole big enough to take the lens of the camera. That was the start of really intimate pictures from a nest site being shown on television. By now we had arrived at Peter Dodson's house.

I asked Peter how he and Manny had got involved in putting cameras on nests and he explained, "It was very tricky to start off with. Manny was making a Honey Buzzard film in the mid-1990s and he used a 16 mm Arriflex camera with a 120 metre magazine – that's ten minutes running time. The camera was attached to the tree and by fitting a periscopic lens Manny was able to film over the edge of the nest. There was a long cable with a switch to start and stop the camera. Manny had video-assist so he could see what he was filming. But he was limited by just having ten minutes of film. He had to be very circumspect about what was filmed. With the advent of video cameras the possibilities were endless. The cameras were small, you could record behaviour at the nest at the crack of dawn without having to re-load, and you could record in infra-red at night. We were always trying to improve the lenses and finding less bulky equipment onto which to record the pictures. That's how the clamshell recorder, a little recorder with a flip-up screen, was conceived. For direct public viewing you'd try and find a nest near your visitor centre and then you'd run the pictures down a cable direct to the screen. But Goshawk nests aren't necessarily sited so conveniently, so we had to transmit across the forest to a receiver which could then transmit on ad infinitum until the signal reached the visitor centre. In 2010 we put a pan-tilt-zoom, PTZ, camera, ten metres away, on a Goshawk nest. We had to have many tractor-sized batteries to power the camera and lens. We covered them with boards and leaf-litter. The batteries had to be changed every week. The lens had a wiper on it. To avoid upsetting the birds we had to raise it slowly to an upright position and only then use the wiper to clean the lens. We got a wonderful sequence when one of the juvenile Goshawks noticed the lens being adjusted. It may have spotted its reflection. It leaned right forward and glared into the lens. A wonderful shot. The future is in HD and 3D. The other big step forward is that cabling and transmitters in trees will become a thing of the past as the new broadband satellite comes into commission. That will make it much simpler and bring the costs down. It means you can put cameras on nests in places that you would never have dreamed of trying before."

It had stopped raining by the time we left Peter Dodson, so we headed off down towards Beaulieu where Eddie remembered seeing Honey Buzzards. My journal entry for that day:

'15/8/12. 1415. Blue sky, sun and wind. Drove past Beaulieu station and parked at Pig Bush. Walked through edge of wood to open area with lone oak. Spotted a flock of Siskins

zipping around. Then looking south-west over woods saw a bird of prey. Pointed it out to Eddie – could it be a Honey Buzzard? We watched it for a long time as it flew over woodland. We hummed and hawed over it – couldn't make up our minds. It reminded me of a Manny Hinge story. We were looking at something that almost looked like a bit of dust on my binoculars and I said, "How do you know it's a Honey Buzzard?" "Oh, it's the 'jizz' it gives you, that sort of thing," he replied. It slowly got closer and closer and it did turn out to be a Honey Buzzard. My friend has never allowed me to forget it.'

We had supper with Manny that evening and as we said our goodbyes he gave me a copy of his Honey Buzzard film. As I thanked him I told him about our progress with Anthony Buxton's film of Honey Buzzards shot in 1929 just outside Geneva. We still did not know whether the footage could be salvaged.

The next day I watched Manny Hinge's superb film, *Honey Buzzard – Wasp Hunter*, which was shot in France. The film vividly portrays the wildlife of the French forests to which the Honey Buzzard flies after spending the winter in Africa. It includes intricate, detailed shots of the life-cycle of a wasp, intercut with the arrival of the Honey Buzzards in early May. We are shown their breeding behaviour, including nest building and shots of an intruder being chased off, copulation, egg-laying and the antics of the chicks in the nest after hatching. The high point of the film, though, is the footage of the Honey Buzzard's determination as it stalks through the long grass along a forest ride, tracking wasps as they return to their nest. It starts digging. The worker wasps swarm around the Honey Buzzard, attacking it. One of them tries to sting it in the eye. The bird's nictitating membrane seals off the eye, brushing the wasp out of the way. The Honey Buzzard, after more furious digging, eventually uncovers the nest and tears off sections of comb which are then carried back to the nest where the grubs are fed to the hungry chicks. It is a quite outstanding film, crammed with interesting behaviour and exquisitely photographed.

A year later, after many false alarms, Eddie Anderson took the reels of film down to London. Here, Prime Focus, a film treatment and restoration facility, successfully resurrected Anthony Buxton's black-and-white film of the Honey Buzzards "Hubert" and "Maria" nesting in the Rhone Valley near Geneva.

The film, which had not been edited, was probably obtained over ten days. The nest was built on a horizontal branch in an oak tree clad with ivy. The single chick was well-grown and was getting ready for its first flight with a prodigious amount of wing-flapping. From time to time this was interrupted by the parent birds flying in and delivering large portions of wasp-nest comb. These the chick grabbed and started picking out the grubs. There were shots of the portable fireman's ladder used for reaching the hide that was precariously set up in the tree, and one shot of the chick being fed from the end of a pole poked out from the hide.

A few days later the chick, now full-grown, had left the nest and was wing-flapping on a nearby branch. As it flew off on its first flight, through the trees down the Rhone valley, I realized how privileged I had been to see such a pioneering film shortly after seeing Manny Hinge's classic state-of-the-art production.

The Honey Buzzard is a very secretive bird and some experts have even called it a sensitive bird. But having seen these two films I realize that, like all birds of prey, if approached cautiously it is very tolerant of disturbance and that it is possible to observe and record its private life and dispel the myth that it is a buzzard that eats honey.

THE RED KITE

British Isles population (2006–10): 1,600 pairs (increasing)

It is May, 1990. Bruce and I park at the RSPB reserve at Dinas, which is ten miles north of Llandovery in Wales. It is a blazing hot day and we are making a quick recce for a film shoot of *Kite Country*, an episode for a new six-part series for Channel 4. *Birdscape* is Bruce's idea – a film featuring his favourite landscapes and the birds that inhabit them. We leave the car park and join the boardwalk that leads into the reserve. Now and then through the alders we catch glimpses of a spectacular fast-flowing river, the Afon Tywi, which runs alongside us.

The boardwalk zigzags uphill and we leave the alders behind. We are now entering a typical Welsh 'hanging wood' dominated by Sessile Oaks. These are more robust than the Pedunculate Oak and are better suited to the acidic soil conditions. We start to see birds in the tree canopies – Blue Tits and Coal Tits, then Redstarts and Pied Flycatchers. Mike Potts, our wildlife cameraman, will be covering these. It is wet everywhere and all the rocks and tree stumps are covered in mosses and lichens.

I tell Bruce we must get a move on, as the camera crew will be arriving soon. We retrace our steps and find a location where we can see the river, which winds round the 'hanging wood' we have just left and a grassy hillside leading into moorland on our right. A range of hills dominate the background. I scan the sky through my binoculars – not a kite in sight.

Bruce decides that this is where he will paint his main episode picture. It is a very attractive scene, with rushing, foaming water and glistening rocks. It is not surprising that we see a Dipper, and moments later a Common Sandpiper picks its way daintily along the edge of the river. Then, just as we are about to return to the car park, we see a Tree Pipit. It is sitting on a fence post and takes off and starts to sing, flying up and up, higher and higher until it is almost out of sight. Then, having proclaimed his territory in such a valiant and vigorous fashion, wings outstretched, he parachutes back to earth still singing lustily. I make a note to add this wonderful bird to Mike Potts's shot list.

Back at the car park our crew are waiting for us. Leaning against the camera car is cameraman Ian Hollands, always known as 'Holly'. He is tall, with wild, straw-coloured hair and beard. His assistant, Peter Pimley, is tall, quiet and studious, and our sound recordist, Steve Phillips, small, blond and cheerful. Beside them is Helga Dowie, production manager. She is a no-nonsense character, has a great sense of humour and is my Girl Friday. I have been working with all four of them for at least three years and with 'Holly' for very much longer. We are all firm friends.

Last to appear is Avie Littler, our executive producer. She is dark-haired, petite and very chic and often dresses in black. Avie is an excellent producer who, above all, creates a good atmosphere in which to work. She does not interfere unless absolutely necessary and she is always there with advice if you want it. I first worked with her in the early 1980s on a natural history series on Japan, and then more recently on a film with Bruce Pearson in Mali. She is a good friend.

It is a beautiful day so there are no hold-ups with our work. We film Bruce starting his painting and then hike off up into the 'hanging wood' to get wide angle shots of the landscape which will be intercut with Mike Potts's wildlife footage. Then we return to record Bruce putting the finishing touches to his painting before going off to a nearby village to meet Tony Pickup, the RSPB warden. As we get out of our car we see our first Red Kites – two of them soaring over the village. Holly quickly sets up his camera and starts tracking the birds in the sky – but they disappear too quickly.

There is bad news from Tony Pickup: one of the kites at a nest we were meant to be filming has been poisoned. Luckily, Rick Price, who is licensed to film the kites, has a hide on another nest, which has two young. We will have a look at them tomorrow.

Mike Potts phones me at our hotel. He is excited, having got some excellent footage of kites feeding on earthworms. "Their eyesight must be phenomenal," he says. "They were wheeling about, high in the sky, before one of them closed its wings and dived down, levelling out just above a meadow in which sheep were feeding. It touched down for a moment, grabbed an earthworm and flew off. Incredible!"

The next day we park at the top of a hill overlooking the Dinas reserve. We film Bruce arriving on a quad bike and then setting up his painting gear. There are kites about and they oblige by wheeling overhead. Bruce starts sketching them and Holly and his team record the moment. "Controlled perfection on the wing as they wheel above me" is Bruce's description of the kites, adding, "They pause on the breeze just long enough for me to grab a quick sketch."

These sketches will be worked up later and be part of a sequence where the live action of the flying kite is blended into Bruce's artwork. Years ago, when I was starting in the film business in London, I used to go in my lunch hour to a cinema in Charing Cross Road called the *Cameo Poly* where they showed newsreels and cartoons. One cartoon was about Johnny Appleseed, an American folk hero and as part of the action a paintbrush appeared on the screen and painted in apple trees onto the landscape. I always remembered this and suggested that we try it.

The technique was simple. First, a film shot had to be taken of the wheeling kite. Then Bruce had to make an exact copy of the chosen live-action frame of the kite wheeling in the sky. Next, his moving paintbrush was filmed against a blue background and the three layers were blended or 'morphed' together at the point where the live action mixed into Bruce's sketch. It was a first in wildlife filmmaking and the result was much admired.

We had to tear ourselves away from the wheeling kites to keep an appointment with Rick Price at the nest he has under surveillance. While the crew have their lunch, Bruce sets up his telescope and we spend an hour watching the pair of Red Kites going about the process of rearing their two young. The adults look identical although I know that, in common with many other birds of prey, the female will be the larger. Their plumage is spectacularly beautiful, in sharp contrast to their refuse-tip of a nest.

Looking at the female's head, her bill and cere are quite normal for a bird of prey her size. But it is her eyes that attract my attention, the iris being very pale yellow, almost colourless. The head and back of the neck are pale grey streaked with dark brown. Her upperwing coverts are dark brown with chestnut-red edges, her primaries very dark brown and her distinctive forked tail chestnut-red. Her feet are quite small. In flight, seen from below, the kite's forked tail and the white patch at the base of the primaries are distinctive.

The two young, which were about ten days old, have had a good feed while we have been watching and it is time to rejoin the unit and meet Peter Davis, the kite recorder for Wales.

Bruce is eager to know how the Red Kite population in Wales is progressing. Peter tells us that there has been a steady increase but that egg collectors are still a real problem. Ten out of 40 nests were robbed last year and six out of 63 nests this year, 1990. The penalty of a fine of £2,000 per egg does not seem to be a deterrent. Bruce is incensed by this and lets rip, "It's perverse. There's a weird fetishness about it. It's a male thing, men getting together in secret to admire their collections of eggs. It's dark. It has an almost pornographic ring about it."

Nevertheless, Peter reassures us the situation is improving. At the end of this season, there will be another 60 or 70 juveniles on the wing, making a grand total of about 250 Red Kites living in Wales. In 1990 Wales is their stronghold but 700 years ago it was all very different. At that time the Red Kite was one of the commonest birds of prey in the United Kingdom. Vast areas of forest that had previously covered the land had been cleared for farming. Kites bred and roosted in the woodland and they would have been a common sight as they wheeled and soared over the never-ending plains and heaths searching for carrion or earthworms.

The *Glead* or *Puttock*, as the Red Kite was known in Anglo-Saxon times, was also a welcome visitor to cities and towns where its scavenging habit helped rid the streets of rotting garbage that, if left, would be a ready breeding ground for disease. William Turner, writing in 1544, gave a detailed description of London kites in a letter to the Swiss naturalist Gesner: 'We have Kites in England, the like of which I have seen nowhere else. Our birds are much larger than the German birds, more clamorous, tending more to whiteness, and much greedier. For such is the audacity of our Kites, that they dare to snatch bread from children, fish from women, and handkerchiefs from off hedges, and out of men's hands. They are accustomed to carry off caps from off men's heads when they are building their nests.'

Kites in towns were afforded royal patronage for their 'winged bin men' role but their popularity in the countryside was on the wane. In 1678 Francis Willughby and John Ray wrote in their book *Ornithology*, 'They are very noisom to tame birds, especially Chicken, Ducklings and Goslings for which cause our good housewives are very angry with them and of all birds, hate and curse them most.' In 1758 Carl Linnaeus classified it as *Falco milvus*, although the name was later changed to *Milvus milvus*, as it is known today.

As sanitation improved and the streets became less noisome, the Red Kite lost its royal protection. It was tolerated in towns but the Vermin Acts of 1532 and 1566 put a price on the Red Kite's head in the countryside. Roger Lovegrove, in his meticulously researched book *Silent Fields*, published in 2007, reveals that churchwardens were not only responsible for the ecclesiastical affairs of their parish but also took on civil duties. In particular, they had to raise monies for the destruction of vermin, a bounty of one penny was paid for the head of each kite brought in. Churchwardens' accounts show that the killing of kites was intense, and particularly so in Devon and Cornwall. At Lezant in Cornwall, 1,245 kites were killed between 1755 and 1809. Bounty was paid out on 698 Red Kites killed in just eight years at Bunbury in Cheshire – of these, 256 were killed in just one year, 1720.

But the killing was not universal. Twenty-eight counties showed no bounty payments for the killing of kites. Red Kites still were numerous enough for Oliver Goldsmith (1730–74) to pen this description: 'The Kite, that may be distinguished from all the rest of this tribe by his forky tail and his slow flying motion, seems almost forever on the wing. He appears to rest himself upon the bosom of the air, and not to make the smallest effort in flying.' Thomas Pennant, the eminent zoologist, in a letter dated August 1777 writes: 'I thank you for the young Kites from the Rooks' nest from an elm in the garden of Gray's Inn Square. Their stomachs contained young frogs. The locality is interesting, but I find that the Kite has bred in Hyde Park in two instances.'

It was the rearing of game for shooting, the Game Act of 1831 and the perfection of the double-barrelled shotgun that relentlessly drove the Red Kite to near extinction in Britain by the end of the nineteenth century. Roger Lovegrove suggests that the Red Kite was extinct in England by the early 1870s, and in 1900 it was gone from Scotland too. It was only in the remote valleys of central Wales, albeit a less suitable habitat for the Red Kite, that a handful of pairs survived and continued to breed.

The roller-coaster ride of the Red Kite's fortunes in Wales is well documented and I am particularly indebted to Peter Davis for pointing me in the direction of his article in *British Birds*, 'The Red Kite in Wales: setting the record straight.' The turning point came in 1903 when Professor Salter of Aberystwyth wrote to the British Ornithologists' Club asking for help in protecting the kite in Wales. A committee was set up and funds were raised so that nests could be watched and guarded against egg collectors. During the early twentieth century there were 17 occupied territories, of which five pairs reared six young. For the next 25 years the number of occupied territories averaged 15 a year, with an increasing number of young fledged.

Despite the efforts of the Kite Committee, the 1920s and 1930s were dominated by egg collecting. Corruption amongst paid kite-watchers was uncovered; they were taking eggs from the nests they were meant to be guarding and selling them on to egg collectors. The impact of egg collecting and the deaths of adult birds, caused by scavenging on poisoned baits set for crows and foxes, meant that the 1930s saw the population of breeding pairs sink to its lowest level – an average of just ten, with only seven young fledged during that period.

During the Second World War, records of the Red Kite population in Wales were sparse. The population is thought to have remained stable during this period because travel restrictions prevented egg collectors from searching for nests, and many gamekeepers had joined up to fight for King and Country.

The period 1950–1960 saw a breakthrough for the Red Kite. There were up to 14 breeding pairs, plus another four non-breeding adults, and 62 young were fledged. Figures remained stable despite the impact of myxomatosis in 1954, which wiped out the rabbit population, a key food source for the Red Kite.

By the early 1970s, the Red Kite population in Wales was still below 24 pairs. The late Barbara Handley, former chairman of The Hawk and Owl Trust, takes up the story: "In 1972 all the nests in the Ystwyth valley in mid-Wales, six or seven pairs, were robbed of their eggs. I had a house above Cwmystwyth so I invited friends, either in the music profession or members of the Hawk Trust, which I had recently joined, to help me. The Hawk Trust had been started in 1969 by Philip Glasier to breed Peregrine Falcons in captivity to help bolster the wild population that had been badly affected by the organochlorine pesticides used by farmers in the early 1950s. Starting in 1973, the next spring, from the end of March to mid-May, which covers the incubation period, we would have four volunteers per week staying in the house, on duty in pairs alternately from dawn to dark watching the kite nests and walking the valley. Kite nests were in deciduous trees and easily spotted as well as visible through binoculars from higher ground. We could not by law go very close or

climb the trees, but we could speak to walkers and visitors, ask them to detour if necessary, question anyone too near a nest, and keep an eye on cars and their number plates. Almost everyone was keen to help the kites and already on our side. Would-be eggers were deterred by knowing that a watch existed and not knowing how many pairs of eyes were watching them. Every few days Peter Davis of the Nature Conservancy Council, the permitted recorder, climbed the trees with a kites' nest and inspected them to reassure us that no eggs were missing. I believe this was the very first project of the Hawk Trust. It stopped all the robberies in the Ystwyth, although egg collectors probably moved elsewhere for easier pickings. The RSPB took up the campaign soon after, joining with farmers, landowners and residents in other parts of Wales already in the field. From then on there was widespread effective volunteer wardening of kites' nests."

Through the 1980s and 1990s, the Red Kite population in Wales increased steadily to a point where there were 104 breeding territories, 62 successful pairs and 155 young had been fledged. This success was undoubtedly due to the birds extending their range into areas that provided better opportunities for hunting and scavenging. One surprising fact to emerge from research undertaken in the 1980s was that all the Red Kites breeding in Wales were descended from just a single female.

Even though the Red Kite in Wales had staged a recovery, it was a slow one. In 1986 the then Nature Conservancy Council and the RSPB set up the UK Red Kite reintroduction programme with the aim of re-establishing Red Kites in suitable areas of England and Scotland. But before the project could go ahead, five criteria had to be met: (1) There was historical evidence of former natural occurrence; (2) There was a clear understanding of the factors causing extinction (and that these factors no longer applied); (3) There was suitable habitat to support the reintroduced population; (4) That natural re-colonization was unlikely within a reasonable timescale; and (5) A suitable source of birds was available for release.

The Red Kite ticked all the right boxes and by 1989 preparatory work at two sites, the Chilterns in southern England and the Black Isle, by Inverness in northern Scotland, was under way. Release aviaries were built in which the young birds would be kept until they were old enough to be released.

The young kites being released in England came mainly from nests in Spain and those for Scotland were brought from Sweden. The young were taken at four to five weeks old and then kept in captivity for another six to eight weeks. Initially, the young were placed in an artificial nest under cover and fed remotely so that they did not become imprinted. For the first fortnight they received small gobbets of food, which they could easily handle, and then progressed to larger hunks of prey that they could tear up themselves. Perches within the aviary enabled the birds to exercise and build up their pectoral muscles ready for their first flight out into the wild.

After the birds were released, food was still put out for them every day. This process is known as 'hacking back', a centuries-old technique adopted by falconers. Young falcons, such as Peregrines, that are 'hacked back', released into the wild to fly free, always develop better flying techniques more quickly than those that are not. They are fed each evening, watched carefully and, at the right time, are caught up and are ready for training.

Before release each kite was ringed and wing-tagged. On one wing a colour tag was fixed denoting the release site and on the other a coloured tag indicating the year of release. The bird's individual number, letter or symbol is on both tags. The tags were big enough to be read through a telescope at almost one kilometre in good light but not through binoculars unless the bird was very close. Since it is vital to monitor the whereabouts of the released birds in a reintroduction scheme like this, a small radio-transmitter was attached to the upper side of the two central tail feathers, the 'deck feathers', of each bird. Radio-tracking the birds, if there is a direct line of sight, allows them to be located up to 80 kilometres away. However, due to undulating topography and the presence of trees and undergrowth, radio-tracking is generally only possible up to about five kilometres away. The transmitter falls off when the tail feathers are moulted out the following year.

The release at the site in the Chilterns was a great success, with 76% of the birds surviving their first year. On the Black Isle site, only 51% made it through their first year, mainly due to persecution. The first successful breeding in both areas was in 1992, just two years after the first release, when four pairs reared nine young in the Chilterns and one pair reared a single chick on the Black Isle. By 2000, there were an estimated 112 pairs in the Chilterns and 32 pairs on the Black Isle.

The Red Kite's wheel of fortune had turned full circle. Now, thanks to the dedicated efforts of conservationists, this majestic bird was once again soaring over the United Kingdom. I think everyone welcomed the return of the Red Kite, but none more so than Richard Mabey, one of our foremost nature writers: 'Suddenly the air was full of kites, a shifting mesh of flight-lines that stretched as far as I could see. It was, I guess, one of those excited gatherings that, for so many species, are part of the ritual of roosting. But that explains nothing. This was a wilful, gratuitous relishing of the wind. All birds of prey love the wind. It is when they become what they are truly made for. Reach a kind of epiphany. Yet this awesome, communal display was more than that. These birds were dare-

devilling, taking their flight skills to the edge. I was rooted to the spot. I couldn't count the birds. There were 30, 40 in front of me, and, when I turned round, just as many behind. They were exalted, falling out of the sky like peregrines, skimming the fields, stooping, spiralling, stalling, their forked tails fine-tuning their balance so effortlessly that it looked as if they were juggling the wind. Each time one rose or fell, I felt myself rise and fall with it. I was deep-breathing in sympathy. I didn't want to fly, or be up there with them, but they transported me back to being six years old again, rushing down a hill with my arms held out – back, maybe, very much further than that.'

Richard's last two sentences immediately remind me of my prep-school days in Northamptonshire during the war. During the afternoons we either used to play 'cruisers and battleships' or stage imaginary 'dog-fights' in a meadow that rolled down the hill to a valley below. Because I was tall and rather awkward, I was always bullied into playing the part of a slow-flying Heinkel 111 bomber while the boys of normal height zipped around me like gadflies pretending to be Spitfires or Hurricanes, vocally spraying me with bursts of machine-gun fire. Coventry was not far away and for several nights, lying in bed in our dormitory, we were wakened by the bombing. The headmaster, Oliver Wyatt, came round and told us to lie under our beds just in case a stick of bombs dropped nearby. Lying in bed at night, we became expert at identifying friendly or enemy aircraft as they flew overhead. Our aircraft droned; German aircraft approaching or returning home throbbed because their engines were not synchronized.

Less than fifty miles east of my prep school was a patchwork of forest and farmland over which German bombers would have passed on their way home. A thousand years earlier, what was then a dense area of woodland became known as Rockingham Forest. Following the Norman Conquest, it was designated as the Royal Forests of Narborough and Rockingham, where the King would hunt deer and wild boar. Red Kites resident then would have feasted on the entrails of any game that was hunted down.

Areas of woodland around the villages were cleared and farmed as pasture, plough and fallow. This would have favoured the local Red Kites. They would have scavenged local rubbish tips and taken advantage of any farm animal carcasses rotting in the fields. Much more clearance occurred when the forest lost its legal status under the Enclosure Acts in the nineteenth century. Those Acts and the Game Act put paid to the Red Kite in Rockingham Forest.

Lord Lilford, in his book *Notes on the Birds of Northamptonshire*, published in 1895, says that 'till about 1844 or 1845 the kite was common and bred in many localities. The latest record I have of the appearance of a kite in these parts is from Mr. G. Edmonds, of Oundle, who informs me that in November 1868 one of these birds suddenly rose from a ditch within a yard of him, where it was regaling upon a dovecot Pigeon.' He went on to say: 'The species has been all but extinct in our district for nearly fifty years, and is now a rare bird in all parts of Great Britain.'

In the 1920s, the Forestry Commission started buying up blocks of woodland. In those days, this meant clear-felling existing trees and planting conifers, which were then harvested on a strict rotational basis. By the 1990s, the Commission was responsible for 250,000 hectares of woodland. Towards the end of the century, English Nature (now part of Natural England) divided England into 120 distinctive 'Natural Areas' based on an assessment of the distribution of wildlife and natural landscape features. Each area had its own *Natural Area profile*, which included nature conservation goals. Rockingham Forest was one such area, the immediate aims being to clear-fell Norway Spruce plantations to make way for broad-leaved species; to manage the existing ancient woodland, largely oak and ash; to benefit wildlife in general; to retain both fallen and standing dead trees in ancient woodland; and to reintroduce coppicing as a regular management practice. The vision for the landscape in the *Natural Area profile* for Rockingham Forest is for it to '… delight the senses and be cherished by present and future generations.'

It was against this background that there was an exciting development. Karl Ivens, a Forestry Commission ranger, told me this story: "It was 4 May 1994. I was out stalking deer when suddenly my Hungarian Vizla dog stopped dead, its muzzle sensing something over the brow of the hill. I moved forward very carefully expecting to see a deer. To my amazement, it wasn't a deer but a Red Kite feeding on a dead Rook. It was only twenty yards away. Luckily it had its back to me so I could watch it easily. I could see that it had been tagged but couldn't read it. I also saw that it was carrying an aerial. It dropped a tail feather, which I picked up and gave to Derek Holman, one of my volunteers and an outstanding ornithologist."

I met Derek in 2012 and asked him to take up the story. He explained, "I was lucky enough to see the kite with the aerial the next day at Wadenhoe Great Wood, which incidentally is where the last kites in Northamptonshire bred in 1843. Because I knew him, I phoned Ian Spence, who was the Project Officer for the Chiltern site that was in the fifth year of its release programme. We discussed with him the possibility of Rockingham being the second English release site." The idea was put up to the UK Red Kite Committee and in 1995 it was given the go-ahead.

At the same time, Ian Carter was appointed as Project Officer. He told me, "I was working for English Nature at the time. It was a five-year contract, which sounded ideal to me. I've always been interested in wildlife, ever since I was a kid. I did a bit of egg collecting, 'til it became illegal, and I always loved watching birds. Eventually I took a degree in ecology at the University of East Anglia."

That summer, Ian Carter and Karl Ivens went out to Spain to pick up the young Red Kites which, when fully grown, would be released into the wild in Rockingham Forest. Having flown to Madrid, they drove up to Salamanca and Segovia where there was a healthy population of Red Kites.

Ian Carter gave this account: "The landscape where we went to collect the kites was mind-blowing. Everything was just on a much larger scale than back home in southern England. There were big, rolling plains, now and then dotted with woods. Most of the farming was cereals, but some was pasture. This was where they raised fighting bulls for the ring. The open land was ideal for foraging kites." Karl Ivens expanded, "Our opposite numbers in Spain had done quite a lot of preparatory work and found active nest sites. Most of the nests were in Cork Oaks, poplars or pines. I did a lot of the climbing and one day I was all clobbered up with gear and about to go up a tree when I heard a lot of shouting. I looked round and there was a fighting bull advancing rather ominously towards me. In the background our Spanish hosts were waving their arms and shouting. I had so much gear on, ropes, safety harness, carabiners *etc.* that I couldn't even think of running. Luckily there was a guy with a bull whip who ran in, cracked his whip a couple of times and drove the bull away."

At the end of a week, only ten young kites had been collected and unfortunately it was time to return to England, via Madrid airport. As Ian Carter explained, "This was easily the most stressful part of the trip. The young kites were travelling in flight kennels. At the airport a vet checked out each of the birds before they were conveyed to the pressurized baggage hold of the aircraft. I'd arranged for someone to meet us at the quarantine area at Heathrow airport and I was only able to relax when I saw the vehicles driving away from the airport on their way up to Rockingham Forest and the release pens."

A daily roster was organized so that Karl, Ian and Derek could share the responsibility of looking after the kites. Karl shot rabbits, squirrels and pigeons and brought in road kills. There was quite a difference in age between the kites and, to start with, some of them had to be force-fed. The kites always had more than enough to eat and they all settled in well.

A few days later there was a new arrival. It was a male Red Kite that was known as 'Orange £' because of the tag that it was carrying. On 3 April 1995 it was found injured at a farm near Watlington. It had been shot. The bird was taken to London Zoo where it

was successfully treated and made a full recovery. 'Orange £' was to be a key player in the Rockingham Forest release programme.

Seven weeks after they arrived from Spain all the kites had been ringed, and tagged. They had also been fitted with transmitters so that they could be monitored and were ready to be released.

The big day arrived, 24 July 1995. An imposing list of dignitaries had been invited, the press were there and photographers and TV crews jostled to get the best camera angles of the moment of release. Ian Carter had mixed feelings: "I was a bit worried that the kites' release in the full glare of the media was going to be a bit tacky. I felt that with everyone peering into the release pens there was a danger of people not treating them as truly wild birds. But I knew it was important that local people, estate owners, farmers, gamekeepers, should know what we were doing – that we could reassure them that the kites weren't going to be a threat."

Karl and Ian shared the honour of releasing the kites. Ian said, "Considering that this was their first proper flight, they flew amazingly well. Some of the kites just took off

and disappeared into the trees. Others demonstrated their aerial ability and circled high overhead. One put on a show and circled really low over the assembled dignitaries. One or two stayed in the pens and had to be shooed out. I was relieved when they'd all gone.' Derek said, "We continued to feed the young kites at the release pens over several weeks and stopped when it was obvious that they were self-supporting."

Release of kites at Rockingham Forest continued for the next three years. On a national scale, there were new releases at Harewood Park in Yorkshire from 1999 to 2003, in central Scotland from 1996 to 2001, in Dumfries and Galloway from 2001 to 2005, in Tyneside from 2004 to 2006, Aberdeenshire from 2007 to 2009 and finally at Grizedale Forest in the Lake District from 2010 to 2012.

In 1996, at the Rockingham Forest release site, the rehabilitated male 'Orange £' mated with one of the released Red Kites from Spain, 'Grey/H'. Unfortunately this pairing failed when the nest was deserted just when the eggs were on the point of hatching.

In 1997 eight young Red Kites were fledged at Rockingham Forest. Every year the numbers of young fledged continued to rise. In 2006 over 100 young were raised for the first time. 'Grey/H' had raised ten fledged young between 1997 and 2001 but died in 2002. 'Orange £' continued to breed and probably helped to raise broods between 2003 and 2005, but sadly died in 2006. He was a unique bird and made a tremendous contribution to the Rockingham Forest release scheme.

By the end of the 2011 breeding season over 1,100 young Red Kites had been fledged from the Rockingham Forest release site. It was a great success.

During 2012 I made contact with Geoff Williamson, who was the organizer of the Hawk and Owl Trust's East Midland group and also a volunteer at Rockingham Forest, and asked if I could come over and watch the kites and talk to those involved. As well as Geoff, I also met Derek Holman and another volunteer, Steve Thornton, to watch the kites gather before they went up to roost at Fermyn Park Woods. An extract from my journal reads:

> *'7/3/12. 15.45 The wind has dropped a bit. The park in front of us is divided up into paddocks. The grass is cropped short. The venerable trees scattered across the parkland are a major feature. They've seen much service – they are old enough to have provided wood for boat building as well as for the building of Fermyn Woods Hall. Their shape reminds me of the baobab trees that I saw in Mali. Beyond the park is Harry's Park Woods. Several of the poplars bear enormous clumps of mistletoe trailing from their upper branches. The kites are just beginning to arrive. They come in twos and threes and settle in the upper branches of the oaks. Steve and Derek, who've got 'scopes, point out those that have been tagged. Again they are mostly White-White tags, birds fledged last year.*

> *I asked how important the tagging system is. Derek said it was important for two reasons: to keep track of the dispersal of young birds and of any fatalities. Steve and Derek then launched into a double-act about kites not being faithful for life, contrary to popular belief. They cited the instance of a female, Red-Red 15, mated with Red-Red 18, dying at a nest site on the Drayton estate. They had tried to save the young but they died. On the other side of the road at Lowick there was a pair, White-Red 16 and White-Red 2. Their nest had failed. Red-Red 18 quickly 'pulled' this White-Red 16. It was so quick they thought the birds might breed again that year. And it had a knock-on effect because the jilted White-Red 2 male went and stole White-Red C from the next pair. A bit like humans, added Derek.'*

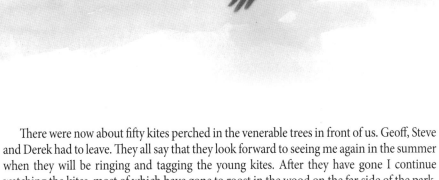

There were now about fifty kites perched in the venerable trees in front of us. Geoff, Steve and Derek had to leave. They all say that they look forward to seeing me again in the summer when they will be ringing and tagging the young kites. After they have gone I continue watching the kites, most of which have gone to roost in the wood on the far side of the park.

'1730. It's a beautiful evening. The wind has dropped almost completely. It's well past sunset and the sky is a pale lemon with the tall poplars of Harry's Park Wood silhouetted against it. A kite perches on a branch near the top of the nearest oak. It has grass in its bill. Perhaps it grabbed that as well as the worm that made up its pre-roost snack. As I'm watching the kite through binoculars I see in the background, on the right-hand edge of Harry's Park Woods, an eruption of kites climbing up into sky. They wheel around. Some descend quickly, others continue climbing higher and higher and I lose them against the darkening sky. I call my wife to tell her that I'm okay. She's tending her pony and tells me there's a wonderful full moon. I ring off and turn round. There's the full moon. It seems huge. Silhouetted against it are about a dozen kites wheeling in the sky. Perhaps someone has disturbed them. Kites are very 'edgy' when they are roosting, the slightest hint of danger sends them rocketing up through the branches. I'm very lucky to have seen this wonderful image.'

I stay overnight in Fermyn Woods Hall. I wake early and, looking out of my bedroom window, see a kite flying low over the parkland. Now and then it drops down for a second to pick up an earthworm. It is competing with a flock of Fieldfares. They are building up

71

their fat reserves ready for their long migration north to their breeding grounds in Norway and Sweden, and seem quite unfazed by the presence of the kite.

During breakfast I have a perfect view across the parkland to where I saw the kites silhouetted against the moon. There is a wood there with kites wheeling above it. Some are displaying and seem to lock together and come spinning down like sycamore seeds. A hen Sparrowhawk appears and has a brief tussle with one of the kites, talons grappling for a moment.

At eight o'clock sharp Steve arrives to take me off nest hunting. All birds of prey start refurbishing or nest building early in the day and we are visiting a wood to see what the kites have been up to. On our journey out I tell him about the kite I saw earlier feeding on earthworms. Steve says the kite's eyesight is phenomenal and recounted the occasion, some time ago, when the cricket pitch at nearby Brigstock was covered with surface water and a tractor and aerator was brought in to spike the ground. The next morning there were 40 kites there feeding on the earthworms that had risen to the surface. While Steve has been extolling the kite's incredible eyesight we have arrived at the wood.

> '8/3/12. 09.30. There are two kites and two buzzards circling over the wood. The understorey is thick and there are big trees. Steve's old dog keeps on getting tangled up in the brambles as we push further in. Eventually Steve stops and points, "There it is." It was quite a substantial nest and, looking through binoculars, I could see fresh, broken ends of twigs that had been added. It looks promising. On the way back we talk about the effect of second generation rodenticides. Steve says several kites have been picked up dead after one of the farmers had a 'blitz' on rats in his grain store. The poison needs to be used very carefully and a thorough search for bodies made afterwards.'

Back at our cars I say goodbye to Steve after promising to visit Rockingham in the summer to see the young kites being ringed and wing-tagged. In the meantime, Steve leaves with me a tape he wants me to watch. It is of Closed Circuit Television (CCTV) footage taken at a Red Kite nest in 2006 at Fineshade Woods, the Forestry Commission's local headquarters in Rockingham Forest.

Back at home I watch the tape and take notes.

> '20/5/06. I'm looking down on a Red Kites' nest in the fork of a tree. It is change-over time as the male and female swap places on the nest. One of the four eggs has just hatched revealing a wriggling, white down-covered chick. The nest is beautifully lined with a hare's pelt and other furry remnants of carrion brought into the nest. The male treads delicately down into the nest, picks up the eggshell and moves it out of the way. The female watches him for a moment and then slips away. The male gently pushes the chick in under his breast feathers, sinks down and settles down to brood. Later the male walks round the nest picking up various items brought in earlier and arranging them around the chick to keep it warm – a tangle of moss and feathers, part of a hare's pelt and a hank of wool – a very dutiful parent.'

> '21/5/06. Female standing over the chick in the centre of the nest. Her feathers are a bit damp. Very carefully she shifts her taloned feet, all scrunched up to avoid injuring the chick, and walks to the edge of the nest. She selects a rotting carcass and starts pulling at it. She tears off a morsel and, stretching right down into the nest, very tenderly feeds the chick. The amount offered is minuscule but avidly taken.'

'22/5/06. *Both parents present and peering down into the nest where the second egg has hatched. Both chicks look up towards them. The third egg is 'pipping.' Female moves to the top edge of nest where there's now a fresh carcass. She pulls at it, feeds the chicks. The male leaves and the female moves down to brood the chicks. She waggles from side to side, settling down in the nest.'*

'26/5/06. *There's been rain overnight and the female is soaked. She looks down into the nest at the two wriggling chicks. There are still 2 eggs that haven't hatched at the bottom of the nest. The female moves to the top of the nest and starts to break into a rat carcass. The chicks struggle towards her. She feeds them tiny portions of flesh and makes sure they get equal shares.'*

I fast-forward the tape over the next four days. The two chicks have made steady progress and the down on their backs has turned a dusky grey – a first sign that feathers will soon be appearing.

'30/5/06. *To my amazement I see that there are now three chicks in the nest. The two original chicks are being fed by the female. Overnight one of the two remaining eggs, which I thought were infertile, has hatched. The new chick looks puny besides its siblings. Its head with black button eyes is enormous in relation to its body. The ten-day difference in hatching puts the new arrival at a big disadvantage. Will it survive?'*

'2/6/06. The two biggest chicks are being fed by the female who is perched at the far side of the nest. The smallest chick is at the bottom of the nest by the remaining egg. Amazingly it has survived. It works its way forward but remains trapped behind the larger of the two chicks which are golloping down big beakfuls of flesh.'

'15/6/06. Sunny. Nest full of sleeping, well-fed chicks. Primaries, wings coverts and tail feathers much more developed. Female flies in. Two eldest get a good feed. The youngest, going through the grey body phase, doesn't get a look in. A bit of wing flapping, staggers about. Two eldest chicks wing flapping and strutting about. Second eldest turns and defecates over edge of nest. This is quite instinctive to prevent nest being fouled. Nevertheless it is filthy and buzzing with flies compared to nearly a month ago. Both adults arrive with a squirrel carcass. Large chunk of flesh handed over to eldest chick who swallows it whole.'

'24/6/06. The female is at far side of the nest breaking into a Carrion Crow carcass. Black feathers blow away across the eldest chick, which is nearest her, then past the youngest in the middle and then on to the middle chick on the far side. I can see that the tails of the two eldest chicks are developing really well. The female finally breaks into the crow's body and starts feeding the youngsters. Their crops drum tight with food, the chicks are either hunkered down, wing flapping or like the youngest, picking at a rabbit skull. It is a beautiful evening.'

'31/6/06. A sunny day. The three chicks are lying rigid in the nest. The only reason I know they are not dead is that I can see their backs moving gently as they breathe. What has happened? A gloved hand appears over the side of the nest and, one by one, the chicks disappear. Shortly afterwards, they are replaced in the nest. First to re-appear is the eldest chick. He's got a white tag on his left wing with the number 85, on the right it's 85 on green. The youngest is next with an 87 tag and last is the middle chick with 86. White indicates the birds are from Rockingham, green signifies the year and the number is individual to the bird. Later, the two eldest chicks have settled down and are busy preening around their tags. I can see that 85 had been fitted with a transmitter. The youngest is lying down at the edge of the nest. They are all fine.'

'3/7/06. The three chicks have come on so well that life in the nest is definitely crowded. The female flies in with food. It is grabbed immediately by the eldest chick which mantles over it. Later there is much wing-flapping. Room to exercise is at a premium and the youngest chick gets a bit of a battering over its head. The eldest chick flaps and flops onto a nearby branch and then disappears from view.'

Over the next fortnight the two eldest chicks are often out of the nest and are presumably honing their flying skills. The youngest ventures a short distance from the nest onto the surrounding branches. They all come back to the nest to be fed.

'17/7/06. It is sunny with a little wind. The eldest and youngest chick are in the nest. One of the adults brings in food, then leaves. The eldest chick follows. This is not the first time the youngest has been left in the nest alone. Today the vigorous wing stretching and flapping has a purpose about it. A few flecks of down remain on her rump but otherwise the young kite looks fit to fly. An aircraft flies overhead causing a distraction. There's a last stretch of the wings and a couple of steps to the edge of the nest. A short pause and then, with a couple of flaps, the young kite defies gravity and flies out of sight. The deserted nest is like *a charnel-house. Its filthy state is a testament to the adult's care in raising the three young kites from hatching to a state, seven weeks later, where they can leave the nest and take their place soaring over Rockingham Forest.'*

The tapes have given me a privileged view of the kites' breeding behaviour. Now, in 2012, I'm off to watch this year's young kites being ringed and tagged. With me is my step-son, Thom and I am very glad to have him with me so that he can understand what is involved in writing this book. He has followed in my footsteps and is a very good filmmaker. We meet Sam Higgins who will be doing the climbing and follow him to a wood on the other side of Bulwick village where there is a kites' nest, and where Steve Thornton and another climber, Dave from Derbyshire, are waiting. The following is an extract from my journal:

'22/6/12. 10.30. Light, intermittent rain. Thom and I climb a wire fence and follow Steve into the wood. Very green underfoot. The two climbers, Sam and Dave, are ahead of us. We make our way towards the nest site, which is about fifty yards into the wood. The nest, which is large, is at the top of an oak tree. We join Steve who is setting out his ringing and tagging kit on a tarpaulin laid out on the forest floor.

I ask Steve what the kite's breeding success has been this year. He explained, "It's not been a good year for young production. We've only had about a dozen nests with three youngsters. We've certainly lost young birds. It's not necessarily due to the wet but to the extreme cold this year."

Sam has reached the nest. There are two chicks and he puts them in bags and lowers them down to Dave at the bottom of the tree. Steve gently removes the first chick from the bag and places it on the tarpaulin. It lies there as if mesmerized. It is about four weeks old and its feathers are still growing; the quills are full of blood. Thom records the scene on his camera and seems very interested, asking the right questions. The chick is ringed and tagged and returned to the nest.

While Sam is returning the chick to the nest Steve tells us that there have been one or two instances of kites attacking climbers on their way up to nests. He shows us a scene recorded on a mobile phone of a kite swooping in and hitting a climber's helmet with an audible *thwack!* I tell him that I have been in touch with a Dutch researcher, Rob Bijlsma, who has written a paper on raptors attacking people. This refers to six species as doing so but there is no mention of Red Kites. I had always thought they were too timid and promised to let Rob know.

Steve picks up the second chick and very efficiently rings it and puts a tag on each wing – left wing orange with red stripe at the bottom, right wing red tag with orange stripe. A bold figure 28 in white is on both tags. Lastly, Steve weighs the chick and says, "It'll have to lose some weight if it's ever going to fly!" Its parents have obviously fed it well. For the next four weeks it will be kept in a flight aviary with 29 other chicks. This is the final phase of a three-year project, started in 2010, to translocate 90 Red Kites to Grizedale Forest in the Lake District.

Already some of the birds released in 2010 will be mature enough to breed. Soon, bird lovers will be able to watch Red Kites, perhaps one of our most spectacular and beautiful birds of prey, as they float over the forests, lakes and mountains of the Lake District. It is one of the great conservation success stories of modern times and all those who have taken part in it should be very proud of their achievement.

THE WHITE-TAILED EAGLE

British Isles population (2010): 64 pairs (increasing)

I am standing on the edge of a meadow in Hokkaido, Japan's northernmost island. It is the middle of winter. Mrs Watanabe, the farmer's wife, appears carrying a bucket of grain. She is well wrapped up against the cold. I am here with a film crew making a film about the Japanese attitude to wildlife. This particular episode is about the Red-crowned Crane, a symbol of happiness to the Japanese. Every day during the winter, when the land is locked solid by snow and ice, Mrs Watanabe puts out corn for the grateful cranes which come to her field to be fed.

I can hear the cranes calling before I see them. They are flying low, having left their winter roost on the river about a mile away. It is safe there and never freezes because of the hot springs. The flock of 15 birds clear the belt of trees surrounding the meadow and plane down to land by Mrs Watanabe. The prospect of food excites them and they dance, jumping up in the air, trumpeting to one another. Another flock arrives. Eventually there are about 60 birds picking at the grain and scraps of fish that have been scattered in the snow.

I am fascinated by the scavengers that now appear. Crows, foxes and eagles vie for the tasty morsels. The eagles are White-tailed Eagles and I watch a pair of juveniles honing their flying skills, grappling with each other's enormous taloned feet. One of them sees a fox snatch a morsel of fish and swoops down on it. The fox instantly drops its titbit, cowers, ears back, and slinks off.

Later I travelled on icy roads up to the Shiretoko Peninsula to film the eagles flying in from the pack ice off the fishing port of Nemuro to a big communal roost in fir trees inland. There was a seemingly endless stream of Steller's and White-tailed Eagles flying in. They perched as many as 15 birds to a tree, calling out as other birds approached. Some of the Steller's were carrying fish, clutched aerodynamically, a midnight snack against night starvation. It started snowing and through my binoculars I watched an adult White-tailed Eagle settle down for the night.

In England, I once handled a White-tailed Eagle and on another occasion filmed a Golden Eagle for a TV commercial. It is only when you see a bird that close that the difference in size between the White-tailed Eagle and the Golden Eagle is so apparent. Just compare the size of their bills – the White-tailed Eagle's being enormous. Also, up-close you will see that a White-tailed Eagle's eyes are yellow, whereas those of the Golden Eagle are hazel.

Apart from size, the main difference between the two birds, which makes identification simple, is that the White-tailed Eagle's wing is straight-edged like a plank or, as some say, like a barn door. Anyone who has seen Anthony Gormley's 21 metre high steel sculpture *Angel of the North* just off the A1 outside Gateshead will understand what I mean. Its angel's wings are a dead ringer for those of the White-tailed Eagle. The Golden Eagle's wings, on the other hand, are much more conventional, like a Buzzard's.

The tail of the adult White-tailed Eagle is white and shorter than that of the adult Golden Eagle, which is dark. For both birds there are in-between phases – the White-tailed Eagle's tail gradually moults out to white when the bird reaches maturity at five years old. A juvenile Golden Eagle has a white tail tipped with dark brown and moults it out over four to five years until the white has gone. Viewed at close quarters, the colouring of the two adults is quite different. The White-tailed Eagle's body is a uniform greyish-brown with lighter feathers on the head and neck. The Golden Eagle is an overall dark chocolate-brown, apart from the cascade of golden feathers flowing from its head down and around the neck.

The White-tailed Eagle's call is a Fox Terrier-like yelp. They are particularly vocal when approaching their nest site bringing in food, shouting greetings to each other, and in territorial disputes. The lower part of the legs of the White-tailed Eagle are bare and its toes are almost completely covered with scales. In contrast, the Golden Eagle has completely feathered legs and very few scales on its toes.

It is these differences that have led to the two birds being classified quite differently: the Golden Eagle belonging to the genus *Aquila* (eagles) and the White-tailed Eagle to the genus *Haliætus* (sea eagles).

According to Derek Yalden and Umberto Albarella in *The History of British Birds* published in 2009, the White-tailed Eagle was much more numerous in the British Isles than the Golden Eagle in Mesolithic times (10,000 years ago). There were perhaps 1,800 pairs of White-tailed Eagles against 400 pairs of Golden Eagles. From archaeological remains, the White-tailed Eagle appears to have been much more widespread as a breeding bird.

The first descriptions by Aristotle and Pliny of the White-tailed Eagle are confusing because the Latin word *haliaeetus* and the Greek *haliaetos* are both used to describe the White-tailed Eagle and the Osprey. This account by Pliny must refer to the former: 'that Eagle haunteth standing waters to prey upon Water-fowl, which now and then dive under the Water; but she seizeth them as they become wearied and confounded. The Contest is worth looking at; while the Bird endeavours to gain the Shore for Refuge, especially if it be well covered with thick Reeds, and the Eagle for her Part drives her from thence with a Blow of the Wing; and whilst the Eagle striketh, and in so doing falleth into the Lake, the Fowl that swimmeth beneath the Water, sees the shadow of the Eagle hovering above the Shore, riseth up again in another Place, where her Pursuer could least have looked for her. This is the Cause why these Wild-fowl commonly swim in Flocks; for when they are many together, they are not troubled.'

When Gavin Maxwell, author of *The Ring of Bright Water,* visited the great marshlands and lagoons in southern Iraq in the late 1950s he saw White-tailed Eagles, whose behaviour was uncannily similar to Pliny's account. As he wrote in his book *A Reed Shaken by the Wind*: 'The dark line was formed of coots, many, many thousands of them, bunched together under the repeated attacks of five eagles. Under each attack the whole mass spread their wings and scuttered forward for a few yards, driving a frothing wave before them, and as each eagle pulled out of his dive and began to climb again the coots bunched tightly together so that one could not have dropped a pin between them. These were the White-tailed Eagles that breed in the reed-beds, and, when their young are in the nest, often terrorize the hashish-gatherers who trespass on their territory.'

It was in Anglo-Saxon times in Britain that the White-tailed Eagle first appeared in print and as a totem. Francesca Greenoak in her book *All the Birds of the Air,* a treasury of the names, lore and literature of British birds, published in 1979, tells us that in the Orkneys and the Shetland Isles it was known as the *erne,* from the Anglo-Saxon word meaning a 'soarer'. She quotes from a beautiful Anglo-Saxon poem *The Seafarer:*

*Storms there, the stacks thrashed, there answered
them the tern
With icy feathers; full oft the erne wailed round
Spray feathered ...*

I was at Corpus Christi College, Cambridge, from 1951–54 and in their world-famous Parker Library there is an eighth century Northumbrian Gospel book in which there is a very graphic image of an eagle. The bill is huge, the eye is fierce and the lower parts of the legs are unfeathered. The present librarian, Christopher de Hamel, kindly checked for me and confirmed that the tail was white. So it was definitely a White-tailed Eagle and it may have been based, as John A. Love points out in his excellent book *A Saga of Sea Eagles*, published in 2013, on an earlier carving in stone from the Knowe of Burrian in the Orkney Isles.

The White-tailed Eagle appears as a devourer of carrion in the epic poem celebrating 'The Battle of Brunanburh' in 937 AD. A unified England under King Aethelstan inflicted enormous casualties on the Picts and Vikings. The survivors fled to Ireland, leaving the battlefield strewn with the dead and dying:

*They left behind them, to enjoy the corpses,
the dark-coated one, the dark horny-beaked raven
and the dusky-coated one,
the eagle white from behind, to partake of carrion,
greedy war-hawk, and that grey animal
the wolf of the forest.*

The site of this battle has now almost certainly been identified as taking place in Merseyside, so the distribution of the White-tailed Eagle in England must have been widespread. In those days no land drainage had taken place and there would have been vast areas of inland water fringed with reedbeds as well as estuaries rich in fish.

Roy Dennis, one of Britain's foremost present-day ornithologists, thinks that the White-tailed Eagle's predilection for fish was what caused it to be persecuted in the Middle Ages. Like the Osprey, it probably preyed upon the 'stew ponds' where fish were farmed so that people could have fish on Fridays. There would have been carrion for them to feed on too, since the White-tailed Eagle is by nature an ardent carrion-feeder. At this time farming was primitive: each parish had three huge fields, two of which were sown with crops and the other was left fallow. Each family also kept a few cows, goats and sheep and casualties were bound to occur amongst the sheep, especially through foot-rot. There was no fodder available to keep the livestock through the winter so they had to be slaughtered. There were, therefore, rich pickings for carrion-feeders.

Gradually, farming practices improved and intensified. More and more land was cleared, wet land was drained and Viscount 'Turnip' Townshend's practice of four-course rotation of crops was increasingly being implemented. Hitherto, there had been a wasteful fallow year but now turnips were drilled and folded with sheep; in the next year the land was put down to barley or oats; the year after to clover and rye grass; and in the fourth year to wheat. Turnips as a fodder crop meant that cattle could now be over-wintered instead of being slaughtered in the autumn. The face of England was changing and by the beginning of the eighteenth century, the White-tailed Eagle in England was reduced to its last stronghold in the Lake District. Roger Lovegrove, in his book *Silent Fields*, published in 2007, reveals that the churchwardens' accounts for Borrowdale show bounties being paid for the destruction of 34 eagles between 1713 and 1778.

It was during the final elimination of the *erne* from England that Thomas Pennant (1726–98) in his *British Zoology* formally identified the Sea Eagle. Unfortunately, he identified the juvenile as the adult Sea Eagle and the adult as another species altogether, the *erne* or *cinereous eagle*. The Swedish taxonomist Carl Linnaeus classified it as *Falco albicilla* in 1758 but in 1809 Marie Jules Caesar Savigny (1777–1851), a Frenchman, created the modern genus *Haliæetus* and the White-tailed Eagle was officially classified as *Haliæetus albicilla*.

By the beginning of the nineteenth century, the White-tailed Eagle was reduced to its last stronghold – Scotland. In the *A Saga of the Sea Eagles,* John Love chronicles in great detail the decline of the White-tailed Eagle into extinction. It was the human re-colonization of Scotland in the middle of the nineteenth century, and the subsequent increase in population, that led to the White-tailed Eagle's extinction. Sheep farming increased, there were grouse on the moors to be protected and the proliferation of the railway system meant easy access for those wanting to shoot or fish for salmon. The White-tailed Eagle was indicted for taking lambs and fish and persecuted as a result.

Fortunately, there were writers who extolled the virtues of the White-tailed Eagle, and who viewed them as rightful inhabitants of the natural world. Gray and Macgillivray were two such writers. This is Gray in 1871 beguiling us with a story of a White-tailed Eagle that was kept as a pet: 'A few years ago, Dr Macgillivray had a pet Sea Eagle which was exceedingly interesting. He had a house made for it on the face of a hill about a 100 yards from his house. Here it spent the night, but during the day it was generally abroad with the doctor's two boys. It would come at their call and feed out of their hands, fly above their heads and follow them wherever they went. I am not sure if ever it went alone in search of prey, but nothing seem to delight it so much as to get the boys away rabbit-hunting. When an unfortunate rabbit showed itself the eagle would swoop down upon it with amazing rapidity and power.'

Here Macgillivray, writing in 1886, describes the power of the bird in flight: 'The Sea-Eagle is now on wing, and as he gradually mounts in wide curves, sailing at intervals, you cannot fail to gaze on him with delight. With his feet concealed among the feathers of the abdomen, his head drawn close to his shoulders, and his magnificent wings spread out to their full extent, and even seeming to curve upwards at the points, he sweeps along the sides of the hills, advancing with apparently little effort, and, should he spy a carcase, hovers over it in short curves until satisfied as to his security should he alight upon it. On alighting, he stands for a time, then clumsily leaps up to the carcase, perches upon it, and begins to tear open the abdomen.'

Because the White-tailed Eagle was a carrion-eater it was easy for farmers to lace lamb carcasses with poison to kill several eagles at a single sitting. The poison strychnine was discovered in 1818 in Saint-Ignatius's beans *Strychnos ignatii* and would have been readily available over the counter. It is deadly. Death by strychnine is horrific: within 20 minutes violent convulsions take place in which the body is arched and the head bent backwards before the animal sinks down exhausted. Thereafter, the convulsions recur every few minutes until death occurs from exhaustion or suffocation.

It was the diligence of John Alexander Harvie-Brown (1844–1916) who, between 1887 and 1906 in collaboration with others, wrote *Vertebrate Faunas* of all of Scotland's regions.

His writings allow us to appreciate the rapid decline of the White-tailed Eagle to extinction. He compares the White-tailed Eagle with the Golden Eagle: 'At one time commoner than the Golden Eagle, the two species have rapidly exchanged places in faunal value. It had not and has not the advantage of the other or "mountain eagle". It does not receive the fostering care of our deer forests. It is more predacious in its daily life. It affects the sea coasts, where it is more open to attacks by sea, and less insured against molestation even by land. It is even more of a wanderer, it is more subject to periodic fits of lamb-stealing, and certain old birds whose teeth get blunted, no doubt do occasionally help themselves to the easiest obtainable supplies. It is even more easily trapped than the Golden Eagle, as being certainly more omniverous [sic] in its diet.'

The perfection of the double-barrelled breech-loading shotgun was another weapon in the keeper or farmer's armoury, but was not so effective as poison. Harvie-Brown describes one keeper's expertise: 'All Macdonald's Sea Eagles were shot with a double-barrelled shotgun and BB shot. He could kill eagles at all times, but the springtime was the best. He had a little bothy of turf built on a green hill in Glenbrittle. Leaving home between four and five he used to wait in his bothy from six to ten, and often the eagle, attracted by the dead sheep, would pitch on the very bothy itself. He waited until the bird began to feed, and then despatched it, shooting at the head. Once he killed three in a morning; another time he shot one Sea Eagle and seven Ravens in the same time.' Macdonald killed 62 White-tailed Eagles on Skye in this way.

As its population declined, the rarity of the White-tailed Eagle made it a target of egg and skin collectors. The most infamous of these collectors were Lewis Dunbar, a bird skin collector and taxidermist, and John Wolley, egg collector. Harvie-Brown, rather like a 'spy master', kept in touch with the situation through a circle of informants and wrote 'In 1849 Mr Dunbar offered 10 shillings each for eagles throughout the county of Sutherland; and Bantock – at the time the gamekeeper to the Duke of Sutherland – 10 shillings each for eggs. Mr Wolley obtained eggs in 1849 from Dunnet Head, and the following year the birds shifted their position about a quarter of a mile west.'

On 2 May 1849, in Sutherland, John Wolley wrote this account while sitting in a White-tailed Eagles' nest that he had just robbed: 'These two eggs are curiously stained, and much smaller than those I took 23rd April. They were some days sat upon. In the morning a shepherd's son led us to the nest site. As we approached the rock we saw two Ravens, which had evidently a nest, and I feared this was a bad sign for Eagles. However, immediately afterwards, I saw a noble White-tailed Eagle moving on the face of the rock, which convinced me he had a nest. I made a circuit, and climbed very quietly, yet with the greatest of ease, till I was immediately under the nest. Here I cocked my gun and took breath. I kept myself in readiness, and threw a bit of stick, when out tumbled the Eagle. I fired, the bird flew on, and would, I feared, escape. But in about a hundred yards she failed, fell over, and lay dead, with her eyes closed.'

Wolley then skinned the bird and observed that she had a shot through her heart: 'On getting above the nest, I can look down into it from about 12 feet, and I can see there are eggs; but it looks impracticable, or nearly so, without a rope. A stake is planted, and soon, with the rope fastened under my arms, I am lowered into the nest, in which I write this account. The nest is made chiefly of dead heather stalks, with a few sticks for the foundation, the largest of which are about an inch in diameter, and two feet long. It is lined with a considerable depth of moss, fern, grass, and *Luzula*. The hollow is small for the size of the bird, and very well-defined. After having blown the eggs, written upon them, and finished my journal, I climbed up without hauling, going round a corner, which would, however, be impassable without a rope.'

Thirty years later, Harvie-Brown wrote: 'The rarity of this fine species for years back may be instanced by the fact that Mr. L. Dunbar has received none for preservation since 1878, the date at which he began to keep records of everything sent to him for stuffing.' Harvie-Brown concludes with the following epitaph: 'Where eggs have been systematically taken for years, it is, I think, reasonable to conclude that, at last, these old birds of a disappearing species may become disgusted at their old homes, and leave the district, as is so evidently the case with the White-tailed Eagle. If, besides, one of a pair of an old eyrie be killed, it is reasonable to conclude that there will be more difficulty for the remaining bird, to obtain a young mate, or a mate at all!' He ended with a plea for the White-tailed Eagle: 'What seems infinitely more to the purpose is to "put up a little prayer" to the proprietors and shooting tenants of lands formerly and presently occupied by White-tailed Eagles to take active measures for their future protection.' The last clutch of White-tailed Eagle eggs in Sutherland was taken by the Reverend F.C.R. Jourdain in 1901. He was a dedicated egg collector determined to have a collection of eggs representing all the birds breeding in the Western Palaearctic, an area covering Europe, North Africa, the north and central parts of the Arabian peninsula and part of Asia including the Ural mountains.

For some little time the White-tailed Eagle lingered on in Scotland as a breeding bird. A pair, one of which was albino, nested in the Shetlands, despite being raided by egg collectors, until 1910. In that year the nest was robbed by a collector who was locally reputed to have been an English clergyman and the albino's mate died. Another pair of White-tailed Eagles survived to breed in Skye, their stronghold, until 1916. The albino White-tailed Eagle, protected for 30 years, was cut down as she soared the skies looking for a mate. The crags, stacks and headlands of Shetland no longer echoed to its cries. In less than 100 years the White-tailed Eagle had been annihilated with the ease of snuffing out a candle.

In the conclusion to his *Vertebrate Fauna of the North West Highlands*, Harvie-Brown optimistically wrote 'Our natural sense of regret at the extermination of this Eagle in Skye is tempered by the consideration that the wide range which it enjoys renders it almost impossible that it could ever become a lost species, since it ranges from Greenland to Siberia and from the fiords of Norway to the forests of Hungary.'

Harvie-Brown was a shade optimistic in his forecast. Persecution and the effect of pesticides made deep inroads into what was once a healthy population. The remotest regions of the Northern Palaearctic, Arctic Russia, Greenland and Norway are still the White-tailed Eagle's strongholds but it has recovered steadily and recolonized traditional breeding areas in Europe. Was it possible that some of these White-tailed Eagles might make their way to the British Isles and re-establish a population here? All the facts suggested that such a scenario was unlikely, particularly since they are not migratory birds, although juveniles do occasionally wander west from Europe and land up, as we shall see later, on our east coast.

Reintroduction seemed to be the only option open. There had been two early attempts: an unofficial one in 1959 by the late Pat Sandeman; and in 1968 an RSPB-backed reintroduction on Fair Isle, run by Roy Dennis. Roy wrote: 'I remember the excitement of waiting for the plane carrying the four eaglets to arrive. It was a brand new aircraft, an Islander. The eaglets, which had been taken from nests in Norway, were in travelling boxes and I'd already built two big release cages for them to grow up in. Watching them develop from 8 weeks old to 18 weeks when they were released was fascinating. I released them by pulling a long line which opened the doors to the pens. Three flew out immediately but one walked out and kept on walking till it reached a hillock and then took off. One of the eaglets disappeared at once and I'm pretty sure it flew back to Norway. It's not far away, closer than Aberdeen. The others hung around, came back for food and gradually became self-sufficient. On a good day you'd see them soaring up to two thousand feet – brilliant. So three of them survived but one was so badly oiled by Fulmars that it subsequently died. In retrospect, the location was a bad choice. It was too small and the Fulmars were a big problem. It was a partial success but it did show that to be a complete success many more birds had to be released as only fifty percent were expected to survive through their first year in the wild.'

The next attempt was masterminded by Professor Ian Newton from the then Institute of Terrestrial Ecology. The location chosen was the island of Rum in the Inner Hebrides. Rum was ideal in that it was a reserve, owned and run by the Nature Conservancy Council in Scotland (now Scottish Natural Heritage). There were plenty of deer and wild goats so there would be carrion for food, there were few Fulmars and the mainland and other islands were close by, providing an opportunity for the young White-tailed Eagles to disperse when independent. The new reintroduction scheme would start in 1975 and run for ten years to ensure success. Roy Dennis was attached to the project because of his specialist knowledge and his contacts in Norway. Annually, White-tailed Eagle chicks would be taken from nests in Norway and brought to Rum.

It was the Nature Conservancy Council who masterminded the whole project and appointed John Love as the project manager. As an undergraduate, John had, quite by chance, been on holiday on Fair Isle in 1968 when the Islander aircraft carrying the four White-tailed Eagle chicks from Norway had landed. He was born in Inverness and was a member of the Inverness Bird Club, where he had listened to lectures by Seton Gordon, probably the most dedicated Golden Eagle watcher of all time, and George Waterston, who had master-minded the protection of the Ospreys when they returned to Loch Garten. John trained as a bird ringer and as a volunteer helped protect Scotland's only pair of nesting Ospreys. Later he attended Aberdeen University and wrote a thesis on 'Bird Predators on Bi-valve Mussels'. As John puts it, "I was sent to Rum on a six-week contract and, in the end, lived there for nearly ten years!"

John's first task was to locate a site where the two aviaries could be situated. Quarantine regulations dictated that it must be at least eight kilometres from domestic poultry and obviously out of the way of curious folk. Eventually a site was chosen that overlooked the sea and would allow the eaglets, once released, ready access to the shore for scavenging. The two aviaries would be based on Roy's design for the Fair Isle reintroduction. A 4 metre × 2 metre timber framework covered with wire mesh would be the basic structure, with a shelter at one end and two log perches.

In the meantime, the Nature Conservancy Council approached the Ministry of Defence to ask if the RAF at their Kinloss base on the Moray Firth could help in transporting the eaglets from Norway to Scotland, as their Nimrod aircraft regularly flew training exercises up into Arctic Norway.

With accommodation and transportation all organized, it was off to Norway to locate the White-tailed Eagle chicks. Bodo, a fishing port, just inside the Arctic Circle was where John Love met up with Johan Willgohs, who had been contracted to find occupied nests with young. Over the next fortnight, Johan showed John what he thought were the most suitable sites. This is John's account: 'The eyries we visited were mostly located on broad cliff ledges, some were on steep slopes and one was even lying like a survey trig point on a high spot of a flat, remote skerry. Two eyries had been constructed in trees, one having collapsed under the weight of the structure. All of them were accessible and the eaglets were all about seven or eight weeks old.'

As there was a deadline to meet the RAF Nimrod from Kinloss, in desperation due to the bad weather, John and Johan were forced to take four chicks from two of the nearest eyries. These were rushed to the designated airbase, packed in cardboard boxes and whisked off to Scotland. Just 11 hours after leaving Bodo, the young White-tailed Eagles were on Rum. For some reason John was not allowed to travel with them and it took him two days to return to Rum, via Oslo, London, Inverness and then, the last leg, by road and sea.

The four eaglets were already in their aviaries when John got back. They had to be fed remotely so that they did not associate humans with food and become imprinted. All the food given to them was fresh and was either fish caught locally, bird carcasses or the remains of deer obtained during the stalking season. They were perfectly able to tear up the food offered and feed themselves. Two weeks later they were wing-flapping and soon flying from perch to perch in the aviary. The eaglets were kept in the aviaries for six to eight weeks, longer than necessary but a requirement of the strict quarantine restrictions that had been imposed. There was one male, named Odin, and three females called Loki, Freya and Karla. The project had its first set-back when Odin died just after fledging, although thankfully all three females fledged successfully.

In his book *A Saga of the Sea Eagles* John described Loki's release: 'On 27 September 1975 I opened up the door of Loki's cage but frustratingly found her reluctant to emerge. A fresh attempt was made the next morning by removing the wire from one wall of her cage. We watched from afar as she leapt at where the wire had been and literally fell out of her cage to freedom. Frantically flapping her wings, she became airborne and found herself carried across the glen, with her legs dangling absent-mindedly, before crash-landing on the far slope. Before dusk she only made one or two brief exploratory flights, but the next morning I spotted her soaring competently at the top of the glen. Twice she was attacked by a juvenile Golden Eagle but skilfully avoided it in the air.'

Karla and Freya were released on 24 October and 1 November, respectively and a food dump was set up on the nearby shoreline. Sadly, Loki's body was found beneath power lines in November. The other two birds remained on Rum throughout the winter but disappeared in the spring. The following year, 1976, Harald Misund had taken over the task of collecting eaglets and ten birds were delivered from Norway. Six birds were released after fledging and quarantine and the remainder kept for a captive breeding programme.

The four birds destined for captive breeding were named Colla, Sula, Ronan and Beccan. Falconry equipment proved useful whilst handling these birds. They were fitted with leather jesses on their legs. The far end of the jesses were united on a metal swivel and a light nylon leash about one metre long was attached to the bottom ring of the swivel. The other end of the leash was attached to a metal ring through which passed a six metre long tether.

Each end was secured, allowing the eaglets to fly from log perches to their individual shelters. The site was enclosed in fencing to prevent disturbance from deer and cattle, and there was a food dump that all the birds could reach. The three birds that had already been released in 1975 would, from time to time, fly in and sneak extra rations.

The four tethered birds destined for the captive breeding programme were never 'manned', a falconry term for taming, which meant that the early leather jesses were inadequate to withstand the constant flying up and along their tethers. Colla was the first to escape. Luckily, John was able mark her roosting place and after dark with the aid of a torch dazzled her and caught her up in a net. Beccan escaped in October 1976 and was free for three days before being recaptured in the same fashion as Colla. Beccan broke free again in May 1977 and this time it was for good. All attempts at recapture failed and, trailing jesses and leash, she flew to freedom. The dangling falconry gear did not stop her fishing and were obvious enough for John to receive reports charting her progress. Cathal, from a batch of four eaglets imported in 1977, was drafted in as a replacement for Beccan, but in 1978 and 1979 there were two further losses: Colla became ill and died a few days later and Shona, imported in 1978, broke both her legs and, although she recovered, eventually died from pneumonia in 1979.

The deaths of Odin, Colla and Shona and the remoteness of Rum with no veterinary facilities on hand made John reconsider the captive breeding programme. He had also been conscious that Harald Misund had always wanted the eaglets to fly free so in the spring of 1979 Cathal, Sula and Ronan were set free. By the summer of 1979, Harald Misund had delivered 32 eaglets to Rum, three of which had died. What had happened in the meantime?

In June 1977, Mick Marquiss, a research scientist, came to Rum to demonstrate radio-telemetry. Gigha, imported in 1977, had a small transmitter weighing only 20 grammes attached to her central tail feathers. She was set free and eventually disappeared from view. Using the portable receiving equipment, John was able to pick up a signal and, by taking a cross-bearing, plot her position. If Gigha was in a glen or on low ground picking her up was relatively simple, but if she moved to higher ground locating her was difficult. In 1978 another trial took place with transmitters fixed to two eaglets named Risga and Kieran. They were tracked as they came to feed at the food dumps but after a month the radio transmitters failed during a spell of very wet weather.

White-tailed Eagles are much more sociable birds than Golden Eagles. John observed how one bird, Beccan, acted as a foster mother to birds still awaiting release. Her lighter plumage, yellow bill and eye stood out against the dark feathers, black bill and brown eyes of the eaglets.

It was not unusual now for John to see several White-tailed Eagles in the air at the same time and they had started to wander. As he explained, 'In early January 1979, during a period of exceptional frost and snow, Beccan and at least three other eagles turned up on one of the neighbouring islands where they were seen to feed on a sheep carcass. Gigha and Ulva remained on Rum to be rejoined two weeks later by Beccan and the obsequious Fingal. Ulva and Fingal were from the batch of ten birds imported in 1978. I once watched Sula leap at Beccan angrily to keep her at bay, but after two or three such attacks Sula had moved sufficiently far for Beccan to pounce on her food unmolested. Beccan gained height with her ill-gotten prey, inducing in Ulva some unrewarded food-begging behaviour.'

The Return of the Sea Eagle film was made by Hugh Miles at about this time. It was part of the long-running series *Wildlife on One* on BBC 1 and was very elegantly produced. There were superb scenes from Norway of White-tailed Eagles displaying and talon-grappling and of the relationship between otters and White-tailed Eagles; they eat the otters' left-overs. Harald Missund was shown taking young eaglets from nests before despatching them by air to Scotland. Then in Scotland, on Rum, there were sequences of the eaglets prior to release: flying on a tether, being hooded and finally released into the wild. There was also a superb shot of a White-tailed Eagle flying towards camera, throwing its head back and calling excitedly.

The first phase of the reintroduction of the White-tailed Eagles to Rum had proved a great success and John was able to write: 'On one memorable day I watched seven eagles in the air together. Several attempted to talon-grapple, but only the pair of older birds could successfully interlock, cartwheeling out of the sky amid excited screams.'

Over the next five years a further 43 eaglets were flown in from Norway, making a grand total of 55. There were only six casualties in the wild along the way, far fewer than if they had been reared by their parents in Norway. The project ended in 1985, by which time a total of 85 eaglets had been imported from Norway, 82 of which had been introduced back into the wild. A few stayed on Rum but the majority dispersed to colonize the islands nearby, Mull and Skye in particular. Some of them were now mature enough to breed. How soon would it be before the first White-tailed Eagle reintroduced into Scotland nested and reared young?

In the meantime, I had a most interesting but sad experience with a juvenile White-tailed Eagle in Norfolk. On my birthday, 11 May 1984, my great friend Eddie Anderson rang and told me that a White-tailed Eagle had been found between Wighton and Eggmere – was I interested? I dashed over there and located Eddie, who was holding this enormous eagle. It was a bird that had fledged last year, a juvenile. It had a metal ring on one leg, indicating that it had been ringed in Schleswig-Holstein, and a coloured ring on its other leg. To my eye it seemed as though it was suffering from some kind of paralysis. When Eddie stretched out its wings it offered no resistance and the pupils in its eyes were pinpoint sharp. Had it been poisoned?

I had worked with Dr Derek Ratcliffe, the Chief Scientist at the Nature Conservancy Council, on a BBC film about Peregrine Falcons so I immediately rang him and asked if he could do anything to help. I told him that I suspected the bird might have been poisoned. He sent up a van overnight from the Monks Wood Experimental Station near Huntingdon to collect the bird and asked me to ring him in the morning. Derek's diagnosis over the phone shocked me, "It's certainly paralysed but its not been poisoned. It has been shot!" He went on to say that there were eight shotgun pellets in the bird's body and one had lodged against the spinal cord, paralysing it. Eddie made some enquiries and found out that there had been a fox shoot the previous day and that it might have been shot then, either accidentally or on purpose. A sad end for a majestic bird.

There was better news from Mull. After a few abortive attempts in 1983 and 1984, in 1985 a pair of White-tailed Eagles finally raised a chick that fledged successfully. It was a female and would eventually come to be known as 'Blondie'. Twenty-seven years later I was on Mull with Eddie and his wife Tina, eager to see the eagles and to talk to Dave Sexton, the RSPB officer on Mull. I had received an email from Dave letting me know that although he was busy ringing White-tailed Eagle chicks at the moment he would find time for a good chat. These are some extracts from the journal I kept:

'6/6/12. Long drive from Aviemore to Oban where we catch the ferry to Craignure on Mull. Very quick crossing and then short drive to Salen where we are booked into a B&B run by Simeon and Heather Hill. Comfortable rooms, then off to find supper and then to bed.'

'7/6/12. At breakfast the other guest in the B&B tells us that the best place to see the eagles is on the north edge of Loch Na Keal. There's a nest in a conifer plantation about a quarter of mile from the road. We head off and have no difficulty in finding the site. There's a lay-by and it's jammed with photographers with long lenses. We carry on and drive to Ulva Ferry, a tiny fishing port. It is from here, every day, that a boatman carries out photographers and bird-watchers to see the White-tailed Eagles catch fish thrown out from the boat. We hurry back to the viewing point by the nest site and scan the loch for the arrival of the boat. Eddie points out the eagles perched on different branches, one above

the other, in a conifer tree. The female is 12 years old and fledged from Wester Ross, and the male is 17 years old and fledged in Mull. The eagles see the boat before we do and start yelping. One of them takes off and for the first time I can appreciate the breadth and length of wing as straight as a plank. Its white tail very conspicuous. It rows through the air pursued by a Hooded Crow. It avoids it easily and disappears towards the boat. Ten minutes later it's on its way back carrying a fish. Its mate calls to it. This time the eagle is harried by the Hooded Crow and its mate. It flies past and drops down out of sight to the nest. Eddie is very excited, "You can see every feather – this is cracking good." Three minutes later the bird is off again for another fish. Six minutes later he's back and drops it off at the nest before joining his mate perched in the tree. Now they both take off and soar. The female finds it harder to get lift. They fly off to Ulva together as a Buzzard harries them. It hits one of the eagles. They look the size of Chaffinches alongside them. Honour is satisfied and the Buzzard sheers away. Both eagles return almost immediately carrying fish and head for their nest. The male returns to perch in the tree. There's some yelping from his mate and off he goes again. This time he's followed by Buzzards and Hooded Crows. One of the Buzzards really giving him gyp – very fierce. The eagle hits an updraft and floats up with hardly a wing flap, leaving them behind. Circling, just the odd wing flap. A Raven comes up to harass the eagle, which flips over on one side to avoid her. The Buzzards still wheeling around. The eagle's mate watches the unequal contest from the luxury of her ringside perch in the conifer tree.'

To get a dramatic view of the thrown fish being scooped up, we move back towards Ulva to set up opposite the sightseeing boat.

'The White-tailed Eagle appears over the brow of hill with the forestry plantation in the background. The inevitable Buzzard is shadowing it. As it approaches the boat it starts to circle, positioning itself. The boatman throws the fish out. The eagle slips sideways, losing height rapidly, and lines itself up perfectly like a jumbo jet coming in to land. Its legs go down, head thrust forward. Blazing yellow eyes fully focused ahead. Feathers from upper part of legs skimming the water. At the last moment, its legs shoot right forward underneath the head and the huge black talons grab the fish. Immediately those huge wings start rowing through the air to lift the eagle and its prey from the water. It slowly makes its way back to its nest site mobbed by its attendant Buzzard.'

The show is over so I ring Dave Sexton and he says he will meet us at our B&B about four o'clock and take us to the hide. I had learnt a bit about his background. He went to university in America and graduated in 1983 with a degree in anthropology. While there he worked on a project to reintroduce Peregrine Falcons to the east coast and monitored Bald Eagles and Ospreys. In 1984 and 1985 he protected the first White-tailed Eagle nests on Mull. From there he went to work for Sir John Lister Kaye at the Aigas Field Centre, near Inverness. After a year there he worked as a researcher at the BBC Natural History Unit before returning to Scotland and the RSPB. He did a spell in Edinburgh, got to the top of the ladder, and then decided he wanted go back to Mull.

On cue, Dave's Land Rover rolls up and we are off. I start interviewing him straight away. When did he first come to Mull? When did he see his first White-tailed Eagle? Dave tells me, "It must have been spring 1980. But then in 1982 I was hiking through a glen on Mull when two huge dark birds caught my eye over the far ridge. Two immature White-tailed Eagles were soaring along the ridge. Often with their legs down they looked like hang-gliders drifting back and forth. One was bigger than the other. I'd stumbled across a young pair (at that time, it was the only pair) and they looked to my inexperienced eye to be prospecting a potential nest site. By 1985 they were fully mature. The female was particularly striking. Her pale sandy head just gleamed in the sunlight, her eyes and beak a rich yellow and her white tail just dazzled as she soared just where I'd seen her all those years before. She quickly became known as 'Blondie'. She was set to become one of the most famous White-tailed Eagles of all time. With her faithful mate beside her, they would raise the first wild-bred White-tailed Eagle chick in Scotland for 70 years."

As the news spread, visitors poured into Mull to see the eagles. Unfortunately, some of these visitors were unwelcome. There are not many egg collectors left nowadays but the Strathclyde police and volunteers are always on the look out, checking cars for the number plates of known offenders. Nevertheless, some eyries have been robbed – although thankfully a number of the thieves have been arrested.

As we drive through Forestry Commission Scotland land, Dave recalls the anxiety of watching that first chick, "We were still on 24-hour protection duties. It had gone on for 12 weeks. We were working to one goal, one aim. We wanted that first chick in living memory to take to the skies. And so that dawn finally arrived. A quick check through the telescope

and there he was. Flapping hard on the nest, jumping up and down. Can't be long now. Five minutes and another check. He was gone! We'd missed it. A quick search. Yes, there he was, sitting on the ground wondering what to do next. As we watched, he launched off again, straight out of the wood and away out over the loch. A bit wobbly but strong enough. Then came those awful, horrible, dread-inducing words which will live with me forever, "What's that in the loch?" "Where?" "There – in the middle of the loch." The head of some creature kept appearing and disappearing in the waves. Our chick – the only chick – had ditched in the very centre of the huge loch. The chick we'd watched over day and night, fretted over through wind and rain, was struggling and virtually submerged hundreds of metres out in the cold grey waters. All that was visible was 'Blondie' and her mate circling low over the water, calling out in desperation as they searched and searched. By now it was virtually dark. We stood for what seemed like hours, unable to think or act. We had to go home. We longed for the dawn to come. I raised my binoculars and started to scan, far and wide, across the loch, down to the water's edge (half dreading what I'd find), anywhere, everywhere. Nothing. I could see the others arriving. We made contact on the walkie-talkies. Two hours later, we had all but given up hope. It was probably time to call it a day. My eye caught a movement over the wood. It was 'Blondie', circling low over the tops of the trees. Then there was the male. The pair of them together – but alone. That's it, I thought. With that, 'Blondie' closed her wings, legs down, and swooped earthwards, closely followed by the male. Had they spotted something? It was another, very long, 30 minutes before the radio crackled into life: 'Dave, I've got him! I've got the chick!' He was alive, sitting on the edge of the loch with both parents nearby. He must have struggled ashore, out of our gaze, as the light fell last night. The chick – our precious chick – was alive!"

We were still stunned by the roller-coaster of emotions in Dave's story as we pulled up at a clearing in the conifer plantations. The eagles had left the original public viewing site on Loch Frisa, so a new hide had to be found. Dave led us into a cabin where bird-watchers are briefed before filing down to the hide. It is supported by the Forestry Commission Scotland, the RSPB, Scottish Natural Heritage, Strathclyde police, the Mull and Iona Trust and local volunteers. He emphasized that the Mull Eagle Hide was set up to divert attention away from other sites, and because of that they had to give the public something special to see.

For those who do not want to go into the hide, there is a big screen on which pictures from a CCTV camera on the nest are transmitted. We were told by Dave to keep quiet and followed him down a rocky path before turning into a stand of conifers. A natural hide had been fashioned amongst the trees. A viewing slit, three metres long by one-and-a-half metres high, had been cut at shoulder height through the lower branches of a tree. The view through it took your eye up a clearing in the plantation to where the eagles' nest had been built in a tree. It was bulky and two dark-coloured chicks were lying in the nest. The female was perched about six metres above them, on guard. Dave told us, "The female is a wild-bred bird from Skye and she got together in 2001 with a Norwegian male from the Wester Ross reintroduction. They had two failed attempts and then hatched and reared their first chick in 2005. They've had a chick or two every year since."

I asked Dave what they fed on and he said, "They eat everything, especially sea birds, such as Eider Ducks, Guillemots and Razorbills, and hares and rabbits. They're not fussy. If they can carry it – even a Red Deer calf – it'll be on the menu." I said I had bought wildlife cameraman Gordon Buchanan's film *Eagle Island* and remember him registering astonishment as he filmed one of the White-tailed Eagles flying into the nest with a lamb. Dave replied, "Living with these big predators can be a problem if you're a sheep farmer. There is a positive management scheme run by Scottish Natural Heritage for farmers if they farm within 5 km of a nest and sign up to improve husbandry, and so reduce exposure to eagle predation. They can get between £1,000 and £1,500 a year out of it. Some feel they're very lucky to have any scheme at all in the current climate. Nevertheless, there are still some farmers that wish these birds were still extinct."

I said I knew that the White-tailed Eagles had boosted the economy on Mull and Dave fills in some details: "Wildlife tourism on Mull is actually now the backbone of the local economy. One of the biggest draws is the White-tailed Eagles. BBC TV's *Springwatch* is what catapulted these birds into the public eye. They did a live broadcast in 2005 with Simon King, Kate Humble and Bill Oddie. People poured in to see the two eagles on Loch Frisa, and some also just to see where Simon King had sat! To sit on the famous stump and have their photographs taken. And we must be grateful, for while the TV crews are here, they are eating in local restaurants and renting self-catering cottages. The eagles bring £3–5 million pounds a year into the local economy."

I ask Dave about the money they take at the hide and am told, "Every penny that's taken here – we charge £6 for adults, £3 for children and we get 3,000 to 5,000 visitors a year – goes back to the Mull and Iona Eagle Community Trust. From that they fund a part-time job on the island and the rest goes out in small grants to groups that apply for it – the Girl Guides, local schools, war memorials, the MOD Club, the young Mull Musicians, the Mull Bagpipe Society and so on. The White-tailed Eagles are putting money back into society and it may just stop someone going out and doing something horrible to them."

When I ask whether this implied the eagles were persecuted, Dave responds, "Up to now, on Mull they are safe. But there's persecution strongly suspected and proven in Scotland. When the young fledged on Mull spread out, because there isn't room for them here, they are at risk. Poisoning is the biggest risk to this whole project today."

As we leave the hide, I ask him if he thinks the White-tailed Eagles will ever be reintroduced to England and he replies, "As a project it is dormant at the moment. White-tailed Eagles could clearly flourish throughout the UK. We only associate them with mountains and Scotland because that was their last refuge from relentless persecution in the nineteenth and twentieth centuries, ending in their extinction in 1916."

I tell him what Mark Cocker, author of *Birds and People,* published in 2013, says about the White-tailed Eagle: 'People have got lost in arguments about the historicity of eagle presence in southern England. Which species was it? When were they there? Did they ever breed? We should perhaps set all those arguments aside for a moment, because what seems indisputable is the strong proof that the species thrives very well now in lowland coastal environments adjacent to the Baltic and North Seas, an ecological zone of which East Anglia forms a part. Why can they have the bird, but we can't?'

We are on our way back to our B&B and Dave tells me that he feels so lucky to have been involved with this project. He brings me up-to-date with Blondie's story. "In 2000 I watched her at that year's nest. She'd just hatched her latest chick and was brooding it carefully as she'd always done. It was always a great comfort to see her each time I visited Mull. It was like visiting an old friend. As I turned away to continue my walk, I couldn't have known it would be the last time I'd ever see her. A week later I was called to be told that Blondie was missing, presumed dead. Her mate had carried on brooding the chick as long as he could before he was forced to leave and get food for himself and the chick. But he couldn't do everything and

during a spell of wet, cold spring weather, Blondie's last chick succumbed to the elements. He would often sit nearby and just call and call – but there was to be no answer."

We pull up at our B&B, Eddie, Tina and I feeling rather down. Dave tries to cheer us up. "But look at what has been achieved. Since 1985, 463 White-tailed Eagle chicks have fledged into the wild. Now, in 2012 there's 60 pairs on the west coast of Scotland and 14 of those are on Mull. Sixty chicks fledged. We've every reason to be proud of Blondie! She's the matriarch!

Dave continued, "In the autumn of 2000 I went back to the original nest wood where Blondie and her mate had reared that first chick 15 years previously. The place they'd courted and built their early nests. I thought I'd scan across the loch anyway, just out of habit. The image that filled my binoculars momentarily took my breath away. There, sitting on Blondie's favourite oak, was her mate. He looked content enough and was preening in the soft fall sunshine, just as she always used to. Often they'd sit there together. On this October day, with the bellowing of the stags echoing round the hills, he had come back to look one last time. Perhaps he thought he'd find her there. Perhaps I did too. She was a true pioneer in every sense of the word and it is no exaggeration to say that without her and her mates' productivity, the whole Sea Eagle reintroduction project would not be the success it is today."

We thanked Dave for sharing his thoughts on the project with us. The return of the White-tailed Eagle is a heart-rending yet heartening story; the recolonization of the cliffs and islands of western Scotland by this wonderful bird of prey is a dream that has been forged into reality.

THE MARSH HARRIER

British Isles population (2006–10): 320–380 pairs (increasing)

In 1952 I was at Corpus Christi College in Cambridge reading zoology, botany and geology when Dr Morton, my mother's family doctor, rang me. Would I like to go with him to Horsey in Norfolk to see the Marsh Harriers? I knew that they were rare, very rare, with only three pairs breeding in the British Isles. I had heard that Major Anthony Buxton had only bought Horsey because there were harriers breeding there. I said yes straight away.

Early the following Sunday, Dr Morton called for me at the porter's lodge and off we went. I assumed that Dr Morton knew Anthony Buxton well because when we pulled up by Horsey windmill two-and-a-half hours later George Crees, Anthony Buxton's keeper and boatman, was waiting for us. He helped us into a punt and then poled us off into the marshes. We travelled in silence along wide, open channels through water meadows studded with wind-blown Hawthorn bushes before coming to a junction where we turned into the reedbed proper. Crees eased the punt effortlessly on its way, a Moorhen scurried away in front of us and the reeds towered over us.

About ten minutes later, Crees pulled into a well-worn landing place. He jumped out, secured the punt and helped us scramble up the bank, where he installed us in a reed-built duck-shooting hide. He pointed out the direction of the harrier nest and told us he would collect us in four hours. Dr Morton and I decided on the different arcs we would watch so that we did not miss the harrier coming in and settled down to wait. While we did so, Dr Morton enlightened me on the history of the Marsh Harrier in the British Isles. He said it had been a common bird of prey up until the nineteenth century. Then, within 50 years, the relentless persecution by gamekeepers and collectors of skins and eggs reduced it to the status of a rare bird.

Nevertheless, the Marsh Harrier bred in Wales until 1877 and hung on in the Norfolk Broads up to 1899, By 1900 it was extinct as a breeding bird in the British Isles. It may have been the conscription of gamekeepers at the outbreak of the First World War that allowed Marsh Harriers a chance to recover. In 1915 they bred successfully again at Hickling, and again in 1921. From 1927 onwards there up to four pairs of Marsh Harriers breeding in Norfolk, by 1939 it had expanded its range into Suffolk, and by the early 1950s was nesting in Dorset. Hickling and Horsey, where they were protected, were their strongholds. "That's how it is now, David – what about some lunch?" Dr Morton produced his picnic basket. There were pork pies, tomatoes, cheese, fruit cake and bottles of cider. It was a feast and we tucked in.

It was very hot in our hide. Dr Morton nodded off and I was just beginning to doze when, out of the corner of my eye, I saw the 'V'-shaped silhouette of a large brown bird approaching. I gently touched Dr Morton's arm and whispered, "Harrier, I think, coming up behind you." We raised our binoculars and there was the female Marsh Harrier – flap, flap, flap, glide. Dangling from one of her talons was a young Moorhen. She swept past the hide 30 yards away and about 15 feet up. After a few more flaps she spread her tail and hung in the air for a moment, wings flapping, before dropping down into the nest. We could hear the harrier chicks squabbling as they jostled to be fed. A momentous day and one for which I will always be in debt to Dr Morton.

As soon as I returned to Cambridge I rushed back up to my room and grabbed my sketchbook. In those days I aspired to be a bird artist and wanted to get down my impressions of the Marsh Harrier – the 'V'-shape of the cranked-back wings reminiscent of a *Stuka*, the Junkers 87 dive-bomber. Little did I know that I was doing exactly what Neolithic Man had done long ago. In the caves of Tajo Segura near the Laguna de la Janda in the province of Cadiz in Spain are crude drawings of birds, including the Marsh Harrier. Finger-painting, using black and red pigments, the inhabitants sought to portray animals in the wild. Some of these were the animals they depended upon for food, whereas others, like harriers and eagles, they probably regarded as power animals – animals that acted as guardian angels that helped in all sorts of ways, particularly with hunting. Today, there are still waterfowl of all sorts in the area, as well as cranes, storks, a wide variety of birds of prey including eagles and Montagu's and Marsh Harriers.

William Turner (1508–68) in his *Avium Praeciparium* gives a very exact description of the Marsh Harrier, or Bald Buzzard as he calls it, which could only have been made from observations in the wild. To quote, 'With a white patch upon the head, and nearly fuscous in colour, always haunts the banks of rivers, pools, and swamps: it lives by hunting Ducks and those black fowls which Englishmen call Couts. If anywhere a little ground rises among the reedbeds, there the bird is wont to make a nest, that, since in power of flight it is not very strong, it may not be far distant from its prey. It suddenly attacks birds, and thus takes them. It also sometimes butchers coneys.'

For the next two centuries the Marsh Harrier was variously called Bald Buzzard, White-headed Harpy, Duck Hawk, Moor Buzzard or Marsh Hawk. In 1758 Carl Linnaeus in his *Systema Naturae* classified it as *Falco aeruginosus*. Soon after it was designated as a harrier in common with the other two British harriers, Hen and Montagu's. The Marsh Harrier, as it was now known, was re-classified as *Circus aeruginosus*. *Circus* from the Ancient Greek *kirkos*, meaning circle and thus describing a circling hawk, and *aeruginosus* meaning copper or rust-coloured.

Circus aeruginosus, the Marsh Harrier, is widely distributed as a breeding bird through lowland wet areas from the British Isles and across Europe, east as far as Lake Baikal in Russia. It comes to us mainly as a summer migrant, although increasingly it tends to over-winter here. The specific scientific name *aeruginosus* is very apt if you view a Marsh Harrier perched in a tree with the naked eye. It is a big, brown or rust-coloured bird of prey with no obvious distinguishing features. Seen through binoculars, an adult female Marsh Harrier is a jigsaw of different shades of brown, highlighted with much paler, straw-coloured patches.

Marsh Harriers are dimorphic – the male having a different plumage pattern and colour from that of the female. Birds generally do not start breeding until their second or third year, gradually acquiring their adult plumage as they mature. Starting with the head, both sexes have a black bill black, a yellow cere and orange eyes that turn to yellow as the bird gets older. They also have a pronounced bony ridge above the eye, which protects the eye when pouncing on prey in thick cover.

The male's head is pale, with longitudinal rusty streaks running from the crown to the nape. A much lighter brown streak than in the female runs from the bill through the eye to the edge of the ear coverts. The mantle, scapulars and back are brown, leading to a pale grey area on the rump. The tail is silver-grey. The breast and the inner leading edge of the wing are rusty-brown with darker streaks. The outer leading edge is a silver-grey, which merges into a distinctive silver-grey, almost lavender-blue, wing panel that covers all but the innermost secondaries and primaries. This panel is a key identifying feature when viewing a flying male from the side or above, the five dark outer primaries showing as a black wing-tip. Since male Marsh Harriers do not assume their full adult plumage after the first moult, there can be some confusion in identifying two or three-year-old males when they first appear at the beginning of the breeding season. A recent paper in British Birds (March 2013) points out that many males never develop the typical 'adult male' plumage even when they are many years old, and look essentially like females. Nevertheless, a normal five- or six-year-old-male Marsh Harrier is a very handsome bird indeed.

I remember bird-watching with Andy Bloomfield, then a part-time warden at the Holkham Nature Reserve, as a male Marsh Harrier swept past the hide. Its silver-grey upperwing panels flashed in the sun as it jinked to avoid the attentions of a mobbing crow. It was gorgeous. Andy told me that this male was six or seven years old and that it was polygynous, having two separate females. I could fully understand why, as it had certainly turned our heads.

In females, the head is straw-coloured but there is a chocolate-brown stripe stretching from the base of the bill through the eye to the top of the ear coverts. The facial disc is owl-like. The chocolate-brown of the eye-stripe continues down the nape to the rump. The wing coverts are the same colour brown but the secondaries and primaries are darker. There is often a thin line of pale feathers on the leading edge of the wing and the upperside of the tail appears a lighter, rusty brown. The breast and belly are paler than the back and wings and there may sometimes be a straw-coloured patch across the top of the breastbone.

The 'trousers' covering the thighs are rust-coloured. The legs are long, yellow and scaly, and the large, yellow feet have black talons. As with most birds of prey, the female is larger than the male.

The juvenile Marsh Harrier is a somewhat darker bird than the adult female. It has a similar dark eyestripe but the remainder of the head, straw coloured in the adult, is a striking orange.

The wings of the Marsh Harrier are broad, enabling it to fly very slowly when hunting. It quarters a reedbed or water meadow rather like a gun dog searching for a 'winged' pheasant. Flying about five to seven metres above the ground, it hunts mainly by sight but is also able, like all the harriers, to locate prey by sound alone, its ears being positioned symmetrically behind the facial disc. When prey is located the harrier stops dead in the air, tail spread and wings beating, before dropping, legs outstretched, onto its unsuspecting target.

Occasionally, the harrier will not notice prey until it has overshot and then carries out a spectacular 'cartwheel', wings flailing, tail spread, before plunging down. Sometimes it will even flip over a hedge to catch unwary prey on the other side. The harrier's feet are big and its prey is killed as its sharp talons pierce the body. Females are powerful enough to dive deep into a reedbed to secure prey, but the slightly smaller male generally prefers hunting over water meadows, where the vegetation is more open.

The Marsh Harrier's diet is extensive and includes amphibians, reptiles, mammals and birds. In the spring, when birds arrive at their breeding grounds, frogs are one of their main food items, but then it will be Moorhen and Coot chicks and ducklings. Later they move on to feed on mammals, such as young Rabbits and leverets, voles and Brown Rats. Small birds, such as Reed Buntings, Skylarks and young Pheasants, also feature.

Game preservationists in the 1950s prevented Marsh Harriers from extending their breeding range much beyond Norfolk and Suffolk and a few other counties. Then something much more sinister occurred, as the Marsh Harriers in their stronghold areas ceased to breed. The cause of the crisis is now well known. Organochlorine pesticides – DDT, aldrin and dieldrin – used in agriculture had entered the harrier's food-chain, leading to a reduction in the thickness of their eggshells. After a voluntary ban in the UK on these pesticides in the spring of 1962 the Marsh Harrier staged a comeback. John Buxton, Anthony Buxton's son, told me that they nested again at Horsey in 1972. By 1980 numbers had increased to 20 breeding pairs.

I had moved to Norfolk in the 1970s, and in 1984 was able to watch Marsh Harriers at first-hand. That winter a rare Red-breasted Goose, following Brent Geese from their breeding grounds on the Taimyr Peninsular in Arctic Russia, had fetched up on the north Norfolk coast near Burnham Norton. Every day the Red-breasted Goose, with the small flock of Brent Geese that were its constant companions, used to fly to a freshwater pool on the Burnham Norton meadows for a 'wash and brush up.' I was given permission to set up a straw-bale hide to photograph it.

I spent a lot of time in that hide, the main attraction being that there was always something happening. Marsh Harriers had started to over-winter and there were always one or two birds slowly hunting up and down the reedbeds that separated the sea wall from the water meadows. There were flocks of Wigeon that flew in to hoover up the sweet grass on the water meadows, the drakes with their chestnut heads topped with a golden forehead whistling to their sombre brown mates. You could always tell when a harrier was approaching. Up would go all the heads, the ducks on full alert. If they sensed that the harrier was going to hunt them, they would rise up in a flock to seek safety in the air.

One day when I was waiting for the geese to arrive I noticed some Fieldfares in a nearby hedge, contentedly chattering away, golloping up the last remaining berries. For a split second they stopped their chattering. Out of the corner of my eye I saw the 'V'-shaped silhouette of a Marsh Harrier slip over the hedge in full pursuit of one of the Fieldfares. As I turned to look out of the back of the hide the Fieldfare flopped in, shrieking hysterically. A shadow passed over the opening and I heard a scrunching thump as the harrier landed on top of the straw-bale hide. I held my breath, the Fieldfare lay panting by my gum-booted feet. After what seemed a very long time, but was actually only a moment, I heard a rustling in the straw roof. The harrier had gone. I waited a moment or two before gently picking up the Fieldfare and sending it on its way.

I was intrigued by these over-wintering Marsh Harriers and quite by chance was able to watch them in two of their traditional winter quarters. Richard Mabey, the renowned writer and a great friend of mine, had been penned up for quite a long time and I suggested a trip to the Camargue to set him free again. It was in early December when we went there and the *mistral* was blowing. At Les Baux our only map was torn from my hands by the wind but we did see Wallcreepers and an Eagle Owl.

On our second day we drove out into the Camargue proper, saw flamingos and got lost. At dusk we arrived at the headquarters of the Parc Naturel Régional de Camargue, the huge Étang de Vaccarès, and watched Marsh Harriers coming into roost. The *mistral*

was still blowing and the harriers were being tossed about as they came into land. After 50 we lost count. There was movement all the time: the reeds were being blown almost horizontal, a harrier would drop in on what was its favourite roosting spot only to find it occupied. Up it would go, before being blown downwind to turn and slowly beat upwind to an alternate roosting spot.

A few years later, Bruce Pearson and I made a film for the BBC, *Beyond Timbuktu,* about the area in Mali where our summer migrants spend their winter. We were shadowing the herds of cattle as they followed the retreating flood-plain to the banks of the river Niger. The heart of the flood is around Lake Debo, where there are vast stretches of *bourghou* grass, food for the cattle. Channels and waterways, criss-cross this area and piroques, canoes, over-laden with *bourghou* are poled through the marsh towards Lake Debo. We had pulled into the side of one of the channels so that Bruce could paint this bustling scene. All around us, patrolling the marshy area were harriers galore. They were mostly Marsh Harriers but now and then a Montagu's Harrier would cross in front of us. This is one of the Marsh Harrier's traditional wintering areas.

In July 2000, an event occurred that would have a great impact on my life. Nigel Middleton, the Hawk and Owl Trust's conservation officer for East Anglia, was watching two newly fledged Marsh Harriers as they perched in an Elder bush on the edge of Sculthorpe Moor. Nigel knew that these birds had originated from Guist Common about seven miles downstream on the river Wensum. By now the Marsh Harrier population in Norfolk had recovered to 59 breeding females that had fledged 122 young. What a wonderful place for a reserve, Nigel thought. Discreet enquiries revealed that the lease was available. It had been known as the 'Doctors' Shoot' but as the doctors got older and the moor got more and more impenetrable they decided to call it a day.

Quite by chance, my wife Liza and I were staying with Jemima Parry-Jones, expert falconer and conservationist, at Newent in Gloucestershire when Nigel phoned. Also there was Barbara Handley, chairman of the Hawk and Owl Trust. Should we take on Sculthorpe Moor? There was unanimous approval. Liza was already President of the Trust and I agreed to be a trustee with special responsibility for the new reserve.

About a fortnight later, in torrential rain, Nigel introduced us to Sculthorpe Moor. It was like entering a jungle. Nigel led the way following a deer path. Machetes would have come in handy. There were brambles, saplings and reeds everywhere, ditches and fallen trees to scramble over, and roots to trip you up. I could quite understand why the doctors had given up the shooting rights. And all the time Nigel gave a running commentary of what he was going to do. This was where the first hide would be, here a bridge would have to be built, this was saw-sedge which we would cut and sell commercially, and this was the reedbed proper where the harriers had nested. At the end of this magical mystery tour we were exhilarated, exhausted but completely in thrall to Nigel's vision.

The lease was signed and rent paid. The task facing Nigel and his volunteers was a daunting one. Volunteers, Eric Adnams and Derek Jennings, were the trailblazers. Eric explains what it was like: "We had to start with the track into the reserve. It was completely choked with undergrowth. We had to cut a way through it, even though it was littered and blocked with fallen trees, old cars, washing machines, all sorts of rubbish. All that had to be cleared away. One side of the track had a ditch running alongside it and the banks were quite unstable. Nigel and his vehicle ended up in the ditch and we had to borrow a Tirfor winch to haul him out. Once we'd dealt with the track we had to put in a field gate at the entrance to the reserve proper – that was a big job."

Once the entrance to the reserve was secure, Nigel and his band of volunteers had to face up to restoring the reedbed, which was choked with birch, willow and alder. Working with reeds is in Nigel's blood. His great-great-grandfather, George Cox, was a reed-cutter on Barton Broad. Nigel's holidays were spent on Oulton Marshes, fishing and bird-watching. He had a pet owl and carried a Grass Snake around in his jacket; he was obviously a bit of a lad. He would frighten female shop assistants with the snake so that he could nick bubble-gum. His family told him to get a job and pushed him into catering. Later he did a spell in the Norwegian merchant navy. But he was not happy and so came home wanting to work in the countryside.

In 1985 a chance meeting with Dr Roger Clarke at Blickling Hall, where the Hawk and Owl Trust had set up its base, was a turning point in Nigel's life. Roger became Nigel's mentor and, combining their skills, they were the first to breed Marsh Harriers in captivity. When Nigel wrote a paper on the ecology of winter-roosting Hen Harriers Roger, of course, supervised him. Together they wrote the management plan for the fen restoration at Sculthorpe Moor and the rest, as they say, is history.

By 2003, the majority of the fen had been restored and there was a hide and an 800 metre long boardwalk through the wet and dry woodland at the north end of the reserve. Eric and Derek took charge of its building and told me about some of the trials and tribulations. "It was quite a job. Keeping it level was the difficult part, adjusting to the contours of the ground and the tree roots. We didn't cut any trees down, instead weaving our way through them in a sinusoidal kind of way. We were very proud of it. One weekend some of the volunteers had a go at it on their own. They didn't start where we had left off, they simply started where they felt like it, just following the contours of the ground. When we saw it on the Monday it just didn't look right. So we ripped the whole lot up and started all over again!"

On a day when volunteers were working on the reserve, I went over to talk to some of them. Geoff Clark, the volunteer organizer, said, "It's a passion for me. I've been doing it for four years. I came down here on a volunteer recruitment day and stayed. I prefer the winter work – it's just too hot in the summer. Even in winter I'll be working in a T-shirt felling trees with a chainsaw. There's still a terrific lot to be done to clear all the trees that have smothered the reedbed."

Graham Blanchfield, one of the volunteers told me, "I was taking the dog for a walk on the other side of the river and saw all these people working. I went to the Visitor Centre and asked what they were doing. I was invited to help and have been a volunteer for three years now. I come on a Tuesday or Thursday, though not necessarily for a full day. I enjoy the manual work and it's good to see what's been done over the last ten years. It's an asset to Fakenham and the area around and good that its been restored to its natural habitat."

Vic Gerrard, volunteer mechanic, explained, "I enjoy doing the job – it's a very good reserve and we get a lot of praise from visitors. It's good to give something back to society. My job is looking after the equipment – quad bike, chainsaws and strimmers – and I like to think they're more reliable now than they used to be."

Tim Smith, assistant warden, said, "I came from a shooting background and got to know Nigel who wanted the Grey Squirrels controlled. I'm happy with that, they're not a native species and they take birds' eggs. Since I've been controlling them there's been a positive change in Long-tailed Tit and Treecreeper numbers. I have also moved on to habitat management and now, through working closely with Nigel, I know much more about conservation and how Marsh Harriers fit into the ecosystem on the reserve."

Four years later, in 2007, an aerial view of the 40-acre reserve showed a complete transformation. There was an Education Centre, four hides, two boardwalks meandering through the wet woodland, giving access to all, new dykes and sluices to control the water levels in the reedbed and a scrape to attract waders and wildfowl. By then, up to three pairs of Marsh Harriers generally nested on the reserve.

Over the period 2006–10 the number of breeding Marsh Harriers increased prodigiously and the RSPB estimated that there were between 320 and 360 pairs in the British Isles. In 2010 the *Norfolk Bird and Mammal Report* recorded 62 breeding females fledging 57 young but stated that numbers must clearly exceed this. That was a healthy situation but at the same time there had been an increase in persecution. On 12 June 2004, a man out in his garden at Loddon in Norfolk saw a Marsh Harrier shot. He telephoned the police, who scrambled a helicopter and were promptly on the scene. Two men who had been shooting pigeons were arrested, but despite having a witness to the incident they escaped with a caution after pleading that they thought they were shooting a Rook.

Every year there are similar incidents of Marsh Harriers being shot, some of which are not killed outright and are left to die in agony. There have also been incidents of gas guns being deliberately sited near harrier nests where females are incubating in order to make the birds desert. In 2008 alone, four nests are known to have been interfered with in this way.

In the summer of 2008, Nigel and his team placed a mini-cam at one of the Marsh Harrier nests. There was an anxious wait to see if the female would accept it. Thankfully she did and as a result visitors to the reserve were able to watch close-up shots of the three young being reared, a classic 'first'. We were worried whether the smallest chick would survive, and viewers of the BBC Television series *Springwatch* were equally concerned. On the third evening there was a storm and the camera was hit by lightning. Had the female and her three chicks been killed? Two days later we were able to reassure viewers with pictures of the three chicks being fed. I think these scenes created a lot of empathy for Marsh Harriers – raising a family of chicks in a hostile environment was not as straightforward as some people may have supposed.

Nigel was not slow to realize that the recordings taken by the mini-cam were unique and should be analysed scientifically. Quite by chance, a group of students and their supervisor from Leicester University visited the reserve and were asked if they would be interested in such an opportunity.

David Laithwaite, one of the students, took on the project as a thesis for his PhD. He studied all the recordings for the years 2009, 2010 and 2011. His PhD was called *The Breeding Ecology and Behaviour of the Marsh Harrier*. Because David had access to full coverage of the nest day by day, interrupted only occasionally by malfunctions, he had a unique opportunity to analyse the parent birds' time spent at the nest for different tasks. He was able to note the total number of departures made by the female each day and the time she was absent from the nest. Information was also gleaned on the number of visits to the nest to remove waste materials by the male and the female, the number of visits by both birds bringing supplementary material to refurbish the nest, and the number of 'empty-handed' arrivals by each of the two birds.

Even though the camera was high definition I think most of us found it difficult to identify conclusively some of the prey that was brought in. David concentrated on the number of prey items brought in by the parent birds per day and itemized them as birds, rodents or Rabbits or leverets. He also identified the total time spent by the male and female eating prey. What particularly fascinated me was that he was able to show that the six harrier chicks developed more slowly in 2010 when less prey was brought in than in 2009 (five chicks) and 2011 (six chicks).

The breeding behaviour of the Marsh Harrier, as seen through the mini-cam, may attract the most attention from our visitors but there are, throughout the reserve, other Closed Circuit Television (CCTV) cameras relaying pictures to two big TV screens in the Education Centre. There is one by the woodland hide, where in the evening Golden Pheasants can be seen; another at the Whitley hide picks out Willow Tits on the feeder and Water Rails scrounging fallen food below; and at the Paul Johnson hide a camera points at a branch on which Kingfishers regularly perch to fish. There are other cameras in nest boxes recording breeding Barn Owls and Tawny Owls. These cameras are a wonderful way of putting people in touch with birds and giving them a chance to witness behaviour that they might not ordinarily experience.

I was on duty in the Education Centre one day as a family returned from a walk round the reserve. They told me that they had had a wonderful time and had seen a Golden Pheasant. At that moment their grandfather appeared. I had been told that he had gone to Wolferton, near Sandringham, to try to see the Golden Pheasants that frequent the rhododendrons there. When the family asked him how he had got on he shook his head – not a thing. Just at that moment a Golden Pheasant appeared on one of the TV screens. I pointed it out to him and his face lit up. His family clustered round him and one of the children said, "See, Grandad, you should've stayed with us!"

Leanne Thomas is the Education Officer at Sculthorpe Moor and in 2012 I talked to her about her job. She said, "My job is to inspire and educate future generations so that they understand and appreciate the importance of the natural world. Schools that are not more than an hour's drive away come here for a morning or afternoon session and families on holiday are welcome too. Pond dipping is one of the favourite activities as children love the excitement of emptying their catch into white plastic trays. Little fingers dip into the weed and discover the bizarre creatures hiding within – including dragonfly larvae with their cruel, pincer-like mouthparts. It is moments like this that can forge an interest in wildlife for a lifetime. I try to explain to them how creatures live together and depend on one another, and introduce the concept of food chains, of which Marsh Harriers are at the top."

The female Marsh Harrier we filmed with the mini-cam was a particularly good parent. She is familiarly known as 'Mrs H' and first nested in 2005, had been flooded out by heavy rain and then re-laid and reared four young. She has bred each year, sometimes with a polygynous mate, and in 2010 reared six young. At the time of writing, in 2013, she is in her ninth season and has raised 42 young. I had determined to study her day by day as she raised her young in 2011, with the help of the mini-cam.

The male Marsh Harrier's arrival heralds the start of the breeding season and Nigel keeps a look-out each day from 15 March onwards. Bruce Pearson wanted to get sketches of the harriers displaying, so I put him on stand-by to come up to the reserve at a moment's notice. A day or two later Nigel let me know the first male bird had arrived.

The courtship display of a male Marsh Harrier is breathtaking. On a warm spring day, which encourages soaring, he beats his way upwards in tight circles until he is almost out of sight. Then he starts to lose height in stages like a toboggan careering down over a series of snowy ridges, screaming all the while, before closing his wings and diving vertically towards the female, indicating the preferred nesting site.

The area in which the harriers nest is best viewed from the Whitley hide, which is erected on poles at the edge of wet woodland. In front and to the left of the hide is an area of sedgebed. To the far right of the hide, by the river, is the reedbed. In the middle distance, directly opposite the hide, is a copse, to the left of which, but farther away, are water meadows with Highland Cattle grazing. From there, looking right and stretching to the river, is rough woodland. In the background, hard by the river, are two hides overlooking the wader scrape. In the sedgebed to the right are several dead birch trees, good perching posts. Bruce has been busy sketching this view. Here is an extract from my journal:

> '1/4/11. To the Whitley hide with Peter Cooper, fellow fundraiser and enthusiastic birder. Quite a few visitors there. Nothing much happening and I was about to say; "Sorry, Peter – I'll have to call it a day, must get back to the dogs ..." when the harriers showed. They flew up and down in front of us, talon-grappling, and then went over to the far left where I suspect they're going to nest. The female looked gorgeous – this is her sixth breeding season here: the male a bit scruffy, although his silvery-grey wing patches showed up well. Male dropped into the reedbed several times, followed by the female. She eventually perched on a stump before they both flew off past the copse and away.'

This was a sure indication that they had chosen a nest site. Soon the female will be carrying in beakfuls of reed to make the nest platform. In the meantime the male will have chosen one or two 'cock's nests'. These are platforms in the reedbed where he will roost and butcher any food before delivering it to the female at the nest.

I have only once seen Marsh Harriers copulating and that was in 2002. The eggs from one of the harrier nests had been taken and I mounted an early morning vigil on the two remaining nests to ensure that they were not disturbed. While I was watching, one of the female Marsh Harriers flew in and perched on the stump of a rotten Silver Birch tree. She was quickly followed by the male who landed on her back, wings beating to keep in position. It was all over in seconds. The eggs are chalky white and are laid at two-day intervals. Four or five eggs are normal but our 'Mrs H' laid clutches of seven and six in 2010 and 2011, respectively. As incubation starts immediately, the eggs hatch at intervals.

I was in Cambridge, researching at the University's Zoology Department Library, when Nigel phoned to say that the mini-cam had been successfully inserted at the Marsh Harriers' nest. Although the male had flown overhead 'yikkering' in alarm for some time, the female had been back on the nest within half an hour. Theses are extracts from my journal of many hours watching:

> '31/5/11. 10.01: There are six chicks huddled together on the simple reed platform that makes up the nest. The age range is 15 days old for the eldest to seven days for the youngest. The nest platform is about half-a metre square and it is completely enclosed by reeds. The two smallest chicks are at the back. 10.16: The female flies in with food. She feeds the

four largest chicks. The smallest make no effort to push forward at all. 10.40: The female is back with more food and lands between the four chicks already fed and the two smallest. She deliberately singles out the smallest for feeding. They stuff themselves. Male makes a quick visit to check out the situation and leaves. 11.44: Female brings in another feed. She's working hard.'

'2/6/11. 07.52: Nest lop-sided since last viewed. Female is trying to build it up again while brooding chicks. (It slopes down towards camera.) She's doing a bit of preening and now and then glancing up at the sky. Mrs H is a very handsome bird – golden head, dark eye-stripe stretching down to chocolate-brown back and wing coverts, darker primaries which she's pulling through her beak and lighter tail. 08.54: Chicks beginning to slide out of nest. All beginning to show mini chocolate-coloured feathers. Eyes button-black. Most still sitting on hunkers, although eldest comes stamping in after defecating over edge of nest; they know to do this instinctively to avoid fouling the nest. I tell Nigel about the tilting nest. He goes in, rescues smallest chicks and re-builds nest. Disaster averted.'

'4/6/11. 07.45: To the reserve. Immediately see female bringing in food. Male goes off hunting. Chicks cluster around to be fed. (In the Whitley hide I can not only watch activity out on the reserve but also watch nest activity on the CCTV screen.) Male returns from hunting and drops prey into his cock's nest to the right of the copse. Female comes up to meet him as he flies towards nest. No food-pass. Instead they land in water meadow. Male off hunting again, female drops into nest. Prey a young rabbit. Four largest chicks cluster round to be fed, two smallest not seen. Lots of squeaking as they jostle for food. Male flies right to left over reedbed and lands in nest. Female squawks at him. He drops reed and exits. Two smallest chicks reappear and force their way to the front and are fed. They grab

bits that are too big for them. Female takes them back, divides them into smaller bits. Larger chicks very mobile and rampaging around nest.'

'5/6/11. 11.31: All chicks by now are aware of the world outside of the nest. Spend a lot of their time hunkered down, just waiting and watching. All feather tracts plainly visible, facial disc obvious. Nigel tells me that the other two nests in the reedbed have failed, this female's very dominant male has chased them off. 11.56: Chicks look up, start calling as female drops into the nest. Prey is a Brown Rat. She grips it across the loins and butchers head first. Two smallest chicks get a full crop. Dropped scraps of meat are picked up and re-offered. Female keeps the nest scrupulously clean.'

'9/6/11. 08.41: All six chicks now standing up. Largest chick shows off with a burst of wing-flapping. Nest beginning to look a bit crowded. A lot of scrabbling around. They are still covered in baby down but the areas of chocolate juvenile plumage are spreading.'

At this stage, Nigel and Phil Littler, the official registered ringer, decide the chicks are old enough to be ringed.

'10/6/11. 15.15: Peter Cooper and I join Phil and Nigel at the edge of water meadow closest to the nest, which is about 5 metres away. Phil goes in with linen bags to bring back the first batch of chicks to be ringed. The female appears overhead, yikkering away. Measurements are made of leg lengths to determine whether they are male or female. Then they are weighed and ringed. It's always an alarming moment as the ring clicks closed – sounds just as if the leg bone has snapped. Chick's beak gaping, tongue sticking out. First batch measured, weighed and ringed and returned to the nest. Female still "yik-yik-yikking" overhead. Second batch, same procedure. Smallest chick last to be ringed, still covered in a lot of mushroom-coloured down, head white. Primaries, secondaries and wing feathers all sprouting well. Hisses. Devil's tongue, roof of mouth going blue. Nigel says it's getting stressed, get them back quickly. It's taken an hour to ring all six chicks, five males and one female.'

'12/6/11. 07.53: Chicks are really growing fast, ringed just in time. A lot of preening going on, getting rid of down around growing primaries. The largest chick stands up, looking down on the other chicks as they huddle together. He looks up, sees something flying overhead. 11.39: Loads of activity – wing-flapping and jumping in the air. Eldest chick now 25 days old.'

'14/6/11. 06.52: Chicks now widely scattered. They explore the reedbed. Very adventurous leaving the safety of the nest. Some tunnel into reeds, others perch on a bit of a reed-fringed bank at the back of the nest so that they are only seen in silhouette. 15.46: Female at nest, she's mantling over them, wings providing shade. All dozing. Crops full. They've just been fed. It must be boiling in there.'

Nigel has often wondered what happens to the young harriers once they have fledged. Do they winter here, go to the Camargue in France or make the traditional long, dangerous migration to West Africa? He also wonders whether, after migrating, the harriers stay put in the spring or return to the British Isles where they were raised. With this in mind, we started wing-tagging all our Marsh Harrier chicks and a number of others within a radius of 15 miles. The chicks are fitted with vivid green 'V'-shaped tags on each wing – those in the nest I had been watching having the letters AA, AB, AC, AD, AF or AH etched in white on each tag.

'16/6/11. 10.03: The young are too big to be called chicks any longer – they are young harriers. They're preening, wing-tags showing up well. All heads now sporting Johnny Rotten orange crowns. Practically all down has disappeared, primaries and tail feathers coming on well. One preens under wing, pulling out down. Eyes have turned from black to yellow. Legs are yellow too. Female flies in with kill, a Rabbit. The two already there are fed first. Others emerge from the reedbed. They are now quite able to handle bigger bits they grab from the female, turning away and pulling on them, stripping off gobbets of meat. They all get a good feed.'

On 22 June, Nigel reports that the eldest chick, 35 days old, made its first flight. It was a bit of a wobbly affair and it ended up crash-landing in the reedbed.

'11/7/11. 15.50: A beautiful day. Red Admiral butterflies everywhere. Marsh Harrier juvenile perched on mini-cam post. Wing-tag shows up well, but can't be read with binoculars. Another juvenile perched in Silver Birch at front of copse. Juvenile on mini-cam post takes off and circles over nest site. Wings look good, legs now yellow. Disappears behind treeline. Another juvenile appears from right, flies across reedbed and crash-lands in a Silver Birch close to other youngster. Yet another juvenile appears, soaring in tight circles. Stoops at another youngster that flies below it. Copper-red head shows up brilliantly. They fly alongside each other – one turns on its back, thrusting its taloned feet up, grappling with the other. It's a game of tag, good training for later on.'

I had hoped to see a food-pass but was unlucky. I remember one I had seen a few years ago when Liza and I were walking with Nigel to look at some improvements that had been made around the wader scrape. At the time I wrote:

'The male Marsh Harrier appeared in the distance heading for the reserve. He was about 150 feet up, carrying a young Rabbit. From the reedbed on our right emerged five juvenile harriers rising up to meet him. He dropped his prey. The young harriers rose up to grab it like cricketers rushing in to take a steepling catch. The lucky one, who turned over on his back to make a spectacular talon-grabbing catch, dropped down into the reedbed, the unlucky four following him like falling leaves.'

Later in 2011 Phil Littler rings me to say that Marsh Harriers are roosting communally on the reserve. This has not happened before and in my journal I wrote:

'28/8/11. 16.45. Beautiful evening, wind has dropped. Family of Jays floppily fly across reedbed to copse. Male Marsh Harrier appears and is joined by female, they talon-grapple. A juvenile, which had already gone to roost, is flushed out and goes to perch in a birch tree. Male and female soaring together now. Playing together before roosting. They and a juvenile drop into roost. 17.10: Another male and female appear, deck feathers missing in male. They go into playtime routine before roosting, talon-grappling and aerobatics. They circle up high over the copse and disappear. 19.30: Juvenile arrives, followed by very dark juvenile with no orange on head, which flies on towards Fakenham. 19.40: Tatty-tail male and female come in to roost. Cock Pheasant puts up male harrier with terrific "cock-cock-cocking." 19.43: Two juvenile wing-tagged harriers come in to roost.'

'9/9/11. 1730: To the reserve. 18.35: Very dark juvenile with golden crown appears flying left to right, followed by adult male. They disappear. Wing-tagged juvenile next, drops into sedgebed by birch tree and is followed by un-tagged bird which roosts by it. Dark

juvenile seen earlier flies in, goes to roost. 18.50: Male Goshawk flies over reserve towards Fakenham. Quite bulky. Soon after, four harriers appear very high from the east. They soar over the reedbed but don't roost. Two juveniles drop in to roost by old nest.'

'23/9/11. 17.15: With Nigel to watch roosting harriers. Watchers in the hide tell us that two have already dropped in. A Kestrel and a Sparrowhawk are about. Very tatty male Marsh Harrier comes into roost, followed by dark female which roosts opposite the hide. Stunning feather-perfect male flies in, couple of circuits and off. 18.07: Second-year female, ragged wings, flies in, roosts. 18.12: Juvenile, wing-tagged, drops in. Last two get up as gorgeous male reappears, roosts. All settle down again, juvenile perched in birch tree. In background Pied Wagtails roosting at wader scrape. Nigel graphically describes them as "Coming in like rain falling". Sparrowhawk makes a pass through them. They all flare up before settling again. On its way back Sparrowhawk makes a jesting stoop at the harrier in the birch tree.'

It is the beginning of autumn now. The hot weather we have been denied all summer is with us for ten days. I go and look at the old nest:

'27/9/11. 14.55: As I walk through the sedgebed to the old nest site, Mrs H, the female Marsh Harrier, appears, circling over me. Through the binoculars I can see she's in excellent condition, feather-perfect. I stand looking down on the old nest. It's bleached white and very clean. There's no greenery at all save for a large clump of Hemp Agrimony growing at the back. I can see the depression at the forward edge of the nest which caused it to tilt early on.'

Early the following year we go to Horsey to look for roosting Marsh Harriers.

'7/1/12. My wife Liza and I, and Nigel and his wife, Trine, go to Horsey. John Buxton takes us out to a dyke which separates the water meadows from the reedbed. It is a quite brilliant day, low sun and moon rising behind us as we walk out along the dyke to an opening in the willows where we can watch out over the reedbed. The sun is dropping down towards Stubb Mill. There's a brisk breeze blowing up the reedbed, away from us. The first Marsh Harriers appear, floating up and down, silhouettes against the setting sun. As they come towards us I can tell that most of them are juveniles, very dark in contrast to the one lone male with its pale blue upperwing patches. None of the juveniles have our bright green wing tags on them. John Buxton joins us as a pair of Cranes fly over the reedbed and into the gathering gloom. The Cranes bred at Horsey after not breeding in the British Isles for 400 years. Their success is entirely due to John's guardianship. As we walked back, I thought we not only owed a great deal to John for safeguarding Horsey but also to his father, Anthony, who had the foresight to buy Horsey and its one pair of Marsh Harriers nearly 90 years ago.'

As we leave Horsey I cannot help thinking about the six young Marsh Harriers from our reserve. The wing-tagging has been a great success –some of the tagged birds have been seen at the nearby Lakenheath, Titchwell and Holme reserves, whereas others have ventured down through Wales to Somerset. Perhaps because of the increased population, more Marsh Harriers appear to be over-wintering here. Will our six youngsters do that or will they fly on through France, perhaps over-wintering in safety at the Camargue reserve? One bird, we know, was seen in Portugal. Or will they push on, crossing the Mediterranean to face the danger of being ambushed by shooters, and fly down across the Sahara to over-winter in West Africa – a six-week journey fraught with danger? My thoughts go with them, together with the hope that they survive to return and lift our hearts again in years to come.

THE HEN HARRIER

British Isles population (2010): 630 pairs (declining)

When I first became involved in conservation in the early 1970s I joined a number of organizations, including The Royal Society for the Protection of Birds and the Hawk Trust. The Hawk Trust particularly interested me, as it was the only body dedicated solely to 'Working to conserve wild birds of prey and their habitats.' Later in 1987 the Hawk Trust published Colin Shawyer's epic report *The Barn Owl in the British Isles - Its Past, Present and Future*. It showed that the Barn Owl's population had declined dramatically since the previous survey 50 years earlier. The Barn Owl became the Trust's flagship bird and the Trust was renamed the Hawk and Owl Trust. The report suggested a number of measures to help the Barn Owl, amongst which were the creation of rough grass margins on farmland and the siting of nest boxes in barns or trees.

About half a mile from where I lived was a tumbledown wreck of what had once been a farm. There remained the chimney-stack, the skeleton of some outbuildings and a shed with most of its tiles missing. I replaced the tiles and in the darkest corner of the shed secured a nest box to one of the beams. Nothing happened for several years until one day I saw a Barn Owl carrying food and flying straight in to where the nest box was. They have nested there ever since.

In 1993 my wife Liza and I had been away working all summer so it was autumn before we could check out the site. As we walked through the overgrown yard in front of the derelict farmhouse I could see something dangling, fixed to the door. As I moved forward I could see that it was a bird – it was a female Hen Harrier, which had had its feet, cut off and nails driven through both of its wings. Its crucified body was one of the most horrific images I have ever seen: it was an image that reeked of persecution and brought to mind the phrase in the poem *A Sparrowhawk's Lament: Timor mortis conturbat me*.

The Hen Harrier is a bird that has been persecuted more ruthlessly in modern times than any other British bird of prey. Before the nineteenth century Game Act which ushered in almost 200 years of continuous persecution, the Hen Harrier was a common bird, the most common of the British harriers.

Wherever there was open grassland, heathland or moorland in the British Isles, the Hen Harrier must have been a resident breeding bird. It would have been largely ignored, its languid, almost owl-like flight resulting in it being of no interest to falconers. The population throughout the British Isles at that time was perhaps as high as 2,000–3,000 pairs.

It was not until 1544 that a description of the Hen Harrier appeared in print. This was in William Turner's *Avium Praecipuarum*. Turner's starting point was to try to work out what the birds of prey were that Aristotle (384–322 BC) had described in his book

Historia Animalium: 'The Rubetarius I think to be that Hawk which English people name Hen Harroer. Further it gets its name among our countrymen, from butchering their fowls. It exceeds the Palumbarius in size and is in colour ashen. It suddenly strikes birds when sitting in the fields upon the ground, as well as fowls in towns and villages. Baulked of its prey it steals off silently, nor does it ever make a second swoop. It flies along the ground the most of all. The Subbuteo I think to be that hawk which Englishmen call Ringtail from the ring of white that reaches round the tail. In colour it is midway from fulvous to black; it is a little smaller than the Buteo, but much more active. It catches prey in the same manner as the bird above.' William Turner treated both birds as if they were different species. All ashen-coloured harriers, the male birds, were known as Hen Harriers and the brown 'subbuteos', with white around the tail, were called Ringtails. Much later, in 1758, *subbuteo* became the specific name for the Hobby, *Falco subbuteo*.

In his *Systema Naturae* of 1776, Linnaeus classified the Hen Harrier as *Falco cyaneus*, blue falcon. It is truly surprising that this ornithological riddle, the dimorphism of the harriers, remained unsolved for almost 300 years. In 1807 George Montagu in Devon properly described them as two different species, the silver-grey male Hen Harrier and the silver-grey Montagu's Harrier. Their attendant females and juvenile birds were all referred to as Ringtails. In 1817 the Hen Harrier was given its present scientific name *Circus cyaneus*.

Now that a proper classification has been arrived at for the Hen Harrier it is time to examine the bird in more detail. The beak of the male is black and the cere yellow. Bristles cover the area between the cere and the eyes, which are a clear yellow. There is a distinct facial ruff edged with short, very distinct feathers and the head, nape, upper back and upperwing coverts are silver-grey. The rump is white, contrasting with the tail feathers that are light grey with dark transverse bars and have white tips – apart from the two central tail feathers which are plain grey and unmarked. The first five outer primaries are black. The underside is grey, becoming lighter towards the vent. The legs are yellow and long. In comparison to the male, which is a spectacularly handsome bird, the female Hen Harrier and the immature males are rather dull. Her head and nape are light brown with dark streaks and the back is dark brown. The secondaries are barred and the primaries are dark. The rump is white and the tail feathers have three narrow transverse dark bars and a much broader bar at the tip. The underside is pale brown with longitudinal dark brown streaking. The female is slightly larger than the male.

A Hen Harrier out hunting, whether over moorland or a sugar beet field, is supremely methodical. It flies predominantly into the wind at a height of less than seven metres, looking down. Its flight action is to flap its wings perhaps three times and then make a long glide. During the glide the wings are held in an upright 'V'. This is a very economical way of hunting and, as Donald Watson remarks in *The Hen Harrier*, the harrier quarters a field searching for prey as diligently as a pointer searching for game. If it spots prey it makes an instant turn, the tail fans out to cut speed and it drops vertically. The harrier's head points down, eyes fixed on the prey, its long legs, with taloned feet spread, thrust forward for the strike.

The Hen Harrier can also catch prey by sound alone. The facial ruff conceals large, oval ear openings, the forward edges of which are slightly raised and directed backwards towards the edge of the ruff. Rows of stiff, short feathers that are attached to a fold of skin running along the back of the facial disc direct sound waves back into the ear. The silent-flying harrier can easily pinpoint a Meadow Pipit by the rustle of heather or a Field Vole squeaking in tussocky grass.

The first big threat to the Hen Harrier came at the end of the eighteenth century with the Enclosures Acts and the reclaiming of land that followed. According to the book *Coke of Norfolk & His Friends,* published in 1912, when Thomas Coke took over Holkham in 1776 'it was little better than a rabbit warren. All you will see is one blade of grass, and two rabbits fighting for that!' Gradually, using the his friend 'Turnip' Townshend's new 'four-course shift' system, Coke turned infertile heathland into vast acreages of cereal growing farmland. Many landowners followed this approach and it is not hard to imagine the impact that this had on the Hen Harrier.

Nevertheless, in the early part of the nineteenth century the Northamptonshire poet John Clare often used to see Hen Harriers hunting over the heaths and fens near his home in Helpston, near Peterborough. Clare glimpsed something of the character that would soon turn them into victims: 'There is a large blue (hawk) almost as big as a goose they fly in swopping manner not much unlike the flye of a heron you may see an odd one often in the spring swimming close to the green corn and ranging over an whole field for hours together.' Clare saw the harrier as a gypsy – stealthy, cunning, patient, wedded to open spaces and 'the wind on the heath.' It was an association that would spell its downfall, twice over. As the wild wasteland it haunted vanished under the Enclosure schemes implemented by landowners, so did the harrier.

Worse was to follow, as The Game Act 1831 sounded the death knell for many birds of prey, some of which became extinct in the British Isles. Keepers on the grouse moors in Scotland and the north of England waged war on the Hen Harrier. They were easy to shoot when nesting and the young or eggs were simple to destroy.

Research by Donald Watson led him to believe that the greatest decrease in the Hen Harrier population in southern Scotland and northern England took place between 1820 and 1850. The most startling evidence he found of mass killing by gamekeepers was of 351 birds said to have been killed on two south Ayrshire estates between 25 June 1850 and 25 November 1854. By 1900 the Hen Harrier was virtually extinct as a breeding bird in England and Wales, although they were still nesting in the south-west of Ireland, and in Scotland there were small breeding populations in Argyll, the Outer Hebrides and Orkney.

What was it about the Red Grouse and the Hen Harrier that demanded such drastic measures? I felt I needed to know much more about the Red Grouse, how grouse were shot and the management of a grouse moor during those times and began my investigation. Seton Gordon (1886-1977), Scotland's premier naturalist, writer and photographer between the two world wars, wrote about the Red Grouse: 'The one and only bird which Great Britain, and more especially Scotland, can claim for her very own.' The Red Grouse is one bird with which most people are familiar today, featuring in animated advertisements on television extolling the virtues of a particular brand of whisky. It has also long been the logo of the *British Birds* periodical.

It is in the New Year that grouse start their preparations for the breeding season. Seton Gordon, in his book *Hill Birds of Scotland*, published in 1915, sets the scene: 'One hears on every side the deep guttural calls of the cocks as they "display" before the lady of their choice. Often they rise almost perpendicular into the air, descending onto some boulder or knoll with loud cries.' The hen grouse makes a very rudimentary nest, a scrape in tall heather lined with moorland grasses. Six to ten eggs are laid, pale brown with dark chestnut splodges. Incubation doesn't start until the full clutch has been laid and lasts about 25 days.' Seton Gordon continues: 'A few hours after hatching the young grouse are full of life and activity. Grouse with young vary greatly in their behaviour when disturbed.

The cock is usually near the hen and both birds may fly off so unconcernedly that they might well have children in danger. More often, however, the cock grouse flies right away, while his mate flops and flounders over the heather in her attempt to decoy the intruder from the whereabouts of her family.'

The growth rate of young grouse is quite astonishing and within a fortnight they are capable of short flights. At this time they are feeding mainly on insects but soon graduate to heather shoots which thereafter remain their staple diet. They also ingest grit, which facilitates the digestion of their food and is essential for their wellbeing. By July the young grouse are strong on the wing. If they are disturbed the cock bird utters his familiar alarm call, "*Go back, go back!*"

The double-barrelled, breech-loading shotgun introduced in 1852 had put the shooting of flying birds within the grasp of anyone keen on killing 'game birds' – Pheasants, Partridges and Red Grouse. The proliferation of the railway system in the nineteenth century also gave easy access to the grouse moors in northern England and Scotland. Originally, grouse were shot by walking guns following dogs (pointers and setters) which found the birds and then, at a signal, put them up.

Brian Vesey-Fitzgerald, in his *New Naturalist* series book *British Game,* published in 1946, very aptly describes the next stage in grouse shooting: 'Owners (of the moors) soon discovered that the rich men who came from the south wanted to do much more than just shoot grouse: they wanted to shoot lots and lots of grouse, grouse in hundreds. And so moors were managed so as to produce the greatest possible number of birds.' Driven grouse met that requirement and walking up, shooting over dogs, now only happened at the end of the season. The attraction of shooting driven grouse lay in its difficulty. The up to eight guns were stationed in a line of butts at intervals of about 30 yards. Each butt was a semi-circular, waist-high, embrasure of stones covered with peat turfs. Each person would be shooting with a pair of guns and slightly behind and to the right would be a loader holding the second gun already loaded. A section of the moor was then driven by beaters towards the butts. The driven grouse, in packs rather than family coveys, flew, hugging the contours, straight at the waiting guns.

I asked George Winn Darley, owner of a grouse moor in north Yorkshire, what the attraction was, and he explained, "The birds are incredibly fast and come at you very low. You've got to have your wits about you. It's the best bird-shooting sport in the world. It's unique. If you're a golfer you'd like to play a round at St Andrews in Scotland. If you're a footballer you'd dream of playing at Wembley, a tennis player at Wimbledon, and so on. So, if you shoot, I think you'd always hanker at having a day at driven grouse."

I consulted *Record Bags and Shooting Records* by Hugh S. Gladstone for information on numbers of grouse shot. In this I discovered that on 12 August 1915 at the Little Abbeystead beat in the Forest of Bowland in Lancashire eight guns shot 2,929 Red Grouse in six drives – that is the record. Even more remarkable is that on 20 August 1872 at Wemmergill in Yorkshire Sir Frederick Milbank killed 728 grouse to his own gun, 190 in one drive. The total number of grouse shot that day was 2,070. Sir Frederick was the great-great-grandfather of Anthony Milbank, who now owns Barningham Moor in North Yorkshire.

In 1974 I filmed a grouse shoot on the Milbanks' estate at Barningham. This was for a film I was making for the BBC on the Peregrine Falcon, in which grouse were a very important part. We were blessed with beautiful weather and I had with me a wonderful cameraman, Hugh Maynard. I told him beforehand that the birds would be flying "like the clappers" but that didn't faze him at all. Hand-holding the camera, he filmed some wonderful shots – one in particular, I remember, of a grouse crumpling up in mid-air. He managed to pan with the falling bird until it bounced to a halt right in front of him. Hugh was crouched to the right of the butt and he remembers the gun telling him to cross over to the next butt. There were more birds being driven over there and perhaps that gun was a better shot. There were other fantastic shots in the sequence: the driven grouse flying low over the heather, the guns shooting, dogs retrieving and the grouse killed laid out for inspection. A gesture by one of the guns during a drive impressed me: a pair of Short-eared Owls was put up by the beaters and flew towards one of the butts. The gun in question shouldered his gun, saluting the owls, acknowledging that he knew they were predators beneficial to man.

There were lots of grouse in Yorkshire that year but the Game & Wildlife Conservation Trust told me that the numbers shot each year between 1911 and 1980 had fallen by 82%. A particularly severe long-term decline occurred after the Second World War and after the mid-1970s in Scotland and Wales. One of the major causes of a declining grouse population is a 30% loss of heather between 1950 and 1980 through overgrazing by sheep and conversion to forestry. Since then, grouse numbers have remained stable on English moors and 2011 was a particularly good year, with counts showing an average 23% increase. So what, nowadays, I wondered, are the guidelines that provide the maximum number of grouse and still allow the moor-owner to make a profit? George Winn Darley told me, "A grouse moor is probably the only primary land use in the uplands that is not subsidized. Our income comes from grouse shooting – people taking a day's shooting and paying for it. And also because there are people like me who want to invest in the conservation side of things, making sure that the moor is attractive to grouse."

Red Grouse eat heather shoots throughout the year, so the top priority is heather management. Heather is burnt on a grouse moor in order to provide food for grouse. The aim should be to burn patches of heather on the moor when it is about ten years old, as burning at this age will stimulate regeneration of growth from the roots to provide the green shoots which grouse like to feed on. If the heather is not burnt until it is 15 or 20 years old there will be a very hot burn due to the long, woody heather stems, and no regeneration. The burning, which starts in October and continues until April, should produce a mosaic of burnt areas (some areas burnt this year, others burnt last year, and so on), these patches becoming greener and greener as the heather regenerates.

George Winn Darley explained how he prepares for heather-burning that gets out of control: "The North York moors are probably the world's driest heather moorland so what we've done is to put in ponds, scrapes – different kinds of water features – so that if there is a wildfire we can tackle it straightaway rather than waiting for the fire service to arrive. As well as serving that function, these water bodies provide a ready source of water for wildlife, not only grouse but for different kinds of waders and, of course, sheep."

Heather-burning is vital if grouse stocks are to be kept stable, as is the tackling the two diseases that affect grouse: strongylosis and louping ill. The deadly part of the life-cycle of the strongyl worm starts when the adult grouse pecks at a heather shoot and inadvertently ingests a strongyl worm. These worms burrow into the gut, causing bleeding, a reduction in digestive efficiency and a consequent loss of condition. Nowadays, as George Winn Darley explains, there are effective countermeasures: "I think we've got a better chance of managing the strongyl situation than ever before. We've instigated a network of gritting stations throughout the moor, since grouse need grit to aid their digestion. Birds shot in the autumn are assessed for their worm burden. If it's low there's no need to worm. If it's high for about six weeks of the year in winter we substitute high-strength, medicated grit to counteract the strongyl worm, which is very effective. If the levels are moderate then either a high-level dose could be used or a low-level dose grit put out in February and removed no later than mid-July, 28 days before shooting starts on August 12." More drastic treatment is to catch up grouse in January and February and dose both hens and cocks directly. This has to be done at night by torchlight, when the birds can be dazzled and easily caught up in a net.

Louping ill is a virus that is passed from a host mammal, generally sheep, via ticks to grouse. The virus is extremely virulent, with up to 80% of the grouse that are infected dying. The strategy for controlling louping ill is to reduce contact between ticks and grouse. As George Winn Darley explains, "I don't actually have any sheep but I work closely with our graziers. What they do is to pour a chemical, often a synthetic pyrethroid, along the sheep's spine and in that way it eventually covers the whole body – in the same way as you'd treat a dog for fleas. Products you can pour on last from eight to 12 weeks and are a very effective treatment programme."

Managing heather-burning and protecting grouse against the strongyl worm and ticks are the responsibility of the head keeper if a healthy grouse population on the moor is to be maintained. "The gamekeeper," says George Winn Darley, "is your biggest single expense. That's £50,000 a year to cover wages, vehicles and equipment so that he can do his job. Then, if you take on another man, that'll be another £40,000."

The keeper's other important job is the control of predators: Foxes, Carrion Crows, Stoats and Mink. All these predators can wreak havoc during the grouse breeding season. *The Red Grouse and Moorland Management* handbook produced by the Game & Wildlife Preservation Trust in 1995 is very explicit on the laws that protect British birds of prey. They are all covered by the Wildlife and Countryside Act of 1981. Some, but not all, receive additional protection and are known as Schedule 1 birds. The penalty for killing a Schedule 1 bird is a fine of up to £5,000. The Hen Harrier is one such bird and the relentless persecution of this beautiful raptor is at the heart of the conflict between conservationists and the owners of grouse moors. By 1946 the Hen Harrier was still extinct in England and Wales and the breeding population in south-west Ireland had diminished. In Scotland, however, there were signs of a recovery mainly thanks to the dispersal of birds from the Hen Harrier's stronghold in the Orkneys.

In the 1950s, large areas of moorland were converted to forestry plantations. Helped by the Forestry Commission and supported by the RSPB's payment of rewards for successful nests, the Hen Harrier prospered as breeding bird in Scotland. By 1975 there were estimated to be 500 pairs in the British Isles. It was then, once the population started to recover, that the Hen Harrier's habit of roosting communally in the winter was rediscovered.

Sir William Jardine, who published the popular *The Natural History of the Birds of Great Britain and Ireland* between 1834 and 1838, had been one of the first to observe and describe winter communal-roosting Hen Harriers: 'At night they seem to have general roosting places, either among the whins or very long heath, and always on some spot of open ground. On a moor of considerable extent I have seen seven in one acre. They began to approach the sleeping ground about sunset; and, before going to roost, hunted the whole moor, crossing each other, often three or four in view at a time. When they approached the roost they skim three or four times over it, to see if there is no interruption and then at once drop into the spot.'

In the 1960s, Donald Watson and other observers in Scotland began to notice the return of this behaviour. After several false starts trying to find the best vantage point, Donald Watson describes in *The Hen Harrier* a special evening watch: 'On 19 March 1967, a day of gusty north-west wind tossing the old shreds of purple moor grass about the sky, we found a good vantage point and waited without much expectation. It happened to be one of the rather rare nights, after occupation of breeding grounds has already begun, when turbulent weather seems to force a late resumption of communal roosting. From 50 minutes before until 20 minutes after sunset we made a cautious estimate of ten to twelve ringtails and two adult males.' Donald Watson found that the area in which the harriers choose to roost is generally boggy. In such an area there will, however, always be enough vegetation that can be trampled down by the roosting harriers to make dry sleeping platforms.

So why do Hen Harriers roost communally in winter? This behaviour is not unique since many other raptors also roost communally. The reason is almost certainly due to safety in numbers, the advantage being several sets of eyes and ears to watch and listen for predators, to which they are very vulnerable while roosting on the ground. Reports of Hen Harrier communal roosts were sporadic until the severe winters of 1977/8 and 1978/9. Those winters saw a big increase in the discovery of new roost sites.

In 1983 *The Hen Harrier Winter Roost Survey*, funded by The British Trust for Ornithology, was launched by the late Donald Watson. All county bird-recorders, wardens and known roost-watchers were contacted and asked for information on the sites they were monitoring. Individuals were then appointed to watch each site and issued with observation sheets on which the details of all sightings on a particular day were to be noted.

The results for the first two years were encouraging. Observations came in from 756 watches at 111 sites in 1983/4 and 998 watches at 127 sites in 1984/5. In Scotland it was discovered that most roost sites were fairly close to breeding areas. Coastal roost sites in the east and south of England made up the largest proportion of sites reported and there were also important inland sites in the north Midlands, south-west England, Wales and Ireland. A total of 214 sites was identified.

In October 1989, Colin Shawyer remembers meeting the late Dr Roger Clarke at a talk Colin gave on Barn Owls at St John's College, Cambridge. Roger came up to him and said, "Well, that's taken care of Barn Owls. What about other predators, what are we going to do about Hen Harriers?" I also met Roger at this meeting and urged him, as did Colin, to join the Hawk and Owl Trust. Roger always seemed rather uncomfortable in gatherings such as this but he was a different person out in the field. He came late to bird-watching, having originally been a mad keen fisherman, inspired one day in the late 1970s when, returning from a day on the river bank, he saw a Hen Harrier flying over Wicken Fen. He was captivated by its elegant flight and from that day on he was hooked. He sold his rods, invested in a pair of binoculars, and for the rest of his life focused all his energy and considerable intellect on harriers, and particularly on the Hen Harrier.

Roger and I were in complete agreement that the Hawk and Owl Trust should be defending the Hen Harrier against the renewed persecution in Scotland and the north of England. I persuaded Richard Mabey, now our greatest living nature writer, to prepare a treatment for a film on the Hen Harrier extolling its virtues but not shying away from the fact that on grouse moors it did have a predilection for grouse chicks. Anthony Milbank was chairman of the Moorland Association at the time and he sent us a letter supporting our venture.

We needed money and I remembered that David Connell, one of my best friends at school and a keen bird-watcher, was vice-president of the Distillers Company. I asked him if he would mind getting in touch with the *Famous Grouse* whisky people and ask if they would help. David obliged and the answer came back: 'We're friends of the Red Grouse but not friends of the Hen Harrier.' So for the moment the film was put on hold.

The owners of grouse moors were becoming more and vociferous in demanding a solution to what they perceived as the Hen Harrier's ever-increasing population. In 1992 the Institute for Terrestrial Ecology (ITE) and the Game Conservancy Trust undertook a five-year project, known as the 'Joint Raptor Study', to establish whether a grouse moor with breeding raptors could be a viable proposition. The other interested parties in the study included English Nature, RSPB, the Moorland Association and the National Gamekeepers' Organisation.

One of the study areas chosen was Langholm Moor, owned by the Duke of Buccleugh. Roger Clarke took part in this project as a volunteer and over the five-year period the population of all breeding raptors increased, Hen Harrier numbers rising from two to 14 pairs. The increased number of raptors led to a 50% decline in the autumn grouse stocks and shooting was stopped. It was exactly what the grouse moor owners had expected and they had a field day over these findings, putting the maximum spin on their argument in the press. The RSPB argued that the increase in raptors could not be wholly blamed for the decrease in grouse stocks, pointing out that Hen Harriers only increased after 1990. On the other hand, grouse stocks had been declining for many years due to loss of heather and as a result of an increase in the sheep population.

In 1998 the British Hen Harrier population was stable at around 570 pairs. A new project was launched in that year at Langholm to ascertain whether predation by Hen Harriers on grouse chicks could be reduced by diversionary feeding involving putting out a supply of dead rats and day-old chicks at a feeding station close to the nest site. The results were astonishing, with predation being reduced by 86%. This approach surely provided a way forward. Yet grouse moor owners argued that the practice would only attract more predators, and had issues with the practicalities and long-term consequences of this approach.

Meanwhile, *The Hen Harrier Winter Roost Survey* was going from strength to strength. My nearest roost site was at Roydon Common, near King's Lynn. Run by the Norfolk Wildlife Trust, Roydon is the largest surviving open heath in north Norfolk. I was first taken there by Roger Clarke immediately after he had run a raptor recognition course in the nearby hotel at the Knight's Hill roundabout. There were about a dozen of us and Roger led us from the parking area along a sandy track, once an ancient drove-way, to some low hills that gave sweeping views across the heather to the roost site.

The roost was situated in a boggy area edged with swathes of Purple Moor-grass, which was blowing gently in the wind. I could see grey-green patches of *Sphagnum* moss, some reeds and stunted birch trees, and the whole roost site was enclosed by a carpet of heather. About 30 or 40 black sheep moved slowly across the common pulling at tufts of grass. This was the Norfolk Wildlife Trust's 'flying flock', which could be moved from reserve to reserve to keep heathland in good condition. Beyond the heather and running alongside the road that formed the northern boundary of Roydon Common was a line of trees. This was generally where the harriers coming in to roost first appeared.

For the moment the group busied themselves finding comfortable places to sit before setting up tripods and telescopes. The sun was setting behind us and it was a beautiful evening. I readied my old 8×30 Zeiss binoculars and scanned the tree line. Suddenly Roger called out "There's a Ringtail!" Everyone wanted to see it and very calmly Roger, using a reference point, was able to make sure that we were all able to lock onto it. The harrier was flying right to left, about halfway up the treeline. It flew the length of the common, turned and made for the centre of the common opposite us. After making a couple of unhurried passes, checking that it was safe, it dropped into its chosen roosting place.

Over the next 40 minutes another four Ringtails dropped in. We also saw a Merlin streak across the common and a Marsh Harrier appeared from behind us and flew high above the common making for the reedbeds behind the sea wall at Dersingham or Snettisham. By now it was quite gloomy and we were just about to call it a day when Roger called out

"Coming in right – cock bird!" I peered through the gloom to where Roger was looking. There it was – a silver ghost, a male Hen Harrier, flying elegantly past a stand of birch trees. It made one precautionary circuit before dropping into its own special roosting place. This was the first of many memorable visits to Roydon Common. Donald Watson died in 2005 and Roger took over *The Hen Harrier Winter Roost Survey* with Nigel Middleton, the Hawk and Owl Trust's conservation officer for East Anglia, as his assistant. At about that time I filmed Roger at Roydon Common watching Hen Harriers coming in to roost. It was a bitterly cold day and Roger was well muffled up and wearing a splendid flat cap with ear flaps. He set up his telescope and peered through it. His point-of-view shots of harriers coming in to roost, all Ringtails, had been taken previously by Martin Hayward Smith, a local wildlife cameraman. Then I asked Roger to set off towards the roosting place as if he was going out at dawn to retrieve the pellets that the harriers would have regurgitated before flying off to hunt.

Later I filmed Roger in my office meticulously dissecting the pellets he had retrieved. By now he was acknowledged as the world authority on pellet analysis and had an awe-inspiring encyclopaedic knowledge that enabled him to determine what a particular harrier had been feeding on the previous day. With mounted needles, he teased through the pellet until he found a feather or part of a beak that enabled him to identify the prey. I remember him stressing that weeds on the edges of field margins, plants like Fat-hen, were essential for the survival of small birds in winter. They, in turn, were a vital food source for harriers

A new survey in 2004 showed that the Hen Harrier population in Scotland had peaked at 633 pairs. Roger died early in 2007 following an illness that lasted several months.

Right up to the end of his life he was working on a new edition of Donald Watson's book *The Hen Harrier* and also on a chart that would be an aid in the identification of the contents of Hen Harrier pellets. A further survey in 2010 showed a decline in the Hen Harrier population in Scotland to 505 pairs – a 20% drop since the 2004 survey. Brian Etheridge, leader of the Scottish Hen Harrier survey, states that the evidence from ongoing annual monitoring by members of the Scottish Raptor Study Groups indicates a continuing decline, driven by relentless persecution by moorland gamekeepers in both Scotland and England affecting breeding and wintering birds, respectively.

The Hen Harrier Winter Roost Survey in 2011–12 recorded 49 roosts in England and Wales. Andy Dobson at the British Trust for Ornithology in Scotland and Nigel Middleton in East Anglia found from ringing recoveries that a significant percentage of birds in eastern England were juvenile birds from Scotland. The report also stated that the majority of these birds were adult females or juveniles ('ringtails') and that a larger percentage of the adult males ('silver birds') migrated to the south-west of England for the winter. The majority of the wintering birds originated from within the British Isles but small numbers also came across from continental Europe.

During the 2011–12 winter, while watching wintering Hen Harriers, I had been looking forward to seeing them nesting. I knew exactly where I wanted to go – the Forest of Bowland in Lancashire, their last stronghold in England. Stephen Murphy was Natural England's man on the spot, whom I had met in 2006 when he had put radio-transmitters on two of the young Marsh Harriers that fledged from the Hawk and Owl Trust's reserve at Sculthorpe Moor. Later I rang Stephen and asked him if my wife Liza, who was performing in a play at the Grand Theatre in Blackpool, could spend a day with him watching the Hen Harriers. Liza came back bubbling over with enthusiasm, how kind Stephen had been to her, what a wonderful area the Forest of Bowland was and what spectacular fliers the Hen Harriers were. She asked me whether I realized that the 'Welcome to The Forest of Bowland' signs depicted the Hen Harrier as their icon.

Fired by Liza's enthusiasm, I arranged with Stephen to visit Bowland towards the end of May. He was a bit cautious and said, "At the moment it really is dire for Hen Harriers in England. Perhaps this is the year Bowland will lose its breeders." To make up for being a bit gloomy, he told me about 'Bowland Beth', also known as 'Bowland Betty', named after the character Bet Lynch in the TV soap opera *Coronation Street*. She had fledged at Bowland in 2011 and Stephen had fitted her with a satellite transmitter. Satellite-tracking, he explained, has revolutionized our knowledge of the Hen Harriers' comings and goings and as a result we are now much better placed to develop a strategy to protect them. I had seen the video recording made at that nest and knew that Beth was the most precocious of the four chicks, the first to fledge.

Stephen was full of Beth's exploits. On 23 July 2011 she had left the Forest of Bowland and flew to the Yorkshire Dales, spending the autumn and early part of the winter on a grouse moor between Grassington and Pateley Bridge. I wondered whether she had some ancestral map in her brain that enabled her to pinpoint the best foraging areas, and also the best places to roost. She returned to Bowland on 2 February 2012 and in mid-March again headed back to the grouse moors in Yorkshire before returning to Bowland. In April she returned to the grouse moors in Yorkshire and, to Stephen's amazement, within the next ten days travelled 450 kilometres to a point just north of Inverness. Remarkably, two days later she was back in Bowland. Stephen said, "We can only marvel at the mobility of this fine bird and celebrate her return. RSPB staff saw her sky-dancing and ripping up bits of heather so it looks like she is ready to breed if she can find a mate."

Inspired by Stephen's enthusiasm for Bowland Beth's exploits, I watched the RSPB's excellent film *Skydancer*. The film follows in great detail a pair of Hen Harriers from when they meet in spring through their courting display, nesting, the rearing and fledging of their young and the eventual dispersal in the autumn. It was the harrier's aerial courtship display that whetted my appetite – the silver male seeming to go into a frenzy of diving, climbing, somersaulting and corkscrewing in the air, a quite reckless performance just to indicate to his mate what a fine fellow he was and where she should nest.

On 21 May 2012, Eddie Anderson and I met Mick Carroll at Clitheroe. Eddie had been my companion on our expedition to Falsterbo to watch migrating Sparrowhawks and Mick Carroll, from Yorkshire had taken me to see the Honey Buzzards near Scarborough. Mick drove us to the Hark the Bounty inn in Slaidburn where we would be staying for the next two nights.

Stephen picked us up at 9 a.m. the next day and immediately pitched in, telling us about Bowland Beth's latest exploits. On 1 May she had left Bowland heading for Drumnadrochit, passed through Forsinard in the flow country, which would have been a good place to stay, and reached Thurso on 8 May. Over the next 12 days she wended her way back south again and was in the Grampian mountains by 20 May. What an adventurous, feisty lady she was although there was no sign of a mate yet.

During the drive to our first port of call, I asked Stephen how he got interested in birds and conservation and he told me, "I have loved birds since I was a child, even though I was brought up on the outskirts of a city. I bought the Observer's book of birds for my eighth birthday and my parents bought me a pair of Aintree De-Luxe 8 × 30 binoculars and I was hooked. My headmaster, Mr McKay, encouraged me to study birds and I owe a great deal to him. I first visited Bowland in the mid-1970s and can remember the exact spot where I found my first Curlews' nest. It wasn't all plain sailing, we had a few run-ins with keepers. On one occasion I can remember a keeper showed up with his gun under his arm and a black Labrador at his heels. We, as always, were very polite and as my friend went to stroke the dog, the keeper raised his gun at him and said 'don't touch the dog and **** off!' We were off that hill in double-quick time."

Stephen added, "I saw my first Hen Harrier – the first of anything is always special – on one of those lads' days out in North Wales. Up a small valley, in the distance, a ruined cottage peaked through the mist. Then, from the right, a ghost-like grey bird flew past us. It was a male Hen Harrier, no doubt about it, and we gasped. We saw it for only about ten seconds and it was gone. Fast forward to 2002 and the first day in my new dream job working with Hen Harriers in Bowland for English Nature, The Hen Harrier Recovery Project. I'm in a meeting with all the landowners and gamekeepers from the grouse moors in the Forest of Bowland. Luckily I know Ian Grindy, 20 years earlier he'd been a keeper on Lord Leverhulme's estate near my home and I had a foot in the door."

Stephen pulled up at the headquarters of the United Utilities Company at Stocks House, where we met its Managing Director, Ian Grindy, Phil Gunning, renter of the grouse moor, and Jude Lane from the RSPB. They all told me that they were 100% behind Stephen's efforts to maintain Hen Harriers at Bowland and, as far as they were concerned, the United

Utilities land was a safe haven for them. Phil said, "What I like doing on a Sunday is going up onto the moor, park, switch the motor off and just listen and watch. After a bit, little heads start popping up and if I'm really lucky I'll see a bumblebee-sized creature, a grouse chick, scuttling about."

We left the United Utilities headquarters and Stephen drove us up onto the Forest of Bowland proper. The weather had now cleared and we were in brilliant sunshine as we pulled up and parked at the top of the moor. The rolling hills were a patchwork of purple heather set against areas of grass split up into tiny fields by fences and stone walls and I could quite understand why it had been designated an Area of Outstanding Natural Beauty. Stephen pointed out a valley with Rowan trees where Hen Harriers had nested and explained, "Bowland had once been the stronghold of Hen Harriers in England. In the 1980s there had been 20+ pairs. Then there'd been severe declines so that by the early 2000s it was down to single figures. I soon realized it was a poisoned chalice I was accepting as it was also a place where there were often heated exchanges between keepers and the raptor study groups. On top of that the landowners were reluctant to talk with the conservation groups and *vice versa*."

Stephen was interrupted as Eddie spotted a pair of Merlins climbing up to chase off a male Kestrel that had invaded their airspace. Stooping at it in turn, they swiftly sent it on its way. Stephen continued, "It was 6 a.m. on 1st March 2002 when I saw my first harrier in Bowland. There was a stiff westerly blowing off the Irish Sea and bright, excellent viewing conditions. I was watching a colony of Lesser Black-backed Gulls when from the bottom of my view through the binoculars a fine adult male Hen Harrier lifted into frame. It was seemingly motionless, but lifting vertically and I could see how he twisted one or two primaries – it was as though he was in an elevator. I watched this fine bird playing in the wind for the next two hours, what a privilege. So Bowland had at least one harrier. Two weeks later he was joined by a female and within a month I had located at least six breeding pairs, two of which were on private moors and four on land owned by United Utilities."

We got out of Stephen's car and looked across the valley at a colony of Lesser Black-backed Gulls. This was the very spot where Stephen had seen his first Hen Harrier on Bowland. Fences and a gate indicated that we had reached the boundaries of the United Utilities moor and Stephen pointed to the skyline to the right of the gull colony. Like a scene from a Western movie, a dozen figures appeared on the skyline. "Keepers," Stephen said, "They want to know why we're here and what we're up to."

Stephen told us that Hen Harriers have always been persecuted and that the situation has become worse and worse. He put it to us that it is all down to accessibility and explained that because they now have 6-wheel drive Argocats and quad bikes, there is no part of a moor that a keeper cannot reach quickly. It only takes five minutes to put a handful of ice cubes around a clutch of Hen Harrier eggs and 30 minutes later the eggs will have been fatally chilled. Stephen also explained that keepers are kitted out with state-of-the-art night vision goggles and 'scopes and thermal imaging equipment. The latter used at a harrier roost at night projects an image of a Hen Harrier glowing like a Belisha beacon.

This is a hard-hitting image, but not as aggressive as Jeremy Deller's mural confronting visitors to the Venice Biennale in 2013. A huge Hen Harrier swoops down with a red Range Rover crushed in one of its taloned feet. On 28 May 2013, *The Daily Telegraph* reported that Jeremy Deller's inspiration for this vision of the natural world taking revenge on mankind came from an incident that occurred on the Queen's Sandringham Estate in Norfolk in October 2007, when two Hen Harriers were shot in plain view.

We discussed what was being done to save the Hen Harrier from extinction in England. As long ago as 2006, Natural England had set up a Hen Harrier Stakeholders Group Committee facilitated by the independent Environment Council to try and resolve the conflict between the conservationists and the owners of the grouse moors. There were many meetings but, as George Winn Darley put it, "The process seems to have been held up by an unwillingness or perhaps fear on both sides to move away from their entrenched positions. What I can tell you is that any of the Pennine grouse moors could lose 300 brace of grouse a year to Hen Harriers and not feel the pinch. Here, for example, historically there were five Hen Harrier sites on the North York Moors. The last pair nested in 1997."

Grouse shooting is a very important part of the local economy and if there were not enthusiasts like George Winn Darley heather moorland would disappear. Any areas that were left would be intensively grazed by sheep, wind turbines would blight the view and conifers would march in insidiously from the margins. All that the conservationists are asking is that the Hen Harrier be allowed to reclaim its rightful place in the delicate ecosystem of the heather moorland in England. They point out that there is suitable habitat on the English grouse moors to support 330 plus breeding pairs of Hen Harriers.

The Stakeholders Group had made some progress discussing a brood-management scheme whereby Hen Harrier chicks would be taken from nests, reared in captivity and then relocated back to their original sites in the autumn. Then one of the interested parties suggested a quota, at which point the RSPB pulled out. They argued that a body led by an independent facilitator was not the most appropriate forum for getting agreement on a

way forward. Shortly afterwards the Northern England Raptor Group and the Hawk and Owl Trust also withdrew. The status of the Hen Harrier as a breeding bird in England hangs by a thread.

'Hen Harrier extinction: looks bad on the old C.V.,' wrote Simon Barnes in *The Times*. 'Extinction. It's a big word, a big concept. Extinction can be local or it can be global; local extinctions generally prefigure global ones. To get close to wiping out the breeding population of an entire nation is a remarkable achievement, especially since the whole process is against the law. Are we going to accept this, I wonder? Or will we do something to stop it?'

In 2013, armed with the government's commitment that 'by 2020 we will see an overall improvement and status of our wildlife and will have prevented human-induced extinction of known threatened species', Defra took over and reconvened the original stakeholders knowing that the Hen Harrier was dangerously close to extinction as a breeding bird in England. As you would expect there were still a wide range of views on the problem.

I spoke to Jeff Knott, the lead spokesman for the RSPB, who said, "My primary focus is to stop illegal persecution. We've got to protect the birds at the winter roosts and provide effective year-round protection, particularly during the breeding season. We are talking about a critically endangered bird in England and we can only talk about other schemes such as brood management and translocation when we've got an English breeding population of 50 pairs of Hen Harriers."

Simon Lester, head keeper at the Langholm project in Scotland said, "I can put my hand on my heart and say that harriers aren't a problem. Harriers aren't limiting grouse at Langholm because diversionary feeding works. What's stopping us shooting grouse is Buzzard predation. Medicated grit has stopped grouse crashes but when stocks are low any predation from raptors is bad news."

Anthony Milbank, former chairman of the Moorland Association said, "Hen Harriers last nested with us ten or 15 years ago. If they came back I'd definitely go for diversionary feeding. The trouble is nobody trusts anyone. This new Defra initiative needs good leadership, someone to bang the drum and who is much respected and admired by all the moor owners and keepers. Someone who could tell everyone to stop messing around. So far it's completely unacceptable to reduce Hen Harriers to the level that they have been in England. It's asking for all sorts of trouble and we're going to end up with vicarious liability and God knows what if we don't pull ourselves together."

Stephen Murphy believes that gamekeepers can be enlightened: "This year, 2013, one of our volunteers located a pair of breeding Hen Harriers in Northumberland. I went and met the head keeper who asked 'What should we do?' I mentioned Simon Lester's success with diversionary feeding and arranged for him and his under keeper to go Langholm and talk to Simon. They were completely sold on the idea. Their boss invested in a massive chest freezer and we supplied frozen day old-chicks and mice. So everything was geared up for diversionary feeding. Then the nest failed. But that keeper really wanted those harriers to succeed. It would have been a real shot in the arm for grouse shooting in that part of the world and it's through keepers like him that Hen Harriers may breed successfully in England again."

The thrust of the Defra initiative must remain focused on the plight of the Hen Harrier. The legal and illegal killing of all predators and the success of 'gritting' has meant that mass-production of Red Grouse on the central Pennine moors has exceeded all expectations. The stock of birds left to overwinter is at record levels and there is now absolutely no excuse for the continued illegal persecution of the Hen Harrier. Moreover, the Defra initiative must not be side-tracked by reference to other birds of prey such as the Common Buzzard.

Just before lunch Stephen drove us down to Dunsop Bridge, where we met the two Bills, Bill Hesketh and Bill Murphy. Beforehand Stephen had told us that they were fanatical conservationists and excellent birders. In 1975, when the Bowland harriers were down to one pair, they had mounted a 24-hour watch on the nest to make sure the young fledged successfully. We arranged to meet them on the morrow.

In the afternoon Stephen took us on a different route along a river and up through forestry plantations. We saw a Red-breasted Merganser on the river and two Common Buzzards circling high overhead. The forestry started to thin out and Eddie pointed out a female Goshawk, flying low over the trees on our right-hand side. It was cavorting in the sky but not displaying. That was the end of day one.

The next day we picked up the two Bills and retraced the previous day's route. We saw the Goshawk again and a Merlin flying hell for leather away from us over the forestry plantations. We stopped and looked down on the same valley. A male Kestrel settled in a Rowan tree and as it turned to peer down there was a brick-red flash as the sun caught its shoulder feathers. I asked the two Bills what they thought was behind the lack of Hen Harriers. They said they had both been told by a well-informed source that persecution, up until seven or eight years ago, had been co-ordinated at roost sites. On a selected day, on the Pennine grouse moors, mist nets would be set up at the roost sites and as soon as the harriers flew in and had settled a shot would be fired. In the confusion the harriers flew into the mist nets and then had their necks rung. It was a sobering thought and made me wonder whether Bowland Beth would survive.

Unbeknown to us, as we left to catch our train home, Bowland Beth was homing in on the Forest of Bowland. When we had last heard she was in the Grampian Mountains but was now back in Bowland and quite close to the nest site where she fledged in 2011. We had missed her by about five hours. Beth stayed at Bowland for a couple of days and then, on 25 May, headed north-east, using the prevailing wind to settle on the grouse moors around Pateley Bridge. This is where she had spent her last autumn and winter. It seemed as though she had found a good billet for the summer and her immediate future seemed secure.

In the meantime I had travelled up to Scotland for a meeting with Roy Dennis, the Osprey expert, and then went on to talk to Dave Sexton, the RSPB Officer on Mull. When I got back there was a message from Stephen telling me that on 3 June Beth was still near Pateley Bridge and he ended by saying he thought she was fine. Stephen takes up the story: "Another fix from Beth's transmitter on 11 June showed that she had contracted her foraging range to the grouse moors around Nidderdale and Colsterdale. This was probably due to several days of prolonged rain. It was one of the wettest Junes in living memory. Heavy cloud cover meant that for several days we couldn't get an accurate fix on her. On about 14 June I started to be really concerned for her. Maybe the transmitter had failed. I contacted the manufacturers and asked whether the last fixes were reliable. They confirmed my suspicions that Beth had died sometime between 8 and 11 June. I was therefore able to plot the approximate position of Beth on a map. Working for Natural England I wanted

to make sure that I did everything by the book. I contacted the landowner who couldn't have been more helpful and co-operative. He arranged for the head keeper to help me search. Using a hand-held scanner, I managed to locate Beth at 11 a.m. on 5 July. She was lying face down in a patch of heather and Bilberry. The satellite tag was plainly visible. A post-mortem showed that she had probably been shot as one of her legs was broken and her femoral artery had been nicked. She may have been able to fly a few miles before she bled out and collapsed onto the grouse moor where she was found. Later, cutting-edge scientific analysis showed fragments of a lead pellet or bullet embedded in the leg bone. She had definitely been shot."

After a pause, Steve adds, "Beth was a beautiful bird, an amazing bird and I feel so privileged to be the only human to have held her while she was just a bundle of earth-bound feathers and attitude. Her story is remarkable. We should be celebrating her life now and her becoming a parent and tracking her sons and daughters."

We will probably never know exactly what happened. Perhaps this fearless, naïve bird went a wing-beat too far and had to run the gauntlet to regain the grouse moor that she knew as home. We grieve that she was cut down illegally in the prime of life. I hope she has not died in vain and recall the phrase *Timor mortis conturbat me*.

I gloried at her short life, and was so mortified by its ending that I asked David Harsent, poet and friend, to compose a requiem in her honour.

Bowland Beth

That she made shapes in air

That she saw the world as pattern and light
moorland to bare mountain drawn by instinct

That she'd arrive at the corner of your eye
like the ghost of herself going silent into the wind

That the music of her slipstream was a dark flow
whisper-drone tagged to wingtips

That weather was a kind of rapture

That her only dream was of flight forgotten
moment by moment as she dreamed it

That her low drift over heather quartering home ground
might bring anyone to tears

That she would open her prey in all innocence
there being nothing of anger or sorrow in it

That her beauty was prefigured

That her skydance went for nothing
hanging fire on empty air

That her name is meaningless
your mouth empty of it mind empty of it

That the gunshot was another sound amid birdcall
a judder if you had seen it her line of flight broken

That she went miles before she bled out

David Harsent

THE MONTAGU'S HARRIER

British Isles population (2006–10): 12–16 pairs (stable)

In the 1980s, when I lived much closer to the coast, I often used to walk my Springer Spaniels, Nathan and Gatsby, along the sea wall from Burnham Deepdale to Burnham Norton. This stretch of sea wall was the final link in reclaiming land from the sea by the Holkham estate and was completed in 1825. It was a good walk, five miles there and back, and whatever the time of year there were plenty of birds to be seen.

In the winter there were big, densely packed flocks of Brent Geese feeding inland on Alastair Borthwick's winter wheat. Looking out east there was Scolt Head Island. In the winter you might see the arrow-head silhouette of the resident Peregrine Falcon as it cut through a twisting flock of Dunlin. Six months later, in the summer, Common, Little and Sandwich Terns would be fishing the creeks and returning with their catches to feed hungry chicks in the sandhills on the island. On the inland side of the sea wall, fields of wheat or barley rippled and glistened in the summer sunshine. Running alongside the sea wall was a ditch fringed with reeds. There was one point on the ditch where several drains from the fields converged and where a small reedbed had formed, 30 metres wide, jutting out into the arable land.

I remember one summer seeing a pair of Marsh Harriers nesting in this area. They had staged a big comeback and were breeding not only in the marsh reedbeds but also in fields of cereals or oilseed rape all along the Norfolk coast. Much more exciting, though, was a pair of Montagu's Harriers, Britain's rarest breeding bird of prey, that nested for two years running in arable crops on the hillside beyond the coast road. Several times I saw the male

bird, silver-grey with black wing-tips, hunting just above the sea wall for voles. Flap–flap–flap, then a glide with its wings held above the horizontal. If it overshot potential prey it had the amazing ability to 'stand' on its tail, turn through 180 degrees and give a couple of quick flaps before plunging, legs outstretched into the grass. After a successful kill, the harrier would lift off, the prey tucked under its tail, alternately flapping and gliding as it made his way towards the nest site on the hill in the distance.

It was against this background that one morning, early in September 1986, the telephone rang in my study. It was Paul Letzer, a fisherman who operated out of Wells harbour. He told me that the previous evening as he was driving home from the coast to Burnham Market he had seen a bird of prey lying on the grass verge. It was obviously a road casualty and although he had not stopped he had seen a wing move, so knew it was still alive. He thought I would know what to do and gave me exact instructions to find the bird.

Armed with gloves, a towel and a cardboard box, I drove slowly down the hill from Burnham Market towards the coast, carefully scanning the verge as I went. Paul had said it was on the left-hand side of the road just before an open gateway onto a track into a field. I parked the car and went to investigate. A wing poked out from behind the rows of Alexanders, an edible coastal plant brought here by the Romans, that lined the hedge. As I bent over to examine the bird, it opened its beak and hissed at me. From its head I knew it was a harrier, as it had the pronounced facial disc, reminiscent of an owl, which covered its ear openings. It was wet through, very bedraggled and muddy. As it started to struggle away from me I gently restrained it, wrapped it in the towel and placed it in the box.

As I drove to the vet's surgery in Fakenham, I quickly ran through the possibilities. It couldn't be a Hen Harrier – much too far south from its normal breeding range. It wasn't a Marsh Harrier – not large enough and it didn't have their distinctive straw-coloured crown. There were no other choices – it had to be a Montagu's Harrier, a female. I knew that a pair had nested on farmland fairly close by, although there was always the possibility that it was a bird wandering through on the start of its migration south to Africa.

All this went through my mind as I carried the cardboard box into the vet's surgery, where I was greeted by Gordon Brown, who had just joined the practice. As Gordon gently examined the bird, I stressed how rare it was and asked whether he thought he could save it. He pointed out that the harrier had a broken wing, and unfortunately it was the humerus that was fractured; in birds this is hollow and is notoriously difficult to mend. He also explained that the bird was dehydrated and that he would need to put it on a drip. Gordon realized how important a bird it was and said that he would give it his best shot; if it got through the next 48 hours there was a chance it would survive. Then he would see about setting the fractured bone. I rang Gordon the next day and was told that the bird was holding its own and my hopes rose. But first thing the next morning Gordon rang to tell me that the bird had died during the night.

George Montagu (1753–1815), after whom the Montagu's Harrier was named, is rightly famous for solving an ornithological riddle that bedevilled the scientific classification of two of the harriers since they were first described by Aristotle (384–322 BC). It is easy now to understand how this happened, since sexual dimorphism, the difference in appearance of male and female of the same species, had not yet been recognized in birds of prey. The cock Hen Harrier and the smaller harrier with similar silver-grey plumage were both named as the Hen Harrier, and the female Hen Harrier, and the smaller harrier with dark brown plumage above, pale streaked underparts and a white ring at the base of the tail, were both known as the Ringtail.

Harriers were not used for hawking, binoculars had not been invented and shotguns were not generally available for those of a curious disposition. No progress was made until Eleazar Albin's *A Natural History of Birds* was published in 1731. In it was a plate of what today we would recognize as a male Montagu's Harrier. It must have been drawn from a specimen of an adult Montagu's Harrier. Albin's plate of the harrier was labelled *pygargus,* meaning 'white-rumped', which added to the confusion. Nevertheless, Carl Linnaeus in his tenth edition of the *Systema Naturae* published in 1758, recognized Albin's description and ascribed it to the genus *Falco* with the specific name *pygargus.*

Despite Linnaeus's authentication of Albin's plate of what is now known to be a Montagu's Harrier, the debate continued. Ornithologists changed their opinions day by day. Dissection showed that the grey birds were males and the Ringtails were female. Peter Simon Pallas (1741–1811) spent six years on a scientific expedition through Russia and Siberia. He noted, 'The truth is, that the first year all are dark-coloured, very differently variegated; but at the second change of feathers, chiefly the males grow whitish.' Thomas Bewick in his *History of British Birds*, published in 1797, added a cautionary footnote to his description of the Hen Harrier: 'It has been supposed that this and the following are male and female; but the repeated instances of Hen Harriers of both sexes having been seen leave it beyond all doubt that they constitute two distinct species.' John Latham (1740–1837) made an extremely sensible suggestion that would cut through all the hot air that had been generated – take some chicks from the nest and keep them in captivity for three or four years to confirm the change in plumage.

It was at this juncture that George Montagu entered the scene. He came from an upper-crust background, his father being The Earl of Manchester. He was one of 13 children and, as was expected of him, he joined the army at 17 and was married at 18 to a niece of the Earl of Bute. His regiment was posted to America during the War of Independence, where he was appalled by the stench of death, the scant regard for humanity and the rape of the countryside. As an antidote, he started collecting specimens of American birds. He was promoted to captain and returned home, but left the army and joined the militia and reached the rank of lieutenant colonel before being court-martialled.

Sometime earlier he had met Eliza Dorville. He left his wife and set up home with Eliza, who was also married. The scandal that ensued meant that George was disinherited by his family. Nevertheless, George and Eliza moved to Knowle House, near Kingsbridge in Devon, and settled down. Here George could pursue his career as an ornithologist, backed up by the steady companionship of his Eliza.

His time in the army stood him in good stead, as his observations were always meticulous. Gradually, over time, he collected information on all the birds he studied and these were collected in his *Ornithological Dictionary*, which was published in two volumes in 1802 and in 1813. He gave a description of what is now known as the Montagu's Harrier, stressing that it was smaller than the Hen Harrier, about the size of a female Sparrowhawk, and had a long tail and wings which, at rest, projected beyond the tip of the tail.

He now applied himself to solving the 'harrier problem'. In 1807 he wrote a paper that stated two vital facts. The bird familiarly called a Ringtail and given the scientific name *pygargus,* was in fact the female Hen Harrier, *cyaneus.* In his meticulous way, he described how he had taken a nest of three Hen Harrier chicks and reared them in captivity – exactly what John Latham had suggested. One died but eventually the remaining two moulted into adult plumage, a grey male and a female, a Ringtail. He then went on to describe the 'other harrier', which he called the ash-coloured falcon. He emphasized the critical identification feature thus: 'secondary quills cinereous-brown above, pale beneath, with three remarkably dusky-black bars across them, nearly in parallel lines, each half an inch in breadth; one only of which is seen on the upper side of the wing the others being hid by the coverts. It is probable that this species may be indigenous to us, and that it has frequently been mistaken for a variety of the Hen Harrier.' Montagu died in 1815 as a result of treading on a rusty nail. Nevertheless, from then on the ash-coloured falcon was always associated with his name. The genus *Falco* was subdivided and the name *Circus* adopted, the Montagu's Harrier therefore acquiring the scientific name *Circus pygargus*.

While researching his monograph on the *Montagu's Harrier* during the early 1990s, Dr Roger Clarke had not had time to visit George Montagu's home. However, in 2006, Bruce Pearson and Roger travelled down to Devon, as Bruce put it, "in search of any echoes we could find of George Montagu. In Kingsbridge we found where the original Knowle House that Montagu moved to in 1798 would have been and were invited into a modern house that was built on the site of the old gardens. Back on Fore Street we turned into 'Montagu Mews' and 'Montagu Close'. We posed for photographs by the street signs, and I took a photograph of Roger leaning on a wall that bears the following plaque:"

> *Col. G. Montagu*
> *FLS*
> *Ornithologist*
> *Lived Here 1798–1815*
> *Devon Birdwatching and Preservation Society, 1956*

The unravelling of the riddle of the Montagu's Harrier identity now allows us to study the bird in the field and assess the main distinguishing points. The male Montagu's Harrier and Hen Harrier are both grey birds with black wing-tips. The Montagu's key diagnostic feature is the single black bar on the upperwing, across the middle of the secondary feathers. Seen from below, there are two dark bars. When perched, the Montagu's Harrier's longer black primaries project beyond the tip of the tail. Its shorter legs means that its attitude when perched inclines towards the horizontal, rather than vertical as in the longer-legged Hen Harrier.

In the field it is virtually impossible to differentiate between a female Montagu's Harrier and a female Hen Harrier, and as a consequence they, and juveniles, are often both referred to as 'ringtails'. However, the experienced harrier-watcher will tell you that the light patches above and below the eye in the facial disc are distinctive but, above all, that the three bold, rufous bars down the axillary feathers are the main diagnostic feature setting the female Montagu's Harrier apart from the female Hen Harrier. For me, however, it is the 'delicacy of flight' that tells you that is a Montagu's Harrier.

The juvenile Montagu's Harrier differs from the adult and juvenile Hen Harrier ringtails in having an ochre-red colour to the underside of the body and under-wing coverts. The upper body is dark brown and the primaries are dark grey merging to black. There are excellent plates by Bruce Pearson, with more detail of flying harriers showing different stages of plumage, in Roger Clarke's monograph published in 1996.

The Montagu's Harrier is a rare breeder in the British Isles. Apart from in Norfolk it does breed regularly but in small numbers in Oxfordshire, Dorset and Wiltshire. It does, however, breed extensively throughout Europe and reaches as far east as the steppe region of south-west Asia. As forests were cleared, its range extended into western Siberia. It is a migratory bird and it spends our winters in a broad belt across Africa and down almost as far as the Cape of Good Hope in South Africa. The population breeding in south-west Asia winters in India.

The largest harrier roost in the world is at Gujarat in north-west India. When Roger Clarke visited the area in the early 1990s he wrote the following about what he saw as dawn broke: 'The first harriers! Two were well up in the intense glow already, and then three. I followed them up in my binoculars as they beat their long wings to go higher. Then, looking down, I saw several more heading straight for us into the light breeze and perhaps 15 milling low over the grass beyond. Then more and more harriers rose out of the grass and the first yikkering reached our ears. The yellow sky was littered with flying birds – graceful, flying, gliding Montagu's Harriers. The thought of George Montagu flashed into my mind, the English naturalist who first described the species for science (wouldn't he be astounded to see such numbers), calling, aerial, literally a circus.'

I was very envious of Roger's exciting trip and also wanted to go somewhere that I could be sure of seeing plenty of Montagu's Harriers. Bruce had just come back from a trip to Extremadura in Spain and told me to go there. The breeding population in Spain was estimated in 1995 to be between 3,647 and 4,632 pairs – very different from the one pair I had seen at Burnham Deepdale.

My wife Liza and I flew to Madrid, picked up a hire car and drove down along an excellent motorway past Seville, eventually turning off for the town of Trujillo. It was spring and hordes of Swifts with their shrill cries were criss-crossing above the main plaza, which was dominated by a magnificent statue of Pizarro, the famous Spanish conquistador, mounted on his horse. It was from here that Pizarro set out to conquer Peru. We checked into our accommodation, a parador, that had once been a nunnery. Our room was spartan but adequate and the greatest joy was opening the shuttered window to be confronted by a pair of White Storks nesting on the chimney-stack opposite.

We left the parador and drove down to look at the bullring. Bruce had told us this was the place to see Lesser Kestrels and as we got out of the car we were treated to an amazing spectacle – hundreds of Lesser Kestrels wheeling over the tiled roofs. Now and then kestrels peeled off from the flock to disappear under a tile to their nesting places. We drove a little further on to a fish pond that held a pair of Black-winged Stilts, a lone Avocet and a Green Sandpiper. Then it was time to head back to the main plaza for a drink and to find somewhere to eat. Our lack of Spanish did not help with the menu, but we ordered and ate what turned out to be bull stew – very nourishing. We rounded the meal off with a liqueur made from acorns and went to bed.

After an early breakfast we set off for the Belén Plains. This was where Bruce had told us we would see Montagu's Harriers. We travelled up a dusty road, with the open steppe on the left-hand side, stopping occasionally to scan with our binoculars. I could see Little Bustards close by and right in the far distance a group of Great Bustards. There was no way of getting closer to them so we set off again. I suddenly saw a bird I had never seen before, an Azure-winged Magpie. We pulled onto a farm track to get a closer look. What a beautiful bird: black head, fawn body and blue primaries and tail. There are two populations of this magpie, one in Spain and another in eastern Asia. Why are they so far apart? On my return I learnt that they were considered to be two separate species – end of mystery.

It was time to turn back for Trujillo. As we sped down the dusty road I saw a familiar shape flying across the plain towards us – a male Montagu's Harrier. It hunted along the tall grasses at the edge of the steppe and we were able to keep track with it. My wife positioned the car so that I could follow it perfectly and at one point it was so close that I could see the yellow of its eye. On the upper side of the pale grey wing I could see the thin black line running through the secondaries and the long, thin black primaries. It flew fairly slowly, flapping and gliding, all the while looking down, searching for prey. A big cattle truck coming from the other direction forced us to slow down and pull in. The spell was broken and the Montagu's Harrier swept away from us across the steppes. It had been a wonderful moment.

Bruce and I had made a film together in Mali about his epic journey following migrating birds from England in the summer to their winter haunts in Africa. This a typical passage: 'On the stump of a thorn a Black-eared Wheatear watches the ground silently. This will be a bird from south-west Europe or North Africa, as that population is known to winter in the belt of semi-desert and dry acacia savannas of Sénégal, south-west Mauritania and Mali. But the most exciting migrants down here are the Montagu's Harriers. At one point in mid-afternoon I count five of them in the air at one time, each lightly drifting and floating, wavering on the strong breeze coming in from the sea.'

I remember the pair of Montagu's in Norfolk I watched off and on and I am immediately transported back there... 'It is a long time before anything happens, but then suddenly a female Montagu's appears in the neighbourhood. She begins to drift around the area where the male had been earlier, and then disappears into the grass. But still no sign of the male. When he does appear, the change in his behaviour is extreme and quite magical. From high up he plummets in a steep power-dive at the female, which by now is up in the air again. He twists and turns, diving around her, then rises up, circles once or twice and dives again. The intensity of this "sky-dancing" behaviour and the time of year suggest that the female has only recently arrived at the site. The male will have arrived back from Africa a week or so earlier, normally around mid-April, and would have started prospecting a nest site almost immediately; now he is drawing the female's attention to it.'

This description of the Montagu's 'sky-dancing' was written by Bruce in 1994 when the birds were at their peak in West Norfolk. You have to go back 70 years before that to find the Montagu's Harrier nesting so productively. At Horsey and Hickling in the Broads the number of nests peaked to eight or nine each year between 1924 and 1926. Jim Vincent, the warden at Hickling at the time wrote: 'After all the young had hatched and could fly, one could see 30 of these birds with one sweep-round of the field-glasses.'

There were seven nests in 1929 but from then on it was all downhill. In 1937 Anthony Buxton, who owned Horsey, wrote 'Unless owners of shoots can, at the eleventh hour, be persuaded to give their keepers orders which none could dare to disobey, I think the harriers in East Norfolk are doomed to destruction. Let there be no doubt as to who is to blame.' In 1942 there was a brief respite when two nests were found and thereafter there were one to four nests annually until 1957.

In 1954 at Snettisham in west Norfolk, breeding was suspected on the Sandringham estate. There were suspicions that they may also have bred in 1956 and 1958 but the first definite record of breeding was in 1965, when a pair reared four young. Two nests in wheat fields in 1968 are the first records of Montagu's Harriers breeding in crops in Britain. In 1970, and for the next two years, a pair nested successfully in the reedbed at the RSPB reserve at Titchwell. The female returned for several years thereafter but without a mate.

The importance of the Montagu's Harriers breeding in west Norfolk was realized in 1982 when the RSPB appointed Bob Image as the Harrier Protection Warden. When I spoke to Bob recently he told me, "I was wardening a Goshawks' nest in Yorkshire where Chris Knights, a wildlife cameraman, was making a film. Out of the blue I got a call asking if I'd like to watch over and guard Britain's rarest breeding bird, the Montagu's Harrier, which was nesting in Norfolk. I said, 'Give me a week and I'll let you know.'" For Bob that was the start of over 20 years protecting these elegant birds of prey and, to quote him, "I haven't got fed up with it yet!"

Bob found that the harriers were nesting in arable crops inside the sea wall. Over five years the numbers of nests increased from two in 1982 to four in 1986. The sea wall, reed-fringed dykes and edges of fields provided prey-rich habitats, with plenty of Skylarks, Reed Buntings and Meadow Pipits.

During Bob's second year of wardening, in 1983, he was faced with an emergency. As he explained, "Immediately after the eggs hatched one of the adult female Montagu's disappeared, but we don't know what happened to her. The male kept on bringing in food but the four chicks were too young to feed themselves. We did two things – we put up a little wire coop which the chicks could shelter in and twice a day collected the prey the male had brought in and cut it up into small pieces which the chicks could cope with. We covered ourselves in blankets, anything to break up the human outline, as we didn't want the chicks to become imprinted, and went in and hand-fed them. If we hadn't they would have died. We did this until the chicks, at three weeks old, could feed themselves. It worked and three out of the four chicks fledged."

At the original west Norfolk location there were five Montagu's Harrier nests in 1989, seven in 1990, and a peak of nine nests in 1994, the best total in Norfolk for 70 years. But for some reason the population started to decline and none returned to nest in 2003. Bob Image thinks that this was an innate response to the persecution the birds had suffered in the past. He suggests that it is a survival strategem: don't stay too long in one place before moving on to pastures new.

In 2003 the Montagu's Harriers moved to a new location in Norfolk and it was Andy Bloomfield, a good friend and phenomenal bird-watcher, who saw them first. This is an extract from his journal: 'May 25th. Had a wonderful bit of luck. In the air above the old stone pit was a pair of displaying Montagu's Harriers. The male, which I thought was noticeably smaller than the female, was sky-dancing like a male Marsh Harrier – he was frantically diving, twisting and tumbling down towards the female, while calling like a quiet Oystercatcher, before short bursts of talon-grappling.'

Despite seeing the birds copulating on 27 May, Andy lost contact with them until 20 July when he came across the male soaring around some rough scrub. His journal continues: 'The male was calling a piercing yet quiet "*wiseow*", which seemed to draw the hen bird from a rough, unkempt patch of nettles, brambles and willowherb. After sailing around together, she dropped back down to the same spot – presumably the nest site.'

Andy was well aware that he was watching the UK's rarest breeding bird of prey and noted in his journal 'I feel very privileged to be part of this amazing event, yet always treat the birds with the utmost respect. I limit my visits to about two-hour stints and I remain hidden in the bottom of a hedge. It's a good vantage point that allows me to see all the comings and goings, yet far enough away that no disturbance is caused to the birds and, also equally importantly, so that no one can see me. The last thing I want to do is draw attention to them. For me it has to be kept a secret, the fear of egg collectors or bird-watchers disturbing necessitating such secrecy.'

The following incident, again extracted from Andy's journal, illustrates how susceptible the harriers were to disturbance: 'July 22nd. Watched a perfect food-pass in which the male arrived from the west at a great height with a small mammal. He was calling as usual and this triggered the hen bird to rise up and meet him. She was calling too, a more excitable note, prior to swiftly turning upside down and flinging out her talons expertly beneath the cock bird to catch the prey he dropped. After ten minutes of soaring round the nest site, she dropped lower before stalling in the air with her wings held stiffly upwards and dropping into the nest with the prey. After a brief spell she flew off to the east. Fifteen minutes passed before she returned with what looked like a small bird. However, there was a difference. A man was walking his dog on an adjacent stubble field in full view of the nest area and it took 15–20 minutes after he had left before the female dropped height and took the prey to the nest. This behaviour made me realize just how vulnerable they would be if there had been crowds of bird-watchers present, a situation that might have been disastrous for their ultimate fortunes.'

Another extract from Andy's journal is a testament to the Montagu's Harriers' phenomenal eyesight: 'July 28th. The female was sitting in the stubble for about 15 minutes. She began to look anxious, craning her neck around as if perplexed by something. After a few seconds she repeated this performance before stretching her neck up and then taking to the wing. Around she circled before I noted a tiny speck in the sky, dropping in from the west. It was the male, he plummeted down like a falling pebble, instantly dropping a small mammal, which she caught expertly as ever, upside down and with one taloned foot outstretched. What was interesting to me was that she had obviously seen him arriving from a great distance. There was no need for him to call to warn her of his arrival.'

On the same day, Andy was impressed by the cock bird's ghostly appearance: 'The male usually departs the nest area at a fair height as soon as the food-pass is completed. With his pale, ghost-like plumage, he soon disappears from view, particularly if the weather is grey and overcast. At times he can appear gull-like and even like a falcon. No wonder the old name Ash-coloured Falcon came about. It is also little wonder that the pair remained elusive and their presence undetected by so few people.'

The pair of Montagu's Harriers was very aggressive to any other birds of prey that might constitute a threat to their unfledged young. This is a further extract from Andy's journal: 'When I arrived, I saw the female was in her usual spot in the stubble field waiting for her mate to bring in prey. After 15 minutes she started to utter her usual "wie-erp" call. Suspecting an imminent food-pass I looked up only to see a fresh-plumaged juvenile Marsh Harrier. It was spiralling down quite rapidly, heading for the female Montagu's, almost as if answering her calls – a definite case of mistaken identity?! Instead of receiving a feed, the young Marsh Harrier faced a full-out attack from the super-fast female Montagu's who continued calling as she mobbed it. At one stage she flung herself upside down beneath the Marsh Harrier, her talons raking the impetuous intruder. This did the trick as, after emitting a loud, chattering call, the young Marsh Harrier departing westwards. Almost immediately the male Montagu's arrived on the scene from the east, whistling loudly as always. His mate was swift to greet him and did so enthusiastically. A small

mammal was dropped, caught by her and taken down to the ground to be plucked. Instead of joining her, he sped off after the young Marsh Harrier. With the speed and agility of a falcon, he stooped and flung out his talons in a swift and silent attack. The young Marsh Harrier fled from its smaller attacker amidst a constant volley of aggressive calls.'

Most of the prey brought into the nest site was small mammals or birds, although, as Andy's journal recounts, there were exceptions: 'August 1st. The female arrived late afternoon carrying a large item of prey, the leg of a hare or rabbit. It was a struggle for her to carry it. She flew in low and dropped it in a patch of willowherb about 20 yards east of the nest. I assumed therefore that she was used to collecting road kills as it had come from a creature that was far too large for her to have killed it. Also, it seemed to me, judging from where she left the prey, that the young must be maturing and venturing out of the nest site.'

Two days later, Andy was able to watch the female hunt over some nearby fields and wrote: 'August 3rd. Initially I saw the female quartering back and forth low over the fields. It wasn't long before she plunged purposefully into the grass, although it was three minutes before she emerged with a small mammal. A clear pattern has emerged in her hunting method. Once she seems confident that she's on to something, she seems to carry out very low deliberate passes over her intended victim before flying away at a fast pace then stalling rapidly and suddenly, turning and returning even faster, just like a Sparrowhawk. She then rises slightly, stalls again, with wings stretched up and held back, tail fanned out, and pounces with talons outstretched for the kill.'

That year there was plenty of prey for the harriers to bring in to their rapidly growing chicks. This account from Andy's journal illustrates the wonderful dexterity and flying ability of the parent Montagu's Harriers: 'August 5th. The female arrived from the east carrying a small bird and as usual circled the nest area. She started calling and instead of dropping into the field started to gain height again. Above her the male bird appeared from a great height, also clutching prey, a small dark mammal. How were they going to cope with this? Instead of taking his prey item to the nest, he actually dropped it down to the female. What happened next was phenomenal. She rolled sideways and flung out a leg to catch the mammal, while still clutching her own prey in the talons of her other foot!'

After many days of patient watching, Andy finally saw what he had been waiting for – the first sight of a youngster emerging from the nest: 'August 6th. Having watched the pair see off a male Marsh Harrier that had ventured too close to the nest site, the female returned to her vantage point on the nearby stubble field while the male continued to soar around the area on what turned out to be the hottest day of the year so far. After a few minutes he then dropped down low over the nest and began to fly up and down and round and round seemingly with great excitement. It was a similar display to when he was courting his mate in May. The young could clearly be heard squeaking from the nest and after a few moments I saw what I had patiently been hoping would happen – a fully feathered young Montagu's Harrier flapped up from the nest and quite weakly flew towards the male. It turned slightly, allowing me to see its gorgeous orange underparts and its black-and-white face markings before flopping down into a clump of willowherb. During all the excitement, the male continued to fly higher and higher, still calling "*chek-chek-chek*", almost as if he was attempting to entice the youngster to gain height. After the youngster pitched down, the male continued to circle while calling, which attracted the female's attention. She was soon overhead and again the young bird struggled into the air before dropping back into the nest. The female circled the nest just like her mate had done, calling a rather hoarser "*kerk-kerk-kerk*" as she flew faster and faster. After doing this for five minutes with no more youngsters coaxed from the nest, she returned to her usual spot on the stubble field.'

As Andy recounts, flights by the youngsters became more and more confident: 'August 10th. Within an hour's watching I saw three flights by a juvenile and on one occasion two flew up together, sparring with each other and jostling with talons hanging downwards.

On another occasion one flew up to circle the area and then carried on to quarter the field before returning to the nest.'

On 12 August, Andy saw three youngsters for the first time as they left the nest area to see off a pair of juvenile Marsh Harriers that had strayed too close. Surprisingly, the young Montagu's were just as efficient and aggressive as their parents in seeing off their larger cousins. From then on, Andy's days watching the Montagu's Harriers became rather intermittent. He saw four juveniles, airborne together, on 17 August but by 23 August they were travelling farther afield. On one occasion he had a memorable encounter with the entire family over a sugar beet field beside the main road. He told me that he was amazed that very few bird-watchers had noticed them, as on some days they were very obvious.

The last note in Andy's journal reads: 'September 5th. Beside a narrow lane saw a wonderful sight – three Buzzards, one Montagu's Harrier and one Marsh Harrier wheeling together low over a small copse to the north. It was truly exhilarating as they were all juveniles and locally bred within two miles of my house. Fifteen years previously I would never have believed that I would have seen such a sight!'

The arrival of the Montagu's Harriers near a village in north Norfolk and the fledging of four young was one of the best-kept secrets of 2003 – only a handful of people knew of their existence. However, in 2004 that was all going to change. The previous year, James McCallum, a bird artist, had joined Andy watching the harriers after they had fledged. When I interviewed James in 2012 he told me, "I never told a soul. Then one day in the local supermarket two people I'd never met before came up to me and said, 'Are you James McCallum?' I said, 'Yeah. Yeah.' 'You're the chap who paints birds?' And I said, 'Yeah. Yeah.' 'So have you seen the Montagu's Harriers?' They mentioned the name of the village and I was absolutely flabbergasted. I knew that was it, the whole world now knows."

About the middle of May 2004 I was rung by a friend and told about the birds and the location. I collected Nigel Middleton, the Hawk and Owl Trust's Conservation Officer for East Anglia and we went on a discreet recce. We hid, well concealed, on the forward edge of a pit that overlooked the site but which was far enough away not to disturb the birds. We watched for about two hours. The site was in a rushy meadow through which flowed a small stream. There was a big Hawthorn hedge in the background, a long gap in which had been closed off by posts and rails. We passed the time watching a Sparrowhawk taking food to its nest in a conifer belt on the hill beyond and a Buzzard that was obviously nesting in a copse further away at the top of the hill. Eventually our patience was rewarded when the male Montagu's Harrier sailed over the site. There was a half-hearted attempt at interception by a male Marsh Harrier, that was nesting in cereals on the far side of the hedge. We had seen enough, and left.

As we drove off, we noticed a group of people gathered at a gate that led into the field where the Montagu's Harriers were nesting. Nigel thought we ought to have a word with them. Among them was my friend Marjorie Stabler, a very keen bird-watcher, and Tony Barnham, both of whom Nigel and I knew well. With them was Bob Image, the RSPB Warden. We had arrived just as they were discussing how to safeguard the harriers, now that it was no longer a secret. Although most of the approaches could easily be monitored, there was a weak link – a public footpath with a hedge either side allowed a covered approach to a gap in the hedge which was within a few yards of the nest. Tony offered, with the help of the most reliable members of his bird-watching groups, to monitor this weak link.

Tony died in 2011. I often used to see him walking through the village with either a lurcher or a whippet at his heels. I had never joined one of his bird groups but I wanted to know more about him so I asked Rebecca, his daughter, to help and she told me, "His early life was spent working for Dalgety, the seed and agriculture company. I can remember him ringing me and extolling the virtues of agriculture, but then he changed his view and became quite anti-farming, much more of a conservationist. Later he worked for the National Trust at Brancaster Staithe. He managed a team rebuilding sea defences, making paths, replanting. He was also employed by the Norfolk County Council running bird-watching courses. Eventually he moved away from the coast and built up a life which revolved around his beloved lurchers and whippets and taking people on bird walks."

Marjorie Stabler was a member of one of his bird groups and remembers Tony well. "He was a good-looking guy, neat beard and moustache, grizzled hair always neatly trimmed. My link to him was through our dogs, as we had whippets and greyhounds too. We used to meet him out on the marshes. He always had his lurcher, Bella, with him. There were three bird groups: Mondays was for golf club members, Wednesdays was our lot, and Thursdays was for the left-overs. Tony was one of the small group that knew about the Montagu's in 2003. He said it was very interesting. Everyone saw the Marsh Harriers as they crossed the main road to go off hunting but they never noticed the Montagu's. Even when the secret was out in 2004, I still don't think a vast number of people knew about it, only locals."

Luckily Tony kept a journal, in which he noted how many of his bird group members turned up and some details of his duties as honorary warden (self-appointed) watching over the Montagu's Harriers. The entries in his journal were short, very staccato: '12th April: Watched a pair of Marsh Harriers displaying and saw a hare with a leveret. 22nd April: Saw the female Montagu's and then later in the day the male and female displaying. 30th April: Noted that the male was very pale. Both birds wheeled over the site. 6th May: Marsh Harriers have nested very close to the Montagu's – no interaction. 10th May: Two boys walked close to the nest, Marsh Harriers got up but the Montagu's sat tight. Boys were "noisy." 15th May: Male Montagu's harassing Marsh Harrier that came too close to the nest site. 19th May: A suspicious car, a blue-green Cavalier saloon, number plate GUR, rest of plate unreadable, parked at end of lane. A couple from Sculthorpe? 22nd May: "Battle Royal" between a male Marsh Harrier and the pair of Montagu's. Later the male Montagu brought prey in and passed it to the female, who came up to join him. They both settled in a Hawthorn bush, covered in pink blossom, after cruising around. 1st June: Male Montagu's comes from N.W. and both go to roost N.E. of nest site. 11th June: Saw what I thought was a sub-adult Hen Harrier male chase a juvenile Sparrowhawk. Later I think it might have been a Montagu's in transition. 16th June: The Montagu's eggs may have hatched(?) 22nd June: Male wheels over site until female flies up to accept food-pass. Then goes to perch in Elder bush.'

There is then a gap in Tony's journal until mid-July: '17th July:, Male delivers food to the female at the nest site. '23rd July: Saw the female Montagu's and three juveniles fly up from the nest. 24th July: The female and the juveniles fly up to investigate a passing Carrion Crow. 31st July: Saw a spectacular food-pass from the male Montagu's to the three juveniles. 2nd August: Two of the juvenile Montagu's "bombing" an intruding Marsh Harrier. They outflew it completely.' Tony's last sightings of the Montagu's were on the 19th, 20th and 21st, when he saw the three different juveniles, at separate locations, exploring the Norfolk countryside. A great success!

In 2005 the pair of Montagu's Harriers returned to the same site but were frustrated by the pair of Marsh Harriers, which had nested earlier than in the previous two years. The Montagu's moved away and nested closer to the coast in a field of oilseed rape, where they raised one chick. Another pair nested close by but the nest was predated by foxes. That year the presence of the Montagu's Harriers became widely known throughout the bird-watching world when a Stilt Sandpiper, a rare vagrant, dropped in to the Burnham Norton marshes. Two-and-a-half thousand 'birders' poured into Norfolk to see it and could not avoid spotting the Montagu's Harriers on their way there.

The year 2006 saw five pairs of Montagu's Harriers nesting within a two-and-a-half mile triangle. Although two nests failed, ten young were fledged that year. One of the males was polygynous, looking after a female already on eggs and then servicing another female on a nest in a wheat field two miles away that backed on to a house that James McCallum was renting. I suspected James had a soft spot for Montagu's Harriers, which was confirmed when he told me, "I think, for me, they are the most elegant of the harriers. It's the buoyancy they have. The males are beautiful. It's their lightness, their agile shape. They are a very elegant bird. I remember the first day I saw them displaying. I picked up the male against the blue sky when I heard him calling, a weak little call. He was incredibly high. I just managed to see a flash of silver as he was diving. He was twisting backwards and forwards so every time he turned you'd get a silver flash – it was really eye-catching. The female was sitting on the edge of the field watching. Occasionally she'd go up and join him and they'd lock talons. One day, I remember, they performed a really beautiful sequence. The female was sitting on the top of a hedge and the male came down out of nowhere, really fast and just dive-bombed her. He used to exaggerate his elegance and his shape. It almost looked aggressive. She'd duck and he'd come round again. Sometimes after that he'd come and land next to her and sometimes they'd mate as well. He was a very striking male – incredibly pale.

His upperwing markings were quite restricted, not like a text-book male. I remember watching him on another day. He was flying along the edge of a field and kept coming and coming straight towards me. I just sat there watching him through binoculars. And then he must have chanced upon a leveret, he stalled a bit, and was about to drop down when, running out of nowhere across the field, came the female hare. She was literally up in the air boxing him, striking his talons. You could see the harrier jump. It was like, "hey, what's going on?" Anyhow her attack was enough to see him off."

I knew that James had painted a scene where the male, described earlier, had delivered prey in a food-pass to the four juveniles and he explained the background: "I saw it happen right above the field at the back of our house. It was a beautiful warm day with a bit of a breeze and the thistles were shedding their seed. The male came in with prey and the young flew up, a real scrum as to who's going to catch it. I remember this moment with them all coming up to catch the prey item. The warm gusts of wind and all the thistledown going up, sparkling in the sky as it did so. It was a lovely scene that epitomized the height of summer in north Norfolk farmland." In 2008 James McCallum was awarded a prize for this painting at the annual Society of Wildlife Artists exhibition. It was an award instigated by the Hawk and Owl Trust in memory of Roger Clarke, who died in 2007.

In July and August 2006, Roger, who by then was seriously ill, made several trips to Norfolk, in the care of Bruce Pearson, to see the Montagu's Harriers. I had been watching a pair of Montagu's on David Lyle's land and I suggested to Bruce that the place David allowed me to use on a concrete sugar beet pad would suit them well. Good parking and it was discreet. I said I'd ask David's permission and meet them there.

I had known David Lyles for some time and several times he had walked my wife and I around his farm, showing us where Barn Owls bred and where the Marsh Harriers nested on his land. The year 2006 was very special, as Montagu's Harriers nested on his farm. Six years later, in 2012, I asked David what he had learnt about the birds, and he told me, "Montagu's Harriers have a special relationship with hares – and I don't mean the obvious one of them being a favourite prey item. They are the Montagu's Harrier's best ally. It happens in this way. The hares have meeting places in the crop. They eat the shoots and deposit their droppings there. They wander off, come back again, eat their droppings and eat some more shoots. This creates a circle, perhaps a couple of yards wide, that makes an ideal nesting place for the Montagu's Harriers. There's no danger of the crop collapsing on the nest if there's a cloudburst and it's away from the tractor tramlines. The tractor tramlines are a highway for predators – foxes and badgers. A human track through the crop is an open invitation to the same predators. If there's a nest in a crop which needs harvesting we leave a 50 metre square uncut around the nest. I've done this several times. A three-strand electric fence all the way round will keep foxes away. Harvesting doesn't seem to upset the harrier. Despite the racket, the male Montagu's Harrier still delivers prey to its familiar fence post and the female swoops in to collect it or may drop it to the female so that she has to make a spectacular talon-grabbing catch in mid-air. I am so lucky to have such elegant birds of prey nesting on my land."

It was a boiling hot day in midsummer, when Bruce and Roger returned to watch the Montagu's Harriers. They settled themselves in their collapsible fishermen's chairs in the shade of the windswept beech trees lining the concrete sugar beet pad. Through binoculars and telescopes they watched the patch of golden wheat where the harriers had their nest.

It was obviously a red letter day as Roger's account illustrates: 'We sat a full kilometre from the nest to avoid any hint of affecting the bird's behaviour – they range widely around their nesting territory, as we were almost immediately abruptly reminded as the male Montagu's flashed by over the hedge metres to the side of us, carrying prey and making a bee-line for the nest. Reaching his mark, he began to circle and the female came in from below to take the traditional food-pass. The action quelled. Then we realized that a dark young Marsh Harrier had strayed over the nest field. Instantly it seemed both Montagu's were there, chasing up at the larger bird. Harriers regard their nest site as covered by an inviolable bubble of airspace, out of which any intruder is to be pushed. The aim is to get under the intruder and chivvy them away. After a few minutes of the Montagu's getting under and pushing, and the gauche Marsh Harrier apparently not quite understanding what was expected of it, we realized that the mêlée was fast coming towards us, another totally unexpected bonus. It crossed the far hedgerow of "our" field, the Marsh Harrier now flipping over time after time to present talons as the emphasis of the attacks changed – to coming from above. No longer constrained by directly protecting the nest, the Montagu's had turned defence into punishment. The female was pressing home attack after attack, which caused the Marsh Harrier to flip over in defence each time and the male Montagu's selected his moments in between to dive in from on high. This cacophony of wild action drifted down into a dip of partially dead ground from us at the side of our field and it soon became obvious that the Marsh Harrier was now grounded there in the wheat. The female Montagu's was heckling with a chattering alarm call and swinging in with many successive dives, occasionally seamlessly joined in a pendulum fashion. The male Montagu's was swinging up from one dive, taking station on extended wings, then closing them to slice down again vertically at terrifying speed. The Marsh Harrier stayed down. In fact, given the number of Marsh Harriers cruising around at this stage of the season, this Marsh Harrier's full crime was a bit of a mystery. But, there had been no actual contact and sensibilities had been served. Gradually the onslaughts slowed and the female took to cruising around, though still heckling, and still resuming dives at intervals. Down in this cereal bowl the fierce light both shone through the translucence of her wings and reflected upwards the glistening yellow wheat, making her glow like a wild ethereal being as she cruised still in anger. The male held back more and more until he was away and eventually she followed. The Marsh Harrier still stayed down and we never did see it slip away.'

Roger's account accurately captures the 'cut and thrust' life of a pair of Montagu's Harriers during the breeding season. Once the well-kept secret of the harriers was revealed and the throngs of bird-watchers descended, bringing a boost to the local economy, the people of Norfolk became justly proud of their Montagu's Harriers. A float at the local flower show that year sported a banner emblazoned with the words 'SAVE OUR MONTY'S!'

At this exciting time when the fervour for Montagu's Harriers was at its height, I lived very close to the Sculthorpe airbase, a facility still run by the Ministry of Defence. It had a very long, heated runway and the word was that, if one of the US spacecraft hit a snag, this was an alternate landing site for the shuttle. The huge runway was surrounded by acres and acres of grass. Right against the perimeter fence in the Tattersett Business Park was the workshop of a furniture company. An old guy working there knew of my interest in the harriers, which used to hunt the airfield for Meadow Pipits and Skylarks. At the beginning of each breeding season he would ring me and let me know when he had seen what he called "the silver bird."

One day my wife and I were driving home and our route took us through a village. As we drove up the hill away from the village a male Montagu's Harrier appeared immediately in front of us. Alternately beating and gliding, it was hunting the hedge alongside which we were travelling. It seemed quite unaware of us as we followed slowly about five yards behind. I felt that we were almost near enough to touch it. What an elegant raptor – its grey plumage, as it floated ahead of us, reminding me of the morning suits worn at weddings. It was a very sharply turned-out bird.

As we reached the top of the hill, the site of a Roman fort, the harrier cut across in front of us, heading off left across the fields. Instantly I knew where it was going. We shot off past the turning to our home and into the Tattersett Business Park. We pulled up in the furniture company's parking area and rushed up to the perimeter fence. There was no sign of him. Had I got it wrong or had we beaten him to it? No, there he is, a couple of extra flaps and he is hunting over the airfield, head down, searching, listening. The Montagu's Harrier's buoyant flight carried it effortlessly in a search pattern backwards and forwards across the airfield.

What was it that had drawn us together at that moment? For our paths to coincide as it hunted up that hillside hedge was quite uncanny. It was as though it had been predestined, or maybe I had been thinking so hard about this particular bird that I had almost willed it to appear. Meeting that male Montagu's Harrier, whatever it was that brought us together, was a magic moment and I shall never forget it.

THE GOSHAWK

British Isles population (2006–10): 280–430 pairs (increasing)

It was early August 1983 and just beginning to get dark. A Tawny Owl called in the distance. I was standing in the road opposite Glebe Farm on the edge of the village with Cliff Howard. He and I lived nearby and Cliff had always been interested in birds of prey. He knew that I had trained a Goshawk and had seen the film I had made on television, an adaptation of T.H. White's book *The Goshawk*. Cliff had started in the right way, by training a Kestrel, an excellent bird for a beginner. But he lusted after a Goshawk and in the end I gave in and promised to get one that we would both take part in training and would own 50:50. So, there we were, looking up into a Sycamore tree where, 20 feet above us, was perched a juvenile female Goshawk being anxiously scolded by a Blackbird. Through my carelessness, she had escaped the previous day. She had killed recently and her crop was bulging, and she had resisted all my attempts to lure her down

I had told Cliff that I was confident I could secure her. We had a ladder and torch at hand and my plan was that, as soon as it was really dark, we would place the ladder against the tree and Cliff would shine a torch on the hawk while I climbed up and very carefully put my gloved hand under her tail. With luck, she would step back onto my glove. At the same time, and this was the tricky bit, with my other hand I would have to find her jesses and transfer them to my gloved hand. I had done this before and knew it would work.

To lose the bird now would be hard to take – it was almost fully trained and I just had to get it down. I owed it to Cliff. As we waited for it to get really dark I harked back to how I had obtained this bird that was now playing so hard to get. I was a member of the British Falconers Club and I knew that John Fairclough, the secretary of the club, was importing some juvenile Goshawks from Finland. I rang him and was told that they would be £50 each and that I could collect one in three weeks' time. Meanwhile, Cliff built a mews, a special lockable shed in which the hawk would be housed, and showed me where the key would be kept. On the due date we drove to John's house near Tamworth. He was in a hurry and led us straight to a barn in which there was an aviary holding what seemed to me about 50 juvenile Goshawks – some perching quietly, some on the floor and some flopping around. One of the birds was caught and carefully placed in the suitably lined laundry basket we had brought with us. I handed over a cheque and the Goshawk was ours.

When we got back we went straight to Cliff's hawk house, carefully shut the door, and placed the basket containing the Goshawk on the floor. Cautiously, I opened the basket and managed to get my gloved hands around her before she could burst out. Cliff had a towel ready, which he wrapped around the hawk's body so that she could not flap her wings. I then busied myself attaching leather jesses to the hawk's legs. These were attached to a swivel, through the bottom ring of which was passed a yard-long leather leash. This was either wrapped round the falconer's glove when carrying the hawk, or used for tying the hawk to a bow perch if outside or to a screen perch in the hawk house. When I had done this Cliff removed the towel and the hawk immediately 'bated', flapped off the perch, and hung there for a moment before regaining it. Panting, she regarded us with a jaundiced eye.

I could see that she had a faint hint of a pale stripe above the eye. Otherwise her head feathers were dark brown with thin, toffee-coloured edges. Her back was the same dark brown colour with only the faintest of pale edging to the feathers. The primaries had a light background traversed with dark bars and there were four broad, dark bars across the tail feathers. The breast feathers were a warm toffee colour with dark vertical streaks.

Tomorrow there would be bells to put on, one on either leg and one on her tail. But now we left her in the dark to settle down and get used to the screen perch. The training went well. I had already taught Cliff how to keep a diary of the hawk's weight, behaviour, food given and any kill made. We shared the first week's 'manning' of the hawk. With two of us involved the training could be much more intensive, with quicker results than could be achieved by either of us on our own. The hawk responded well, jumping to the fist for food, and at the end of the second week was being carried around outside and did not bate (fly off the fist) at everyday sights and sounds. By this time she was flying 20 yards on a line to the fist.

The third week was more of the same. At the end of the week the Goshawk would fly free 70 metres to the fist and had been called down from a tree on a line. We had hidden a dead Rabbit in the grass and as Cliff walked up I pulled on the line attached to the Rabbit and the hawk grabbed it without hesitation. As we walked back to Cliff's house I told him that, by the end of next week, we should be able to try for a Rabbit in the wild.

Cliff was away on the Monday of the fourth week and I had agreed to take the hawk out in the afternoon and just restrict myself to calling her off. This involved placing the hawk on a fence or other perch before walking some distance away, turning and whistling while holding out my gloved fist on which was displayed a tasty morsel. In the event I was delayed and did not leave until late in the afternoon. She was not very keen so I walked her around for half an hour. She roused (shook her feathers) to show she meant business. I removed her swivel and leash and started calling her off – 40, 50, 70 metres, no trouble at all. I should have left it at that as the light was fading but I decided to have one more go before calling it a day. I put her on the fence and walked away. I turned, extended my gloved hand holding a rabbit's forepaw as a lure, and whistled. She leant forward to take off and hesitated. There was a sudden gust of wind and she was off and soon out of sight. The wind increased, I couldn't hear her bells and, before I knew it, it was dark.

So it was that 24 hours later I was standing next to Cliff looking up at the faint outline of our hawk in the tree. It was quiet and the anxious Blackbird had long ago disappeared. We extended the ladder and gently positioned it on the tree trunk just below the hawk. I whispered to Cliff to keep the beam of the torch full on the bird and to stand to one side so that my body did not cut it off. I gave him a thumb's up and moved towards the ladder. As I looked up I saw a dark form fly silently in from right to left and crash-tackle our hawk. It was a Tawny Owl and it hit the hawk right between the shoulders, '*thwack!*' There was a tinkle of bells and Cliff tried to follow her with the torch – but she was gone.

I have told this story at some length because in the mid-1970s only a handful of Goshawks bred in the British Isles, having been relentlessly persecuted into extinction in 1889 by game preservationists and egg and skin collectors. I hoped that our bird would survive to join this nucleus and eventually breed. Most of my knowledge of Goshawks has been confined to trained birds. In chapter 1, I compared the characteristics of the Sparrowhawk as a killer to that of a Medici assassin with a thin, razor-sharp *stiletto* and those of a Goshawk to a Samurai warrior with a damask-toughened *katana* sword. The Goshawk is a thug. The Goshawk's scientific name is *Accipiter gentilis* (*Accipiter* meaning hawk and *gentilis* meaning belonging to a clan or species). It was John Ray in 1678 who first called it a Goshawk.

Like most birds of prey, the male Goshawk is only two-thirds the size of the female but apart from that they are very similar in appearance. In the adult bird the tip of the bill is black, merging to bluish as it turns up to the yellow waxy cere. The top of the head running back from the cere is dark grey. Above its orange-red eye is a white eye-stripe running along the supra-orbital ridge. This stripe is wider at the back of the head and is especially prominent when the bird is in yarak (keen to hunt) or aggressive. The ear coverts below and behind the eye are also dark. From the bird's nape down the centre of the back the plumage turns to a lighter grey and the wing coverts, secondaries and primaries become progressively darker. The upper side of the tail is also dark with four darker transverse bars, the final one being much broader than the rest and with a white tip. The adult Goshawk's underparts are white, over-scored with black horizontal bars. The markings are finer at the throat and increase in intensity from the chest downwards to include the flanks, although the vent is white. The underside of the tail is pale with four or five transverse dark bars. The Goshawk's legs are in stark contrast to the Sparrowhawk's, being shorter but much thicker and more powerful; the rear and inner front claws are the 'killers'.

The Goshawk is a killer *par excellence* and has the great advantage that it can be flown by one person on their own to take game for the table, unlike the Peregrine Falcon which requires horses, dogs and a retinue of helpers. Since the dawn of falconry over 3,000 years ago it has been one of the falconer's favourites. It was so esteemed by Attila, King of the Huns, that he bore the Goshawk as an emblem 'crowned on his badge, his helm and his helmet.'

Falconry arrived in England with the Saxons and Goshawks are mentioned in the *Saxon Chronicles* between the eighth and ninth centuries. It was the practice then for falconers to release their trained hawks in the spring, allowing them to breed. Later, in the autumn, they would catch young birds and train them. The value of a Goshawk then was three shillings. Ethelbert, the Saxon King of Kent, was presented with a hawk (presumably a Goshawk) and two falcons in the middle of the eighth century by Boniface, Archbishop of Mons in Belgium. In the *Domesday Book* (1086 AD) there is a register of Goshawk nests: Buckinghamshire 1, Cheshire 24, and so on. The British Isles were well wooded then and the population of Goshawks could well have approached 10,000 pairs.

By the twelfth century, falconry was firmly established. It was *de rigueur* to be seen with a hawk on your fist. 'Many citizens', wrote William Fitz-Stephen in his account of London life, 'take delight in Sparrow-hawks, Goss-hawks, and such like and in Dogs to hunt in the woody ground.' William Fitz-Stephen was in service to Thomas à Becket and witnessed his murder. Hawks or falcons, not money, were another way the Exchequer had of levying taxes. In 1139 Outi, a gentleman of Lincolnshire, was asked to find in lieu of tax 'one Hundred Norway Hawks (Goshawks) and one Hundred Girfals (Gyrfalcons).'

The Kings, Edward II and Edward III were all fond of hawking and their royal courtiers were not slow to follow suit. The eulogy of the Franciscan friar, Bartholomew de Glanville,

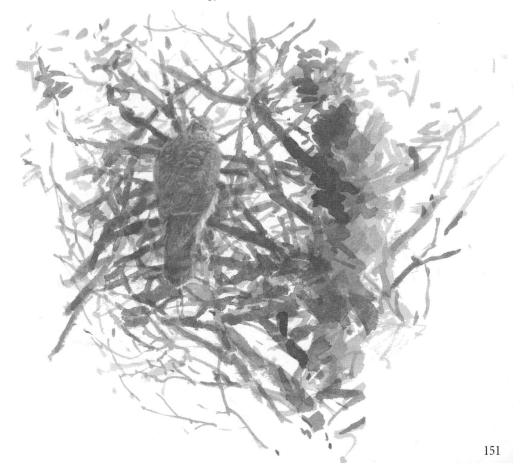

to his Goshawk shows the esteem of a falconer for his bird. She was a royal fowl, 'armed more with boldness than with claws.'

On 21 September 1472, John Paston writes to his brother, "I ask no more goods of you for all the service that I shall do you while the world standeth but a Goshawk. If I have not a hawk I shall wax fat for default of labour, and dead for default of company, by my troth." Sadly, the bird when it was delivered was found to be lame in both legs (perhaps due to the way in which it was caught) and was released back into the wild.

The Boke of St Albans, supposedly written by Dame Juliana Berners in 1486, described in order of rank the persons worthy of different birds of prey. It ranges from an Eagle for an Emperor to a Kestrel for a Knave. The Goshawk was fit for a Yeoman. It seems crazy that such a highly prized bird should be entrusted to a Yeoman, and how could he have afforded one?

The first detailed account of a hawking establishment occurs in the sixteenth century at Hunstanton Hall, the home of the le Strange family. The Goshawk was a firm favourite. One bought in 1533 cost 40 shillings, a good sum in those days. They were valuable birds and nothing was spared to ensure their welfare. Ten shillings was paid to John Maston for looking after Goshawks from 14 September until 15 November, a good wage for just two months' work. Even so, the Goshawk was good value. Flown from the fist, the le Strange Goshawks provided sport and welcome additions to the larder – hares occasionally and plenty of Rabbits, Pheasants and Partridges.

Henry VIII was a very keen falconer. Gordon Robinson's excellent book *The Sinews of Falconry*, published in 2003, tells us that 'Regal establishments required a Master Falconer with administrative ability, able to delegate responsibilities of the mews.' Henry VIII's mews were at Charing Cross in London. Such a paragon of all these virtues was Robert Cheeseman, Master Falconer to the King. In 1533 Henry VIII commissioned Hans Holbein, whose main assignment was to paint portraits of the royal household, to prepare a portrait of Robert Cheeseman. The attention to detail is meticulous: Cheeseman, who is looking out to the left, is wearing a red silk jacket over which is an overcoat lined with sable. He wears a fashionable black hat. On his left, gloved, hand sits a hooded, grey-phase Gyrfalcon. The ringed fingers of his right hand are stroking the upper part of the falcon's breast, soothing it. The painting as a whole reveals the sure touch of the master.

Although Cheeseman's portrait shows him with a falcon, the Royal Household accounts indicate that the King favoured one species in particular, the Goshawk – it occurs nine times in the household accounts. One day he saw a Goshawk on a cadge, a wooden frame for carrying hawks. He liked the look of it so much that he bought it for £3. Out hawking on foot, when he was 34 years old, he nearly lost his life, as described in the 1809 edition of *Hall's Chronicle*: 'The King following his hawk leapt over a ditch beside Hitchin with a pole and the pole brake, so that if one Edmund Mody, a footman, had not leapt into the water and lifting up his head, he had been drowned; but God of his goodness, preserved him.'

Shakespeare (1564–1616) makes many allusions to falconry in his plays. Hawking was sometimes called 'birding'. In *The Merry Wives of Windsor,* Master Page says, 'I do invite you to-morrow morning to my house for breakfast; after, we'll a-birding together; I have a fine hawk for the bush.' I used one of Shakespeare's most famous falconry quotations in the first film I made for BBC Television, a dramatization of T.H. White's book *The Goshawk*. I cast Duncan Carse as T.H. White because he looked somewhat like him and he had a beautiful speaking voice. He had had a remarkable career, surveyed South Georgia in the

South Atlantic, been one of the first presenters on television and been one of three actors who had played *Dick Barton – Special Agent*.

Shakespeare's *The Taming of the Shrew* has the following six lines, which I used in the scene where T.H. White played by Duncan Carse is watching the hawk for three days and nights:

> *Another way I have to man my haggard,*
> *To make her come, and know her keeper's call;*
> *That is, to watch her, as we watch these kites,*
> *That bate, and beat, and will not be obedient.*
> *She eat no meat to-day, nor none shall eat;*
> *Last night she slept not, nor to-night she shall not.*

Eventually the Goshawk accepted the gloved fist as a natural perch. The brilliant orange-red eye closed over, but jerked open as a book on Duncan's knee slipped down. He, too, was asleep as the hawk's eye closed over finally in sleep.

The book on the floor was a copy of the first book written in English on how to train a hawk. *The Approved Treatise on Hawks and Hawking* by Edmund Bert was published in 1619, three years after Shakespeare's death. Bert was a very accomplished falconer, very sure of himself, and some of his advice and methods for training Sparrowhawks and Goshawks are as valid today as they were 400 years ago.

Manning a hawk, the process of taming a hawk so that it accepts your gloved fist as a natural perch, has never been better described than by Bert: 'I continue her upon my fist ten days or a fortnight (unless in a shorter time I find her a sound hawk), which I shall the sooner understand. She shall well be assured to find no other perch than the fist, from that time I rise until I go to bed, when she shall go with me.'

I have a facsimile of Bert's book with a foreword by the late Philip Glasier, one of the best falconers of modern times. In 1954, just after I had come down from Cambridge, he got me my first hawk, an eyass, a newly fledged, female Goshawk. It came from Sergeant Bill Ruddock stationed in Germany and cost £5. Philip said he would write me a weekly letter telling me what to do on a day-to-day basis. If I followed his advice, he told me, he was sure that at the end of three weeks the hawk would be well enough trained to catch a Rabbit.

This was a joint project with my friend, Noel Cunningham Reid. His mother had a large estate at Six Mile Bottom in Suffolk with big open fields, ideal for training a hawk. Six Mile Bottom, six miles from Newmarket and at the bottom of a hill, has always been regarded as one of the premier game shoots in the country. It is light land and the 11,000 acres were laid out and farmed for shooting. Shelterbelts line the edges of the fields, providing excellent cover for nesting game, and also providing sporting shots at the birds as they were flushed towards the waiting guns.

Back in 1954 the arrival of the Goshawk was imminent and we commandeered part of the game larder as our mews and covered the windows with hessian to reduce the light level and set up a screen perch on which the hawk could perch and sleep. A phone call from Philip Glasier told us the hawk was on its way. On 2 July, Noel and I went to London Airport to pick up our Goshawk, Tanya – so named because during the journey Noel had decided that the hawk should be named after Tanya Crouch, a ruthless 1950s stock car driver!

In the darkened mews, back at Six Mile Bottom, I took Tanya out of her travelling container and we wrapped her in a towel so that we could fit her with jesses, bells, a swivel and a leash. Now she could be carried around. At first Tanya bated and gently was replaced, but again she bated. I remembered that we had to weigh her and slowly carried her over to the specially adapted scales and placed her over the perch until she could feel it on the back of her legs. She stepped backward onto the perch. Noel carefully adjusted the weights until the scales were balanced, 2lb 1oz. Philip Glasier had instructed us to keep a day book noting the bird's weight, behaviour, amount of food given and, if everything went to plan, kills made, so Noel entered details of her weight. I took her off the scales and continued walking around slowly with her on my fist. Noel took over for a spell and when I took her up again she was much calmer. I offered her the hind leg of a Rabbit but again she bated. Finally, after two hours on the fist, she took a medium-sized crop off the Rabbit leg. We were relieved and I gently placed her on the screen perch and secured her leash with a falconer's knot. This meant that she was secure but still had the freedom to bate and return to the perch via the hessian screen.

Because there were two of us sharing the manning process, it could be intense and good progress was made. After a week I was able, when I whistled, to get her to step from her perch onto my fist for a bloody morsel of Rabbit liver. Now there was an irritating intrusion. I had to leave Noel in charge while I went off for a Territorial Army camp near Scarborough. I left him with some rather bossy notes about how to continue: 'Gradually increase the time you take her out. First, take her out where there won't be people about and then, by the end of next week, one or two people can see her at a time. Keep her away from dogs and windows. Always keep a good grip on the leash. Weigh her every day, just before you feed her, and consult Glasier's notes on how important the day book is.'

A fortnight later, I returned to my grandmother's house near Malton for the final few days' training. As I got out of my mother's car I was delighted to see our Goshawk resting on her bow perch on the lawn. Noel had worked very hard. Tanya sat well on the fist, didn't bate and was coming eagerly five or six yards on a line when called. Each day the distance was increased. Eventually, flown free, she would fly 100 yards when called to the fist. Her best flying weight had stabilized at 2 lb 2 oz. Philip stressed that before we tried for a kill the hawk must be successfully called down to the fist from a tree. We found a dead tree, and with the hawk on a line for safety, called her. She shuffled along the branch and leant forward, but was distracted by something for a moment before launching herself down to the fist.

Tanya had already acquitted herself well with a dragged dead Rabbit, so on 27 July we set out for our first kill. She was very keen, feathers fluffed up, talons clutching my glove with an iron grip if I gave a squeak. Nearby there was a quarry where Rabbits were always to be found in the early evening. We quietly made our way there. The leash and swivel were released from the jesses. Tanya fluffed up her feathers, shook them. It was her signal to me that she was in yarak. We turned into the quarry. There were Rabbits everywhere. Suddenly, from cropping the grass contentedly, they were streaking for their burrows. But there was a half-grown one dawdling and Tanya had seen it. She threw herself off my fist, flashed across the close-cropped turf, cut a corner and had him, one taloned foot across the Rabbit's loins and the other convulsively gripping its head in a death grip. I moved in cautiously, stopping every time the hawk looked up. Slowly I stooped down to kneel beside her and gently secured her jesses with my gloved left hand as she plucked fur from the luckless Rabbit. She looked up at me and I was in awe. She had done it – made her first kill 25 days after her training started – and I now felt that there was a bond, a palpable bond, between us.

Philip had told me to split open the Rabbit's skull and allow the hawk to feast on the brains, the ultimate reward for a faultless flight. Edmund Bert, 350 years earlier, gives similar advice: 'I let her take all her pleasure, but by little bits of warm meat I sup her from my hand, letting her wholly see what I do, until I see her ready to forsake the quarry to catch my hand, then I deliver up more covertly until I have her jump to my fist, where with plumage and tiring I end her supper. You shall hereafter find a better benefit to many purposes hereafter by your dealing with your hawk thus.'

After her first kill, Tanya, Noel and I returned to Six Mile Bottom. Here we were able go hawking every day and Tanya became a formidable killer. Between August 1954 and January 1955, she caught 128 head of prey, mostly Rabbits, Partridges, Pheasants and Brown Rats. I lost her three times and once had to recover her at night from a fir tree with the help of a ladder and torch. I shall always be in debt to Noel for this wonderful experience. The bond forged between falconer and hawk, one of the wildest of nature's creatures, gives immeasurable delight. The presence of my Springer Spaniel, Chaucer, reinforced the endearing partnership. Sadly Tanya, after going downhill very rapidly, died on 15 March 1955. I sent her corpse to The British Falconers Club vet. The post-mortem revealed that it was pasteurellosis, a bacterium that causes pneumonia. It was a sad end for a wonderful bird.

At the time when Noel and I were flying Tanya, the Goshawk had been persecuted into extinction as a breeding bird in the British Isles. There were occasional reports of breeding but these were never confirmed.

Forestry Commission plantations that were established during the Second World War were, by the 1960s and 1970s, substantial enough to provide suitable Goshawk habitat. Falconers lost birds and these, together with birds released unofficially, took advantage of this new environment and a small nucleus of breeding pairs was established.

I knew that Robert Kenward was the Goshawk expert. He had been involved with the official reintroduction of Goshawks into the wild and was a pioneer in radio-tracking. Robert had written a paper about releasing Goshawks so I rang Carole Showell at the British Trust for Ornithology library and the next day I had the article in front of me. I also rang the secretary of the British Falconers Club and asked if they could put me in touch with Robert. Since he was travelling there was a delay before contact was made but when he did he answered my queries very fully and reminded me that it was all in his book *The Goshawk*, published in 2006.

Reading the book, I learnt that Robert got his Goshawk, the first one he trained, from the same Sergeant Bill Ruddock who had supplied mine. In 1968 he went to Oxford to read zoology, where he was rather overwhelmed by the heady mix of lecturers and demonstrators, who included David Lack, the most famous of the post-war ecologists, and Niko Tinbergen, a ground-breaking animal behaviourist. At the end of his three-year course he was tempted to join the RAF but was persuaded to study for a doctorate at the Edward Grey Institute – a study to see if Goshawks could help reduce crop damage by Wood Pigeons. Fortunately, Robert still had a trained Goshawk, called Foot, and this is his account of a day's research with his hawk: 'At 3.30 his feathers suddenly tighten and both feet grip the branch. I can see that he has spotted a lone pigeon, which is flying rather weakly over the far hedge to land some distance from the flock. As it lands, he is off, wings beating fast as he skims the sprout crowns, no gliding even though the flight is gently downhill. White feathers puff into the air. I note the response of the other pigeons, which again circle and settle farther down the field. The main objective of this research is to record the behaviour of the pigeons in response to successful and unsuccessful attacks, to see whether wild hawks or their effigies might help protect brassica crops.'

Robert's doctorate thesis was published in 1978, at which time he was studying the fate of lost trained birds of prey, a fate that had resulted in the breeding population of wild birds steadily increasing.

The unofficial release of Goshawks into Britain started in the late 1960s and involved birds trapped in Sweden and released on the Welsh borders and other birds brought over by Bill Ruddock from Germany were released in the north of England. From 1970 onwards Goshawks could be imported under licence for falconry and a survey carried out in that year showed that 52% of these Goshawks were lost or released. A later survey carried out in 1978 indicated that the percentage of hawks lost or unofficially released was 33%. In 1970 the British Falconers Club also carried out an official release in two areas of 22 imported birds, ten of which survived. As a result of these lost birds and releases, the Goshawk population in Great Britain increased from nine pairs in 1970 to 59 pairs in 1980. It was slow progress but now, 30 years later, the population is estimated at between 280–430 pairs.

In 1978 Robert moved to the Institute of Terrestrial Ecology at Monks Wood near Huntingdon to study forestry damage by Grey Squirrels. He was one of the pioneers of the use of radio-tracking to locate raptors and formed a company, Biotrack, in 1980. Radio-tracking revolutionized falconry as birds on a kill or lost could now easily be recovered.

What I particularly liked about Robert's excellent book, which is packed with scientific detail, were the personal accounts of research that are a taster for each chapter.

One of Robert's projects was to see how well falconry-trained birds would survive if

lost unintentionally. How many would survive to boost the wild population? Eleven radio-tagged Goshawks without prior experience were released into the wild. Three days later Robert was worried about one particular bird, and wrote: 'This bird had not killed in the last two days. She had not been hunting effectively, and could easily have been called to the fist at any time. That was the intention this morning, to rescue her as a failure. However the signal was unexpectedly weak and coming from within a Blackthorn thicket. I abandoned the cumbersome antenna and crawled under the sharp twigs, with a glove on my left hand in case she would come to me, and the receiver in my right. A paper clip in the antenna socket gave enough reception to show when I was approaching the source of the signals. There lay a Fox, as if asleep, but this half-starved young vixen was cold. Next to her, tail feathers protruded from disturbed ground, I pulled out the legs and back of the Goshawk. The journey back to Oxford was sombre and smelly.'

The post-mortem showed that the vixen probably found the hawk on a kill. The Goshawk attacked the Fox and one of its talons pierced the rib cage, causing fatal damage to the liver from which it eventually died but not before it had killed and devoured the hawk. Four of the 11 hawks released on this project died. As Robert put it, 'Although radio-tagging was an elegant way to find dead hawks, each was a bitter experience.'

Knowing that the Goshawk population was increasing and the conflict that this might create, Robert has always been keen to show that this impressive killer is particularly adept at controlling pests – Wood Pigeons, Grey Squirrels, Rabbits, Carrion Crows and Magpies. Hugh Miles, producer and wildlife cameraman, enlisted Robert as specialist adviser on his Anglia *Survival* special, *Goshawk – The Phantom of the Forest*. Shot on Forestry Commission land in the Kielder Forest on the Scottish Borders, its message is clear – if you are lucky enough to have top predators like the Goshawk in your area you have got a healthy environment.

Mike Richards, a first-class wildlife cameraman, filmed a pair of breeding Goshawks from the time they built their nest to the eventual dispersal of their free-flying young. He also meticulously documented the forest's rich array of wildlife, all part of the Kielder Forest's intricate web of life.

Steve Petty, the Forestry Commission's bird ecologist, has worked at Kielder for nearly 40 years. There was a fascinating sequence in which he visited a Goshawk nest site after the breeding season. At the base of the tree he found a primary feather moulted out that year. He was able to compare it with others collected there over the previous eight years and show that it was from the same bird: the primaries are as unique as a human fingerprint. Although the Goshawk is a deadly killer of pests, there is a downside to its reintroduction: it also preys on other birds of prey such as Sparrowhawks, and between 1975 and 1995 reduced the Kestrel population at Kielder Forest from about 30 pairs to just two pairs.

The flying shots in Hugh Miles's film are superb. I know he was using trained birds flown by a falconer and that is why he was able to get such excellent shots of the Goshawk killing Carrion Crows, Rabbits and Pheasants. There is one shot that is quite outstanding – the first moment a Goshawk appears in the film is a visual masterpiece. The point of view is looking up a ride in a forestry plantation. You hear a Goshawk calling and from behind a hillock in the ride the indistinct shape of a bird flying towards you emerges. There is then silence as the bird, which we can now see is a hawk, rows through the air towards us. It is 'the silent killer' and the shot is just as compelling an image as that of the rider emerging from the mirage in David Lean's *Lawrence of Arabia*.

About the time Hugh's film was made, Goshawks were being seen fairly regularly throughout Great Britain. I remember one early spring looking down across forestry land in the Peak District at Edale, with the Ladybower Reservoir in the background. A pair of Goshawks flew up out of the conifers and started their courtship display. They gave an

intense display of diving and power-climbing as they ascended higher and higher. At the Hawk and Owl Trust's reserve at Fylingdales in North Yorkshire I again saw a Goshawk, a male skimming the top of one of the mature plantations by May Beck. When the Marsh Harriers arrive in the spring at our reserve in Norfolk and start displaying, a pair of Goshawks often appear and join in.

It was to be 20 years before another film on the Goshawk was made. This was a record of the breeding behaviour and feeding ecology of a pair in North Yorkshire. Garry and Mike Marchant studied Goshawks for several years, watching the adults' behaviour and ringing the young when they were old enough before they even considered making a film. In 2008 they felt confident enough to start, and in February had narrowed their search to concentrate on a pair that was building a nest in a 60-foot tall Sitka Spruce.

They had already erected a hide about 60 metres from the tree. While the birds were absent, Garry and Mike ran power and transmission cables to the base of a tree nearby. It was Garry's job as tree-climber to put the camera in position. Mike, watching his computer screen in the hide, told Garry when it was positioned to give maximum coverage of the nest. All that remained was to fix the camera securely to the tree. They kept watch on the birds and started filming towards the end of the incubation period.

I watched the footage from Garry and Mikes' marathon recording session with great interest and this is my interpretation of what I saw, with their help on occasion.

'11/5/08. The nest is large: 4 feet long, 3 feet wide and 2–3 feet deep. The female Goshawk walks in from the edge of the nest. The four eggs, bluish in colour, are in quite a deep depression. She settles down very carefully to brood. She uses her beak to push the eggs under her and has another go until she's satisfied she's covered them perfectly. She's very alert. Her eyes are not as orange as I've seen in adult Goshawks in the past. After a while she stands up in the nest and starts fiddling with the nest material, rearranging twigs, bunching her talons up so as not to damage the eggs. For some reason she places some Scots Pine shoots in the nest cup. Is it possible that they are being used as a disinfectant against parasites in the nest cup? She settles down to brood again, turning through 90 degrees and now facing the tree trunk. The male calls her off for food and she flies away, the male then coming in to take over. He's noticeably smaller than her. The male settles down on the eggs and to make sure they're covered properly has to turn through 270 degrees.'

'14/5/08. The female is incubating. She gets off the eggs and reveals that one has hatched. The chick gapes its beak wide open, calling. Egg tooth can be clearly seen. One of the other eggs is "pipping", the tip of the second chick's beak working away. The female turns, looks at the chick and settles down to brood again. Later the female returns with the hind-quarters of a Rabbit, strips off tiny portions of flesh and very gently feeds the chick. She doesn't over-feed, just three portions this time: little and often spread out over the day.'

'15/5/08. Twenty-four hours later a second egg has hatched. The two chicks are actively calling for food and the third egg is on the verge of hatching. The female comes in from the left and settles down to brood. A few hours later, while the two chicks are being fed, the third egg hatches. The chick flops out, head still stuck in the shell. It is absolutely exhausted after chipping its way out the shell but finally raises its head and then flops down again. Its eyes are open and it is still soaking wet from the fluids in the egg. Remarkably, the female ignores it and continues feeding the first two arrivals.'

'17/5/08. All the eggs have safely hatched and there are now four bundles of fluff huddled together in the nest. The two eldest chicks are calling and the female flies in with a Rabbit's leg, possibly the one she cached the other day. These two chicks push to the front – first come, first served. The third chick pushes forward and gets into a position where it's noticed. Number four chick has no idea what's happening and is left right at the back. Later in the day the female brings in a Wood Pigeon, a neatly plucked, bloody carcase. The four chicks press forward to be fed, the smallest at the front. They all call and gape but the female favours the three eldest chicks. Despite the smallest chick calling and gaping (gaping is the trigger mechanism that encourages the female to offer food) it is ignored. The others are getting a big feed. At this stage every feed is vital and any chick missing out will soon weaken and fall behind.'

'23/5/08. The male is standing on the edge of the nest. He's just brought in another Grey Squirrel. He's had trouble with this one and it must have put up a bit of a fight because *his left leg has been bitten and is covered in blood. If it gets infected this could affect the development of the chicks as he is still the main food provider.'*

25/5/08. The young are now ten days old. It is very windy and nest is swaying alarmingly, backwards and forwards. The female is off hunting, leaving the male on guard watching over the chicks. His beak gapes a bit, he's anxious – a bigger gust of wind and the chicks could be blown out of the nest and wouldn't survive on the ground. He hears the female calling and leaves. Moments later she arrives with a Wood Pigeon. As before, the three eldest chicks thrust forward and are fed in turn. The youngest tries hard and manages to edge forward round the other three, but is ignored.'

'27/5/08. Heavy rain all day. The female is soaked and looks very bedraggled as she spreads her wings, sheltering her young to try and keep them warm and dry. She stays in this position all day. Now and then a chick peeps out from the cover of her breast feathers. There was more rain during the night.'

'28/5/08. After the downpour, today there are only three chicks in the nest. It's impossible to know what happened to the fourth but it most probably became chilled in the rain. Even though the missing chick was one of the three eldest, it wasn't strong enough to survive and died. The little chick, against all the odds, is still alive.'

'4/6/08. The best day for ages – really sunny! The female is feeding the three youngsters from a squirrel. They've positioned themselves around her so that it's easier to grab food when it is offered. Their feathers are beginning to show through – body feathers, primaries and tail feathers.'

'8/6/08. The female has brought in another squirrel. It lies between her and the three youngsters. She makes no effort to break into it so that they can feed. A squirrel's skin is very tough and the largest youngster pulls at one of the legs making no impression. The young are now 23 days old and their feathering is more advanced. Later in the day, and after it has lain there for four hours, the squirrel is broken into by the female and the young are able to help themselves. The female just watches them get on with it.'

'11/6/08. The youngsters are now 26 days old. The largest is a female and is able to stand properly as it pulls at a Wood Pigeon carcase. The smaller chicks are both males and one grabs a gobbet of meat from the carcase. Like the Sparrowhawks I described in the first chapter, the males, although smaller, appear to develop more quickly. This means that they can leave the nest earlier, keeping their distance from the more aggressive female.'

'14/6/08. The three youngsters are standing in the nest. They've just been ringed and are sporting two rings each: a uniquely numbered British Trust for Ornithology ring and a coloured ring that enables individual birds to be recognized. Later in the afternoon a thunderstorm hits the forest. The three young move towards the trunk of the tree. It starts to hail and one of them is hit on the head by a hailstone. They all cluster together and are getting very stressed as there's no way they can escape the hail. The rain and hail continues to pelt down and just when it seems unlikely the youngsters will able to survive the female returns to the nest. Whew! She's followed by an enormous clap of thunder and hasn't arrived a moment too soon, as the rain and hail are now soaking and bombarding the youngsters. The female moves them even closer to the trunk of the tree. There's nothing else she can do as her youngsters are far too big for her to cover them with her wings. They just have to ride out the storm. Soon afterwards the rain and hail stop and the female leaves. The youngsters haven't

had time to dry before the female flies in with a squirrel. The biggest of the youngsters grabs it and won't let go. The female doesn't intervene even though the other two are calling for food. She leaves them to it and flies off, returning after a while with a Wood Pigeon. Apart from the top of her head, she's completely dry. Not so the youngsters. She gives the two males a really good feed. They'll warm up now and dry out quickly with all that protein in them. Garry reckons that the adults have been through this kind of drama before and know what's required of them. They are outstanding parents and have weathered the storm.'

'16/6/08. The youngsters are alone on the nest. All their feather tracts are well developed although their baby down still clings on. They have recovered from the storm and seem much more aware of the outside world. They are full of energy, rampaging around the nest and wing-flapping for the first time. A bit later the female is feeding the young when the male flies in with a Rabbit. The female thinks he's an intruder and chases him off. As she does so, she very nearly wipes out two of the youngsters that are in her way. It could have been a disaster: if they'd been knocked off the nest they would have died for sure. I think it was the male's fault as he forgot to call. At any rate, the female is soon back on the nest and resumes feeding the youngsters.'

'19/6/08. A windy, sunny day. Two of the youngsters are standing up, looking out into the outside world. The other is hunkered down. Most of their baby down has gone and the youngest male is preening, aligning the edges of his primaries and removing tufts of down. The female arrives and starts feeding them a squirrel, the young male getting a really good feed. All that food pumped into him helps produce good, strong feathers. At the moment, the feathers are still "in the blood", they've not hardened off yet. If the young are deprived of food at this stage they develop "hunger traces", pale lines across the quills, weaknesses that could break.'

'23/6/08. The youngest male, the one that I thought was doomed, is now a strong, feisty young Goshawk. He's quite able to feed himself from the squirrel that has been brought in. As Garry put it, "he stood out as a real battler especially when it came to feeding times and he never gave up. It was very much the survival of the fittest." Later in the day the three young are standing about in the nest. One of the males wanders over to the edge, hesitates for a moment, and launches himself across to a branch ten feet away on the next tree. A first flight! Twenty minutes later he's still marooned on the branch. He can see his brother and sister in the nest and starts wailing plaintively. He looks down, realizes how high he is, and moves nervously about on the branch before throwing himself off and flapping to regain the safety of the nest. It was easy.'

'25/6/08. The nest is bathed in sunshine. In the centre lie the three young Goshawks. Their heads are all touching in the centre. They've just been fed and are watching a pair of Chaffinches flitting about above them. It is a scene full of promise. Soon these birds will be independent, killing for themselves. But for the moment they are content, their crops are full and they are happy to be relaxing in the sun.'

'3/7/08. The female comes into the nest with food and is ambushed by the two young males who have already left the nest. This behaviour shows the importance of the males leaving the nest first. It gives them a head start over the bigger, more aggressive female. The small male, which at one time I felt sure was destined not to survive, is the last to leave the nest for good. He's a bit wobbly on a branch of the nearby tree. There is a slight hesitation and then he pushes off to join his brother and sister, which can then be heard calling to each other. In *the background is the empty nest, the scene of such drama over the past 44 days. The male and female Goshawks were certainly wonderful parents.'*

I muse over how those three young Goshawks fared. For the next four or five weeks they will still be dependent upon their parents but will then have to move on. If they stay on Forestry Commission land their future looks good but if they stray off the edge into land where game preservation is practised their future is bleak.

In Britain, the Goshawk's conflict with game conservation is dealt with very negatively. If Goshawks breed on or near estates where Pheasants are reared, the juvenile hawks will always head for the rearing pens, where they are often shot or poisoned. In Sweden, however, a practical solution has been found to this problem. Juvenile Goshawks raiding rearing pens are trapped under licence and translocated to a suitable location at least 30 kilometres away. Young Pheasants at rearing sites can also be given better protection by improving the ground cover and removing any neighbouring trees that may provide lookout points for hunting Goshawks. Much greater effort and co-operation is needed between the shooting fraternity and wildlife conservationists if this problem is to be solved.

Robert Kenward concludes his excellent book *The Goshawk* with the following words: 'Can everyone accept that the more ways in which an animal is loved, as a free spirit or a companion or even as a delicacy, the more human resources can be available for its conservation? I don't know. However, co-operation requires tolerance, which starts with knowledge.'

THE COMMON BUZZARD

British Isles population (2009): 57,000–79,000 pairs (increasing)

I am watching Gordon Brown, our vet, preparing a male Common Buzzard for dissection. We are hoping to find out what made Aristotle (384–322 BC) state that the Buzzard had three testicles, *triorchis* in Greek. This mistake was perpetuated for centuries. Aldrovandus (1522–1605), who dissected a male Buzzard, supported Aristotle by stating that he had found three stones (testicles). A little later Christopher Merret (1614–95), who published the first comprehensive list of British birds, compounded the mistake calling the Buzzard *Buteo triorchis*. John Ray and Francis Willughby's *Ornithologia,* published in 1678, put the record straight after they had carried out a dissection: 'The third stone appeared not to us, though we diligently sought it.'

Carefully, and with great precision, Gordon opened up the abdominal cavity and removed the intestinal tract. Then, alternating between scalpel and clippers, he cut away the bird's rib cage and removed it. He took samples from the pectoral muscle, kidney and liver, which would later be despatched for analysis to determine whether there were any environmental contaminants. Gordon pointed out the three-lobed kidneys that were attached to the back of the abdominal cavity. With a mounted needle, he indicated the pair of testes attached to the kidneys. Although they were small, I could see there were only two. "Thank you, Gordon," I said, "but where is the organ that might have been mistaken for the third testis?" Gordon showed me the adrenal glands, which were attached to the anterior lobes of the kidneys. It was possible, he suggested, that if one of the adrenal glands had a tumour on it or was over-active someone might wrongly identify it as a third testis.

Francis Willughby, who had rubbished the idea of a third testicle, opted for the scientific name *Buteo vulgaris* and his co-author, John Ray, gave it the English name Common Buzzard or Puttock. Carl Linnaeus, the Swedish taxonomist, classified it as *Falco buteo,* later changed to *Buteo buteo,* which is how the species is classified today.

I saw my first Buzzard in the spring of 1947 when I was at Stowe School in Buckinghamshire. That winter, 1946/7, was one of the worst in living memory. The ground was frozen solid and there was a foot of snow, so there was no rugger or hockey but plenty of opportunity for my friend, David Withers, and I to go bird-watching. I saw Bramblings for the first time and we found a Barn Owl dead beneath its roosting perch in the Oxford Lodge at the entrance to the school. On the day etched in my memory, freezing cold with a clear blue sky, we were striding out like Scott of the Antarctic, boots squeaking in the snow, making our way across the South Front back to the school. David stopped, grabbed my arm and pointed across to the stand of cedars that mask Stowe church. Quite low down soaring over the cedars was a Buzzard. It flew effortlessly, wings motionless but thrust well forward and held slightly raised in a 'V', its primaries spread like outstretched fingers. I scanned it with my battered binoculars and was shaking with excitement as I handed them to David. As I did so, the bird caught an updraft and soared away until it was out of sight. That epic moment, my first Buzzard, was reduced to just over a dozen rather dull words in the Natural History section of the next *Old Stoic* magazine 'A Buzzard was also seen by those expert birdwatchers, D.S. Withers (G) and M.D. Cobham (G).'

I have used four main sources in writing this chapter on the Buzzard: Colin Tubbs's book *The Buzzard* published in 1974, a 1957 paper by Norman Moore on the status of the Buzzard up until 1954, papers by Peter Dare on the population of Buzzards in Devon 1955–93 and papers by Robin Prytherch on the colonization by Buzzards of a 75 square kilometre area in north Somerset including the Gordano Valley, west of Bristol.

The Common Buzzard shares with the Honey Buzzard the characteristic of having considerable variations in plumage. As Colin Tubbs so aptly puts it 'Some individuals are almost uniformly dark brown, above and below, in striking contrast to the clear yellow of their feet, legs and cere. At the other extreme, birds occur which are almost completely white on the underside save for dark markings on the under-wing coverts. Between these two extremes will be found a multitude of variations, though the most common form is intermediate between them, and is rather lightly barred on the underside with a distinct pectoral band of darker barring. The plumage characters remain constant from year to year – they do not change as the bird moults – and can be of considerable assistance to the observer because they enable individual birds to be identified.'

On a day when there are good thermals a pair of Buzzards can soar for hours, regularly giving their distinctive "*wheoo*" call that helps to find them. There they are, silhouetted against the sky, their wings outstretched and held in a 'V', primaries curled up at the tips and tail spread wide. Flying in this way enables Buzzards to cover large distances quickly and with little expense of energy.

The Common Buzzard is an opportunistic hunter and searches for its prey in three different ways. One is to soar at 60–100 metres above the ground, occasionally hovering, and when it spots something, to drop in stages, much like a hovering Kestrel does, before plunging down to make its kill. However, perhaps the most popular method is 'still hunting' from a tree, fence post or a telegraph pole – a technique that saves energy and has a high success rate. Buzzards also hunt on the ground, searching for earthworms and insects.

I once had a grandstand seat for the last two methods of hunting. In the mid-1970s I made a film for the Ministry of Defence on the Scorpion, a new lightweight armoured fighting vehicle. We needed a handsome backdrop against which to demonstrate this new tracked vehicle and were allowed to use the village of Tyneham, a village in Dorset that had been requisitioned by the government prior to the Second World War. The inhabitants were evacuated as it was part of an artillery range and told that they would be able to return to their properties once the war was over. In the event, though, this never happened and when we arrived to film it was a 'ghost village' with only the school and the church having been preserved.

We filmed there for three days in blazing hot weather. There had been a heatwave and all the farmland over which we were putting this brand new fighting vehicle through its paces was tinder-dry. Inevitably one of the meadows caught fire and was completely burnt out. Half an hour later there was an unexpected outcome of the fire. Buzzards started appearing in ones and twos wheeling over the burnt field. They perched on telegraph poles and fence posts, scanning the still-smouldering meadow for prey. Now and then one of them would drop down to capture an unlucky vole. Soon four or five Buzzards were on the ground, poking around in the smoking remains of the tussocky grass. I was amazed at how quickly they could run when chasing prey that had escaped the inferno.

An analysis of the Buzzard's diet shows that they are expert at cashing in on a wide variety of prey as it becomes available. Robin Prytherch who, for many years, has been studying the population of Buzzards in the Gordano Valley, west of Bristol, told me, "The point about Buzzards, as compared with Sparrowhawks, Peregrine Falcons or Hen Harriers, is that they are not specialized feeders – they don't worry about what they eat. They'll consume anything from earthworms to half-grown Rabbits and also like birds. Climb up to a Buzzards' nest and you'll find feathers from a whole range of species, mostly Wood Pigeons. People often say to me, why do Carrion Crows always mob Buzzards? The answer's actually very simple – Buzzards eat Carrion Crows. I remember going up to one nest and there were two big healthy chicks in it. Lying on the side of the nest were four Carrion Crow carcasses completely eaten out. Also, since time immemorial, Buzzards have eaten carrion, sharing a sheep or deer carcass with Red Kites and Ravens."

In Mesolithic times, the time when fossil records would have indicated their presence, Rabbits do not appear to have existed to feature in the Buzzard's diet. Most of Britain at this time was covered by dense forest, the Wildwood. Gradually, grazing Elk and Auroch would

have opened up sections of the forested areas, creating glades. Derek Yalden and Umberto Albarella in their book *The History of British Birds*, published in 2009, have estimated that this habitat would have been ideal for the Common Buzzard, whose population then could have been in the region of 75,000 pairs.

From this healthy estimate, what factors influenced the decline and subsequent resurgence of the Common Buzzard's population? About 4,000 BC settlers from the east occupied the Wildwood, started clearing it, planted crops and brought in domesticated animals. By 500 BC half the Wildwood had been cleared. The Normans, who invaded Britain in 1066, brought with them Rabbits, which were initially confined, to managed warrens. Buzzards came into conflict with the warreners and some were trapped and killed. Inevitably some Rabbits escaped and there was a slow but steady increase in what eventually became a wild population.

This period was the heyday of falconry and *The Boke of St Albans*, 1496, decreed that the Bastard (Buzzard) could only properly be flown by a Baron. Nevertheless, it is a good hawk for a beginner to cut their teeth on. From Norman times through until the end of the eighteenth century, Britain was largely cleared of the remnants of the Wildwood. During the sixteenth century, legislation was put in place for the destruction of vermin and church wardens were responsible for paying out the bounty on hawks' heads. Their accounts show that the Buzzard was not uniformly subjected to persecution at that time.

Roger Lovegrove, in his book *Silent Fields* published in 2007, tells us that Francis Willughby (1635–72) suggested that the Common Buzzard was widely distributed, Thomas Pennant (1726–98) described it as the commonest hawk in England and John Latham (1740–1837) identified it as 'a bird known to everyone.' In the 1760s and 1770s the first Enclosure Acts were passed. The first enclosures occurred on the heavy, clay lands of the Midlands and the second phase, for 20 years at the turn of the century, took in the lighter lands of Lincolnshire, Norfolk and Essex.

The gradual perfection of the double-barrelled shotgun, with the instantaneous discharge of the percussion cap put the ability to shoot flying birds within most people's capability. In 1785 *Phasianus colchicus torquatus*, the Ring-necked Pheasant, was introduced into Britain and is the common pheasant that is reared in great quantities today. It replaced those introduced by the Normans, who first established the Pheasant in the British countryside

Between 1760 and 1840 the number of estates dedicated to shooting more than doubled. A massive wave of tree planting followed as landowners sought to enhance the beauty of their homes and provide good shooting with woods and shelterbelts that allowed six drives a day, with Pheasants and other game birds flushed out by beaters to the waiting guns. There were generally four drives in the morning, followed by a generous lunch, and another two drives in the afternoon. Much effort went into providing a good day's sport, the emphasis being on ensuring plenty of birds that flew well to provide sporting shots.

It is estimated that in the nineteenth century 70,000 Pheasants and 120,000 Grey Partridges were sent annually down to the London markets from Suffolk and Norfolk alone. Added to those figures would be the large quantity sold to local poulterers. The importance of this revenue to the big landowners in Suffolk and Norfolk cannot be overestimated. The passing of the Game Act of 1831 legalized the role of gamekeepers and, in a moment of complete aberration, the place of birds of prey, embedded in our culture over a period of 5,000 years, was eliminated. It is no wonder that gamekeepers, whose jobs depended on a good show of birds for shooting, would come down hard on anything that prevented this from happening, whether poachers, Foxes, Carrion Crows or birds of prey.

It was against this background that in 1865 A.G. More published a paper detailing the results of a survey he had carried out, entitled 'On the distribution of Birds in Great Britain during the nesting season.' This survey was largely based on a questionnaire that More had despatched widely to his many correspondents throughout the British Isles. This is his appreciation of the Buzzard's status: 'By no means common, and nearly exterminated in the eastern and midland counties of England. Still breeds regularly in several parts of the west and north of England and in Scotland, where it has a better chance of escaping the vigilance of the gamekeeper.'

Alfred Newton, Professor of Zoology at Cambridge University, would have been aware of More's paper because he had contributed data for the counties of Suffolk and Norfolk. Kestrels, Sparrowhawks, Buzzards, the Red Kite and even owls were all being hit hard in the name of game preservation. In 1868 Newton asked the British Association for the Advancement of Science if he could present a paper on 'The Zoological Aspect of the Game Laws.' The meeting was held in Norwich and so great was the public interest that special excursion trains had to be laid on to bring devotees in from all over the country. On 26 August at 11 a.m. Alfred Newton addressed the meeting and said, "I wish to ask the game preservers of this country whether they really believe that their stock of pheasants and partridges is materially increased by the destruction of everything that the keepers are pleased to call 'vermin'. Abundance of game has little, if anything to do with the scarcity of birds of prey. In some foreign countries the existence of numerous birds of prey is a pledge for the plentifulness of game. (Hear, hear.) This being the case, I ask what object they have in the destruction of hawks." As a result of Newton's pioneering address, various acts were introduced to protect birds of prey and seabirds and at least provide them with a close season. Later, all the original acts were replaced with the Wild Birds Protection Act of 1880.

Nevertheless, persecution continued unabated. By 1915 the breeding population of the Buzzard was confined to the western edges of the British Isles: Cornwall and Devon, Wales, the Lake District, southern Scotland and the western Highlands and Inner Isles. What had once been strongholds for the Buzzard were now reduced to a few breeding pairs. Only robust protection had ensured that a few pairs survived to breed in the New Forest in Hampshire.

The First World War from 1914–18 helped restore the fortunes of the Buzzard. Gamekeepers were conscripted and persecution of birds of prey in the name of game preservation virtually ceased. The Buzzard population slowly increased and by the end of the war they had returned to many of the areas where they had once bred. Game preservation and shooting on the scale seen before the war became a thing of the past as a dramatic worldwide economic depression began in the late 1920s and continued through most of the 1930s. The Buzzard's population made a slow but sure recovery during this period and by the end of the Second World War was at its highest level for several hundred years.

It was the spread of myxomatosis in 1953 that prompted the British Trust for Ornithology to carry out a census of the Common Buzzard in 1954. Rabbits were an integral part of the Buzzard's diet and the Trust was anxious to analyse population figures before and after myxomatosis had taken effect. Norman Moore was seconded from the Nature Conservancy Council to run the survey.

About 80 observers spent the spring of 1954 checking for territories that were occupied by breeding pairs of Buzzards. The census area was just less than 6,000 square miles and the results gave an estimate of 810 breeding pairs. Although there was a great variation in breeding density, the average was 7·23 square miles for each pair of Buzzards. The area surveyed covered one-fifteenth of the total area of Great Britain so when the figures were extrapolated the total population was estimated to be approximately 12,000 pairs plus 2,000 non-breeders. The survey showed that the Buzzard was common in the west but a rare bird in eastern Britain due to the lingering effects of persecution in the name of game preservation. It also found that the Buzzard fed on a very wide spectrum of food, was very adaptable and was therefore not in conflict with other predators.

A particularly important finding from the survey, which continued until 1957, was that the spread of myxomatosis had an adverse effect on the breeding population of Buzzards. In 1955 there was a dramatic decrease in Buzzard breeding activity in areas where Rabbits had been wiped out, with some pairs not breeding at all. Breeding activity in 1956 was twice as good as in 1955 but less than in 1954. This decline, the report states, was due to food shortage and a change in man's attitude towards the Buzzard. Now that there were no Rabbits, it stood to reason that Buzzards would start taking chickens and game birds. A shotgun pointed in the right direction soon put paid to that threat.

Peter Dare, then living in south Devon, was one of the observers who contributed to the 1954 BTO survey. He went on to read zoology, botany and marine biology at Exeter University and then undertook research from 1955–8 into the diet and breeding ecology of Buzzards to assess how they were responding to the virtual extermination of Rabbits by the myxomatosis outbreak. The external examiner of his doctoral thesis was H.N. 'Mick' Southern, a senior researcher at the Bureau of Animal Population Studies at Oxford, who specialized in predator/prey relationships, notably between Tawny Owls and small mammals. He had taught Peter how to measure small mammal abundance by live-trapping, using the recently invented Longworth trap.

Peter started his original research during the autumn of 1955 and when I asked him why he chose the hill-farming district of Postbridge on Dartmoor he explained, "I went there one day when I was looking for a suitable study area. There were plenty of Buzzards about, there was a good mixture of habitats, human disturbance would be low, and everything was very viewable. Much of it was common grazing land where access was not restricted at all. I could park my Land Rover on ridges and other open places and then scan large areas to follow the activities of the Buzzards."

In 1955 Peter's study area supported 14 pairs of Buzzards, plus a wide variety of prey species, although Rabbits by now had been virtually exterminated. There was competition for what food there was from Kestrels, Tawny Owls, Foxes and Badgers. Peter added, "It was then a very good place for birds, not only Buzzards, but breeding Montagu's Harriers, Merlins, Curlews and other upland species. I started by visiting the farmers who were very helpful and interested and provided much useful information on the local wildlife. They liked Buzzards because they caught Adders.

I asked Peter how he did his watching and was told, "I had a little pocket-size telescope, times 20 magnification, the kind some deerstalkers used to use. It was very lightweight and suited me because I could wedge it against a tree, post or the window of the Land Rover. I could even take it up trees to look into nearby nests." Peter went on to explain that Buzzards are highly territorial and generally hunt over particular areas that they can rely on, doing so every day, other areas being hunted over opportunistically. He confirmed that there were three main hunting methods – 'still hunting' from a perch, from the air when hovering like a Kestrel, and what he called 'grubbing around on the ground'. I asked him how many kills he had seen and was told, "I very rarely saw them catch anything unless I spent many hours watching individual birds hunting small mammals and frogs. I only once saw one carrying a Rabbit." Peter also told me that Buzzards do eat carrion of all kinds, feeding especially on sheep carcasses and placentae when available. He added that they are also opportunistic hunters, farmers occasionally reporting sightings of Buzzards hanging about waiting for small mammals to be flushed out during silage and haymaking.

Peter analysed Buzzard pellets to investigate the prey taken on Dartmoor throughout the year. In winter Field Voles predominated, making up over 42% of the diet, with Rabbits contributing 21% and other small mammals including Moles 25%; birds and early emerging frogs and reptiles provided the remainder. In the spring and summer, Rabbits predominated, accounting for over 43% of the diet, followed by Field Voles at just under 18%, frogs at 14% and other small mammals, Moles, birds and reptiles providing the rest.

Peter told me that the Buzzard's breeding season really starts at the end of winter. The males start their noisy and spectacular displays then, soaring and then diving and calling

excitedly in the vicinity of their mates. This continues through March, by which time they will have built a nest and mated. In April the female will have lined her nest and laid her clutch of eggs. In his Dartmoor study area, 60% of the nests were in conifers and 26% in Beech trees. Most of the nests were approximately 15 metres above the ground, although some were as low as four metres, these being built in a Rowan tree and a Hawthorn. The average distance between nests was one kilometre. Most clutches, of two or three eggs, are laid during the third week of April. As incubation starts after the first egg is laid, hatching is asynchronous. This gives the eldest a big advantage if prey brought into the nest becomes scarce. If this is the case, the eldest chick will attack the smaller, younger chicks and eventually kill one or both of them. Provided food is plentiful, the chicks will be self-feeding at 28 days and fledge about three weeks later.

I asked Peter about tree climbing and he responded, "The first nest I wanted to check to see the young and what food the adults were bringing in was in a Scots Pine in a little spinney close to a farm. I asked the farmer if I could borrow a ladder, and he agreed. A friend and I stuck this great wooden ladder through the roof of the Land Rover and drove over to the tree. That was a memorable occasion, looking at my first Buzzards' nest. In it was one big chick. The nest smelt musty, there were a few feathers and pellets lying about and one dead vole. Eventually I got into a routine. There were some nests that I could watch through my telescope from a hide higher up the slope. I did not use climbing irons – they proved impractical – and instead climbed unaided. I did find three nests in trees that were especially climbable and I used to go up those four times a day and check what prey had been left for the chicks and I'd also check their development and look for pellets under the trees."

During this initial study period, Peter identified 508 prey items brought to the nests. There were 345 mammals, of which 120 were Rabbits and 134 were voles, as well as 73 birds, 15 reptiles and 60 amphibians, mostly frogs. He also emphasized that invertebrates – worms, beetles, caterpillars and leatherjackets – were often taken as part of the parent Buzzards' diet.

The food brought to the nests at Postbridge during 1955–8 was checked in territories where some Rabbits had survived and others where Rabbits were scarce or absent after being eradicated by myxomatosis. In the first category Rabbits made up 33% of the chicks' diet followed by Field Voles at 22% and birds at 14%; amphibians, other small mammals, shrews, Moles and reptiles providing the remainder. In areas where Rabbits were scarce, the prey items brought in were much more evenly represented, with Field Voles being most frequent at 21%, shrews, birds, amphibians, other small mammals and Moles contributing between 17% and 12% each, Rabbits just 4% and reptiles 3%.

Peter summarized the effect of myxomatosis on the Postbridge Buzzards between 1956–58 as follows: out of an aggregate 41 territorial or potential breeding pairs, 31 pairs bred and laid eggs. Only 22 pairs hatched their eggs successfully and of those only 15 sets of chicks survived. The total number of chicks fledged was 20 and the average number of chicks fledged per pair was 1·3.

Peter Dare subsequently followed a career as a government marine biologist on the east coast specializing in commercially exploited molluscs – cockles, mussels and scallops. In his spare time he studied the Buzzards in Suffolk but still found time to carry out follow-up studies at Postbridge in 1961–9 and 1990–3, where he found that losses of complete Buzzard broods fell from 32% after myxomatosis to only 10% in the 1960s and to zero in the 1990s. The proportion of breeding pairs that succeeded in raising young rose from 48% in the late

1950s to 84% in the 1990s. The average total number of young fledged rose by 23% as a result of more pairs rearing two chicks rather than one. In the last period two broods of three chicks were raised, the first time this had happened at Postbridge since Rabbits were wiped out by myxomatosis. Peter's report was a very thorough documentation of the Buzzards' successful adaptation to, and recovery from, the ecological disturbance caused by the disease.

I was telling Bruce Pearson all about Peter Dare's work and how important it was. He agreed but was adamant that we should also talk to Robin Prytherch. Bruce told me that he had done some illustrations for an article on Robin's work monitoring a Buzzard population in the Gordano Valley just to the west of Bristol.

Following Robin's very explicit instructions Bruce and I drove down to Bristol and on 13 May 2013 met up with Robin and settled down in a quiet corner of the local pub with pints of Otter Ale. I asked Robin how he had become involved with Buzzards and he explained, "I've always been interested in birds. I originally worked in London and then the company I worked for moved me to Bristol. It was like having the shades lifted from one's eyes. It wasn't much of a life really, travelling halfway across London to work and back again in the evening. Here, I can just drive out of Bristol and see wonderful birds at the Chew Valley lakes. I got involved with ringing and one day noticed a ridge nearby where there were Buzzards. I found a nest and that experience stimulated my interest in Buzzards. I also noticed that there seemed to be more Buzzards about than were published in the local bird report. So I suggested to the Bristol Ornithological Club that we should do a five-year study, 1980–84, just recording the presence or absence of birds in the breeding season. This should have given us an idea of how many pairs there were. It wasn't a very thorough survey as a lot of the observers were just basic birders. When I saw the grid references recurring, I noticed they were always on a road. Many of the observations weren't where the birds were but where the watchers were standing. By this time I was really interested and decided to keep an area aside and monitor it myself each year. In 1982 I settled on a 75 square kilometre patch and counted 13 pairs of Buzzards and from then on was able to relate all the increases in this defined area."

I suggested that before it was too late we should go and have a look at the area. We drove around, stopping from time to time as Robin pointed out the main features of his study area in the Gordano Valley. The hillsides were wooded, mostly deciduous but with one or two plantings of conifers, and there were rocky spurs protruding at intervals. There were also some quarries. Robin said the rocky outcrops generally marked the boundaries between Buzzard territories. It was a brilliant sunny day but there was not a Buzzard in sight. The bottom of the valley was a patchwork of hedges enclosing improved grass meadows and some arable land, and lines of poplars indicating areas of wet ground. Robin turned down a lane, stopped and pointed out into a field where there was a lone 'stag's horn' oak tree. On a branch projecting at right angles from the main trunk was a huge nest. We looked at it through our binoculars. Was it being used? Robin thought so. We moved on and at last saw a Buzzard just above the skyline. Slowly it climbed higher and was buffeted around by the strong wind. Then suddenly it dived down into one of the wooded areas; it was clearly one of the resident birds.

We drove on through very narrow lanes to see more of the Gordano Valley and as we got out of the car Robin pointed out a very pale Buzzard that had flown down and was just entering the woody hillside in front of us. He was excited, as it was not a bird he had seen before. I asked how he knew it was a new arrival and Robin pulled out a loose-leaf folder with pages and pages of Buzzard sketches and explained, "I've got this Buzzard catalogue, a kind of rogues' gallery of all the pairs in my area. I draw them in my notebook originally and then transfer them to my sketchbook. I'm always looking for the pattern of the plumage. The crescent across the chest is the common feature. The dark brown ones tend to be males and the lighter ones females. The juveniles' plumage is quite streaky until they're two years old. Then they get barring on their bellies and flanks. Individuals vary enormously. Sometimes they are very, very dark like this one that I called 'Chocolate', or very pale like this one I called 'Cream'. 'Chocolate' and 'Cream'. The great thing about these birds is that in March they have this lovely blue bloom on their feathers. They look stunning when you get the right light on them. But some of them have little idiosyncrasies like this bird here. Its wings stick out like that when it's perched. It must have had an accident and didn't last long – it couldn't cope and died in the end. And this one is a fascinating case as it went blind in one eye. His right eye was okay though and he managed to maintain his territory and even helped to rear one young. When the crows mobbed him, got all round him, he would be constantly looking left and then right as he only had one eye to check with."

I asked Robin how he approached the task of checking for pairs of breeding Buzzards and was told, "I go through the woodlands and check all the established nest sites. That one was used last year, it looks worn and not very interesting. You go on, get to another nest and see that it is all built up with a nice spiky green edge to it. And so it's a slow process of elimination. Then you want to know if the nest is being used, you want to see a bird on it. I discovered that if you can walk with the wind in your face the sound of your footsteps will have been eroded by the time it reaches the Buzzard sitting on its nest. As you approach, you should see the tail sticking out, as the Buzzard will be facing into the wind, as that's the most comfortable way for it to sit. I try never to pass under a nest or to look back. It's important to keep on walking. If you look back at the nest the Buzzard will notice the eye contact and fly off."

It is during this period in the spring, Robin told us, that Buzzards defend their territories most resolutely. If an intruder appears the incumbent Buzzard gives a warning call. If this has no effect, the Buzzard will fly up to attack the intruder. When it has gained sufficient height it stoops down, lowering its talons. This aggressive threat will generally deter the intruder but if not the attack is repeated, with the Buzzard's mate joining in as well. Once the intruder has got the message, the male Buzzard escorts it off the territory.

Robin added, "One of the interesting facts I discovered during the breeding season was that in some territories there appeared to be a third bird, although this isn't necessarily bigamy. In one case there was a male and two females; the females each had their own territory and the male was providing for both of them. They each reared one chick. I've come across another case where there was a third bird in the territory. I eventually worked out that it was one of their chicks from the previous year. It stayed around and in its third year it was actually visiting the nest, helping to feed the chicks, I called her 'Nan'. That year they were able to fledge three young because of the helping hand from that third bird. 'Buff', the female, was boss in the territory. She would tolerate another female, but if it had been a male it would have been sent packing. I did wonder if the young female, the helper, had laid one of the eggs because I did see the male, 'Rufous', copulating with her, copulating with his daughter. The next year, the dominant female died and the daughter took her place. Father and daughter lived together for five years and reared four young."

Robin's long-term study of the Buzzards in the Gordano Valley, in which territorial pairs were counted, has continued from 1982 to the present day. There were 13 pairs in 1982. This is an extract from his field notes: '12/4/82. 13.45. Watching Tyntesfield territory. One Buzzard is circling with prey … it rises high then glides/stoops towards nest (in a Larch). It briefly "display flaps" (possibly directed to another Buzzard nearer to me), then continued to glide/stoop to the nest area where it settled at the top of a tall Larch where its mate was perched and receives a food pass.'

Within ten years the population had doubled to 26 pairs. It took only four years to double again to 52 pairs. As Robin put it, it was almost as though the Buzzards couldn't produce enough young to fill up the space. But as the density of the pairs of Buzzards increased, so their productivity decreased. In 2013 there were 106 pairs. Another extract from Robin's field notes reads: '27/5/13. 14.45. Norton's Wood. Territory – new. Extraordinary situation! I have been watching this area in which a beautiful male, with white underparts, has settled, and quite suddenly there is a second, similarly plumaged, bird – a female. Fortunately for me, the male is missing central tail feathers, otherwise – apart from 'jizz' – it would be difficult to separate the two. This is the 106th pair this year, one more than last year.'

I asked Robin if he could give me a reason for this dramatic increase in the Buzzard population and he replied, "This surge in the population must have had its origins in the 1970s. The catalyst could have been the reinforcement in the law 15 years earlier (the Protection of Birds Acts 1954 to 1967, later incorporated into the Wildlife and Countryside Act 1981). Buzzards that avoided persecution were living 25 years, giving the possibility of breeding for over 20 seasons. The other reason was that hitherto the Buzzard had been restricted to the upland areas in Devon and Cornwall, Wales, the Lake District and the western regions of Scotland. These areas were biologically not as good prey-wise for predators as the lowlands. So when the Buzzards spread out from their original strongholds they found there was much more food for them to prey on. As a result they were laying larger clutches of eggs and fledging more youngsters. That, to me, has been the root cause of the Buzzards' expansion."

The flow of Buzzards eastwards across the country resulted in them breeding again in Norfolk in 1992, and by 2001 at least ten pairs were confirmed as breeding. Most of the nests were in the northern half of the county. In 2006 a pair of Buzzards chanced on good updrafts produced by a ridge running south-east to north-west inland south of Cromer, an area that had always been a constant attraction to wandering birds of prey. The pair stayed and searched for a suitable tree in which to nest and were attracted to a group of Scots Pines on the edge of a wood. The following is an extract from my journal in 2012:

'2/4/12. To Templewood, the home of Eddie and Tina Anderson. Eddie takes us for a walk through his wood. Parts of the wood are old; others 50 years old and there are interesting plantings of ornamental trees. We were anxious to see the Scots Pines at the top of the wood where Buzzards had nested since 2006. We turn uphill and Eddie tells us about the three-legged fox, a vixen, which raised cubs very close to where we are. Studying her through a telescope he could see that the stump was clean and beautifully healed. Was it a road casualty that had been taken to a vet and then released, I wondered? We arrive at the top of the slope at the far end of the wood. Here are the magnificent Scots Pines that the Buzzards had favoured since their arrival. Eddie points out the different nests at the top of the Scots Pines that the Buzzards had built. Good solid constructions. As if on cue, the Buzzards appeared circling overhead. Eddie had named the female 'Bianca' because she's pale and the male, which is dark, 'Mr Brown'. He's a textbook Buzzard. We leave the Buzzards and walk downhill, past the pond through the plantings of ornamental trees and back towards the house. Back in front of the house we stumble onto a Buzzard fest. Buzzards appear from all points of the compass. Some are flying north up the coast; others are pairs that are displaying, the males and females soaring round each other. Now and then a male would break off soaring to dive at his mate. Using the impetus of his dive, he quickly regains his station soaring above his mate and repeats the dive again and again, showing off like mad. It was a quite brilliant display.'

Quite out of the blue, in 2012, Defra revealed an astonishing plan to research various options to reduce predation of gamebirds by Buzzards including destroying Buzzards' nests and removing Buzzards from shooting estates and keeping them in captivity. It would cost £400,000. The public had a field day venting their fury on Defra. The arguments against the scheme were ferocious and had teeth. Pheasants are not a native bird, an estimated 40 million of them being released into the British countryside at the end of every summer, and they damage the ground flora of our woods. Motorists kill many more Pheasants than Buzzards do and more pheasants are shot than can be eaten, the surplus being left to rot or bulldozed into mass graves.

In the end Defra held up their hands and surrendered. What I could not understand was why they had not adopted the raptor biologist, Robert Kenward's practical advice set out in a paper he published in 2001, 'Factors affecting predation by buzzards (*Buteo buteo*) on released pheasants (*Phasianus colchicus*)': 'Shoots do not generally expect to harvest more than 50% of released Pheasants, although some estates do recover up to 70%. The estimated loss to Buzzards of 4·3% was therefore a small proportion of total losses. The number of Pheasants available for shooting would have been reduced appreciably at only a minority of pens. Our results suggest that the occasional heavy losses might be avoided by encouraging shrubs rather than ground cover in pens, by siting pens where there are few perches for Buzzards, and perhaps also by high-density releases.'

Robin Prytherch told me that the keepers in his study area took pre-emptive action to avoid the loss of Pheasant chicks: "If a keeper knew of Buzzards nesting near his rearing pens he would actually provide them with food. A couple of Wood Pigeons put on the ground near the nest would do the trick. That would be enough. Buzzards are not going to work hard unless they have to. They'll come down to food on the ground. That solved the problem instantly."

Unfortunately, not all gamekeepers are so like-minded. For example, an RSPB secret surveillance film recorded in 2013 showed a gamekeeper beating to death two Buzzards, which he had caught in an old-fashioned crow trap. The evidence collected did however, lead to a successful prosecution.

On 23rd May 2013 a headline in the Guardian read: 'Government licensed secret buzzard egg destruction, documents reveal.' An RSPB request under the Freedom of Information Act 2000 had revealed that Natural England, the Government's statutory conservation adviser for England, had issued licences for the destruction of four Buzzards' nests and their eggs. The two licences issued were for separate areas and ran from 23rd April to 8th May 2013.

Martin Harper, the RSPB's Director of Conservation, speaking on behalf of the UK Raptor Working Group, said, "We were proceeding collaboratively and that is why we are so angry now. Most people would prefer to see Buzzards soaring in the sky. They are big, majestic creatures in the wild; they are England's eagle."

Jeff Knott, a Species Policy Officer at the RSPB, asked, "The Buzzard has full legal protection, so why are we undermining this when all the available evidence shows they are not a significant source of loss of Pheasant chicks?"

Nigel Middleton, the Hawk and Owl Trusts Conservation Officer for East Anglia, added, "This is a step backwards. We're in the 21st century and shooting estates must look hard at their management practices to ensure there is no negative effect on native biodiversity. They must move on from a Victorian mentality and find ways of managing their sport that does not require the destruction of birds of prey."

On 27th May 2013, Robin Prytherch posted this blog: 'One way to put Buzzards into context is to compare their weight, or biomass, with other animals – say, people or cows. In my study area I now have 106 pairs of Buzzards in 75 square kilometres; they are at maximum density. Their total weight, allowing for an average number of young birds and immatures, would come to about 350 kg. This is equivalent to about six humans or two-thirds of a cow and there are 100s if not 1,000s of those! Or 290 full-grown Pheasants! Buzzards do not normally kill full-grown Pheasants because the Pheasants are too heavy. They may kill young Pheasants (poults) if the rearing pens are not properly managed, but competent gamekeepers have ways of alleviating problems when they happen. Now, here comes the real shock – as many as 40 million Pheasants are released in the UK annually, which equates to 41,000 tonnes (16 times greater than the biomass of any other bird species in the UK) – that is a lot of biomass and it must have a colossal impact on the local environment. Within a few months getting on for half of the released Pheasants will have died, many killed on the roads, but most die simply because at such high densities they cannot all survive despite the hard work of all the keepers who provide food for them. Many of the rest are shot. It is the birds that have died that the Buzzards go for, as they are efficient scavengers. Buzzards do kill some birds, but mostly pigeons and crows (including Magpies), which should please most gamekeepers. So, are there too many Buzzards, or too many Pheasants? Not enough Buzzards, I'd say and definitely too many Pheasants.'

Why has the destruction of four Buzzard nests and their eggs caused such uproar? Licences are issued almost routinely for the destruction of Greater Black-backed Gulls, Brent Geese and Cormorants, which all have smaller populations than the Buzzard. There are plenty of Buzzards so does it really matter if four nests and their eggs are destroyed? What is so special about birds of prey?

Birds of prey are a very important part of our culture. The Golden Eagle, for instance, is a symbol of power. This symbol has been passed on, civilization by civilization, to the present. For centuries, falconry, the use of trained birds of prey, principally Peregrine Falcons and Goshawks, was one of the main ways of putting food on the table. Then, the link between man and bird was a palpable one. The advent of the shotgun and the 1831 Game Act put paid to that and ushered in an era of unprecedented persecution, which still continues to this day despite all British breeding birds of prey being protected by law. But worse was to come. The introduction of organochlorine pesticides after the Second World War decimated the populations of many birds of prey. Once the link between bird of prey deaths and pigeons feeding on winter-sown cereals was discovered the pesticides were banned. Birds of prey were now heralded as prime indicator species – species that were at the top of the food chain and showed us humans what was wrong before it affected us. How dare we think of destroying Buzzards or any of our fabulous birds of prey that are so embedded in our culture?

It was Nigel Middleton from the Hawk and Owl Trust who first told me that there was a pair of Buzzards nesting on the Sculthorpe Moor Nature Reserve in Norfolk. This is the account of Phil Littler, a licensed ringer and volunteer, on discovering the nest: "Sometime in the middle of June I saw a Buzzard fly off from high in a poplar tree. The tree was covered in Ivy but I saw what I thought was a nest in the crutch of the tree. Later in the month I had another look. Again I saw the Buzzard slip away so I presumed it was nesting. I asked Alex Laver, a local tree surgeon and climber, if he could help. On July 7th myself, Alex and John Middleton, group secretary to the North-West Norfolk Ringing Group, met at the reserve and went to the nest site. It was a fine sunny day. Alex climbed an adjacent tree and nimbly crossed to the tree that held the nest. He confirmed that there were three young Buzzards and these were lowered in turn in an old pillowcase to be ringed. The ringing took an average of five minutes a bird and that included the time taken to lower it from and raise it back to the nest. Each bird was fitted with a 'G' ring, the recognized ring size for the species, and placed back in the nest. No further visits were made to the nest site and all three young fledged successfully."

After our visit to the Gordano Valley in May 2013 I mentioned to Bruce that I still had not found any Closed Circuit Television (CCTV) footage of a Buzzards' nest. Robin had told us that Mike Potts, a cameraman with whom we had both worked, had once filmed a Buzzards' nest but could not remember for what programme it had been shot. I said I would try the RSPB to see if they could help. Brian Reed, who is in charge of CCTV operations at the RSPB, thought there might have been footage shot in 2012 up in Scotland and sure enough, two days later, I received two DVDs in the post. RSPB were using a state-of-the-art system that was beyond me and my very old computer. Brian very kindly, and with great patience, talked me through the process of bringing the DVDs to life and I made the following notes:

'5/5/12. The Buzzards' nest is in the crotch of an oak tree, which stands on the edge of a forest. Beyond there's rough grazing with rushes dotted about. No leaves on the oak tree yet. The female Buzzard is incubating, turned slightly away from camera. She gets up, turns the eggs. The male flies in for a moment and pauses. The female gets up and I can see that they both have text book plumage. The male flies off and the female settles down again. I notice that the female has a wing tag, A9. Later I talk to David Anderson, the Forestry Commission's conservation manager, who tells me that they've been wing tagging for eight years and have now tagged over 700 Buzzard chicks. They change the colour of the tag on the left wing each year.'

'29/5/12. The oak tree is in leaf. Male and female are both at the nest as the female feeds a two or three-day-old chick. She rips off small gobbets of meat from the kill and offers them ever so gently to the chick. It feeds well.'

'6/6/12. I can see the chick in the nest struggling about. Female flies in with a spray of oak leaves and settles down to brood. She weaves the oak spray into the edge of nest. She struggles, but eventually weaves it in to her satisfaction. She's clearly a perfectionist.'

'13/6/12. Today there are cattle grazing in the field on the edge of the forest. The female is feeding the chick that now must be over 15 days old. The female tears off bigger chunks of meat from what looks like a rabbit carcass.'

'20/6/12. Male leaves the nest as the female feeds the chick on which feathers are just beginning to show. Chick has a good feed. Female is anxious, flies off to investigate.'

'7/7/12. It is raining. The young Buzzard is now fully feathered and soaking wet as it stands on the edge of the nest looking out into the field below. Beside it is the female Buzzard who is gently pecking around her offspring's beak, a 'wash and brush up' operation. It is raining.'

Robin rang me at the end of that same summer to tell me that the Buzzards' nest in the isolated 'stag's horn' oak in his study area had failed. There was a full clutch of eggs. The female had incubated them almost to the point of hatching and then there was a lot of rain. The nest became waterlogged and she deserted.

An account of Robin Prytherch's work on Buzzards in the Gordano Valley appeared in the *British Birds* journal in 2013. In an introduction to the piece Roger Riddington, the editor, wrote 'Robin is an amateur, and won't mind me labelling him as one.' Thank goodness for that, I thought. Robin is continuing a tradition of amateur naturalists that started with the Reverend Gilbert White of Selborne. Robin would have enjoyed a discussion with White as he called the Buzzard 'a dastardly bird, and beaten not only by the raven, but even by the carrion crow.'

This is Robin's summing up at the end of a day watching Buzzards. It was published by *British Birds* in a compilation called *Best Days with British Birds*: 'I reluctantly closed my notebook. I had to leave – it was ten past six and I was already late for some human social activities. So, in about seven hours of almost continuous watching, I'd seen at least 20 individual Buzzards over seven territories, in four of which I had gained significant extra information. It had been an exciting and rewarding day and one that I will long remember out of many happy Buzzard-watching days.'

THE GOLDEN EAGLE

British Isles population (2003): 440 pairs (stable)

The first time I saw a Golden Eagle I was climbing in the Hochschwab range of limestone mountains in the Austrian Northern Alps. It was a 300 metre high cliff and, slowly but surely, our group made good progress. Towards the end of the climb, Kurt, our guide, who obviously had great faith in me, told me to lead on the next pitch. The last part of the pitch meant traversing right around a huge slab of overhanging limestone. There was a 200 metre drop below and, although there were hand-holds, to keep moving I had to lean out over the void to give my boots purchase on the rock so that I could move sideways like a crab. I scrabbled feverishly for hand-holds and footholds, sweating and swearing. I did not dare look down. I was terrified. Then, out of nowhere, a Wallcreeper, a small crimson-and-grey bird, appeared to my right, scuttling up the slab ahead of me. Calm now, I inched round the rest of the slab and a moment later was standing at the end of the pitch.

I breathed a sigh of relief and started hammering in a piton for the next belay point. As I did so I heard a noise like tearing linen. I looked up and stooping towards me was a Golden Eagle, wings folded in a vertical dive. I froze, mesmerized by the huge shape hurtling in my direction. I felt the rush of air as it passed, missing me by a yard and watched it pull out of its dive and disappear over a ridge on the rock face far to my left. When Kurt joined me, he laughed, pointed at the site of the eagles' nest on the rock face, 200 metres away, and said, "Don't worry, David, he wasn't trying to kill you. He was just giving you a warning – keep out!" This was my first Golden Eagle and it's still the closest view I've ever had of one – perhaps a bit too close for comfort! That was in 1950 when I was doing my National Service in Austria.

Ten years later, Roy Dennis, world authority on Golden Eagles and Ospreys, wrote in his diary '27 April 1960. Cairngorms. My very first sighting of a Golden Eagle! I hiked up through the forest and crossed the top of the corrie to look down to Stac na h-Iolaire, a small mountain. Found a Golden Eagle brooding on her nest high in the rock face. Only her very golden head and huge bill were showing over the edge of the big bulky heap of sticks. She slowly lifted herself off the eggs and left the nest, lumbering away on her huge wings towards the south. Dark brown plumage, with golden mantle, head and tops of her shoulders. Long, heavy wings with upturned primaries. Bright yellow legs. I left quickly so she could return to the eggs.'

In writing this chapter I have used four main sources: Roy Dennis's *Golden Eagles* (1996), Seton Gordon's *Days with the Golden Eagle* (1927), Leslie Brown and Dean Amadon's *Eagles, Hawks and Falcons of the World* (1968), and Jeff Watson's *The Golden Eagle* (2010).

The Golden Eagle's scientific name is *Aquila chrysaetos*. *Aquila*, its generic name, means eagle in Latin and *chrysaetos*, its specific name, translates from the Greek *khrusos*, meaning gold and *aetos*, meaning eagle. In 1735 Linnaeus originally classified the Golden Eagle in his *Systema Naturae* as belonging to the falcon family, *Falco chrysaetos*. It was later reclassified to the family Accipitridae, which as well as eagles, includes buzzards, hawks, kites, harriers and Old World vultures. This family was subdivided and the Golden Eagle assigned to the genus *Aquila*.

In their book, Leslie Brown and Dean Amadon suggest that it is reasonable to believe that birds of prey evolved from the less predatory types of bird and that kites might be the most primitive members of the family. They also thought that the Accipitridae evolved along two separate lines from the kite family. One direction produced the Brahminy kites and from them were derived the Old World vultures, the vulturine sea-eagles and the sea-eagles. In another direction came the snake-eagles, harriers and harrier-hawks, leading to the goshawks and chanting-goshawks. In turn, the harpy eagles, secretary birds, buzzards and booted eagles evolved from them.

The Golden Eagle is a bird that most people will have heard of. It is the head and shoulders of the adult bird that are so striking. The big, blue-black bill, the yellow cere and the deep-set, piercing, hazel eyes, and the golden feathers crowning its head and cascading down its neck all provide a regal image of power and grandeur. The whole of the back is dark brown. The carpal region and wing coverts bleach as the bird gets older and the tail is grey with a dark band at the tip. The thighs and legs are covered by a thick layer of lighter brown plumes, which extend to brush the massive yellow toes and black talons. The juvenile does not have the golden head and neck of the adult and its eyes are brown, the key identifying feature being the white tail with a dark tip. The full adult plumage is acquired over three to four years during which time there is a gradual reduction of the white areas at the base of the flight feathers and on the tail.

For a description of a Golden Eagle in flight I cannot find anything better than this passage in the late Jeff Watson's book *The Golden Eagle*: 'Golden Eagles are most often seen in flight. When soaring they use thermals or up-draughts to gain height and often spend long periods in the air without any movement of their wings. Viewed head-on in soaring flight, the wings are held in a shallow 'V' and, when seen close to, the upturned "splayed fingers" of the outermost primaries are sometimes visible. Seen from below, the shape of the Golden Eagle is distinctive. The tail and head are proportionately longer than either the Buzzard or the White-tailed Eagle. The wings look broad and long but are not parallel-sided. The trailing edge of the wing usually has a slight 'S'-shaped curve caused by the shorter inner primary feathers. This is in marked contrast to the very deep, parallel-edged wings of the White-tailed Eagle, giving that species the apt description of the flying door.'

I have been lucky to have seen Golden Eagles many times in Scotland: while working on a BBC film about Gavin Maxwell, the author of *The Ring of Bright Water*, on the Isle of Skye; with Roy Dennis when we were searching for a Peregrine Falcon's eyrie; and most recently on Mull with my friends Eddie and Tina Anderson. My journal from that visit reads:

'8/6/12. Mull. We drive to the eagle-viewing site that Dave Sexton, the RSPB's Mull officer, had suggested. A mass of people watching. A Golden Eagle had just killed a hare and was struggling to get it up to the eyrie – it was well short of it. A photographer kindly showed it to me through his long lens after I'd struggled to find it with my bins. Eddie eventually had to draw me a sketch map so that I could pinpoint it. Eventually found it. Now and then it flapped its wings – too heavy for it to carry off! Just before catching the ferry we decided to have one last look for Golden Eagles on the east side of Ben Mor. Drove through forestry alongside the river Lussa and out into the open. Found a good spot on the old road and parked. Great view looking up to Ben Mor. After a short wait, I spotted a Golden Eagle soaring along the crest. It had much more swept-back wings than the White-tailed Eagles we'd seen earlier. Eddie was also following one through his bins. It turned out to be my

bird's mate. They eventually dropped down out of sight before re-appearing for a moment as they soared round behind Ben Mor.'

My brother, Richard, remembers watching Golden Eagles in the Cairngorms and being amazed at the height to which they soared. He was on a Territorial Army mountain warfare course and his group had walked from Rothiemurchus, where they were based, to the west end of Loch Avon. They stopped by the 'shelter stone', a well-known landmark the size of a house. The wind was blowing down the loch and had created an effective up-draught, which about half a dozen raptors were enjoying. There were four Buzzards but above them, much larger, were a pair of Golden Eagles. Richard watched them through his army-issue Barr and Stroud 6 × 30 binoculars soar up and up, until they were out of sight.

Golden Eagles catch Rabbits and Mountain Hares. In his *New Naturalist* book, *British Birds of Prey*, Leslie Brown suggests that a human might be able to see one of these animals moving at 600 or 700 metres. A Golden Eagle, with a visual acuity four to eight times that of a human, should therefore be able to see a moving hare anywhere in a whole glen 500 metres or so below. Soaring at height, the Golden Eagle has two methods of hunting: either a glide into the attack or a vertical stoop with wings closed. They are also adept at using the contours of the land to mount a surprise attack on a pack of Red Grouse or Ptarmigan. Golden Eagles may also tail-chase prey such as Mountain Hares or Rabbits if they are flushed in front of them.

Seton Gordon gives a very comprehensive list of prey items in his book, which does, of course, feature Mountain Hares, Rabbits, Red Grouse and Ptarmigan. There are, however, some unusual items that he found in the eyries he visited – domestic cat, small collie dog, Heron, Salmon and Pike. Jeff Watson's interest in the Golden Eagle's diet was prompted by a visit to an eyrie in 1982, after which he wrote, 'The nest was a midden, with carcasses of grouse and Rabbit interspersed with a couple of dozen other items, almost every one of them something different. There was the skin of an Adder, wing feathers of a Kestrel, a Merlin and a Peregrine, spines of a Hedgehog, a Meadow Pipit, a Herring Gull, the foot of a Raven, and a complete nestling Hooded Crow.' In his book, Jeff divided Scotland into nine main regions when researching prey species. He found that in the Outer Hebrides and on Skye the Golden Eagles' favoured prey species were Rabbits, sheep and Fulmars, whereas on Mull, hares and sheep featured strongly. In the north, north-west and west-central Highlands, Golden Eagles depended on deer, Mountain Hares, Rabbits and grouse; in the south-west Highlands, Rabbits, sheep and grouse were the main items of their diet; and in the east Highlands Mountain Hares and grouse were the main prey. Finally, in south-west Scotland, Golden Eagles mainly caught Rabbits and Mountain Hares but also relied on grouse and a variety of other bird species.

Every Mountain Hare's nightmare must be to look over its shoulder and see a Golden Eagle bearing down on it. Todd Katzner, an American raptor biologist, in Jeff Watson's book, *The Golden Eagle*, explains why: 'The feet of a Golden Eagle are remarkable. Large and powerful, they tell a story of power and finesse, blended together to form the weapons of one of Nature's most perfect predators. They inspire in me respect and awe.'

The eagle's awe-inspiring fierceness, its mastery of the air, its acuity of vision, are all physical virtues to which we would aspire. No wonder it is so deeply embedded as a symbol in human culture. In 3,000 BC the Sumerians worshipped an eagle God. This was passed on to the Hittites who used a double-headed eagle as a totem so that they would never be surprised. It has been a strong emblem for successive European empires, the Greeks and the Romans. Caius Marius in his second consulship ordained that the Roman legions should carry an *Aquila*, an eagle standard. It was highly revered and was a rallying point in battle. In the Battle of Teutoberg Forest three Roman legions commanded by Varus were ambushed by an alliance of Germanic tribes led by Arminius, a traitor. The Roman legions were totally destroyed and the three *Aquilae* captured. Upon hearing of this ignominious defeat, the Emperor Augustus was so shaken that he banged his head against the wall "Quinctilius Varus, give me back my legions." Seven years later the Emperor's nephew, Germanicus, led the Romans' massive retaliation against the Germanic tribes. He inflicted huge casualties on them and devastated their land. He retrieved two of the three legions' *Aquilae*. The third *Aquila* was eventually recovered 15 years later. At last honour was satisfied. The strong symbolism of the eagle emblem was adopted by the ruling families throughout Europe. The Russians took it up and it began to acquire a sinister gloss when it was adopted by Napoleon and by Hitler's Third Reich. The Bald Eagle is, of course, the emblem of the United States of America.

Those same physical virtues that made the eagle a symbol in many cultures also meant that falconers aspired to train them. In 1486 Dame Juliana Berners is believed to have compiled *The Boke of St Albans*, which listed the different birds of prey and the appropriate persons of rank designated as fit to fly them. An eagle was assigned to an emperor. I do not think this should be taken too seriously, though: Golden Eagles are notoriously difficult to train for flying at quarry, they are very heavy to carry and the only falconers regularly using them for killing prey today are the eagle-hunters in Kazakhstan and Mongolia. They fly their Golden Eagles from horse-back. The eagles are kept hooded until prey is sighted and then cast off; they can catch Foxes, Marmots or sometimes even Wolves.

Even in the fifteenth century, when falconry flourished, the Golden Eagle would have been absent from lowland England and been confined to the mountainous areas of the Lake District and Wales. A few pairs hung on in the Lake District until the beginning of the nineteenth century but Scotland has remained its stronghold. Although the Golden Eagle's persecution was ordered by James II as early as 1457, the expansion of sheep farming from the middle of the eighteenth century onwards resulted in it quickly being targeted as a sheep-killer, with any shepherd who felt his sheep were threatened taking action.

By the beginning of the nineteenth century the Golden Eagle's population was on an ever-increasing downwards spiral, accelerated by the advent of grouse shooting. The Marquis of Bute in 1808 insisted that his gamekeepers swear an oath to 'use their best endeavours to destroy all Birds of Prey, *etc.* with their nests. So help me God.' The Golden Eagle was tolerated in deer forests because its presence in the sky prevented grouse from flying up in alarm and alerting a stag, being stalked, of impending danger. Because the Golden Eagle also fed on carrion it was easy to poison, a much easier method than shooting as several eagles could be dispatched at one carcass.

As the Golden Eagle became increasingly rare through persecution it became the focus of attention for egg-collectors and taxidermists and orders would be placed for clutches of eggs and skins. Every grand stairway in the big country houses of the time would be lined with cases of stuffed birds, sometimes also featuring a clutch of eggs or young.

At our family home at Boynton in East Yorkshire there was just such a display of stuffed birds. My grandfather, leading me upstairs, would pause by the glass case containing a lone Golden Eagle and tell me the story of how it came to be there. One day in spring towards the end of the nineteenth century a Golden Eagle appeared at Boynton and the local farmers demanded that it be shot. For days the keeper stalked it, but every time it came within range it flapped off unhurriedly. In desperation, the keeper lay out on the hillside as though dead, his gun hidden alongside his leg. Nothing happened on the first day but on the second day, just as it was getting light, the keeper heard the rattle of the eagle's pinions as it flew in to investigate. He jumped up and shot it. When the contents of Boynton were sold in November 1950 there it was, lot 1041, in a glass case, the Golden Eagle shot at Boynton.

The persecution of Golden Eagles during this time was a theme that the great wildlife artist Joseph Wolf explored. In 1874, fully aware that it might upset his patrons, he exhibited a painting entitled *Broken Fetters* at the Institute of Painters in Watercolours. It shows a Golden Eagle escaping and flying away to snow-capped mountains in the background, with a section of chain dangling from its leg. Another picture by Wolf in charcoal showed the melancholy sequel to this event. The eagle has reached his old haunts and has perched in a favourite tree. He spreads his wings again but the chain wraps around a branch and, after a brief struggle, he hangs head downwards, swaying in the wind.

Joseph Wolf was born in 1820 at Moerz, near Coblenz, in Germany. As a young boy he was interested in natural history and was soon drawing the animals that abounded in the countryside around his home. Above all, he was fascinated by birds of prey. Wolf's big break came when he was asked to produce some life-size illustrations of falcons for Schlegel and Wulverhorst's *La Traite de Fauconnerie*. These came to the attention of the Zoological Society in London and he was subsequently commissioned to illustrate their scientific papers and sketch the rare and exotic animals arriving from around the world. Now Wolf had access to bird skins, and his notebooks became crammed with detailed measurements of the spread of wings from above, foot, tail, *etc*. He was the first artist accurately to portray the feather tracts, for example the correct number of primaries, secondaries, tertials, scapulars and coverts on the upper side of a bird's wing.

Wolf did not want to be labelled as a mere scientific illustrator. Perhaps influenced by the Romantic Movement, which stressed the emotions evoked in confronting untamed Nature, he wanted to show that he was capable of producing dramatic pictures with a story to tell. In 1849 he entered a small painting, *Woodcocks Seeking Shelter*, for the Royal Academy exhibition. It was about to be rejected but the eminent Victorian artist Sir Edwin Landseer overruled the hanging committee's objections and it was accepted. An avalanche of commissions followed, but of far greater importance were invitations to sketch the wildlife on the estates of the Duke of Westminster and the Duke of Argyll in Scotland. The solitude, the wild snow-covered mountain scenery, Golden Eagles hunting Ptarmigan and Ospreys fishing the lochs below inspired a new approach that was to influence his future work.

Perhaps Wolf's greatest contribution to bird portraiture was his appreciation of feathers. As he once wrote, 'People have no idea of the difference in feathers. The feather of an owl is a ghost – you can hear nothing. But when an eagle folds up its wings, they rattle like cardboard.' How will Wolf be remembered? Will it be for his immaculate illustrations for Gould's *The Birds of Great Britain* or for a sketch of a Golden Eagle about to take off from a mountain crag, dramatic and romantic? If you look at his artwork, you can almost hear those feathers rattling.

You can certainly hear the rattle of pinions in Tennyson's poem *The Eagle*:

> *He clasps the crag with crooked hands;*
> *Close to the sun in lonely lands,*
> *Ring'd with the azure world, he stands.*
> *The wrinkled sea beneath him crawls;*
> *He watches from his mountain walls,*
> *And like a thunderbolt he falls.*

The Golden Eagle escaped the fate of the White-tailed Eagle, which became extinct in Britain in 1916, for several reasons. It retreated to the fastness of the Scottish Highlands, it was tolerated in the deer forests and, if put off its nest, did not circle round endlessly like the White-tailed Eagle – it made itself scarce.

By the time that the White-tailed Eagle was extinct, Seton Gordon (1886–1977) had already written three books. He was born in Aberdeen and had ready access to the nearby Cairngorm mountains. He went to Oxford University, took up photography and started writing natural history books. It was not until 1927 that he wrote *Days with the Golden Eagle*, in collaboration with his wife Audrey. It was a brave book to write as the Victorian ethos that every bird with a hooked bill should be destroyed still lingered on in the Highlands at that time. The population then was probably less than 150 pairs. His photographs and his prose describing the private life of the Golden Eagle stirred the hearts of the uninformed, making them realize it was better to shoot with a camera than with a shotgun.

Seton and Audrey Gordon set out on a mild April day in 1926 to recce the eagles' nest they were keen to watch, and wrote, 'All at once, high in the blue vault of heaven, I saw the form of a Golden Eagle sailing serenely above the forest. From the fringe of the woodlands a few grouse rose terrified at her approach and scattered wildly. She heeded them not, but as she half-turned in her flight the sun fell upon the golden plumage of her neck and she became a veritable eagle of burnished gold.' They reached a spot on the hillside where they could look down on the nest. It was massive, and had possibly been in use for 50 years or more, and contained two eggs. Seton and Audrey made a pile of fir branches and heather where their hide would be.

On 10 May, having allowed time for the eggs to hatch, they set up a hide overlooking the nest and carefully camouflaged it with the fir branches and heather left there earlier. There were two eaglets. Five days later, hoping that the eagles had become accustomed to the hide, Seton took the first watch. They had already settled on a procedure to hoodwink the parent birds. Seton and Audrey would walk together to the hide, Seton would quickly slip inside and Audrey would retire out of sight, the birds tricked into believing that the coast was clear. Through a tiny peephole in the canvas hide Seton was able watch the activity on the nest and recorded his observations: 'On this day the weariness of sitting for six hours in a cramped position, looking through a small hole with one eye, was lessened by the life-and-death battle between the two eaglets. The larger of the two tormented her smaller brother, pecking him without mercy and several times driving him almost to the edge of the eyrie. There, just as he seemed about to fall, she caught him with her bill and swung him back into the centre of the eyrie. The fate of the weaker eaglet indeed hung in the balance at this time, and since the young hen seemed bent on killing her brother we named her Cain and her brother Abel.'

After this first watch they decided to give the eagles five days' rest and on 20 May Seton entered the hide again. Much to his relief, Abel was still alive: 'It became very dark, and a thunderstorm appeared to be approaching. But after a few drops of rain the clouds drifted over, and as the air became less oppressive the eaglets roused themselves and stood up in the eyrie to preen their down.' A little later Seton had his first close-up view of the female Golden Eagle: 'There was a sudden rush and she alighted at the edge of the eyrie, eyed the camera lens (which projected a fraction of an inch beyond the front of the hide) for a moment, then, her suspicions allayed, picked up a large fir branch and re-arranged it carefully. She then proceeded to feed each chick in turn on the hare. She gave them small pieces of flesh and with great relish swallowed large pieces of bone herself.'

Six days later Seton and Audrey were once again watching the eyrie and wrote: 'The eaglets were now about 26 days old and Cain was already growing the wing and tail feathers, which looked like a black edging to her wing and tail stumps. Abel was also growing finely, and a recent heavy meal had swelled his crop. For an hour-and-a-half the eaglets were quiet, then Cain rose and stood menacingly over Abel, who sullenly awaited the attack. But the bully now appeared to treat her brother with more respect, and on this occasion aimed no blows at him.'

Seton took over from his wife at 1 o'clock on 29 May during a violent squall: 'At twenty minutes past one, at the beginning of a squall, the hen eagle arrived. For the duration of the squall the mother brooded the eaglets, then commenced to feed them, and continued to do so for three-quarters of an hour. I was glad to see that this time she fed Abel first, although Cain as usual attempted to keep her small brother in the background. The eaglets' meal on this occasion consisted of a course of grouse followed by hare – a meal fit for a king! After a really good meal Abel was in excellent form and when a little later on Cain attempted to bully him by pecking at him Abel, to my astonishment, actually retaliated, and to such purpose that Cain was forced to run to the far side of the nest!'

It was 19 June before Seton and Audrey were able to watch the eyrie again: 'Cain by now was well feathered all over; Abel's head was still white, and much down remained upon his body. The eaglets were now about seven weeks old. At a quarter to one the cock eagle arrived with a grouse. He looked a superb figure as he stood, very erect, on the edge of the eyrie, the mid-summer sun shining full upon his light brown plumage. The eaglets were now able to tear up the prey for themselves. Abel had developed wonderfully during the 15 days we had been absent from the eyrie. No longer did he live in terror of Cain; they pecked at each other's bills amicably and never from that day forward did we see them fight, nor Cain attack her brother.'

On 26 June Seton was on watch: 'Cain was engaged in hopping round and round the eyrie, flapping her wings as she did so; these were the first of the wing exercises we were to see so much of in later days. At 4.15 p.m. I saw what at first I took to be an insect against the sky. But in a second the supposed insect was seen to be the cock eagle, who swooped down from the hills at a truly incredible speed. In one foot he held a cock Ptarmigan, unplucked. His meteoric arrival was the most wonderful thing I have seen in the bird world.'

A visit to the Hebrides kept Seton and Audrey away from the hide for a week and the eyrie was now swarming with flies: 'The cock several times brought prey to the eyrie and I could see the fierce flash of his eye as he scanned the glen below. On one visit he had scarcely laid a grouse on the eyrie when Cain seized it in her talons and half-flew with it across the eyrie. Abel flapped his wings excitedly, and I felt sure the eaglets might any day now take their first flight from the home that had given them shelter for close on ten weeks.'

On 7 July a part of the eyrie on which Cain was standing collapsed and she fell to the ground: 'From my hiding-place I did not see the actual fall, for it took place on the side farthest away from me, but to my astonishment I saw Cain, who had seemed safe in the nest a few minutes before, walking along the ground looking scared and wild away from the eyrie. She soon disappeared from my sight, and I did not again see her.'

Abel seemed reluctant to fly and to persuade him otherwise the parent eagles put him on a starvation diet: 'On 15 July my wife took the day's watch in the hide. Abel was still there, half-starved, and with scarce the strength to call for his callous father and mother. Again the eyrie was empty of food, and the eagles never came near it all day. At last, on 16 July, after being alone in the nest nine days, the eaglet took wing and left the eyrie which had been his home for 11 weeks. Hunger drove him forth and, spreading his great wings, he mounted unsteadily into the air on the arms of the breeze and disappeared forever from our view.'

Days with the Golden Eagle was a pioneering book in the same way as Francis Heatherley's *The Peregrine Falcon at the Eyrie* and W.W. Nicholas's *A Sparrowhawk's Eyrie*. As Roy Dennis wrote in a foreword to a new edition of Seton Gordon's book, 'How he would marvel at our new digital cameras that we can attach to our telescopes to obtain incredible images.'

The year after Seton and Audrey Gordon had been studying Golden Eagles, a pair of eaglets were being taken from a nest in Scotland before being sent to the Royal Zoological Society's zoological gardens at Regents Park in London. The partnership between one of the Golden Eagles, known as Mr Ramshaw, and the man who trained it, Captain C.W.R. Knight, was, at that time, to become as world-famous as the bond between George and Joy Adamson and their lioness, Elsa.

Captain Knight, known as 'Chas', was a falconer, a pioneer wildlife cameraman and a showman and, as such, he had been asked to fly falcons in a falconry display at Wembley Stadium for *The Pageant of the Empire*. His first film *Wildlife in the Tree Tops*, made in 1921, had very good reviews and he was soon in great demand as a lecturer. Another film, *The Filming of the Golden Eagle*, followed in 1926. It, too, was a great success and in 1928 Captain Knight set off on the first of his lecture tours to the United States. On his return he took possession of the Golden Eagle that came to be known as Mr Ramshaw. The eagle was trained in the traditional way starting with several hours of carrying on a gloved fist each day to accustom him to the sights and sounds of modern life. He was taught to fly to the lure when called and eventually to kill live prey.

It was on Captain Knight's next lecture tour to America, this time with Mr Ramshaw, that they became a celebrity partnership. Mr Ramshaw appeared at the American Museum of Natural History and flew across the stage to land on a perch draped with the stars and stripes. He was an overnight success and for the next 11 years his life consisted of acting in films, appearing on the stage and accompanying Captain Knight on lecture tours in the United States. Two other eagles, a Crowned Eagle and a Martial Eagle, both from Africa, joined Captain Knight's *ménage*. They were also trained and on occasions all three eagles were flown together.

While Captain Knight was absent abroad, lecturing with Mr Ramshaw, the other eagles had to be cared for and luckily his nephew, Philip Glasier, then a schoolboy, had shown a natural aptitude as a falconer. Thus was a dynasty forged, a dynasty that endures to this day with Jemima, Philip's daughter, flying birds of prey so that the public can appreciate their beauty, their fierceness, their wonderful eyesight and their power of flight.

The partnership between Captain Knight and Mr Ramshaw thrived and survived right through the Second World War, despite the ship in which they were travelling to America being torpedoed by a German U-boat. On their return they embarked on an exhausting lecture tour bolstering the war effort. These tours were arduous and, because of wartime restrictions, it was not always possible to obtain food for Mr Ramshaw. This is Captain Knight's recollection of once such occasion: 'On the following evening we were again to appear at a boys' school and were again without anything for Ramshaw. But when I announced that Ramshaw would not partake of any food that evening there was a murmur of disappointment among the audience. Then one of the boys rose to announce that his pet guinea-pig had got out of its cage that morning and had drowned itself in a tub of water, and that Ramshaw might have that if he liked. At once the cheerful attitude of the audience revived; the defunct pet was fetched, Ramshaw flew about the room, did his tricks and as a final gesture stood to attention above the remains of his dinner.'

Young Philip Glasier progressed to become Britain's most expert and famous post-war falconer. I first learnt of him in 1954 when I saw some of the stunning flying photographs he had taken with high-speed flash of his Goshawk, Medusa. Later he helped me acquire my own Goshawk and was kind enough to write me a letter each week taking me through every step of its training. Film producers often asked for his advice on falconry matters and he appeared as the Royal Falconer in *The Sword and the Rose*, flying a cast of Peregrine Falcons. James Robertson Justice, who had star billing, later employed him as his falconer. Philip and his family moved to the Black Isle near Inverness in Scotland. Every 12 August Philip would arrive at James Robertson Justice's house at Spinningdale on the Dornoch Firth and fly his falcons at grouse until Christmas.

Philip also had time to watch Golden Eagles: 'Behind them came a Golden Eagle. When I first spotted her she was a long way behind the grouse, but her speed was quite amazing and she was rapidly overhauling them. They came overhead, paying no attention. A few seconds later there was heard the rush of the eagle's wings as she shot past. I turned and watched her overtake the grouse with the greatest of ease. I saw a massive foot stretch out and take one of them, and then they all passed out of sight behind the hill. The whole scene has remained etched in my mind ever since.'

In 1966 Philip moved to Newent, near Gloucester, and opened the Falconry Centre. The aim was to allow the public to see birds of prey on display in close-up, to admire their flying skills as different birds of prey were put through their paces in daily falconry displays, and through this to understand the value and importance of them in the natural world in which we live. In his book *A Hawk in the Hand*, published in 1990, Philip describes flying birds of prey for the public: 'I had always been confident that watching a bird flying well to the lure for exercise would be a good crowd-puller, but I was surprised to find that people were equally happy to stand and watch for maybe ten minutes at a time while I tried to persuade a new bird to jump a few feet to my fist. To me it was a commonplace chore that required time and patience. And when the bird finally did what was asked of it and was being rewarded they were often more pleased than I was.'

Philip eventually retired in 1982 and handed over the running of the centre to his daughter, Jemima. As it was the oldest dedicated bird of prey centre in the world, and on which all the others now are based, it was renamed the National Birds of Prey Centre. The captive breeding programme is a vital part of the Centre's work and as Jemima explained, "My father started the captive breeding programme and I've expanded it. We now breed something like 65 species here. We're not breeding large numbers of birds for release or for sale. We're striving to breed consistently, that's the key word, from as many different species as we can. In that way, we can learn about them, understand them much better. The flying demonstrations are also very important – they bring people in. We fly a very wide range of birds of prey – from one of the biggest eagles, the Steller's Sea Eagle, through to the smallest falcon, the Merlin. Owls are also flown – Snowy Owls, Eagle Owls as well as more familiar species such as Tawny Owls and Barn Owls. I give a running commentary and there are plenty of photo opportunities. The visitors really enjoy it and hopefully they're being amused at the same time as being educated. But it's the wider issues of conservation that drive me, which is why I spend so much time in Spain, Nepal and India. That's why I'm involved with the vulture project, setting up a captive breeding programme in India to replace the vulture population wiped out by diclofenac, an anti-inflammatory pain-killer, which was passed on to them through the carcasses of cattle. The vultures were an integral part of the Parsi funeral rites. The deceased's body was placed on a marble slab in one of the five Towers of Silence. All flesh is then stripped off the body by the vultures, thus guaranteeing the deceased an easy passage into Paradise. In the absence of the vultures the Parsis are asking for cremation to be allowed as an alternative."

When I asked Jemima when she was going to retire, she laughed and said, "Of course I'm going to go on forever. I've every intention of living till I'm 130! I'd like to do what Lady Scott (Sir Peter Scott's widow) did, which is to slowly back away and enjoy the company of the people who will take over from me. But I will always be in the background, poking people with my walking stick or zimmer frame saying 'We didn't used to do it like that.'"

I have known Jemima, or more familiarly Mima, for a long time and her public flying displays at the Holkham Country Fairs in Norfolk are legendary. Her Peregrine Falcons wait on, circling almost at the limit of human eyesight, before majestically stooping down to a deftly swung lure. Each bird's flying prowess was accompanied by a running commentary, liberally sprinkled with salty allusions to the bird's suspect parentage if it didn't fly to her expectations.

Mima used to provide birds of prey for filming, carrying on the tradition of her great-uncle and her father. I once asked her to help me with a TV commercial I was making for the Highland Spring water company, which was based just north of Perth. The selling point was to be an eagle soaring above a heather-covered hillside whilst in the foreground was a tray on which were two bottles of Highland Spring water and a couple of glasses. Mima agreed to be part of the project and we were allowed three days to complete it. It rained without stopping for the first two days but on the third day it cleared and the local shepherd spent the next hour moving sheep off the hill in the background so that there was no inference that sheep's urine may percolate through to the underwater caverns from which Highland Spring water was drawn.

Freddie Francis was the cameraman and we soon had the camera set up for the first shot – the money shot – in which the bottles and glasses were in the foreground while an eagle soared over the hill in the background. Mima had sent up Chalky, a Tawny Eagle, for this action. The eagle was cast off and was soon ringing up in circles over the hillside. The shot was in the bag. A longer lens gave us a tighter shot of the eagle soaring. What a wonderful bird. The sun was still out so we pressed on with getting the shot of the Highland Spring water being poured into a glass. It bubbled beautifully, the advertising executives and art director looked through the camera and gave us the thumbs-up so we moved on to the final shot. This involved a Golden Eagle perched on a crag, looking around imperiously before taking off.

Sam was the Golden Eagle and I had been warned not to use him for the flight shots as he was not entirely trustworthy. We had already found a rock on which he could perch and where the heather would conceal the fact that he was still wearing jesses and attached to a leash. Gradually he settled down and shook his feathers with an audible rattle. I told Freddie to run the camera. The falconer held out his gloved fist clutching a rabbit leg and called. Sam lumbered forward and took off. We were nearly through, one shot to go.

All we needed now was a close up of Sam's head. It had to embody all the special qualities of the Golden Eagle – the regal bearing enhanced by the golden feathers flowing down from its head, the fierceness portrayed in the huge, curving black bill and, above all, the unrivalled keenness of vision reflected in its hazel eye. Sam settled again, the falconer made a squeak like a rabbit in distress. Sam's golden head feathers hackled up, his bill thrust forward belligerently and the pupils of his eyes contracted in total concentration. It was perfect. Cut!

The best Golden Eagle film I have seen is the RSPB's *Where Eagles Fly*, made by Mike Richards in 1984. It is a year in the life of a pair of Golden Eagles and begins by introducing us to the Golden Eagle's realm in the depth of winter: deer lashed by a blizzard, Ptarmigan and a Mountain Hare perfectly camouflaged in the snow. An eagle soars and stoops at a hare, there is a chase and the eagle kills. Winter's icy grip relaxes, the snow and ice thaw and mountain streams become raging torrents.

It is in early spring that the eagles start to breed and Mike told me about the problems of filming the eagles at the nest. "Roy Dennis and I looked at over 80 different nest sites between the west and east coasts before we found one that would work. It was within sight of a road, a dead-end road, and that helped because the eagles were used to seeing cars coming and going. So I could drive up in the Land Rover and then walk up the hillside from there to the nest site. I knew that I would have to do fifty-hour shifts in the hide, especially when the female was incubating, so it had to be a sturdy construction. I settled on a steel framework base to which were attached wire netting frame sides thatched with heather. The main thing was that it didn't flap and put the eagles off. Inside the framework was a conventional photographic hide. Deer-stalkers' ponies were used to carry all the parts of the hide to just below the eyrie. It was left there so that the eagles could get used to it and was then gradually assembled."

Golden Eagles generally use the same eyrie each year but they do have an alternative site so Mike was relieved to see them return and start freshening up the nest – a huge structure that looked like a cartload of kindling. The birds carefully added sticks and fronds of heather to strengthen the framework and as a final touch bunches of wood-rush were brought in to line the cup in which the eggs would be laid.

By now Mike was putting in 50-hour shifts in the hide, "It was very uncomfortable sleeping in the hide. I arranged it so I could sleep in my sleeping bag and had an extension added to my chair so that I could stretch my legs right out. I made sure it was bearable but the cold was the worst thing."

On 14 March the first egg was laid and, as Mike explained, "The hide was only 25 feet from the nest and I had real trouble getting the female to accept the lens. I put a piece of gauze over the lens and then whipped it off when she flew away. I was convinced that she could see my eyeball through the lens in the back of the eye-piece. It was a most testing experience to be that close to a Golden Eagle. When she finally relaxed and accepted the lens it was fine."

Winter weather returns and although she is covered by driving snow the female eagle continues to brood. She sits tighter and tighter on her nest as the moment of hatching nears.

By 25 April the first egg has hatched to reveal a fluffy white chick with a head that seems out of all proportion to its body. As though to celebrate the occasion, fresh green sprays of Scots Pine have been brought in to decorate the nest. The chick can barely keep its eyes open after its first feed. A few days later the second egg hatches. This second chick may struggle to survive, as there is an eight-out-of-ten chance that it will be killed by its sibling. Mike remembers the first prey: "A dead lamb was brought in and when the chicks were fighting it was difficult to see which were chicks and which was the lamb. After they'd been fed there's a magic moment when the female goes to brood the chicks. She curls up her talons as she moves forward so as not to harm them when she settles down over them." Next follows one of my favourite shots, a brilliant close-up of the female's head with a dewdrop dangling from the tip of her bill.

At seven weeks old the eaglets have lost most of their fluffy white down, black feathers are pushing through everywhere and they are beginning to look like eagles. Mike spent his longest period in the hide just before they made their first flight. "The eaglets were now 80 days old and wing-flapping madly on the nest. The adults starve them by bringing in less and less food. It became very, very windy and the eaglets were able to open their wings and glide up off the nest without actually leaving. So I was able get them lifting up and going out of frame as though they were leaving the nest. Later I was able to get shots of them flying away and landing on the other side of the glen."

After four days in the hide Mike was in pretty bad shape. "Coming out of the hide was an extraordinary experience. The muscles in my legs had gone and it was just as if I'd been ill in bed for a long time. It was very dangerous carrying anything down the hill. I was very wobbly, quite light-headed. But, as is so often the case, it felt wonderful to be out in the bright light again."

There were brilliant shots of the two eaglets talon-grappling in the sky. It is a bleak world they are entering as the first snows of the winter mantle the landscape. It is an epic film – probably the best portrait of a Golden Eagle ever made. I'll let Mike have the last word: "When I gained the confidence of the female and she went to sleep on the nest with me in the hide only 25 feet away from her that was a magic moment for me. Making that film was a very important part of my life."

Another fine film is Ian McCarthy's *In the Company of Eagles*. It was made 15 years after Mike Richard's film and featured Jeff Watson who had just finished his monograph *The Golden Eagle*. The harsh reality of the winter in the Highlands of Scotland was brilliantly portrayed and into this bleak landscape, already occupied by a pair of Golden Eagles, ventures an immature female eagle.

I felt enormous sympathy for this young eagle as she struggled to survive and her nomadic existence was brilliantly realized in the film. She is immediately given a rude welcome by a pair of Hooded Crows who mob her incessantly. The young eagle eventually recognizes that, although these birds may be irritating, if she listens to them, their calls will lead her to a welcome feed on a dead deer carcass. Ian told me that young eagles on the west coast of Scotland really have a bleak time of it trying to reach maturity. The land is desperately impoverished through overgrazing by deer and sheep. The importance of carrion for the young eagles cannot be over-emphasized.

The role of the deer-stalker in supporting young eagles struggling to survive in this hostile environment is neatly woven into the storyline of the film. Matt Wilson is a deer-stalker and eagle enthusiast, who told me, "They are part of the companionship on the hill and may be the only thing you see all day apart from the deer. As an eagle passes by it looks you straight in the eye. That look goes straight through you and puts the hackles up on the back of your neck, I guess just as it must have done with primitive man."

The eagle soon learns that the crack of the rifle heralds a meal. As Matt explains, "As a stalker on the west coast here we're providers by what we leave behind. The gralloch, the innards of the deer, is a very important food source for the birds. It keeps them going in a landscape that has become so impoverished. A young eagle only has a one-in-ten chance of reaching maturity. Every day is a battle against starvation and she'll be learning all the time, honing her hunting skills, year after year, until aged four or five she's capable of holding a territory."

The film ends with the immature female Golden Eagle having survived her first year – she's now two years old. Air-to-air shots from a helicopter follow her as she soars over the wild landscape with which she is now familiar. Jeff Watson sums up his feelings about the eagle: "After working for 20 years with this magnificent bird I've learnt a few things. It's taught me something about humility. The landscape the bird lives in, and the bird itself, makes you feel quite humble. It's a privilege to learn to be patient. Eagles are not easy to study and you have to give them time. I've only learnt a little and I think it'll be another generation or two before we know a lot more about this most majestic of creatures." Later he adds, "In the Golden Eagle I see what it is to be strong, wild and free – what it means to have hope, energy and opportunities. Enjoy these birds and their evocative haunts, and as you glimpse this king of birds, or find its feather cast from the heavens, whisper a word of thanks."

The Golden Eagle once bred in England from Derbyshire northwards, in Wales, and was widespread in Scotland. Leslie Brown in his book *British Birds of Prey* has said that he cannot believe that there were ever more than 500 pairs in Scotland, another 50 in England and Wales and perhaps 100–150 pairs in Ireland. Intense persecution between the mid-nineteenth and early twentieth century in the interest of grouse shooting and sheep farming wiped out the eagles in England and Wales and reduced the breeding population in Scotland to 150 pairs. Despite a respite during the two world wars, when keepers were enlisted, the situation was still grave in Scotland when Roy Dennis started studying the eagles. I asked Roy why these beautiful birds of prey had been so persecuted and he replied, "The killing of birds of prey in the interests of grouse shooting and sheep farming when I first wandered the hills and glens in the early 1960s, was regarded as routine and no one was particularly ashamed of doing it." He then went on to describe the different methods employed – pole traps, shooting and poison: "The most disturbing way of killing eagles was by the use of poison. Insecticides or rodenticides could be used in concentrated form and injected into a dead Rabbit or the remains of a Fox or deer. It was deadly against carrion-eaters such as Golden Eagles. Today the general public is appalled by the deliberate killing of eagles."

It is hoped that eventually satellite-tagging of eagles will act as a deterrent against illegal persecution. A satellite-tagged Golden Eagle, named Alma by researchers, was found to have been illegally poisoned in Glen Esk in 2009, while other eagles fitted with

transmitters were found poisoned in Grampian in 2011, and in Lochaber early in 2012. On 24 September 2012, the BBC published a dramatic story of a Golden Eagle caught in an illegal trap. The bird suffered a lingering death after its legs were broken. It was found near a lay-by on a road near Aboyne on Deeside. It had been fitted with a satellite transmitter just before it fledged from its nest south-east of Inverness. Over the next ten months it was tracked by the RSPB as it moved away from its natal area. By April 2012 it had moved to Deeside, then through Glenshee, and finally, at 06.00 hours on 28 April, arrived at Glen Esk. Over the next 15 hours a succession of satellite readings, accurate to within 20 metres, showed that the bird did not move from that precise spot until at least 21.00 hours that evening, after nightfall. However, by 04.00 hours the next morning it appeared to have travelled, during the hours of darkness, some ten miles north to the location where its body was found five days later. The post-mortem evidence suggested that the bird was caught in an illegally set trap, smashing both legs. The site indicated by the last satellite reading would have been checked and the RSPB offered a £1,000 reward for information leading to a successful prosecution.

By the time this book is published, it is hoped that Golden Eagles and other tagged birds of prey will be able to receive better protection. Using the existing mobile phone network, field-workers will be able to receive instant text messages on their phones detailing the position of any of the birds they are monitoring. This will allow immediate follow-up of any bird suspected of being unlawfully killed.

The effect of wind farms on Golden Eagles is also now of great concern. This concern is reinforced when you learn that an average of 67 Golden Eagles a year have been killed by wind turbine blades over the last 30 years on the Altamount Pass in California. Although, as yet, there have been no known Golden Eagle fatalities in Scotland, the effect of the wind farms may have caused eagles to be displaced from their territories, with a knock-on effect that might result in death. It was this fact, perhaps, that caused Sigrid Rausing, the daughter of Hans Rausing, the Swedish billionaire whose father built the Tetra Pak packaging empire, to claim that the 33-turbine project on the Dunmaglass Estate will spoil one of Britain's wildest landscapes and pose a physical threat to raptors. Miss Rausing owns the Coignafearn Estate in the Monadhliath mountains, south of Inverness in Scotland and in an interview for the Daily Telegraph in 2011 she said, 'The Dunmaglass approval shows that where a species has been hunted to near extinction, protection, sadly, is irrelevant in the planning process. The Monadhliaths are potentially one of the best areas for Golden Eagles in Britain. That there are no breeding pairs at Coignafearn is due to persecution. Our aim is to restore two or three breeding pairs, but the risk of the eagles being killed when venturing over estate boundaries or killed by the proposed wind turbines, is unfortunately very high.'

Roy Dennis had left a message at the hotel where I was staying with Eddie and Tina Anderson: 'Be at Carrbridge car park at 2.30 sharp. I've got a four-wheel drive vehicle. I'll take you to Coignafearn – it'll be a good trip. Have you back by 5.30.' And so off we went, initially following the line of the Findhorn river. We saw a lot of Red Deer, although Roy told us, as the ecological adviser at Coignafearn, how the glen is being restored after decades of overgrazing by reducing their numbers. Four sites had been fenced to demonstrate natural regeneration in the absence of grazing. Scots Pine, Oak, Ash and Bird Cherry had been planted to restore the natural woodland. After nine years you could see a vast difference, a small patch on the hillside looking as it would have done before the overgrazing took place. We turned up a valley, the Alt Calder, immediately saw a Ring Ouzel and then *plop*, a Water Vole dived to safety as we passed. Roy told us there are over 200 separate colonies of Water Vole on the estate. We were travelling up a newly graded road built in order to get the deer-stalkers up on the hill.

Roy told us that one of the first steps Miss Rausing took when she bought the estate was to ban the persecution of raptors. At the time she said, "There's plenty of food for eagles, with plenty of grouse, hares and Red Deer grallochs." Later in the day, Eddie spotted a Peregrine Falcon perched on a rock. As we got closer, its mate left the eyrie sited on a cliff face. She flew round calling, "*kek-ke*", repeatedly. Roy said that this was where, in the old days, keepers would come, hide up and shoot the falcons with a rifle when they came in to roost.

Roy also said that although there were four or five pairs of Merlins breeding here the heather moors were too high and exposed for Hen Harriers. The weather had closed in by now and there was no chance of seeing any eagles but Roy explained that, so far, immature and sub-adult birds had made Coignafearn their home. It was a kindergarten for eagles, where they felt safe. There was plenty of food and Roy had built eyries for them to use when they were mature. We turned downhill, found a Common Sandpipers' nest under a little bit of a peat hag, saw a Red-breasted Merganser and inspected the static dragonfly ponds full of crystal-clear water that one of the staff had dug with a JCB digger.

We were now back alongside the river Findhorn, past Coignafearn Lodge, and, just as Roy had promised, in time to reach our hotel by 5.30 p.m. That evening I couldn't help thinking of the immature female eagle that had been featured in Ian McCarthy's film.

Coignafearn would have been perfect for it, a safe place where, in the company of other immature eagles, it could complete its education.

Sigrid Rausing is a shining light, part of a growing number of landowners who have realized that the land and the creatures that live there are their responsibility. For far too long the owners of sporting estates have held the view that it is their land and that no one has a right to interfere with what they do.

In my mind's eye, I am watching that same young female Golden Eagle soaring over Coignafearn harassed by a pair of Hooded Crows. She easily slips sideways to avoid them. Half-an-hour later she is feeding on a hare, stripping great gobbets of flesh from it. In the background the crows wait their turn. The tables have been turned. She pauses in her feeding and looks right at me. For a moment, as her gaze seems to bore right through me, I am able to share the awe that primitive Man must have felt for the Golden Eagle – awe at its mastery of the air, fierce wildness, strength and keenness of vision. I am lucky to have shared this moment with her.

I think it is only appropriate that Roy Dennis has the final word: "We must never take these birds for granted, for they are the beacons of our mountain country. But we now need a wiser approach to the management of the land, to embrace the health of the ecosystem and the sensitive development of farming, forestry, sport-related management, tourism and conservation. Then there will be a chance of a richer future, not only for Golden Eagles, but also for us."

THE KESTREL

British Isles population (2009): 46,000 pairs (declining)

Tony Huston, expert falconer and friend, had been flying his Peregrine Falcon at Beacon Hill just outside Burnham Market. I was a spectator, photographer and beater. Tony's Pointer, Nelson (black 'patch' over one eye), had found a covey of Grey Partridge, had held his point while the falcon mounted to 'wait on' 300 metres or so above us. At the critical moment the covey had been flushed. With an awe-inspiring stoop, the falcon had cut out one of the birds and killed it.

Now we were pulling up outside my home ready for a cup of tea. As we got out of the car, I saw there was a Kestrel sitting rather forlornly in the hedge. It did not budge an inch as we gently edged closer and Tony cautioned me to stay put. He took out a dead day-old chick from his falconer's bag, attached it to a length of line and gently tossed it onto the grassy bank. The Kestrel bobbed its head up and down a couple of times. Tony gently jiggled the chick about and the Kestrel flopped down on it. Very slowly Tony crawled forwards, moving only when the bird was feeding. His patience was rewarded as he gently passed his hand behind the Kestrel's legs and picked it up. He felt the bird's breast as he came over towards me. "Its breastbone's as sharp as a razor," he said. "Another couple of hours and it would have been dead."

Tony told me that I'd have to look after it as he was off to London in the morning. He knew I had a supply of day-old chicks, warned me to keep the Kestrel in a dark place, and feed it one chick a day. If all went well, I should be able to release it in ten days' time. We went into the house, the promised cup of tea forgotten. Tony scouted round and settled on the old dog room as a good temporary mews or hawk house. There was a blind that could be pulled down to darken the room and a tea chest would serve as a temporary perch. The Kestrel wasn't strong enough to struggle as I placed it on the tea chest. It grabbed that firmly enough and then tucked into the slivers of chick that I offered it as Tony stood watching from the doorway behind me.

Over the next ten days I established a routine. First thing in the morning I gently opened the sliding door to the old dog room and checked that the Kestrel was all right. There was no other perch in the room; sometimes it was on the floor, sometimes on the tea chest. As the bird gained weight it got feistier and feistier.

On the ninth day, when I looked in, the Kestrel seemed completely restored. He was all fluffed up sitting on the edge of the tea chest. I had by now worked out that it was a juvenile male. He had eaten a day-old chick each evening and, as a result, there was a scattering of small yellowish pellets around the tea chest. That, and the splashes of creamy white on the floor, told me that he was in fine fettle. It was time to return him to the wild.

Late that afternoon I returned armed with my landing net. The Kestrel was on the floor and I quickly caught him up. I gently untangled him from the net, wrapped him in a towel and took him out into the garden. It was an ideal time to let him go. It was fine and there was no wind. I unwrapped him and gently helped him on his way. He flew away from me, getting stronger with every wing-beat, and made for the rose pergola at the bottom of the garden. Here he stayed for the rest of the day. From the living room window I kept an eye on him from time to time. Late afternoon merged into dusk and I watched until his hunched outline merged with the enveloping, kindly night. In the morning the Kestrel was gone.

The origins of the name Kestrel are quite obscure and elusive. Gesner mentioned it in his *Historia Animalium*, published in 1555, calling it *tinnunculus* – Latin for shrill sounding, matching the falcon's "*kee-kee-kee*" call. Mark Cocker and Richard Mabey in *Birds Britannica*, published in 2005, states that it is derived from the French for Kestrel – *Faucon crecerelle*; *crecerelle* means high, rattling call. On the other hand, there is a case for it being derived from the word *coystrel*, a knave or a mean and degenerate hawk. John Dryden used it in his poem *The Hind and Panther*, published in 1687:

> *One they might trust, their common wrongs to wreak.*
> *The musquet and the coystrel were too weak,*
> *Too fierce the falcon.*

Eventually Kestrel was the English name adopted and, in 1746, Carl Linnaeus classified it as *Falco tinnunculus*. Because of its hovering flight when hunting, it is probably the one bird of prey that is familiar to everyone.

As with most birds of prey, the male is smaller than the female. Both male and female have the bluish-black hooked beak, with a 'tooth' for administering the *coup de grâce* to their prey. The cere is yellow and the pupils of their deep-set eyes are surrounded by a brown iris. Below the eye is a short, dark moustachial stripe.

The male Kestrel is a handsome bird with a grey head, rump, upper-tail coverts and tail. His back and scapulars are brick-red coloured with dark markings that vary in size from dots at the top of the back to quite broad bars on the scapulars. The primaries are dark. There is a broad, dark band immediately above the narrow pale edge at the tip of the tail. The yellow scaly legs and feet are armed with razor-sharp black talons.

The female, by comparison, is an altogether much duller brown than the male. She has the same varying intensity of darker markings from the head down the back and across the scapulars and dark primaries. The tail is brown, carrying four or five narrow transverse dark bars with a much broader dark bar at the tip. Both male and female have a straw-coloured breast with bold, dark spotting stretching from the area of the crop downwards. Kestrels in their first year are difficult to sex and are virtually indistinguishable from an adult female at any distance. In close up, males show a greyish rump and tail.

Eleven subspecies of the Common Kestrel have been identified across its broad global breeding range, which runs from sub-Arctic Scandinavia, throughout Eurasia to eastern Russia and as far south as the tip of South Africa.

Many Kestrels breeding in the north migrate south during the winter. On 1 October 2005, Nigel Middleton's brother, Guy, was on passage from Lowestoft to Southwold when a Kestrel, exhausted and disorientated, pitched onto his fishing boat. It had a ring on its leg and Nigel, who is the Hawk and Owl Trust's Conservation Officer for East Anglia, sent the details off to the British Museum of Natural History to discover its origin. Meanwhile the juvenile female Kestrel was placed on a straw bale in our rehabilitation aviary to regain its strength. My wife and I fed it each day and gradually it recovered and began taking short flights from perch to perch in its enclosure. As we gathered round to release the Kestrel, which was now fully fit, news reached us that it had been ringed four months earlier in June near Helsinki in Finland. How lucky it was to have survived that epic 1,000 mile

journey by ending up on Nigel's brother's boat. A count-down began so that the local photographer would be sure to get the Kestrel's takeoff. Off it went, wings beating strongly, for a chance-in-a-million return to the wild!

The Kestrel has three main methods of hunting – the familiar hovering, soaring and still-hunting from a perch. A bird hovering over the edge of an arable field or over the grassy banks of a motorway is the hunting method with which we are all familiar. The rapidly beating wings gave rise to several names that are now obsolete, including Wind Cuffer, Wind Fanner and Wind F***er. The term Windhover was used by John Ray and Francis Willughby in the 1678 English edition of their *Ornithology*. The poem *The Windhover* by the priest poet Gerard Manley Hopkins (1844–89) is probably one of the best-known poems about a bird:

> *I caught this morning morning's minion, king-*
> *dom of daylight's dauphin, dapple-dawn-drawn falcon, in*
> *his riding*
> *Of the rolling level underneath him steady air, and striding*
> *High there, how he rung upon the reign of a wimpling wing*
> *In his ecstasy! then off, off forth on swing,*
> *As a skate's heel sweeps smooth on a bow-bend: the hurl*
> *and gliding*
> *Rebuffed the big wind. My heart in hiding*
> *Stirred for a bird, – the achieve of; the mastery of the thing!*
>
> *Brute beauty and valour and act, oh, air, pride, plume, here*
> *Buckle! AND the fire that breaks from thee then, a billion*
> *Times told lovelier, more dangerous, O my chevalier!*
>
> *No wonder of it: shéer plód makes plough down sillion*
> *Shine, and blue-bleak embers, ah my dear,*
> *Fall, gall themselves, and gash gold-vermilion.*

The first part of the poem is a masterly evocation of the Kestrel's prowess in the air. The images that the poet conjures up are stunning but I was less certain about what the last two verses meant. So I phoned David Harsent, friend, poet and librettist to the composer, Harrison Birtwhistle. David said, "Think of the cruciform shape the falcon makes while hanging on air. The almost ecstatic first line of the second verse which leads into 'Buckle!' This evokes the stoop, wings folding, the spread shape suddenly and dramatically ... well, buckling, but it also seems to me an instruction to the reader to fall to his knees. And so 'the fire that breaks from thee then, a billion times told lovelier, more dangerous...'. Thee being, I'm sure, Christ as the Man of Sorrows, Christ crucified, and the fire of resurrection and demand, that is, the demand made of us by that miracle and that miraculous man. The poem ends with seeing love in labour. The bird works against the wind, the ploughman works against the plough. For the final image, the 'blue-bleak embers' signify Christ's wounds, 'gold-vermillion', blood and water, from the 'gash' in his side. For me, the transformative aspect of the windhover is made more powerful and more persuasive if we first find the poet apprehending bird-as-bird, not least because the sacramental aspect of his poem has more heft when imbued with the bird's sheer purity of instinct, its own measure of holiness."

David Harsent's brilliant exposition contains one telling phrase about the hovering Kestrel, 'The bird works against the wind.' Kestrels need wind if they are going to hover without expending too much energy. It is a delicate balancing act as the forces of drag and mass have to be exactly matched by the lift of the wind and the bird's wing-power. The tail, spread when hovering, also gives lift. The less wind there is, the harder the Kestrel has to flap to maintain its position searching for prey. If there's a good wind the bird can glide into position and by fanning its tail hold that position without expending energy.

One of the best descriptions of a Kestrel hovering is by Leslie Brown in his book *British Birds of Prey* in the *New Naturalist* series, published in 1976: 'In hovering the kestrel swings up to a pitch from level flight, stops with the body held at a rather steep angle, spreads the tail, and winnows the air with its wings. The head remains steady while any variation in the air currents is absorbed by movements of the body and wings. Evidently the large, fan-like spread tail considerably increases the lift obtained. If it fails to spot anything the kestrel moves on a little way and tries again; it may only move a few feet between hovers, or travel 100 yards or more. If it sees possible prey it glides steeply downwards, controlling the rate of descent by varying the angle of its wings, as a parachutist slips air from his parachute, and, when a few feet above the quarry, raises the wings vertically above the back and plunges feet foremost into the grass to grasp the prey. The whole action is beautifully controlled and a joy to watch.'

Kestrels also, on occasion, use soaring as a way of locating prey. If the weather is right, with good thermals, it allows a large area to be searched effectively and economically. The Kestrel has exceptional eyesight; it is said that it can pick out a vole at 300 metres. But once it has sighted its prey, how does it keep it in vision when it is being buffeted around by wind and thermals? John Videler, a Dutchman, tried to answer this question in 1983. Using a Locam high-speed camera running between 100 and 200 frames per second he filmed hovering Kestrels from a fixed position. After examining the film frame-by-frame, he was able to state that one Kestrel he filmed only moved its head by less than six millimetres in any direction while flying in a wind gusting at 17–27 kilometres per hour. Split-second changes in the angle of wings and tail are vital to achieve this degree of stability. He also showed that when Kestrels were hovering and gliding they allowed themselves to be blown backwards. Nevertheless, they kept their heads still by stretching their necks forward by up to four millimetres before they had to flap their wings again. This technique not only

allowed the bird to keep its prey in vision, but also saved energy that would have been expended in wing-flapping.

The final common method of hunting is still-hunting from a perch, a technique that is generally used in winter to save energy. Many times have I seen Kestrels perched on the top of a roadside telephone pole, watching the grassy roadside verge or the field margin on the other side of the hedge. As soon as a Kestrel spots an unwary Field Vole, its head starts bobbing up and down as the optic nerves from each eye relay information to the brain, giving the bird an accurate fix on its prey. It then dives headlong and, when just above the victim, spreads its wings, flaps, fans its tail and, with its head above spread talons, plunges with pinpoint accuracy onto the vole.

The Kestrel's main prey is the Field Vole, also known as the Short-tailed Vole, which thrives in any patch of land or field where there is rough, tussocky grass. Voles are mainly nocturnal but their presence is indicated by holes in grass tussocks where they nest, runs in the grass with holes where they pop up from time to time and remains of grass clippings which they have chewed. Both male and female Field Voles mark their territory and defend it with splashes of urine. It is estimated that the number of Field Voles in the British Isles is 75 million. Their breeding season starts in April or May and continues through to September or October. A succession of litters is produced and young born at the start of the breeding season will breed in the same year. Their average litter size is five. Field Vole breeding success follows a cyclical pattern, a poor year followed by a better one. Then, either in the third or fourth year, there is a peak breeding season. This cyclical pattern is exploited by predators in the good years and has a depressing effect on their productivity during lean periods.

Experiments in 1994 by Finnish researchers showed that Kestrels, whose eyes are sensitive to ultraviolet light, were able to detect voles from urine territory markings on their runs, which reflect ultraviolet light. This has two advantages – it pinpoints the areas of maximum vole density and saves wasting time and energy searching at random for prey.

When voles are in short supply or during hard weather, the Kestrel acts like a highwayman. Patrolling the skies over favourite feeding grounds, it will swoop down and harry successful hunters such as Barn Owls until they drop their prey, or simply grab it out of their talons. I have seen Barn Owls, which use the nest box we have erected on the edge of the water meadow in front of our house, pursued like this several times. In the last couple of years there have been excellent photographs and film clips taken that capture such exciting moments.

It was not until the Mesolithic period, roughly between 8,000 and 2,700 years BC, that archaeological records were plentiful enough and of sufficient variety to show what birds of prey flourished then. These records indicate that Kestrels were not the common bird they are now, with only an estimated 13,500 pairs in the British Isles.

As the forests were felled to provide wood for housing, ships, fuel and farming, so the Kestrel prospered. With the advent of falconry in medieval times there was no place for the gentle Kestrel. It was allotted to a knave or a servant. However, the Kestrel is, without doubt, the best bird of prey with which the aspiring young falconer can learn the art of hawking. For the next few hundred years the Kestrel, like all birds of prey, was protected and continued to increase as more and more land was cleared for agriculture.

The Game Act of 1831 legalized the role of the gamekeeper and set in motion the persecution of birds of prey. To cite just one example, on the Glengarry Estate in Scotland between 1837–40, 462 Kestrels were killed. This was happening on the estates throughout Scotland and, to a lesser extent, in England as well.

Charles Waterton, eccentric, traveller and conservationist, writing in his *Essays on Natural History* published between 1838 and 1857 vigorously defended the Kestrel: 'The windhover is perpetually confounded with the sparrowhawk, and too often doomed to suffer from the predatory attacks of that bird on the property of man. But when your gun has brought the poor windhover to the ground, look, I pray you, into the contents of its stomach; you will often find nothing there to show that his life ought to be forfeited. On the contrary, the remnants of the beetle, and the field mouse, which will attract your notice, prove indisputably that his visits to your farm have been a real service to you.'

Most birds of prey suffered much more severely than the Kestrel. Nevertheless, anything with a hooked beak was anathema to the gamekeeper. Leslie Brown, writing in *British Birds of Prey*, recalls 'One of the minor tragedies that befell me when I was a student at St Andrews was being watched by a gamekeeper when visiting a kestrel's nest in a quarry and later being told with glee by him that he had shot the bird – which he thereafter did every year. Even in 1961, in Berkshire, I found ingrained prejudice against the Kestrel very strong; they would eat all the young pheasants I was told, when I ventured, ignorant as I am, to suggest that they might actually be harmless.' In 1954 all British birds of prey, except the Sparrowhawk, received full legal protection.

In the late 1950s and early 1960s the effects of agricultural pesticides hit all birds of prey that hunted over farmland. The Kestrel was badly affected and became a rare breeding bird in the south-eastern counties of England. The offending chemicals were banned and the Kestrel made a remarkable recovery, a recovery that was undoubtedly assisted by the network of motorways that started to fan out over the British Isles. The grassy banks alongside the motorways provided a good vole-rich habitat for the hunting Kestrel and it became a much more familiar bird to the public.

The Kestrel was projected right into the public's eye with the publication in 1968 of Barry Hines's classic novel *A Kestrel for a Knave*. Billy Casper, the hero, is a troubled teenager growing up in a Yorkshire mining town. Barry described him later in a postscript: 'In academic terms Billy Casper is a failure. He is in the bottom form of a rough secondary modern school. He has "a job to read and write", as he tells the Employment Officer. Yet once he becomes interested in falconry, he acquires a book on the subject, which is full of esoteric vocabulary and technical descriptions. He then goes on to successfully train a kestrel, which requires both intelligence and sensitivity. If there had been GCSEs in Falconry, Billy Casper would have been awarded an A grade, which would have done wonders for his self-confidence and given him a more positive image.' A film adaptation, *Kes*, directed by Ken Loach, followed shortly after the book's publication. The film was a huge commercial and critical success and helped propel the book from adult fiction into being widely read in schools and a set text for examinations.

Barry Hines's book and the film *Kes* fired the imagination of young people, especially those who identified with Billy Casper. They all wanted to train a Kestrel and as a result there was a spate of Kestrels nests being robbed. Barry added in his postscript, 'But we would never have taken a young Kestrel from a nest in the same manner. We knew a Kestrels' nest, high up in the wall of a crumbling medieval hall. Generations of Kestrels had nested in the same spot, and we used to stand out of sight at the edge of an adjacent wood watching the parents return with mice and small birds for the ravenous fledglings. It wasn't just the fact that we had no idea how to raise a young Kestrel and it might die, it was more to do with a feeling of awe and instinctive respect for such a beautiful bird.'

Kestrels featured in three of the early wildlife films I made for the BBC Natural History Unit. The first of these films was *The Vanishing Hedgerows* about Henry Williamson, the author of *Tarka the Otter*, and his ten years' spent farming in Norfolk from 1936–46. John Buxton was the main wildlife cameraman and when he was searching for a Kestrels' nest he was presented with an incredibly lucky bonus. Eric Hosking, the world-famous wildlife photographer, had erected a hide on a Kestrels' nest, an old crows' nest, in a tall hedgerow and offered his hide to John. When John took it over he noticed that there was also a Jays' nest a few feet away and a bit lower down. He did a bit of trimming, got into the hide and waited. The Kestrels' nest held four plump, downy chicks. When the female returned to the nest with food she noticed the Jays' nest and the young it contained. The eldest Jay chick stuck its head up, called and exposed its gaping throat. The Kestrel with a couple of flaps landed on the nest and tried to feed it. Its gape was not big enough. She threw the food to one side and to John's amazement proceeded to brood the young Jays. I had a letter after the film was transmitted from an animal behaviourist saying that he had never seen anything like that before. My explanation was that the nest had previously been hidden, and then John partially exposed it and the gaping of the young Jays acted as a 'trigger mechanism' prompting an attempt at feeding and brooding. It was certainly a thought-provoking sequence.

Another film, another Kestrels' nest. I was making *The Private Life of the Barn Owl* and my friend Eddie Anderson showed me a quite unusual situation, a condominium in an

Ash tree. There were three holes in this ancient tree: the lower one housed a pair of Barn Owls, the middle one was shared by a pair of Kestrels and Stock Doves (the Kestrels had first use of it) and the upper one was the nesting site of a pair of Starlings and then Great Tits. They all lived in perfect harmony, a model housing association!

Two pairs of Kestrels had been filmed in the countryside and now an urban pair featured in a film about London's wildlife, *The Unofficial Countryside*. This pair of Kestrels had nested in a hopper, the moulded cast-iron container into which gutters drain. Four young were raised and they were fed not on voles or mice but on House Sparrows. The cameraman was Alan Parker, a scenes of crime photographer, a rather grisly job from which wildlife filming must have been a welcome relief.

In 1974, when that film was made, there were 74 pairs of Kestrels nesting within 20 miles of St Paul's Cathedral. The most famous sites were at the Law Courts on the Strand, the towers of Westminster Abbey, the Imperial Institute in South Kensington, and at Langham Place opposite the BBC building. Window boxes in high-rise flats were also occasionally used as nesting sites.

The provision of nest boxes for Barn Owls was the main recommendation in Colin Shawyer's painstaking survey of Barn Owls for the Hawk Trust in the 1980s. His report showed a 50% decrease in the British Isles population since 1932 when the last national survey was undertaken. Nest boxes were the main conservation measure that helped halt the decline of the Barn Owl and, as a side effect, were also beneficial to the Kestrel. Colin explains why: 'Graham Lenton's work in Malaysia during the 1970s, setting up nest boxes on poles for Barn Owls, helped the oil palm plantation owners get rid of a plague of rats. The owls, because of the plentiful food supply, were producing three broods a year. In the 1980s we adopted his idea of pole-mounted boxes and took it a stage further with two chambers, one for the male and the other for the female. Quite soon we found that Kestrels were occupying one of the chambers and were quite happy to be alongside the Barn Owls. It was a logical step from there to site a separate box for the Kestrels alongside the Barn Owl box. By doing that we could successfully conserve and study two birds at the same time.'

Colin showed me a photograph of a cock Kestrel that had just moved off five eggs, which was sharing a nest box with a Barn Owl incubating four eggs. I asked him if Closed Circuit Television (CCTV) had been used in their study of the nest box breeding Kestrels and was told, "Eight years ago we tried wireless-link CCTV but it proved unreliable. It was powered by 12-volt batteries that had to be re-charged every three days. We had to rely on local farmers for that and, inevitably, there were gaps in the coverage."

Nest boxes have certainly helped the Kestrels breed in areas of suitable habitat where there are no natural nest sites. Colin, through his Wildlife Conservation Partnership, has erected over 1,000 nest boxes for Kestrels, some of them along motorways. As he explained, "I started putting Kestrel boxes up along motorways and other major roads and then wanted to try this on the back of motorway signs because I saw that in the States they has been successfully fixing nest boxes to the back of traffic signs for American Kestrels. That was alright in the States because the signs were set well back from the motorway, but here they were right on the edge of the motorway or over it. So I considered putting them on poles instead. Our five-year research project for the Highways Agency had clearly demonstrated that although Barn Owls, because of their low hunting methods, were highly vulnerable to road traffic accidents, Kestrels were very rarely affected in this way. Prior to this, in the early 1990s we produced an education pack for the Highways Agency, 'InRoads to Birds of Prey', based on the Kestrel. This helped to encourage the Highways Agency to adopt the Kestrel, alongside the Barn Owl, in their Biodiversity Action Plan, and as part of this I formulated a conservation plan for the Kestrel. Although this was not taken up at the time, the Agency has since been erecting specially designed pole-mounted boxes on wide road verges and around adjacent balancing ponds – areas designed to take the water run-off from major roads and which provide wonderful habitats for many different forms of wildlife. From the outset the results have been quite amazing. On the first 20 km stretch of road that we tried (the A1(M) from Peterborough to Alconbury), there appeared to be virtually no habitat and the only food available that you might have expected would have been insects and earthworms. Yet we put up 20 Kestrel nest boxes and in no time at all eight had been taken up and the breeding productivity was good too. Now a further 40 of these specially designed triangular, pole-mounted nest boxes have been installed on other carefully targeted roads in eastern England and we expect to find about 30 of these used by breeding Kestrels by 2014."

By the 1980s the Kestrel population was estimated at 52,000 pairs and it was the commonest bird of prey seen almost everywhere throughout the UK. Then, alarmingly, there was a sharp decline and between 1995 and 2008, according to Breeding Bird Survey figures, the UK lost one-fifth of its Kestrels.

I asked Colin Shawyer about the decline and he explained, "Originally the British Trust for Ornithology didn't acknowledge that there'd been a decline over the last 20 years. Then they changed their tune and agreed that numbers of breeding Kestrels had gone down drastically in Scotland, North Yorkshire and in the south-west. I knew that was the case as I'd seen an 80% decline in nest box occupation by Kestrels in two of those areas. Why had it happened? Farming wasn't to blame and in my opinion it was due to the rapid expansion of the Buzzard population. The Buzzard is now our commonest bird of prey – estimated in 2009 at 57,000–79,000 pairs. They predate Kestrels and they are in competition for their staple diet, Field Voles." I added that I was aware that the Goshawk was an opportunistic predator of Kestrels and that it was also an occasional prey item of Peregrine Falcons.

Colin knew that on my next trip I was going to visit Nigel Lewis who had been very successful with Kestrel nest boxes on Salisbury Plain. He had a wonderful story to tell me about Nigel: "I went down to Wiltshire to visit Nigel and I was sitting with him in his living room. It was a lovely evening. Nigel had opened the French doors out onto the garden and we were chatting away, both in easy chairs. I can't really have been listening, my eyes were wandering round the room and suddenly I was aware that there was a Kestrel lying under Nigel's chair. Was it a stuffed one that Nigel had put there as a joke? I saw it move. What should I do? At that moment Nigel noticed my eyes staring at a fixed point just beyond his feet and asked, 'Colin, are you alright?' 'Er, Nigel, there's a Kestrel under your chair,' I said. 'Oh, is there?' Nigel responded as he peered under the chair. 'Gosh, so there is!' Quite calmly he reached under the chair, gently picked up the Kestrel, walked to the open doors and released it as though it was an everyday occurrence. 'Now, where were we?....'"

It was Nigel's idea to start the Kestrel Highways Project, which was to be a network of Kestrel nest boxes adjoining eight separate major roads throughout Great Britain. The aim was to erect 240 nest boxes over 240 miles of road and monitoring would start in 2009. Before visiting Nigel, I decided to look at the Kestrel Highways Project nest boxes erected in Norfolk. I contacted Phil Littler, volunteer and bird ringer, and asked if I could join him on his next ringing trip. He kindly agreed and the following are the notes from my journal:

'6/6/12. 09.30. Meet with Phil Littler on a lay-by in Bodham on the A149 Holt/Cromer road. There's a line of coppiced oaks dividing two meadows, in one of which dairy cattle are grazing. The box is in one of the oaks about 15 feet up. Phil erects his ladder and bags up the four chicks. Watching with me is Elizabeth from Melton Constable, a ringer under instruction. Phil places the bags on the grass. He'll ring the first one and Elizabeth will ring 2, 3 and 4 under Phil's watchful eye. The first chick is brought out of its bag. Flashing, angry eyes. Very noisy. It's still in grey down with primaries and tail feathers peeping through. Phil tries to sex the chicks by the colour of the rump feathers – grey is a male, brown is female. Each chick is quickly and efficiently ringed and weighed. They are all in good condition. Phil returns them to the nest box. Job done.

Afterwards, I talked to Phil about the Norfolk section of the Kestrel Highways Project and he told me, "The take-up of the boxes has not been what I expected. We've put up 20 boxes and over the last three years only two have been used – and they are right next to each other. One of them is the box we've just visited. That gives me hope. The young from the original box must have used the other box, which is why I think there will be a better take-up from now on. In time the young birds will become 'fixed' on them and return to use other boxes in years to come."

Back home, there was a comforting email from Nigel Lewis telling me that he would meet my train at Salisbury and show me some nest boxes on the A303 (part of the Kestrel Highways Project) before taking me on to Salisbury Plain to ring some Kestrels there. My journal for this day reads:

'20/6/12. To Salisbury. Met at the station by Nigel, Dave Ovenden (ladderman, cameraman and Kestrel enthusiast) and Nigel's grandson, Charles. He's just finished his GCSEs at Charterhouse School and is at a loose end; he's helped Nigel before. We drive off and join the A303. Luckily it's a Wednesday so the road is not jammed with holiday traffic. At Deptford we turn off onto a chalky lane and stop opposite an Ash tree standing in a meadow. A female Kestrel leaves the tree. Through my binoculars I can see the nest box. There are four young in there which have already been ringed.'

Rather naïvely I ask Nigel if this is part of the Kestrel Highways Project, why isn't the nest box mounted on a pole? His answer is very direct and sensible, "I always prefer to use a tree if it's possible. I'll say this against pole-mounted nest boxes. If a young bird falls out of it there's very little chance of it getting back. With a tree-mounted nest a young Kestrel can claw its way back up the trunk (reverse abseil) as they flap their wings. The other advantage is that the box can be sited near to branches to which the young Kestrels can make their first flights. The Highway Project will take time. Ten of our 30 boxes are occupied. The Kestrel, once it's got a successful breeding site, tends to stay loyal to that site. Any empty nest boxes down the road are for their progeny who've yet to breed. They'll all be used. It'll be 100% in seven years' time."

As we move off again, Nigel explained to me how he started putting up nest boxes for Kestrels. "It was at the Fingringhoe Wick firing ranges in Essex that I started. The Essex bird people said in their annual report that there were only eight pairs of Kestrels in the county of Essex. After three years on the ranges I had 12 pairs on the ranges alone. Boxes make all the difference. A lot of holes in trees look good but when you get up there with a ladder you'll see it's full of water. That's especially true of Beech trees. You go up to ring the young and they're all dead because it poured with rain for a day or two before."

We had now arrived at Salisbury Plain, the main part of which is a Ministry of Defence training area. We're on a chalk plateau and the view looking across the plain reminds me of a rumpled patchwork quilt – large squares of light green grassland interposed with smaller, darker, irregular clumps of Beech trees and conifer shelterbelts. It is the largest known expanse of unimproved chalk downland in north-west Europe so it is no wonder that it has been declared a Site of Special Scientific Interest. Salisbury Plain is also recognized as being of international importance as a Special Protection Area and a Special Area of Conservation.

Nigel's vehicle heads towards a clump of Beech trees. As we arrive the female Kestrel flies off and the team swings into action. Dave and Charles unship the ladder and extend it up to the nest box while Nigel gets his ringing kit laid out on a groundsheet. Dave brings down the bagged-up chicks and they are ringed and weighed, the details being meticulously noted down by Dave. It's all done very methodically and they've clearly done this a thousand times before.

Dave wants to show me a new bit of kit and gives me a demonstration, explaining, "It's a gardening tool which you can extend and on which you can fix various gadgets – pruning saw, container for collecting apples and so on. What I've done is slot on a mini-camera. You can extend it up to a nest box, have a gander, bring it down, play it back and count the eggs. The female will often not leave the box. It's brilliant, no danger of chilling eggs or chicks on a cold day. It avoids the disturbance involved in putting up a ladder."

It is one o'clock and Nigel suggests we pull up for lunch, which his wife has kindly made up for us. We park looking down across the plain, this particular view being littered with rusting tanks used for firing practice. During our lunch break Dave Ovenden shows me an unfinished video of one of the nest sites featuring young Kestrels as they grew up. I ask him if he'll send me a copy when it's completed. Just before we move off again, I asked Nigel how he got started on Salisbury Plain. He replied, "After Essex I moved to Warminster, the School of Infantry Training Centre. I started putting up boxes at the western end of Salisbury Plain and the Military were very supportive. Then I ran out of real estate and so I moved to the centre, the Larkhill area. In both areas we've put up 400 boxes altogether, not only for Kestrels but also for Tawny Owls, Little Owls and Barn Owls. But, because I thought Kestrels would be competing with Barn Owls for the same quarry, I set a limit of 25 Kestrel boxes on the plain and 25 off it. They say there's been a decline in Kestrel numbers and the British Trust for Ornithology published a report stating there has been a massive 60% decline over these last few years. Thankfully this hasn't happened in Wiltshire, which is a good area of habitat – and it's likely that the fact that I've put up nest boxes has helped the local Kestrel population. I know that in other parts of the country Kestrels are not plentiful, perhaps because there's a lack of nest boxes. All I can say is that wherever I've been there have been lots of Kestrels and that I've always left a trail of boxes behind."

We visited two more nest box sites, ringing more Kestrel chicks, before Nigel and his team dropped me at Salisbury railway station for my journey home. We had been blessed with good weather and it had been a magic day.

True to his word, Dave Ovenden sent me the video of the nest box and the pair of Kestrels rearing their young. The box was called 'Charlie's box' and it had history. What I did not know was that 20-odd years ago Nigel's wife, Betty, had rescued a male Kestrel with an injured wing and rehabilitated it. Betty called it Charlie and this, in her words, is the triumphant end to the story: "A kestrel nest box had been placed by my husband in one of a group of Beech trees bordering the lane that runs alongside the paddock where Charlie had begun his initial training. We went to the paddock one sunny afternoon and released the little bird. After half an hour we returned. Charlie flew to my glove and we brought him home. The length of freedom time increased over the weeks. A feeding point was selected in the fence line and finally his anklets were removed. Charlie was now unencumbered and knew where to report for his rations. Winter passed, a mild one, and with the spring came a small miracle. Watching through binoculars, we noted the appearance of another kestrel, a female. It was beyond belief but Charlie had attracted a mate and they had settled in the nest box across the paddock. Now began an exciting time. There were eggs and then there were young, and with a huge family to feed Charlie became impatient and reported to our cottage for rations. Charlie's mate must have been hugely impressed that he had a tame human being who produced food on demand. My husband, a licensed ringer, was able to ring the young, a great delight. We had this amazing experience and pleasure for the next five years, during which Charlie used another nest box in the adjacent parish before returning to the original site in the paddock at home. Then, quite simply, he ceased to appear and we knew that all was over. We never knew how old he was, but this wonderful little falcon had given us such pleasure and we like to think we enhanced his life too."

Nigel enclosed two photos of Charlie and his mate flying into the nest box. The box in the photographs is spanking new, tar-paper roof and several perches for the young Kestrels to scramble out onto prior to their first flight. It is very different from that same nest box today, which although rather weather-beaten is still serviceable. Dave's recording starts when the chicks are two to three days old and this is my interpretation:

'21/5/12. There's a lot of chittering as the male Kestrel lands on the lip of the nest box carrying a vole in his bill. The female immediately snatches it from him. There's a bit more chittering and the male flips away. I can see the chicks now. They are covered in white down, which becomes a pale mushroom colour on their backs. Three chicks, one egg still to hatch. They are very small and their heads seem disproportionately large. Black button eyes. The female feeds them very delicately, tiny portions of vole. Now and then she helps herself to bits of flesh which she deems too tough for the chicks.'

'25/5/12. The three chicks are now between three and seven days old. This is because the female doesn't start incubating until after the third egg is laid – a stratagem known as asynchrony. The male, very handsome, flies in with a vole, perches. No female. He calls. His mate brushes past him, grabs the vole. The chicks have already got their heads up, beaks open wide, ready to be fed. While the female jostles around and breaks open the vole, I can see that there's the egg that didn't hatch lying in the debris at the bottom of the box.'

'2/6/12. 14–15 days old. The female is bringing in a lot of food. The chicks are being very grabby. Several times one of them snatches the vole before the female has time to tear it up. This provokes a struggle while the female tries to reclaim the prey. Sometimes she's successful, sometimes not. The main fact is that plenty of food is being brought in.'

'6/6/12. All chicks are standing, not hunkered down. Dots of feathers showing where the primaries and tail feathers are coming through. The chicks are now 18 days old. There's a deal of scrabbling about when prey is brought in. One of the chicks snatches it and turns its back on the others. Female has to plunge in and it turns into a game of "who's got the vole?" Order is restored and normal feeding is resumed.'

'10/6/12. Chicks starting to look like young Kestrels. There's still a lot of down but feathers on back pushing through, as are secondaries. Pale breast feathers streaked with burnt umber almost complete. The male brings in a vole and is pushed aside by the female. Again one of the chicks grabs the prey and mantles over it. Female retrieves some of it and feeds the chicks individually. She swallows the rear end of the vole, flies off. Chicks now 22–23 days old.'

'11/6/12. The chicks lined up in the box. They're waiting for something to happen. The chick on the right casts up a pellet.'

'12/6/12. There's still down on the chicks' heads and on their backs. Tail feathers are developing well. Food brought in and immediately the largest chick commandeers it and retreats to the corner of the box. Female seems fazed by this but eventually there's a scrummage and she manages to salvage a portion, which she feeds to the other chicks. She swallows a portion of skin and perches while she cleans her talons before flying off.'

'19/6/12. The young Kestrels are now fully grown. They've lost all their down. They are standing in the box, scratching, wing-stretching and flapping wings to develop pectoral muscles. They flop in and out of the nest box. They are hungry and start calling. The female comes in and calls. The male dashes in and one of the youngsters grabs the vole and retreats to try and eat it at peace. All the young Kestrels fledged on this day. They are 30–31 days old.'

'22/6/12. All three young Kestrels stretching and scratching. Tranquillity as they stand looking out onto their new world. Food is brought in. There's a mad scramble, wings flailing around, the spell is broken. The eldest youngster wins and, head down, makes for the corner of the box.'

'26/6/12. The box is empty. The female flies in carrying prey and lands on the top of the box. No young Kestrels in sight. She calls repeatedly for them. No response.'

Over the next few weeks the young Kestrels continued to visit 'Charlie's box'. They associated it with food and safety, a place to shelter in bad weather. All the while, though, there was a greater pull, an instinctive pull, which would carry them away to hone their hunting skills and establish their own territories out on Salisbury Plain.

I can imagine them now, their first attempts at hunting. Perched on a hay bale, pouncing on grasshoppers, then, graduating to hovering. The head looking down, eyes scanning the tussocky grass below. The wings beating vigorously with now and then a pause. The spread tail controlling the angle of flight. It is a miracle of natural aerodynamics. Let Gerard Manley Hopkins, the priest poet, have the final word:

> *Rebuffed the big wind. My heart in hiding*
> *Stirred for a bird, - the achieve of, the mastery of the thing!*

THE MERLIN

British Isles population (2008): 1,200 pairs (declining)

The Stricklands, my mother's family, owned great swathes of land in Yorkshire from Whitby on the edge of the North York Moors down through the Yorkshire Wolds almost as far south as Hull. My great-great-great-grandfather, Sir William Strickland (1753–1834) was a keen amateur naturalist, following in the footsteps of the Reverend Gilbert White, author of *The Natural History of Selborne*. Like Gilbert White, he kept a detailed daily journal. There were columns for details of the weather – temperature, barometric pressure, wind, rainfall, and so on. There was also a larger space for nature notes, for when plants were first in flower, when insects and birds first appeared and so forth. On 16 January 1814 he noted that 'an eagle, probably *A. albicilla*, hovered about for several days.' This would have been a White-tailed Eagle.

Sir William has the dubious reputation of shooting one of the last Great Bustards in Yorkshire, probably in about 1830. There are three feathers preserved in his copy of Thomas Pennant's *British Zoology* – did he feel any remorse, I wonder? I remember, 140 years later, doing something that even today, 60 years on, makes me cringe. It was late afternoon, almost dusk, and I was shooting pigeons over decoys as they came in to feed on newly sown spring barley. There was a blurred image of a blue-grey bird coming in to settle amongst the decoys and I swung through and fired. Almost in that instant I knew I had made a big mistake – it was a male Merlin.

This was a turning point in my life. I sold my gun and never shot again. It was to be another 40 years before I could properly atone for that mistake. Then an opportunity arose that allowed me to ask my cousin Fred, who had inherited Fylingdales, the grouse moor near Whitby, if he would consider allowing the Hawk and Owl Trust to manage it in partnership with English Nature (now part of Natural England). Fred and I had several meetings in York and his enthusiasm persuaded me to contact David Clayden at English Nature to pursue the matter further. While these discussions took place I thought I ought to refresh my memories of Fylingdales. Fred kindly met me at York station and whisked me off to the North York Moors. As we passed the Hole of Horcum, a deep valley gouged out by huge torrents of water from melting glaciers at the end of one of the Ice Ages, a gunmetal grey, tetrahedron-shaped structure loomed into view. This was the Royal Air Force's Fylingdales Early Warning System. It had supplanted the three white 'golf balls' that had originally housed the facility.

I had already been warned by Fred that the previous year, 2003, a fire had swept north-eastwards across the moor from the A171, the Whitby to Scarborough road, where it had started, reaching almost as far as Ravenscar on the coast. Seven hundred acres (280 hectares) of heather moorland had been affected. As we surveyed the charred scene of desolation, Fred told me that the fire had provided a bonus: Fylingdales had always been well-known for its archaeological sites, 150 of them, but the fire had revealed many more, bringing the total to over 2,000.

Restoration work was already underway – grass seed had been sown to stabilize the areas where the heather roots had been seriously damaged. These areas would be re-seeded with heather later. Fred was relieved that a great percentage of the heather was alive and pointed out new green shoots pushing out from blackened stems.

Having absorbed Oliver Rackham's *The History of the Countryside*, published in 1986, I knew that Fylingdales had probably only been a heather moor since medieval times, 1,000 years ago. It would have had its origins during the Mesolithic period, 10,000 years ago, when the Wildwood, a mix of birch, pine and hazel, flourished and covered much of the country. The birds of prey with which we are familiar would have been well established and in better numbers than they are today, with only the Kestrel and the Merlin poorly represented.

Aurochs, a huge wild ox, dominated the Wildwood. A Dutch scientist, Franz Vera, proposed that, rather than a continuous canopy, Aurochs, munching away, produced a cycle of succession from trees to scrub to grassland and back again. Using the clearings, Mesolithic man hunted the Auroch with spears. Wolves and Brown Bears dominated the ecosystem, which included Red and Roe Deer, Badgers, Otters and Foxes. By the end of the Mesolithic period the Auroch was extinct.

Six thousand years ago the Wildwood climaxed with oaks, Hazel, Alder, limes and elms. Sea levels rose and fell and the British Isles became separated from the continental land mass. By the Iron Age, 3,000 years ago, hunting had given way to farming. Inexorably, parts of the forest were cleared to provide land for farming. A cooler, wetter climate meant that the debris from deforestation did not fully decay; it built up gradually and turned to peat. Shade-intolerant plants, such as heathers, Bog Myrtle and cotton-grasses, found ready purchase in the peat.

The heather moors, before the North York Moors National Park was established, were known as the Black Moors. They were bleak and inhospitable and had an awesome reputation, since in the winter the weather could be fearsome. On 5 December 1878, George Baker, a sexton, set out with a companion to walk across the moor in response to an urgent message that someone had died and a grave must be dug urgently. It started to snow and his companion turned back. George Baker carried on but never made it. Despite searches and the offer of a reward his body was not found until somebody walked over it on 26th January. There is a memorial stone, the Baker Stone, on Forestry Commission land just off Fylingdales Moor. It was the Victorians who developed the heather moors for grouse shooting and Fylingdales was a well-known grouse moor until the beginning of the Second World War, when the western side of the moor was taken over as a tank-firing range.

On 6 August 2004, I heard from David Clayden that English Nature were happy for the Hawk and Owl Trust to monitor the moor, provided the information was passed on to the various interested parties such as the North York Moors Merlin Study Group. There had always been Merlins on Fylingdales Moor and I knew there was one man who had vast experience of them. I would be contacting him later.

The Merlin is the smallest of all the breeding birds of prey in the British Isles, the male being not much larger than a Mistle Thrush. Its bill is blue-grey with a black tip, the cere and eye-ring are yellow and it has a white eye-stripe. The crown, ear coverts, nape and wing coverts are bluish-grey with black shaft streaks. The tail feathers are the same bluish-grey colour as the upperparts, with black bars running across them down their length and a broad bar at the tip. The breast feathers are pale brown with small, dark, longitudinal streaks in the crop area and becoming more prominent on the belly and flanks. The legs are yellow. The female is larger than the male and is dark brown with rust-coloured edging to the feathers on its upperparts. The primaries are a much darker brown and the tail feathers are dark brown with five pale transverse bars and a pale tip. The underparts are pale cream with dark brown streaks at the crop turning progressively into arrowhead markings on the flanks and belly.

Leslie Brown gives an excellent description of a Merlin hunting in his *New Naturalist* book *British Birds of Prey* published in 1976: 'A Merlin in full pursuit of agile quarry follows every twist and turn of the prey's evolutions with equally swift manoeuvres. In 1972 I saw one pursuing a wader on Stoer Head, in Sutherland. The two came hurtling over my head from the east, and before I could bring my binoculars to bear on them had disappeared behind a ridge into a dip in the ground 200 yards away; in that distance, in about 20 seconds, the Merlin had risen and stooped at its quarry three times. I did not see the end of the chase, but assume that since the Merlin did not reappear from within the shallow valley it may have finally killed its desperate quarry.'

Aristotle (384–322 BC) and Pliny (23–79 AD), a Greek and a Roman, were the first learned persons to write about natural history and particularly about birds. Some of their observations are accurate, others quite ridiculous. In his *Historia Animalium*, Aristotle makes mention of the Merlin: 'Among the hawks, the strongest is the Buzzard, second the Merlin, third the kirkos.' The *kirkos* referred to the moor buzzard, a harrier. Pliny tells us that he knew of 16 kinds of hawks, one of which 'The Greeks named Aesalon, which alone is seen at all times; whereas the most are gone when Winter cometh.' This referred to the European Merlin that we know in the British Isles. Pliny also gives us a charming introduction to falconry: 'In a part of Thrace beyond Amphipolis, Men and Hawks catch birds together, in a sort of fellowship: for the Men drive the Birds from the Woods and Reeds, and the Hawks, flying over their heads, bear them to the ground.'

According to *The Oxford Dictionary of British Bird Names* (1993), the name Merlin is probably derived from the Anglo-Norman *merillon*, with loss of the unstressed initial vowel from the Old French *emerillon*, their name for the Merlin. Thereafter, there were a succession of variations: Merlyon in 1325 AD, followed by Merlyn, and by 1616 this diminutive falcon is known as the Merlin. The Merlin's scientific name is *Falco columbarius* (*Falco* after its sickle-shaped bill and *columbarius* meaning dove). The subspecies *F. c. aesalon* (meaning hawk) is found from Ireland, throughout Britain and eastwards as far as north-west Siberia.

Falconry was introduced into England by the Normans in the sixth century. In the beginning this was the prerogative of kings and princes, but it soon became a national recreation and a means of putting food on the table. *The Book of St. Albans*, published in 1486 and supposedly written by Dame Juliana Berner, indicates the different species of falcons and hawks allocated to individuals according to their position in society. The Merlin was specifically allocated to a Lady.

There is a captivating poem by Sir Walter Scott (1771–1832), *The Lay of the Last Minstrel*, in which a lady falconer and her Merlin are featured:

> The Ladye by the altar stood;
> Of sable velvet her array,
> And on her head a crimson hood,
> With pearls embroider'd and entwin'd,
> Guarded with gold, with ermine lin'd;
> A merlin sat upon her wrist,
> Held by a leash of silken twist.

At the time this poem was written, the shooting of Red Grouse on the heather moors of the British Isles had just begun. In Scotland particularly, any bird with a hooked beak was classified as vermin and destroyed. On the Glengarry Estate in Scotland, between 1837 and 1840, 78 Merlins were killed in the name of game preservation. Since they use prominent stones among the heather as lookout points, they were easy to trap. In hindsight, however, there is no way such persecution can be justified, as the Merlin's main prey is Meadow Pipits and other small birds. Nevertheless, there was a healthy population between the two world wars, when Merlins bred in the south-west of England on Exmoor and Dartmoor and had strongholds in Wales, North Yorkshire, Lancashire and Northumberland and, of course, in Scotland. However, there was a marked decline in the Merlin population in the British Isles after the Second World War, particularly in the 1950s and 1960s, followed by further declines in the 1970s. Four factors influenced this decline: the use of pesticides at their lowland winter quarters, persecution, disturbance by hill walkers, and the hard winters of 1947 and 1963.

In 1983–84, the first survey of Merlins in the British Isles was carried out and the population was estimated at between 550–650 pairs. Ten years later, in 1993–4, another survey was undertaken and the population estimated at 1,291 pairs. The population had increased and was stable, but the Merlin was nevertheless placed on the Amber list of Birds of Conservation Concern. One of the reasons behind this population increase was that there was now very little persecution, most gamekeepers having at last realised that Merlins had no adverse effect on Red Grouse numbers. Even so, there were some who took the law into their own hands by taking eggs to reduce the clutch size, and by shooting and trapping Merlins.

In 2008 a third survey was undertaken and showed that the Merlin population was relatively stable at 1,200 pairs. Nevertheless, it was noticed that there had been some local declines, specifically in parts of the north of England. A number of factors were identified that may have contributed to these declines. These included land use change, particularly the development of commercial forestry plantations; and declines in the populations of some of the Merlin's prey. In addition, grouse moor management since the 1970s had resulted in the area of new burns more than doubling, resulting in the removal of old, tall heather, the Merlin's preferred nesting sites. Another factor that may have contributed to the declines is climate change, since the north of England is at the southern edge of the Merlin's breeding range. In the future, the effects of climate change may mean that Merlins will have to move north to breed successfully.

It was time to get out on the moor and talk to Wilf Norman, local bird-watcher and Merlin expert, who had been observing Merlins on Fylingdales for the past 25 years. He would know where all the breeding sites were and we had to make sure that they were not destroyed when the heather was burnt during the autumn and winter. My cousin Fred came with me, as well as John Cavana, who had been taken on as a ranger/gamekeeper.

We first walked south from the B1416 road right into the moor to Low Moor, where there was a good stand of tall heather on slightly higher ground. Wilf explained that this was what Merlins looked for in picking a nest site – tall heather and a view dominating the area. John quickly understood that this area was not to be burnt when the burning regime started in the autumn. It was tough walking but we managed to check out all the other potential nesting sites on the moor, giving John a clear understanding of the areas that must be left alone. Unfortunately, we didn't see a Merlin or, for that matter, any Red Grouse all day.

I asked Fred about his views on heather burning and how successful it had been, and was told, "I can remember there was big debate initially about whether we should burn or cut the heather. I was in favour of cutting because it had been used very successfully on an RSPB moorland reserve in Cumbria. Cutting can be done in all weathers, the heather regenerates quicker, sheep do not like the prickly stalks, and the cutting is done by contractors not gamekeepers. Nonetheless, the archaeologists were against it because stones and monuments can be damaged by the cutters. So, every autumn we burnt selected areas of heather. But prior to burning we'd cut firebreaks on three sides of the area to be burnt to reduce the chances of a wildfire starting. The cut, damp heather and grass acted as a very effective fire extinguisher. Nevertheless, we did have one 'wildfire' that got out of hand and burnt 20 hectares although fortunately it recovered quickly."

Fred continued, "We have a target, set by Natural England, of the amount of heather we must burn each year – it's 100 hectares a year on a 17–20-year rotation. We've got into a familiar routine now and Phil Turford, one of the farmers on the moor, helps David Hutton, the keeper, with the burning. They start in October and finish in March. The latest figure I have is that they burnt 115 hectares during the autumn/winter of 2011/12."

Fred added, "It's been the same with our plans for vermin control on the moor. Carrion Crows and Magpies were a problem: perched in a tree they were able to check out the positions of all the nesting birds from Red Grouse to Meadow Pipits. As soon as eggs were laid or young hatched they'd be in there in a flash, gobbling them up. The population of Carrion Crows and Magpies has increased enormously over the last twenty years and these birds have few natural predators. But recently I've learnt that the Common Buzzard, which is currently enjoying a population explosion throughout the British Isles, does take nestling crows to feed their own young. Perhaps in the future they will assume the role of top predator at Fylingdales. Nevertheless, desperate times require desperate measures and the fight against Carrion Crows and Magpies starts with the Larsen trap, which is a very effective means of control. These traps are roughly two-and-a-half feet square and one-and-a-half feet tall and have two compartments. One is for the 'call bird' and has perches and food and water provided. The other is the trap, the door to which is kept open by a split perch. Carrion Crows are very territorial and come to investigate any potential rival. When an intruding crow touches the perch the door closes and the crow is caught.

He concluded by explaining that, "Initially we had problems with the public letting the call birds out and destroying the traps – they didn't understand that Carrion Crows are so harmful to wildlife. We placed notices close to each of the traps, explaining why we were trapping the crows and that what we were doing was legal. We had no more trouble. From a quite modest 33 trapped in 2007, David Hutton, the keeper, really got into his stride and, using the new Multi Larsen Trap, caught a record 269 crows in the winter of 2011/12. Foxes can do just as much damage as crows and at night David and a driver go out 'lamping.' The driver operates the light and positions the vehicle and David uses a ·223 rifle with a night-vision sight to take out the Fox. Stoats and Weasels need trapping too and artificial tunnels with a Fenn trap set inside are a very effective means of control. Stoats can be very destructive, taking the eggs and chicks of Red Grouse, waders and other ground-nesting birds, including the Merlin."

Working with David Hutton is Chris Hansell, the Wildlife Ranger, who explained, "My job is moorland management, maintenance of tracks and so on. I work closely with David Hutton and the two of us, with the shepherd, carry out the heather burning each year. I'm also the contact for various organisations that want to carry out surveys on the moor and for those who want to undertake research projects on some aspect of the moor's biodiversity. I've been getting an increasing number of volunteers out on the moor, more eyes on the ground, and now have a good network of people. We've set up a lot of new nest boxes and started studying the autumn migrants coming through. We've had four Hen Harriers through this year and as there's a lot more food for them on the moor than there used to be, I think it's just a matter of time before they stay and breed. When they do, we'll be ready for them and make sure they are safeguarded."

I needed to see Wilf Norman again, get him on his own and talk to him about his knowledge of Merlins at Fylingdales. When we met he told me, "There are about six different sites on the moor that Merlins use and generally we'll have three pairs nesting. One of the sites was burnt out in the big fire – it'll take a long time to recover. This year has been a bit strange with the weather and several pairs turned up briefly but then disappeared. There's plenty of prey for them – Skylarks and Meadow Pipits. I think it was that really warm weather in March, it was exceptional – up into the 70s for days. Whether that threw the bird's metabolism out or whatever, I don't know. In the previous five or six years pairs have bred successfully and I've been ringing the chicks."

I had been told that Wilf had had an unusual experience when he once visited a Merlins' nest and asked him to tell me more. "Yes, that was in 2005. I'd gone to a nest as I was expecting the eggs to hatch. As I got closer and closer and nothing happened and I wondered whether the nest had failed. I took a few steps more and spotted the female just sat there. She just let me walk right up to her and reach down and pick her up. The reason was that she had two tiny chicks in the nest and an egg that was chipping, actually in the process of hatching. She was one of the birds that had been ringed on Bransdale Moor five years before, providing the first evidence that our birds come back to the North York Moors to breed. I replaced her very gently back on her chicks and the egg and she just stayed there. It was a wonderful experience, I must admit."

I then asked Wilf to recount his Adder story, which I had heard before. "It happened on Spaunton Moor in the early '90s. I knew there was a Merlins' nest somewhere but couldn't find it. So I just sat down and watched. The female came by and had a look at me and then, all of a sudden, I saw the male sitting on a mound about 15 metres away. I got up and he flew in an arc a short distance and landed on a rock nearby, just looking at me. I thought this was very odd and concluded that the nest must be close by. I walked forward about ten yards and there was the nest. And in it was an Adder with the head of a tiny Merlin chick in its mouth, trying to swallow it. The chick was cheeping away and I didn't know what to do. In the end, I stamped on the snake's tail and it dropped the chick and scarpered. The chick was okay but it was bald. I would love to say that the chick survived but the next time I went to the nest site it had gone. It was a stretch of moor that was rocky – classic Stoat habitat. The loss of the chick was very disappointing but I wish I'd had my camera with me when I saw that Adder trying to swallow it". I asked Wilf if he had any other memories of Merlins and he told me, "One time I was walking on a footpath that ran along a ridge when a Meadow Pipit came over the skyline being chased by a Kestrel. The pipit quite nonchalantly dodged out of the way and the Kestrel changed its tactics and started climbing above it and stooping at it. It made no difference as the pipit just side-stepped, no trouble at all. And then, all of a sudden, there was a blue blur as a male Merlin cut through and just grabbed the pipit. I'll swear the Merlin looked up at the Kestrel as much as to say – that's how it's done, mate!"

I said to Wilf that I thought Merlins were difficult to spot and that you had to be lucky to see one. I was concerned that, as Fylingdales was now a reserve, visitors, if they had not seen a Merlin, would perhaps go away feeling disappointed. He told me to go and talk to Brian Walker, the Forestry Commission's Environment Manager. My meeting with Brian was a real eye-opener. When I expressed my concerns he said, "I know what you mean. Just to look at heather moorland you wouldn't think it was a fantastically diverse habitat. Where the interface of lime and acid come together you get a fascinating variety of plant life. There are myriad little pockets containing interesting species. In my job as Environment Manager of the Forestry Commission in north Yorkshire I've been able to bring environmentalists together, at whatever level of expertise – academics, organisations and individuals – to help understand and protect forest ecosystems. This has helped the conservation effort at Fylingdales. The big ecological opportunity is that it's got forest to the north and south of it and it's got quite differently managed land in and around RAF Fylingdales."

Brian continued, "There are two wonderful streams, the Jugger Howe Beck and Blea Hill Beck, which support Water Voles – a species that has now virtually disappeared from our North York Moors National Park. I can remember seeing them down near Scarborough on Scalby Beck. It was like *Tales of the River Bank* – there were loads of them going back and forth. I discovered that the North York Moors National Park didn't have a Mammal Group. But there is one now and we bring everyone together for a meeting every

18 months or so to share their knowledge, find out what they've discovered. Laura Winter is the best surveyor of Water Voles in the North York Moors. Every year she'll visit the best sites to see how they're doing. There are a lot of questions still to be answered, though, particularly about the dynamics of the population."

Brian also explained, "Fylingdales Moor supports a particularly important population of the Large Heath butterfly, a northern butterfly that is more or less at the edge of its range here. It is found in damp places on moorland feeding on Purple Moor-grass and cotton-grasses and is being monitored by Dave Wainright from Butterfly Conservation. Another rare butterfly is the Small Pearl-bordered Fritillary, a headline species of which there's a really important population at Fylingdales. It is found on the banks of all the streams running off the moor and can sometimes be seen settling on Marsh Violets, one of the caterpillars' food plants."

I had heard that Fylingdales Moor was also home to a particularly rare snail found in only four places in the British Isles and asked Brian whether this was true. He replied, "Yes, it's a whorl snail, *Vertigo geyeri*, that likes cool, damp places fed by spring water. Jugger Howe Beck stream is perfect for it. The snail is tiny and when snail expert Adrian Norris said he'd show me one, I thought to myself, hang on a minute, if it's that tiny how's he going to find it? Anyway, Adrian walked alongside the stream and now and then pressed his hand down into areas of wet moss. After a bit, he stopped and held out his hand. I couldn't believe it, as there were five of these rare snails lying there. It was pure magic to find a snail like that, only 1·8 millimetres across the shell!"

Brian also told me that there were groups surveying Adders, beetles, moths, bees and crickets, and that if I wanted to know about birds I would be best off talking to Professor John Edwards. After an initial year as a trustee of Fylingdales, I had handed responsibility for the moor over to John for safekeeping. When I did do I had suggested to him that it was a bit of a poisoned chalice. Some time later, with a wry smile, he said, "A poisoned challenge, I think you meant. When I started I knew nothing about moorland management. More importantly, I didn't know what was on the moor, particularly what birds were there. So that's why we started the annual surveys; they will be in their eighth year this year. We have a group of volunteers, whose only qualification is that they must be good birders, very good birders. We use the system devised by the British Trust for Ornithology for their Breeding Bird Survey. We cover 22 one-kilometre squares, that's nearly 90% of the moor. I can tell you that Red Grouse have increased and Skylark have decreased after three bumper years from 2008 to 2010 and Curlew also increased. The Meadow Pipit has always been the most plentiful species since the surveys began. Four new species (Nuthatch, Fieldfare, Raven and Short-eared Owl) were recorded in 2011. The weather plays an enormous part in the breeding success of our birds of prey. A pair of Montagu's Harriers was washed out by rain in 2007, and in 2011 two pairs of Merlins attempted to breed. One pair failed, the other fledged two chicks."

John's meticulous wildlife monitoring was a significant factor when the Court Leet, after many years of negotiations, succeeded in getting Fylingdales Moor into the Government's Higher Level Stewardship (HLS) scheme. The Court Leet is made up of farmers and residents of the parish of Fylingdales. Two members of the Court Leet are on the board of the company that manages the HLS agreement, along with cousin Fred and the sheep farmers who now stray sheep on the moor. Meadow Pipits and Skylarks benefit from the insects that thrive as a result of the presence of the sheep. This is all down to the HLS agreement, which has strict targets to be reached. The HLS funding has enabled the Hawk and Owl Trust to employ three part-time staff at Fylingdales: an education officer, a wildlife ranger and a moorland keeper.

Not so long ago, John Edwards and I were sitting at the top of the Jugger Howe Moor steps. It was a brilliant, crystal-clear day in June and I was bemoaning the fact that we had not seen a Merlin all day. John was explaining how the weather affected them but his voice trailed off when he noticed that I was not listening. My lack of attention was because, looking past him over his shoulder, I had just seen a speck in the distance. It rocketed towards us and, with an audible "*whoosh*", a female Merlin flashed past his shoulder and continued, contour-hugging, to the far south end of the moor. We looked at each other and laughed. An epic, shared, experience!

John relies on a wide variety of folk to help him with his surveys. John Knight is just such a person and is a volunteer member of the North York Moors National Park Merlin Survey Group and an ecologist and photographer. Mick Carroll, a member of the Northern England Raptor Forum, kindly took me up to meet John at his home near Guisborough on the edge of the North York Moors. I asked John how he had become involved with Merlins and he explained, "One day I was walking over the moor and as I crossed the brow of a hill a male Merlin shot off a nest containing four eggs. This first finding of a Merlin nest started me on several decades of interest in, perhaps addiction to, the Merlin. The gamekeeper at that time loved Merlins, which he used to call 'his Merlin', and was very helpful to me. That was in the early 1970s, when there were a lot of Merlin on the moors, and I remember finding five nests in one weekend in quite a small area. I soon started photographing Merlin and have since taken hundreds of photographs of them, though admittedly most are only fit for the bin. Sometimes I've spent ten hours in the hide and not taken a single photo all day."

Thus, John Knight embarked on a pursuit that carried him in the footsteps of pioneer wildlife photographers such as Richard and Cherry Kearton. The first photographs they took were of a Song Thrush and its nest and eggs. Cherry Kearton was an excellent rock-climber and at considerable risk dangled from cliffs to photograph nesting seabirds. Their equipment was clumsy, not exactly portable but they lugged it everywhere to get the right shot. They even used a stuffed cow as a portable hide, each day moving it forwards until the camera was in range of the nest. It was very hot in there and one day when the temperature was up in the 70s, Cherry fainted. The stuffed cow fell over, feet in the air and Cherry was marooned for several hours before he could be rescued.

The Keartons' photographs of a Merlin at the nest were probably the first taken in England. The nest is in a slight hollow situated in deep heather. The Merlin is facing left and looking back over its shoulder. In their book *With Nature and a Camera*, which was published in 1898, the Keartons describe an incident in the home life of the Merlin: 'One day, whilst waiting for a Merlin to come back to her fast-feathering chicks, a violent thunderstorm broke over the hills. When the hail and rain descended in earnest the youngsters appeared to get frightened and began to call out "*tway, tway, tway*" in the most pathetic tones. This had the desired effect, for the old bird soon faced the ordeal of the lens; but although I secured two or three photographs they were of very little use on account of the miserably wet and bedraggled condition of the bird.'

The Keartons were born and spent the early part of their lives at Thwaite in Swaledale in North Yorkshire. Less than 50 miles south, as the Merlin flies, were the moors near Skipton where William Rowan in 1918 undertook the first in-depth study of the breeding biology of the Merlin. That summer one of the keepers told Rowan of a brood of newly hatched Merlin, which he offered to spare if he wished to watch them. Rowan went to look at the site and wrote, 'The young were quite small and still unable to walk. They were clad entirely in white down. They had a most ferocious mien, and lay on their backs and presented their claws and their beaks when we attempted to handle them.'

A hide was erected and Rowan started his vigil. He quickly discovered that the only way to avoid missing the most interesting behaviour was to stay all night in the hide: 'Once indeed I was in there for 36 hours on end without coming out and without a chance of stretching my aching limbs. Sleep was, of course, out of the question.'

No matter whether it thundered and rained or was blisteringly hot, Rowan never saw the hen Merlin brood her young: 'At night they huddled together, but just anyhow. For a moment one would see a large beady eye shining out from some corner of the soft, downy pile. But as night fell all movement would cease. With the earliest streak of dawn, first one head and then another would jerkily appear.'

The hen Merlin, nevertheless, day and night kept a watch on the nest site from her nearby boulder perch. The cock bird flew in with food every two hours or so, the hen flying out to meet him. Rowan noted 'Both birds were always so low, and the transaction so swiftly executed, that it was exceedingly difficult to see whether he dropped the prey or whether she snatched it from him. The prey included the following birds: Meadow Pipit, Skylark, Ring Ouzel, Snipe, Spotted Flycatcher, Willow Wren and Song Thrush, though the first constituted 90% of the entire supply.'

The feeding at the nest took a quarter of an hour when they were young, but was completed much more quickly as they grew older and stronger. Rowan noted the blood-filled

quills emerging from the down and that the youngsters were starting to stand. They were responding to the hen bird's alarm calls and would 'freeze' no matter what they were doing. By 1 August the backs of the young were well feathered and they were strong enough to stand on prey and pull it apart. They were becoming adventurous, climbing up the heather. As Rowan put it 'It was as though they were trying to get used to the sensation of being in the air. Instead of scrambling down they would now jump the last few inches with wings outspread. On 2 August the down was disappearing visibly. The colouring of their first winter plumage was apparent. On 5 August the three biggest could fly for about 100 yards.'

The keeper had asked Rowan several times when he thought the young would fly but was not satisfied with Rowan's answer and shot two of the young Merlins that had ventured farthest from their nest. The other two were caught and the keeper promised Rowan that if he took the young away he would spare the adult birds. Two weeks later Rowan released the two surviving chicks on wild heather moorland in Wales.

Twenty years later one of the greatest wildlife photographers of all time, Eric Hosking, was in Scotland erecting a hide ready to photograph the Merlin. At that time in the early 1940s, he had become famous because a Tawny Owl he was photographing had attacked him and as a result he had lost his left eye. Eric Hosking's photographs of Merlin were taken near Aviemore in Scotland and appear in his book *Birds of the Day*, which was published in 1944. The most famous one is of a hen Merlin standing alongside her clutch of eggs, one of which has been displaced. This is Eric's account of the story behind the photograph: 'It was kicked there by the hen as she left the nest hurriedly to go to take food from the cock, and it caused her a great deal of embarrassment when she noticed it on her return. She tried to rake it back to the nest, but it was rather deep in the heather and was not easily rolled, so reluctantly she turned to the nest and brooded the other three eggs for a while. She was, however, obviously concerned for the missing egg and tried again and again to recover it, till presently she succeeded in getting her bill well underneath and rolled it back into the nest.'

Chris Knights, a wildlife photographer who farms in Norfolk, told me a story about photographing a Merlin in February 2010: "There was a light covering of snow on the ground and I went to photograph some Skylarks that were feeding in the centre of a great big field that had been sown with winter barley. When I drove up they flew away but dropped down at the end of the field. I followed them in my vehicle and slowly drove around the headland before setting up to photograph them. Suddenly I was aware of a blurred shape flashing past me. It was a hen Merlin heading hell for leather towards the Skylarks. They shot up in the air and the Merlin followed them up and caught one just as easily as that. It settled about 150 yards from me on a little hillock where a Hare had scratched at the soil and removed the snow. I left it to feed for a few minutes and then gradually edged in until the Merlin was filling the viewfinder of my camera. When she flew off all that was left were the Skylark's feet lying in the snow."

In the 1980s, there was concern that the widespread afforestation of moorland areas would affect the ground-nesting Merlin. Between 1986 and 1989, Jack Orchell studied the Merlin in the Galloway Forests, supported by the Hawk and Owl Trust. As he explained to me, "In 1980–81 my Merlin study led me in a new direction. Merlins were conspicuous by their absence from their traditional hillside haunts. Armed with a Schedule 1 Merlin licence from the Nature Conservancy Council, which allowed me to look for Merlin nests as long as I kept disturbance to a minimum, I searched far and wide for them but without success. Invariably, Merlin-like birds, glimpsed dashing low across heather-covered hillsides or through forest glades, turned out to be Cuckoos. So what had become of the region's Merlins? The answer surfaced rather unexpectedly in 1982. I had been watching a boulder-strewn ridge near a moorland road in April and one morning noticed a male Merlin perched prominently on a large rock. He made two ground-hugging flights down a slope towards a Meadow Pipit displaying near the moorland track. His first flight was unsuccessful, for the pipit found cover in a patch of Bog Myrtle at the last moment, but his second attack ended in a capture. I watched him ferry his prey back to his boulder perch, where the hapless victim was plucked for several minutes and various parts were consumed. I resolved to return later in the year to look for the Merlins' nest."

Jack continued his story, "June brought disappointment. I failed to find any Merlins nesting among heather on the recently planted boulder ridge, so in desperation resolved to check out the deep heather above the tree line on a mountain some way to the north where several years earlier a Merlin had dashed past me in a power-dive. I waited until July for my recce of the mountain slopes, for that is when the female Merlin would be most vocal in defence of her nest site and chicks. The uphill trudge through conifers was exhausting and a prolonged exploration of the higher slopes yielded nothing. To make matters worse, it started to rain and the ground became dangerously slippery underfoot. I was forced to take cover in the heather and remained there assailed by clouds of tormenting midges until the rain cloud passed and sunlight flooded down. Almost immediately I heard the faint begging calls of a female Merlin far below me in the forest. Her calls were swiftly answered by the higher-pitched yikkering of the male. Before I knew it, the female's calling became louder and louder as she flew uphill in my direction and eventually alighted in a tall Sitka Spruce growing a few metres below me. After half an hour she returned with prey to the very same tree. I noted its exact location and decided to revisit with a couple of trusted friends to confirm that I had actually found a Merlins' nest in an alien

conifer. Barry Holiday and Geoff Shaw had been forest rangers for some years and both were knowledgeable about birds of prey. Barry was an expert tree-climber and Geoff was a skilled bird-ringer. Two days later they accompanied me to the 'Merlin tree' that stood at the end of a narrow ride in the forest. As we approached, I found encouraging signs on the ground – a few flight feathers plucked from fully grown Meadow Pipits. Before long Barry had scaled the lofty spruce and had found an old crows' nest near the crown containing four partly feathered Merlin chicks. They were lowered in a bag to Geoff, who duly weighed and ringed them as I took a few photographs to record the find. The chicks were quickly replaced in the nest and we left them in peace.

Jack concluded by remarking, "That discovery provided the impetus for a pioneering Galloway-wide search for tree-nesting Merlins, with the full support of the Forestry

Commission and other interested parties. Thankfully, more tree-nesting Merlins were found scattered along woodland edges across the region. My study formed the basis for the conservation guidelines for both moorland and forest-nesting Merlins alike. It also established beyond doubt that Scotland's commercial forests, whose creation had been strongly opposed during the 1980s, did have some benefit to wildlife."

The Merlin was brought right into the public eye by the advent of BBC Television's *Springwatch* and *Autumnwatch* programmes. In 2006 Simon King, a bird of prey enthusiast and expert presenter, crouched in the heather, extolling the flying powers and hunting prowess of this diminutive falcon that we see zipping low across the heather and then harassing an intruding Red Kite. In his words, "This is the smallest bird of prey in the British Isles. They're very powerful flyers and they punch well above their weight when it comes to hunting, taking Meadow Pipits and other birds. Just look at the speed they reach... And this is the moment when the male Merlin chased a Red Kite, an iconic bird of Wales. But look at the size of it compared to the kite – a tiny little gnat, with absolutely no qualms about taking on that big beast." Simon stretches both arms out to demonstrate the kite's wingspan and then indicates that the Merlin is not much bigger than his hand and wrist. "Now if you look at my arms stretched out, that's about the wingspan of a Red Kite. The Merlin is a tiny guy by comparison. So, that shows just how feisty they are. That Merlin was nesting about 100 metres away from a Hen Harrier. You'd think that's kind of extraordinary, why so close? It's thought that they benefit from each other's company because the Merlin, as you've seen, is quite a bolshy character. It chases off predators like Red Kites, Ravens and others that would steal eggs or chicks from either of their nests. And the Hen Harrier has a very different method of hunting – it flies low over the heather and suddenly flushes birds and, if it's lucky, catches one. Often it doesn't and those birds that are flushed the Merlin can often chase and take. They have a reciprocal relationship."

We are back with Simon in the heather and follow a Merlin in slow motion as it wheels and stoops trying to outfly a Skylark. "Now we haven't filmed a Merlin hunting since we've been here, but a few years I did film a Merlin hunting for a series called *Trials of Life*. Their method of chasing prey is to follow its every move, to shadow it, and on this occasion it's chasing Skylarks. The soundtrack isn't erroneous, the Skylark is singing, which may seem really curious when it's within an inch of losing its life, but it's a communication from the Skylark to the Merlin saying, 'I am so fit, I am so strong that I can afford to sing my little heart out despite the fact you're chasing me.' And more often than not, Skylarks that sing well and strongly while they are being chased, do get away, albeit with a crash into the vegetation."

Now we return to Simon sitting on some tussocky grass with the coastline of the Shetland Islands below him. "We've been lucky enough to introduce cameras to a Merlins' nest. Let's see what's been going on with them." A view is then shown from a Closed Circuit Television camera pointing into the nest as the female Merlin returns to her clutch of eggs – it is a privileged glimpse of the private life of the Merlin, quite unique. The nest is in deep heather and there is a view from it across rolling heather moor to the coastline beyond. "That's the female Merlin, just hopping onto the nest of five eggs. She does the majority of the incubating. What a great view, fantastic to be able to see them in such detail. She does a lot of egg-turning, it's important she keeps them on the move." We see the male Merlin skimming fast across the heather hillside to deliver food to the female before taking over

the incubation of the eggs in the nest. "The male has been great. He's a fantastic dad. And he's doing the majority of the hunting at the moment, not just for himself but he also feeds his mate. A quick food-pass. And while she's off having 'brekky' he goes off to do his share of incubation. The male is much smaller than the female and he's got a bit of a problem when it comes to incubating the eggs because he can't squeeze them all under his breast feathers. Try as he might, he can't cover them all so it's just as well that the female's doing the majority of the incubation."

John Aitchison was the wildlife cameraman and told me, "Both adults accepted the hide very quickly. We'd moved it slowly into position over a few days. Someone always walked us into the hide and walked away again. I remember the hide being full of cables, batteries and a recorder and monitor for the nest camera. Having the nest camera meant we could check exactly what was going on in the nest so we were confident that the female was comfortable with us. And of course there was the usual tripod and long-lens camera set up. My abiding memory is the speed at which the male Merlin had to roll out of the way of his mate when she grabbed food from him."

Back to Simon a few days later: "Fantastic news from our Merlin nest. This is hot off the press. Just a few hours ago this was going on in our Merlin nest." The female Merlin leaves the nest to reveal two newly hatched chicks. "Here's the female bringing a meal in, possibly a Meadow Pipit. All the chicks hatch at different times because the Merlin doesn't start incubating until the second egg is laid. That means there's a big age gap between the first chick and the last. Just look at how weak this chick is compared to its sibling. Incredibly weak, it can't even take food yet. We'll keep a camera team watching them over the weekend."

Simon, Shetland coastline in the background, brings us up-to-date on the Merlin family: "Let's find out what's been going on with them over the weekend." Back to the CCTV camera as the female Merlin leaves the nest to reveal five chicks. "There you go!

Five beautiful chicks. A lovely, lovely sight. They do quite well up here in the Shetlands, Merlins. Very rare birds but they are doing okay. The male has been a model dad bringing in food to the female. She's been very attentive too, trying to ensure that each of the chicks gets a meal. Their youngest one, the one that hatched most recently, is on the far left and it can barely lift its head. We hope it does well, we'll certainly be keeping a very close eye on that family and bringing news of them throughout the course of the week."

Several days later Simon briefs us on the progress of the Merlins: "We've had tremendously strong winds, so strong that we couldn't record the Merlins without disturbing them – the hides would have been buffeting around. But today we've put in a new camera, giving us a new viewpoint... This is the female Merlin as she returns to the five chicks. You hear the wings of mum coming in; you can hear the chicks calling. Beautiful stuff. A very attentive mum."

The male lands on a fence post, he's clutching a Meadow Pipit. The female approaches at speed to grab the pipit. She misses first time, tries again and succeeds. As Simon explains, "The male has been hunting small birds and the food-pass between him and the female is completely astonishing. Picks it up – oops, she misses it – and takes it from his beak with her feet. Got to be careful she doesn't take an eye out. And then straight back to the nest and feeding the youngsters. All five are alive and growing. I'm a bit concerned about one of the middle chicks. There, if you look at the new camera position you can see the bird in the bottom left, it's got a scratch on its back. How did it happen? Did one of the siblings do it? Perhaps it was mum. I really can't be sure. We are going to have another look tomorrow and hopefully all these chicks are going to make it through the night."

Sadly, *Springwatch* did not return to the Merlins' nest. I talked to Simon about it and he thought that since it was near the end of the series, and satellite time is very expensive, the BBC just pulled the plug. He did assure me, however, that the Merlin chicks all fledged successfully.

Back with John Knight in North Yorkshire, I asked him what he had learnt in all the years he had been studying Merlins, perhaps starting with when the birds return to the moor to breed. He told me, "The males arrive first and they are faithful to a site they've used previously and they'll defend it against all incomers. What makes a good nest site? Tall heather is important for shelter and cover. In one direction there needs to be a good view over the moor. There needs to be good look-out positions, boulders, near the nest that the male Merlin can use. One concern of mine is the hillocks of turf that are put up on grouse moors to hold medicated grit. Merlins use these as vantage points or plucking posts. Birds of prey occasionally ingest grit to clean out their crops – are Merlin taking in medicated grit, will it affect them?"

"What about the food supply," I asked, and John explained, "It is vitally important. Merlins depend on Meadow Pipits as their main food source. On the moor there are resident and migratory Meadow Pipits. If there's been a terrible winter, like some of the ones we've had lately, the resident pipits will have been killed off, starved to death. So the breeding season is put on hold until the migratory birds arrive. You can tell the difference by the plumage: the resident bird's plumage is braided and dull from contact with the heather; the migrant's plumage is pristine. This is my explanation for the variable breeding success of our Merlin. After they have settled down to breed, the male carries out practically all the incubation for the first week to ten days. I think this is because the female has lost about half her body weight in laying her clutch of eggs and needs to recover. So she spends the time feeding on Mistle Thrushes, Fieldfares and Starlings, building up her reserves again. When I've been in my hide photographing a pair of Merlin I've twice come across a case of polygyny. In one instance the male had brought in food to the nest. Two hours went by and he hadn't reappeared. The female was getting anxious and in the end she disappeared. About 20 minutes later the male came in with food and I was able to photograph him feeding the young. I reckon the female had got very upset because no food had been brought in, so went off and gave the male a piece of her mind to make sure he brought food to the nest. I'm sure the male's long absences were because he was looking after two females."

I had hoped that Bruce would be able to use John Knight's hide to sketch Merlin chicks in the nest but unfortunately his pair of Merlins failed to breed. Garry and Mike Marchant, who made the excellent film on the breeding biology of the Goshawk, stepped into the breach and offered to let Bruce tag along while they ringed some Merlin chicks from a nest they had been watching. This is Bruce's account of his day with Garry and Mike:

'27/6/13. I left Cambridge at 4 a.m. and arrived at Helmsley where I met Garry and Mike. As we drove up onto the moor through patchy light rain and low scudding cloud we were hoping that all would be well for ringing the chicks – although a spell of heavy rain at any moment would mean abandoning the chance of ringing today. But fortunately, as we left the car and kitted up, the weather cleared enough so we quickly set off across the moor guided by Garry and Mike's experience and a hand-held GPS device. After about 10 minutes we heard the alarm call of the female bird first, and after a short while the slightly shriller call of the male as they swept high overhead, but at a distance, alert and defensive as we approached the nest. After a moment or two of careful treading, there in a shallow dinner-plate-sized depression hollowed out under a wiry tangle of lank heather were three Merlin chicks – about 25 days old I was told. They were still downy in patches with plenty of rufous feathering showing as they leaned back in a collective bundle with talons clenched like boxer's fists. I hung back a little behind Garry and Mike and unpacked my sketchbook as they set themselves up for a spell of processing the young birds – weighing, measuring wing length, and putting a ring on the left leg of each chick. For the 20 minutes or so it took Garry and Mike I crouched alongside them sketching rapidly as they handled the birds, or leaned towards the nest noting as much detail as I could as each bird was processed. Fabulous birds and, thanks to Garry and Mike, an exceptionally memorable day – except for the weather.'

A few days later I phoned Garry and asked if I could visit the site with him. He kindly agreed and the following is my journal entry for that day:

'6/7/13. I catch an early train from Peterborough, change at York and arrive at Thirsk, where Garry meets me. We drive through Helmsley and up onto the moors. Long winding road, moorland either side. Television mast looms up out of the mist. The odd barn here and there, wherever there are some stone-wall-enclosed fields, and now and then an isolated farm. Bleak! As we pull up it starts to rain. We hear grouse nearby and we wait. I'm hoping to see a nest containing Merlin chicks, the ones that Bruce sketched while they were being ringed. Garry has been keeping tabs on them. After about twenty minutes, we think it's getting brighter and we set off. To start off with it is hard going as it is uphill. After half a mile we reach the top of a ridge and Garry gets his GPS out to set a course for the nest site. We see some grouse scuttering along through the heather. The moor is obviously well managed, a mosaic of burnt heather – differing heights of heather re-growth and some bare patches with standing water. Grey rocks everywhere with sphagnum moss and bright orange fungi in between. The female Merlin suddenly appears and cuts across the sky in front of us. It's much brighter now and Garry tells me that we're nearly at the nest. "Go slowly," he says as we approach a belt of taller heather. We push forward gently and after a few steps Garry points downwards. I inch forward cautiously, peering through the tall heather and there they are, three Merlin chicks crouching down in a shallow depression with splashes of mutes decorating the area around the nest. Their primaries, wing coverts and tail feathers are beginning to show well. On the nearest bird I can see the brand new BTO ring on its leg. I signal that I've seen enough and that we ought to go and cautiously we move away from the nest. I'm so glad I made the effort to join Garry and see the chicks before they fledged.'

As we walk back to the car we see the female Merlin in the distance, clearly keeping an eye on the nest. I thank Garry for the opportunity to see the chicks and he tells me that having checked the nest he thinks the three young Merlins will fledge in the next few days. They should be safe as there is no persecution of Merlin on this moor. It had been an exciting day with a satisfying ending. A week later Garry called to let me know that he had just visited the area again to check on the Merlins and that he had seen all three chicks flying over the moor close to the nest.

THE HOBBY

British Isles population (2009): 2,800 pairs (increasing)

It was hot and I was resting on the swing-seat at the back of the house. Shading my eyes against the glare I checked for any signs of activity. Nearby, a Spotted Flycatcher sat, hunch-backed, on its usual perch, the handle of a neglected spade. Beyond the two Sycamores at the bottom of our garden the water meadows bordering the river Wensum shimmered in the heat. With an audible click the flycatcher zapped an unwary insect. I watched it flutter up to its nest in the Wisteria behind me. Mason bees buzzed to-and-fro as they excavated galleries in the soft mortar of the cobblestone wall. Summer had been a long time coming but it was here at last. I made a mental note to water the plants that evening. All was well.

I was jerked out of my reverie by a commotion. Rooks from the nearby rookery were mobbing something out on the water meadows. I caught a fleeting glimpse of a bird of prey, a Kestrel, I thought. I dashed inside, grabbed my binoculars and hurried to see how a Kestrel had upset the tranquillity of the rookery. I was wrong – it was not a timid Kestrel as I had first thought but a swashbuckling Hobby scything through the sky, invading the Rook's airspace. I caught a glimpse of long dark wings, black head with matching moustachial stripe, slate-grey back and a slash of fox-red along its thighs and beneath the tail. That morning there had been a hatch of Mayflies and the Hobby was taking full advantage of it. Through my binoculars I could see the Mayflies bobbing and weaving over the gently waving meadow grasses.

The Hobby's hunting technique was breathtaking. After each stoop, successful or not, the falcon powered up, wings cutting through the air to regain its pitch, 100 feet above the ground. For a moment it was in limbo, suspended. Then the Hobby turned and sliced vertically downwards. As it raked over the meadow grasses its taloned feet shot forward to grab its prey. It was a yo-yo of a flight. I could see the prey transferred to the Hobby's beak as it climbed for height again.

While I watched, the Hobby carried out 30 or 40 hunting parabolas across the water meadows. By now she was opposite the rookery again and the Rooks renewed their harassing tactics. She led them on and just when it seemed that she might be overwhelmed she slipped with a flick of wings and tail between the top and middle strands of barbed wire fencing that ran along the banks of the river. Discombobulated, the Rooks scattered, overwhelmed by the Hobby's death defying flight.

It is only when viewed in close-up, rather than glimpsed in the cut and thrust of a hunting flight, that one realizes that the adult Hobby is an exquisite bird of prey. It is the intricate markings on the head that catch one's attention. The tip of the bill is black, shading through to blue-grey. The cere and orbital ring are yellow and the eye is dark brown. The head and nape are grey-black and the cheeks are white, emphasizing a black moustachial stripe and downward extension of the ear coverts. The Hobby's back is dark grey-black merging into the upperwing and tail coverts and tail feathers. The primaries are black. The breast feathers are pale buff with bold dark brown streaks. The bird's 'trousers' and undertail coverts are a striking fox-red. The underside of the wings and tail are pale with dense, dark spots, forming bars, and the flight feathers are greyish with dark bars and a dark tip. The juvenile is similar to the adult but the feathers on the head and back, and the primaries and tail, are darker with buff edges. The breast feathers are also slightly darker

than in the adult with the same bold dark brown stripes but they lack the fox-red 'trousers' and undertail coverts.

It was not until the twelfth century that the Hobby was first identified and named by Giraldus Cambrensis (*c.*1146–*c.*1220). W.B. Lockwood's *The Oxford Dictionary of Bird Names* published in 1993 states that the name Hobby comes from the Old French word *hobé*, to jump about. It goes on to suggest that the name probably arose in relation to hawking, referring to the well-known agility of the Hobby in pursuit of its prey. Giraldus Cambrensis was also the first person to identify the Merlin in his *Topographica Hibernica* written between 1183 and 1186. He travelled extensively and was principally concerned with birds of prey (falconry was then at its apogee). But he has two other claims to fame: he was the first to recognize sexual dimorphism in birds of prey, demonstrating that the female is usually bigger than the male, and also described population limitations in birds of prey. A translation by Forrester reads: 'It is, however, a remarkable fact in the history of this tribe of birds, that their nests are not more numerous than they were many centuries ago; and although they have broods every year, their numbers do not increase.' Put simply, this means that a certain area of land can support only so many birds. The supply of food limits the population and young birds therefore have to disperse or will die.

Sir Thomas Browne (1605–1682) in his notes on the natural history of Norfolk made one of the first recorded observations on migration: 'Beside the ordinairie birds which keep constantly in the country, many are discoverable both in winter and summer which are of a migrant nature, and exchange their seat according to the season, those which come in spring coming for the most part from the southward, those which come in the autumn or winter from the northward.' He went on to note: 'The Hobby and Merlin would not be omitted among hawks the first coming to us in the spring, the other about the autumn.'

Sir Thomas Browne undoubtedly provided information and sketches for Willughby and Ray in their *Ornithologia* (1678). Here we find the first full description of the Hobby and mention of the use of Hobbies in catching larks: 'The Hobby is a bird of passage, yet breeds with us in England. Its game is chiefly larks, for the catching of which birds our fowlers make use of it thus. The spaniels range the fields to find the birds: the Hobby they let off, and accustom to soar aloft in the air over them. The larks espying their capital enemy, dare by no means make use of their wings, but lie close and flat upon the ground as they can, and so are easily taken in the nets they draw over them. This kind of sport is called daring of larks.' Eleazar Albin (1692–1742) copied this account of 'daring' of larks, word for word, when describing the Hobby in his *Natural History of Birds*. Alongside the text is what is probably the first accurate illustration of a Hobby in colour.

The Hobby was given its official name, *Falco subbuteo*, by Carl Linnaeus in 1758 in his *Systema Naturae*. The term *subbuteo* was used by Aristotle (384–322 BC) to describe a group of birds of prey that he called 'half buzzards of the broader kind.' He was hedging his bets, grouping together a number of different species, probably including the Hobby, which he could not identify.

The Hobby arrives in the British Isles to breed during the last two weeks of April and the first two weeks of May. It breeds over a very large area in the northern hemisphere – from the British Isles in the west right across Europe, Scandinavia and Russia to Kamchatka in the east and the island of Hokkaido in the north of Japan. The Arctic Circle is its northern breeding limit and in the south it breeds from Spain through the Mediterranean to China but to the north of the Middle East, Afghanistan and India.

Hobbies migrate south to their winter quarters from the end of September to the middle of October. The majority of birds breeding in Europe, Scandinavia and western Russia head for Africa. Leslie Brown in his *New Naturalist* book *British Birds of Prey*, first published in 1976, gives this eyewitness account of Hobbies in their winter quarters in Africa: 'I am not familiar with the Hobby in its British haunts, but I see far more Hobbies in Kenya each year than most people in Britain see in their lifetime. I have seen as many as two hundred Hobbies in a large scattered flock, hunting flying termites, and have driven for miles through country where rainstorms had recently brought out these insects, seeing a Hobby every few minutes. Especially I remember one evening in November 1948, when I was lounging at dusk, enjoying a sundowner outside my tent in a remote part of the thornbush of Embu district. A flock of Hobbies streamed overhead for ten or fifteen minutes, going to roost on a steep hillside behind me. I did not count them, but suppose that two or three hundred must have passed over in that time. They had been hunting flying termites in the evening, following a rainstorm, and were all going to bed with full crops.'

Where Hobbies nesting on their eastern limit migrate to remains a mystery. Some may make for Africa, others may head for India, Nepal, Bangladesh, Burma and southern China.

The Hobby used to be considered a rare bird in the British Isles, a survey undertaken in 1967 giving an estimate of fewer than 100 breeding pairs. In his monograph *The Hobby* published in 1999, Anthony Chapman meticulously charts the factors that favoured increasing numbers of Hobbies breeding in the British Isles. The late Peter Prince and the late Dr Roger Clarke, who undertook research from 1993–5 at a study area just outside Cambridge, found that several factors helped the Hobby population to expand. Reduced numbers of gamekeepers allowed the population of Carrion Crows to increase, providing second-hand nesting accommodation for Hobbies, warmer conditions due to climate change may have caused an increase in insect prey, and flooded gravel pits and old peat diggings may have provided better hunting areas. More recent research has shown that the increased abundance of two dragonfly species, the Common Darter and the Migrant Hawker, in August and September has resulted in increased post-fledging survival rates of young Hobbies.

It was Steve Parr, working for the Countryside Council for Wales, who found that the number of breeding Hobbies reported to the Rare Breeding Birds Panel had risen dramatically between the mid 1970s and the end of the 1980s. From just 65 pairs in 1973 the figure had risen to an estimate of 500–1,000 pairs in 1990. Dr Mark Eaton of the RSPB recently told me that the latest survey, carried out by the RSPB in 2009, estimated a total of 2,800 pairs in the British Isles and was still increasing.

With the Hobby population booming, Bruce Pearson and I wanted to watch the birds as they arrived in the British Isles at the end of their spring migration. Everyone told us that the National Nature Reserve at Shapwick Heath in Somerset should be our destination. This was a regular site where good numbers of Hobbies dropped in to feed up after the rigours of the long flight from Africa before departing for the areas where they would nest.

Shapwick Heath National Nature Reserve was once covered by the sea. As the ground dried out reedbeds took over. They, in turn, were replaced, successively, by sedgebeds and wet woodland, the rotting vegetation building up and turning to peat. Neolithic man colonized the area 6,500 years ago, settling on the dried-out land, and built wooden tracks to cross the wet areas. One such track is now known as the Sweet Track, named after Ray Sweet who discovered it in the 1970s. It was probably the Romans who first realized that Shapwick's peat when dried out was an excellent source of fuel for cooking and keeping warm, and for hundreds of years peat continued to be cut out by hand. It was in the 1950s that peat harvesting for horticultural use began on an industrial scale at Shapwick, using heavy-duty caterpillar diggers. The large-scale extraction of peat left large expanses of open water and, in 1961, the areas where the peat had been exhausted and the surrounding land, were designated as the Shapwick Heath National Nature Reserve.

You do not have to be in a hide to view Shapwick Heath's most famous attraction – its murmuration of Starlings. Every evening between November and February millions of Starlings in great flocks put on an aerial display at Shapwick that is unsurpassed. Like iron filings in thrall to the artistic passion of a magnet, they twist and turn before being released to drop and settle in the reedbed to roost. But what Bruce and I wanted to see were Hobbies, and lots of them. We checked with the reserve office and were originally recommended 10 or 11 May as the most suitable dates, but because of the cold spring it was subsequently suggested that we postpone our visit until the following week. The following are extracts from my journal:

> '13/5/13. 10.30. Driving along the A41 past Bicester Bruce suddenly shouted, "Hobby! Hobby! Hobby!" Wonderful. I couldn't see it of course as I was on the wrong side of his car. I hope it's a good omen for our trip to Shapwick.'

> '14/5/13. We stayed with Linda Bennett and her husband, David, who made us very welcome. Left at 09.00 and arrived at Shapwick at 10.15. The weather was fine at first but turned to rain with strong wind. Met by Simon Beard (Education Officer) and

Simon Clark (Reserve Manager). Taken on a recce of the reserve, which is enormous. An industrial site, abandoned after all the peat destined for gardeners had been dug out, was how Simon Clark described it. Great care has been taken to retain any original features – wet woodland, grassy meadows, ditches and drains and, at the same time, take advantage of the outcome of the peat extraction that had created open stretches of water, islands and reedbeds. We were taken to the Decoy Hide (there are five hides altogether) where we had an excellent view over open water to reedbeds, skeletons of trees dotted about here and there and willow scrub. In the background was Glastonbury Tor. Hundreds of Swifts, Swallows and House Martins were hawking for insects over the water, but no Hobbies. A Marsh Harrier wafted across the reedbed and we heard a Bittern booming. We left the Decoy Hide and drove along the track that runs alongside the main drain. At the wader scrape we saw a Great White Egret – they nested here last year for the first time. On the way to another hide we saw an exceptional stretch of wet woodland, a mix of Alder, Hawthorn and Oak. The grassy meadows are dissected by drainage ditches which are edged by stands of Alder. The wet woodland habitat is excellent for butterflies. Then we returned to the visitor centre so that I could interview Simon Clark.'

I asked Simon how big an area the reserve covers and he told me, "The National Nature Reserve here at Shapwick is 500 hectares but if you take into account the other partner reserves around us, RSPB, Somerset Wildlife Trust and the Hawk and Owl Trust, you're probably getting on towards 1,500 hectares altogether."

Apart from the Starling roosts what else is Shapwick famous for, I asked? Simon explained, "The public associates Shapwick with the Starling roosts, these big roosts have probably been forming here for 15 years and the area is quite famous for that. But, in general, Shapwick is particularly popular with the bird-watching community for the variety of species they can see, Great White Egrets, Marsh Harriers, Bittern … and that's just around the reedbeds. There's also a rare dragonfly, the Hairy Dragonfly. We've got open water, areas of fen, wet meadows that are packed full of wildflowers and wet woodland. White Admirals, Purple Hairstreaks and Silver-washed Fritillaries and Argent & Sable moth are just some of the butterflies and moths found on the reserve. The Lesser Silver Diving Beetle is a rare beetle that thrives in the ditches running through the meadows and there are also Great Crested Newts. We monitor their population by trapping them in empty two-litre coke bottles. You immerse it in the water so there's an air bubble at the top of the bottle. The newts investigate but can't get out. So you check the bottles in the morning and release the newts."

I was aware that Shapwick had a thriving Water Vole population and asked Simon about this. He explained, "Yes, Shapwick is one of the key national indicator sites for Water Voles and we do have a very strong population. John, one of our reserve managers, has just started monitoring a series of dedicated ditches, checking for signs of feeding, the use of burrows or males marking their territory. It is a burgeoning population and we often get reports of herons and otters predating them. On one of the lakes there's an island with an old tin shed on it. A pair of Barn Owls nest there and when we went out to collect owl pellets we found there was a colony of Water Voles below the owls' nest box. They seem quite happy to be there despite the ferocious predators perched above them."

I asked if people came to Shapwick with the sole purpose of seeing Hobbies and Simon said, "Certainly. I met a gentleman on the reserve the other day from South Africa. He'd come all the way here to see the Hobbies because he'd been told it was the best place to see them." What was the most he'd ever seen in one day? "About 50, in one patch of sky, in one go. The most we've seen so far this year in a day is 25. At this time of year we have early emerging dragonflies and damselflies and St Mark's Flies. For the Hobbies it's a kind of fast-food restaurant – they come here to build up their reserves again after the long migration flight. Then they will fly on to nest elsewhere. I hope you have better luck tomorrow." The following is an extract from my journal for the following day:

'15/5/13. 10.00. Sunny with blustery wind. We're at Shapwick Heath National Nature Reserve overlooking Noah's Lake. It's a large expanse of water dotted with islands, on one of which is the shed used by nesting Barn Owls. On the far side of the lake there are meadows in which cattle are grazing. Shapwick village with its church nestles in the wooded hillside beyond. Bruce is sitting sketching on the edge of the lake. I'm watching from the car. It's cold. There's plenty of activity over and around the lake. Swifts, Swallows and House Martins are hawking for insects low over the water. One Swift flashes past the vehicle, flicks over in a quick half-turn narrowly missing Bruce. There's a Mute Swan nesting on one of the islands and there are plenty of duck out on the open water – Mallard, Gadwall, Tufted Duck and Pochard. Bruce shouts "Hobby!" and points towards the right-hand shore of the lake. It is overgrown with clumps of willow, out of which dead trees are etched against the brightening sky. "There's another one – low down – right to left!" Bruce shouts. I get an excellent view of it as it flashes past round a reedbed studded with scrub. Bruce then points out where a Hobby is perched in one of the dead trees. I get an excellent view of it, black head, white throat with moustachial stripe, dark vertical stripes on its breast and a hint of foxy red by its legs. After a while we work out what the Hobbies are doing. On the right-hand edge of the lake there's a break in the clumps of Willow, forming a glade about 50 yards long. At either end of it are fallen dead trees projecting out of the scrub and sedgebeds. The Hobbies are using this sheltered area, a pocket of warm air, flying from one dead tree to another to hawk for insects. A Great White Egret flies in from across the lake and lands in the left-hand dead tree which the Hobbies are using as a perch. The egret looks very elegant. One of the Hobbies completes a hunting circuit and lands in the same tree as the egret but lower down. The four Hobbies are now hard at work flying back and forth in a loop pattern across the glade, snatching up insects as they go. At the end of a hunting flight one of the Hobbies lands in

the dead tree close to the Great White Egret and receives an admonitory tap on the head for its impudence. It flies off. We had enjoyed a good morning's birding. We had seen Hobbies hunting, and the Great White Egret administering a reminder to the Hobby of its place in the great pecking order of birds was a splendid bonus.'

After a lunchtime snack Bruce and I head off with Simon Beard, the Hawk and Owl Trust's Schools and Community Officer, to be shown round the Trust's 130-acre Shapwick Reserve. I can see that it has great potential but at the moment it is just a vast expanse of closely cropped meadows intersected with ditches. One area was on slightly higher ground and looked particularly interesting. In the background was a stand of willows and Alder and in front of that cattle were grazing on a rough meadow with good grass, plenty of docks and rushes in profusion. It would be good for Snipe, I thought. On the boundary of the reserve a hide had been built that looked down and across the rushy meadow. There was a prominent sign indicating that this was a Hawk and Owl Trust reserve, with a map showing where you were. On our way back I saw there was a Badger sett and suggested to Simon that it might be worth building a viewing platform so that visitors could watch Badgers and their cubs in the spring.

Simon Beard dropped us back at the visitor centre and I went off to find Chris Sperring, the Hawk and Owl Trust's Conservation Officer for the south-west of England, as I knew he wanted to talk to me about the reserve. We sat down and I asked Simon how it got started. He explained, "One day I was driving along one of the droves, that's what roads are called on the Somerset Levels and because of the peat foundation you can literally feel the road going up and down as you drive along. They're not very wide and as I was going round a corner one day I almost hit a vehicle coming the other way. In it was one of the wardens from the Shapwick Heath reserve, Melvyn Yandell. Melvyn jumped out of his car, came running over, and said 'Chris, thank God I've seen you – would you like to buy a reserve?' That's how it all started. Melvyn told me that there were 130 acres of arable land for sale on the edge of his reserve. I had this vision of turning land that had been intensively farmed into an area that would be a major bonus for wildlife. I went to see Barbara Handley, the Chairman of the Trust, and asked her what she thought. I think it only took half an hour to hatch a plan about how we'd raise the money – and the rest is history. So, we've now got the reserve, and it's going through a period of arable reversion. This means that it has to be intensively grazed, which is against my nature of course because I'm keen to encourage voles and voles need lots of long, tussocky grass. I've got to be patient, though, as the land has got to go through this process to reduce the nutrients in the soil that have resulted from growing arable crops. It is work in progress, a transition from arable land to an area that will eventually become totally wild. It's going to be absolutely fascinating."

After we had finished, Chris asked what luck we'd had with the Hobbies. I told him that the better weather this morning had brought them out and we had had some good sightings. Chris wondered whether we would like to hear his Hobby story. "Of course," I said, and Chris explained, "Very late autumn, 2012, we had an amazing Hobby incident. We don't normally get Hobbies where I live in Portishead, which is in north Somerset but that day in a particular field that we call the Old Primrose Field – because it's the only field locally that has Primroses – a group of seven Hobbies, obviously just passing through, suddenly appeared. But what happened next, which my partner and I saw, was a pure coincidence. While we stood there, two Sparrowhawks – both females – came out of the wood separately and started attacking the Hobbies. We then witnessed a battle between two predators – the low-level ground-hugging Sparrowhawk and the aerial Hobby. What was interesting was that, after each attack, the Sparrowhawks would retreat to the woodland – their domain – and the Hobbies would rocket up into the sky – their domain – as fast as they could. Then, when you could only just see them, they'd turn and stoop vertically like a miniature Peregrine Falcon, almost striking the Sparrowhawks as they patrolled the edge of the wood. It was absolutely unbelievable and one of those experiences that, as a naturalist, you have once in a lifetime. It's something you treasure forever." Chris told me that he had taken photos that day but acknowledged that they were not very good: the action had all taken place at breakneck speed and in poor light. Bruce and I thanked him and made our way home.

The next day I remembered hearing of some brilliant photographs of a Hobby catching dragonflies taken by Martin Hayward Smith. He's not only a photographer but also a very successful wildlife cameraman. I rang and asked if I could come over and talk to him. A few days later I went to meet Martin at his cottage in Norfolk. It is an idyllic situation with a good sized garden, which has a pond that is often used as a film set, and a small stream that wends its way behind his house. There are various barns and outhouses, one of which has been converted into a holiday home, and nest boxes everywhere. It's a fabulous place and little wonder that Martin's called his home Tickety Boo Cottage.

Before I started interviewing Martin I was anxious to see his tame Stoat and her three young, known as 'kits'. Martin took me into one of his outhouses, gently pulled down a shutter and there she was lying in her den with the kits snuggled up to her. Martin pointed out the Closed Circuit Television (CCTV) cameras monitoring her every activity. Inside his cottage Martin switched on his computer and there on the screen was the Stoat's den. It looked totally realistic and was not over-lit. The Stoat and her kits were relaxed and they were behaving completely naturally, as they would in the wild. Martin told me that he could actually sit at his desk in front of his computer and record the behaviour of the Stoat family, zooming in and out as he wished, without them being aware of it at all.

I asked Martin how he became interested in wildlife photography. He explained, "I suppose my love of nature came from living in the countryside. As a young school lad of about eight or nine, I used to go off down the river, down to the reedbeds, into the woods, all on my own. My parents didn't mollycoddle me at all. The only time I got scolded was if I was late and our tea had got burnt in the oven. I'd come back with a few birds' eggs in my pockets which I'd identify from my *Observer's Book of Birds' Eggs*. It's up there on the shelf somewhere with little ticks against eggs I'd collected. It would be illegal nowadays but it's just one of the ways you learnt about birds and fieldcraft."

"What about photography, how did you become interested in that," I asked? Martin replied, "My father was a press photographer for the Eastern Daily Press. As a lad I used to go into the Fakenham office and watch my dad at work. Later he would let me help with the processing of his films, the fixing of the black-and-white prints. To me it was pure magic watching this image appear in the tray of liquid in front of me. I was lucky to learn in that way, but of course it was ages before I could combine photography and my love of wildlife."

I said that I could understand how Martin's two interests melded together but asked him how he took his wonderful shot of a Hobby catching a dragonfly? He replied, "A couple of years ago I was walking round the Sculthorpe Moor Nature Reserve just checking what was around when I spotted this little silhouette on the top of a tree that overlooked the wader scrape, a man-made lagoon. As I watched, it left the branch, came swooping across the water, and grabbed a dragonfly. I thought this is fantastic. I quickly nipped into the Paul Johnson hide opposite the wader scrape and got set up. The wind direction was right, the sky was blue and there wasn't too much ripple on the water. I waited and while I did so I was thinking how I associated different birds of prey with Second World War aircraft. Buzzards, to me, are Lancaster bombers, Sparrowhawks are like Spitfires, and I think Hobbies as they come stooping out of the sky are like Hurricanes. At that moment the Hobby came out of the sun and straight down across the water. Although there are dragonflies above the water, you're not looking at those, you're tracking the Hobby through the camera and then taking photographs. You're on the fastest shutter speed possible to freeze the action, with hopefully the dragonfly in shot as well. So you're taking these photographs and it's not until you've stopped – again, thank God, for digital cameras – that you can look at the screen on the back of the camera and think, 'Yeah, what a fantastic shot I've just got!' It was amazing to see this one solitary bird doing its aerobatics over this very small lagoon. It would fly straight towards you and bank, perhaps four metres away, that's what made it so special. It would fill up on dragonflies and then go back and sit on a dead branch in the willow tree preening itself – and then after 15 minutes would just do it all over again. It was just absolutely out of this world to watch this small falcon manoeuvre over the reedbeds, come in, spot what it was after and nail it. Photographing that Hobby was very, very special. A couple of days later, off it went and I was left with some fantastic photographs. It's great to share them with you because, to be honest with you, no one else has seen them; they've just stayed on my computer."

The photo I picked out, which I considered to be the best, showed the Hobby flying over the lagoon towards the camera, slightly left to right. Studying it carefully, I could see that it was a juvenile as it had no foxy-red trousers. The shutter had closed catching the Hobby's wings halfway through the down beat, its legs were lowered ready to strike, and its eyes were locked with laser-like accuracy onto the dragonfly a yard away from death.

Bruce Pearson and I made a wildlife series in the early 1990s for Channel 4 called *Birdscape*. For it we needed film of a Hobby catching dragonflies so I immediately contacted Simon King, as he was the acknowledged expert at filming Hobbies. In 2013 I asked Simon how he got started and he explained, "I started my apprenticeship as a wildlife cameraman with Hugh Miles. He was making a film about British raptors and he asked me to go and film Hobbies catching dragonflies on the lagoons and boggy places on Dorset heathland. I love Hobbies, I love their athleticism, their aerial skills. They are small, not thugs like Peregrine Falcons, so manoeuvrable. They have loads of spirit. They are masters of the air. They stoop down, line up on their prey, steady themselves with their tails, stretch their taloned feet right forward until they are almost under their beaks and grab their prey. They tear the dragonfly apart on the wing and are then off on another hunt."

I was to learn eventually that the contest between Hobbies and dragonflies was not as one-sided as I had originally thought. Years later, there was a BBC *Springwatch* sequence featuring Simon as he was filming a Hobby catching dragonflies. The background was a wide stretch of water, willow scrub, sandy heathland and a spinney of conifers. Simon was using a high-speed camera and starts by telling us, "Having just had a quick review of the shots I've taken, it amazes me how often the Hobby misses the dragonfly. The dragonfly taking evasive action is a real battle of aerial aces, it's a dogfight." Simon starts filming the

Hobby as it stoops down to catch a dragonfly. Excitedly he swings round to address the camera: "I've just seen something amazing. I've seen a dragonfly, and I had no idea they could do this, taking evasive action, diving into the water to escape the Hobby. I don't think this has been documented before, it's unbelievable. The dragonfly is flying and goes straight into the water as the Hobby turns in for the kill. That's mind-blowing."

I asked Simon whether he thought this tactic was a calculated risk, whether it was better to risk getting stuck in the water rather than flying up to avoid the Hobby's clutching talons, and he told me, "I saw it happen so many times that it wasn't purely coincidental. The dragonflies learnt that if they took evasive action and dived into the water the Hobby would abandon its attack. They were much more likely to survive that way than if they flew upwards. There was a risk of course that they might not be able to break free of the meniscus, the surface tension of the water, but it's a better risk than being grabbed and eaten."

I used some of Simon's footage of Hobbies catching dragonflies to intercut with Bruce sketching Hobbies nesting nearby on Canford Heath in Dorset. Bruce described the difficulty of sketching such a fast-moving bird: "Sketching birds in flight is something that always excites me, an attempt to catch the very essence of the bird. The single, sudden dash of a passing Hobby is not enough and the action must be repeated. The longer the observation and the more frequently the actions are repeated, the nearer I feel to distilling that essence of the bird. I've missed out this time in my quick thumbnail sketches, I've made the wings too pointed."

A few days later Bruce returned to Canford Heath to catch up with the Hobbies again. "I had more luck when I was lying on a warm bank in the sun watching dragonflies flying around a boggy hollow. Suddenly, there was a flash of wings and the Hobby sped past. I was too slow to see what happened but as the Hobby slowed and gained height I could see it bring one foot forward to its beak and start dismembering one of the dragonflies I had been watching."

The Hobbies that Bruce had been sketching were nesting in a nearby spinney of conifers. Hobbies are late breeders, nesting in July and August. This is a good time for them to nest as by then there are plenty of small, inexperienced birds on the wing, easy prey for an aerial predator like the Hobby. A local firm erected scaffolding, stage by stage, so that Maurice Tibbles, a great character and a wonderful wildlife cameraman, could film from a hide the Hobbies rearing their three chicks. One of the Hobby chicks was still covered in down, unlike its siblings which looked almost ready to leave the nest. As Bruce pointed out, this was a kind of insurance policy; if there is plenty of food the youngest will eventually get a meal – if not, it will perish.

I remember that at this stage in our filming schedule for *Birdscape* we were desperate for a shot of a nesting Nightjar as we could not find one in Dorset. Maurice suggested calling Chris Knights, farmer, wildlife cameraman and stills photographer, and offering him a day in our Hobby hide if he would film a Nightjars' nest in Norfolk for us. Chris agreed, got the Nightjar shot for us, and then went down to Canford Heath. As he described, "It was a massive platform on top of professionally erected scaffolding – very health and safety conscious. By now the young were quite big and more or less ready to fly. Both adults were bringing in food, small birds, I think. That tower platform was luxurious, very different from the one I once built for Hobbies in an Ash tree – that hide was really rickety! People always ask me why it takes so long to get photos from a hide and I have to explain that it's no good at all trying

to hurry. If you put up a hide, you've got to let the birds get used to it and this takes time, especially with a bird like the Hobby. I remember one particular Hobbys' nest, though – we'd put up half the scaffolding, taking it very easy, and when we came back one day there was the male Hobby perched on it. On another occasion, we'd built a hide in a tree where there was a Sparrowhawks' nest. I was climbing up the scaffolding with another person behind me carrying the camera and when we got in the hide the Sparrowhawk came back, stood on the nest, which was about 15 feet away, and glared at us for about ten seconds. Then, as though nothing had happened, it settled down and started brooding. That just shows you how some birds are. They are all individuals, like human beings, and none of them react the same."

Some of the best films I have seen featuring birds of prey have been made from hides perched on scaffolding. There are limitations, though, and it requires great fortitude to be penned up in a hide for 72 hours. There is always the chance that you may miss the 'money shot' for which you have been waiting because you are uncomfortable, checking the camera or just nodding off. Peter Dobson of Carnyx TV specializes in wildlife monitoring and installs tiny cameras based on those used for 24-hour CCTV surveillance of garage forecourts. Recently he was kind enough to send me a DVD showing his coverage of a Hobbys' nest in the New Forest. The following are the notes I made while watching it:

'10 July. The nest is in an old crows' nest in a Scots Pine. The first of a clutch of two eggs has hatched. The female arrives at the nest with a small bird and feeds the newly hatched chick minute slivers of flesh. Nearby, perched on a dead branch, is the male Hobby on look-out.'

'13 July. The second egg has hatched. The female settles down to brood the two chicks. The next day the female brings in the carcass of another small bird that the male has caught and plucked. The eldest chick grabs at the food. Is the younger chick going to get fed? It suddenly perks up, gapes and is fed.'

'15 July. There's a change-over. The female takes over from the male, which has been brooding. She has just settled down when she suddenly becomes alert and then with the speed of light, calling incessantly, speeds off the nest. Her calls as she circles round and round the nest site become more and more aggressive. The two chicks acted instinctively, have frozen and made themselves as small as possible. What is it that threatens her and the two chicks? Later it pours with rain. The female returns, spreads her wings out halfway, acting as an umbrella. The chicks, their downy feathers dry, keeping peering out from under the female's bedraggled, soaking wet wings.' Afterwards I asked Peter Dobson what had caused the disturbance. He thought it was probably a Carrion Crow being inquisitive or a Grey Squirrel on the prowl.

'21 July. The female Hobby and her two chicks have dried out. The male calls to signify that he's brought in a kill. Over the next four days we see how much food the chicks pile in.

Six feeds a day. This is a critical time and they are growing fast. Their feathers are pushing out through their baby down. Any deprivation now will weaken the shafts of those long primaries soon to be scything through the sky.'

'25 July. More rain.'

'28 July. When the male or female now brings in food it is just dropped into the nest. Chicks have become very 'grabby'. Sometimes the female holds onto the food so that it's shared out properly.'

'3 August. The two chicks are alone in the nest. The primaries, wing coverts and tail feathers of the eldest chick are well grown. There is some down still on the head and back. The other chick has still got a lot of down on it and is wing-flapping vigorously. The female brings in food and leaves. A terrific fight ensues between the two chicks as the eldest chick grabs the food, mantles over it. The smaller chick holding on to the other end of the prey item is completely smothered by the other chick's wings and body. The female Hobby flies in. That is enough of a distraction for the larger chick to let go. The smaller chick grabs the food and backs into a corner of the nest.'

'8 August. Both chicks are ready to fledge. More and more wing-flapping to develop pectoral muscles. Parent birds call to them now, trying to entice them off the nest. The larger chick makes a short flight off the nest. It will return to roost on the nest at nightfall.'

'13 August. The smaller chick backs up to edge of the nest, squirts out a jet of faeces and, flapping madly, moves across the nest and takes off. Later, against the evening sky, it is seen walking along one of the uppermost branches of the Scots Pine.'

Four weeks later the two youngsters set out on the 8,000 kilometre flight to their winter quarters in Africa.

It is when they start hunting on their own that juvenile Hobbies suffer casualties. In 2012 Bruce and I visited the Raptor Foundation just outside Cambridge where there was a male Hobby with a broken wing that was being cared for. Simon Dudhill, trustee and manager of the raptor hospital, met us and told us about the bird's history. The Hobby was brought in on 25 August and was diagnosed as having an injury to the carpal joint on its left wing. The wound was cleaned and because the bird was dehydrated it was given a critical care formula. It had to be force-fed with dead mice and day-old chicks and on 31 August was seen by a vet specializing in birds of prey and x-rayed. It was found to have an open fracture to the left wing that had to be pinned with a steel rod. The bird remained with the vet until it was returned to the Raptor Foundation on 11 September. The wing could then be fully extended and was expected to heal. Over the next ten days the Hobby was self-feeding and doing well. On 26 September it was returned to the vet and the steel pin was removed. There was some concern about the bird's overall condition and blood tests were taken. On 28 September the Hobby was collected from the vet, fed well and cast up a pellet. To give the bird more exercise it was moved to a slightly bigger aviary, where it was able to flap its wings well. On 10 October the results of the blood tests came back showing that it had parasites in its blood. The Hobby was put on a course of Lariam but unfortunately didn't improve and was found dead. As Simon concluded, there was only so much one can do. A simple blood parasite can hamper a bird's ability to get strong enough to fly again in the wild.

The following year, Steve Thornton and Derek Holman, whom I had met when I was studying the Red Kites at Rockingham, and who knew that I was interested in Hobbies, asked me whether I wanted to watch Hobby chicks being ringed. Three days later Nigel Middleton, The Hawk and Owl Trust's Conservation Officer for East Anglia, and I met Steve and Derek at Fermyn Country Park. This is an extract from my journal:

'20/8/13. 14.00. Steve and Derek first took us to Lowick Wood. We parked about 150 yards away from the wood in which a pair of Hobbies had nested. The two young were perched in a dead tree. Luckily Derek had his telescope with him and I was able to get a good view of the rather drab young. One of the adults brought in food. What a contrast to the juveniles with its slate-blue back, Johnny Depp pirate's moustache etched against the white collar and russet pantaloons. Then we were off to Lilford Park. On the way I spotted a Hobby flying along the hedgerow. It power-climbed and then stooped down – presumably to catch a dragonfly that it had spotted in the meadow grasses. We followed Steve and Derek into Lilford Park. Immense trees, beautiful parkland and Lilford Hall in the background. We parked near the old aviaries. The nest was in an oak tree, in an old crows' nest in the crown of the tree. For the past three years this pair of Hobbies had nested within 50 yards of this tree, always in an old crows' nest. Sam, the climber, was quick to get organized and in no time at all had lowered two bags containing the two chicks. Derek was set up on the tailgate of his car. The chicks, which were still downy with tail feathers and primaries just showing, were about 14 days old. They were measured, weighed and then ringed. Nigel, under instruction, was allowed to ring one of the chicks. He was delighted. It was a very good day.'

Lord Lilford (1833–1896) was an enthusiastic amateur ornithologist. He was brought up at Lilford Hall and the surrounding countryside provided ample opportunity for exploring the natural world. He kept all kinds of animals – Badgers, armadillos and eagles, to name but a few. When he inherited Lilford he built a series of aviaries to house the birds he had collected. Lord Lilford is most often remembered for bringing Little Owls to the British Isles from Holland during 1888–1890 and releasing them in Northamptonshire. They spread from there to Rutland by 1891 and to Bedfordshire the following year. His greatest achievement was the production, between 1885 and 1897, of the *Coloured Figures of the Birds of the British Isles*. There were seven volumes and Archibald Thorburn was his principal artist. Bruce gave me his thoughts on Thorburn: "I was very influenced by him when I started painting birds. I slavishly copied his bird illustrations in my copy of T. A. Coward's *Birds of the British Isles and their Eggs*. I think a lot of his work was done from skins. He got the overall look of the bird right but it wasn't a study of character." Lord Lilford was a perfectionist and was quick to point out errors but was also lavish with his praise. The following are extracts from some of his letters to Thorburn. '8 July 1888: The angle of eye in Teal is rather too acute. 17 April 1889: The eagle is perfect with the exception of the iris, which should, I think, be a shade lighter in colour. 2 May 1890: We are both delighted with your beautiful picture of the eagle, which has just arrived. I most gladly retain it, and shall always treasure it, for my heart is very often in the Highlands amongst the eagles and the wild deer.'

Lord Lilford was keen on all field sports, particularly falconry. In a letter dated 3 August 1888 he writes, 'My falconer took two very young Hobbies yesterday from a big nest in a tall oak tree about 150 yards from that out of which he took three on 28 July in 1886 and 1887.' Lord Lilford found it very frustrating that his falconer could not train Hobbies to fly well and offered a good price for any trained Hobby that would do so for larks; the difficulty being in getting them to fly at all. Lord Lilford always used to refer to Simon Latham's book on falconry *The Faulcons Cure and Lure*, published in 1633. Latham was extravagant in his praise for the Hobby: 'She will show herself a hawk to please a prince, for you may fly her twenty times in the afternoon when no other hawks will fly, but must be waited on.' He goes on to say that the Hobby will fly partridges, quails, larks, and all in the most perfect manner.

I asked Jemima Parry-Jones, expert falconer and conservationist, for her opinion on the Hobby and she told me, "They are dynamite birds to fly to the lure. They never seem to tire and I've flown them until I thought my arm was going to drop off. They never look as if they are going to catch feathered prey. Wild Hobbies are insectivorous until they've got young to feed and will then go after Swallows and House Martins that have just left the nest. My father, Philip Glasier, once trained a Hobby, a rescue bird that had fallen out of its nest. That definitely used to go up high, but only to catch insects."

I am standing by the old aviaries at Lilford Park and can see the hall across the parkland in the background. I can imagine Lord Lilford at his desk writing a letter: 'Is there yet a chance? Will someone read up Latham and other old hawking books, try if they can to extract a hidden hint, and give their whole mind to practice in the field?' As I stand looking through my telescope at the crown of the oak tree I can see two Hobbies, newly fledged from the crows' nest in which they were hatched. They are fluttering from branch to branch. I realize that I am very lucky to be watching Hobbies at Lilford in the shadow of a man whose constant daily endeavour was to encourage interest in living creatures and, quite humbly and simply, to help others through what he himself had learnt.

How Lord Lilford would have enjoyed Philip Glasier's account of watching a family of Hobbies at Kingley Vale near Chichester in West Sussex. It is a final paean to the flying ability of the Hobby: 'These four, consisting of Mum and her three offspring, were chasing a Swift. The Swift easily avoided the youngsters' efforts, eluding them with deft twists as they endeavoured to foot him. Mum, obviously fed up with her children's fumble-footedness, decided that a demonstration was called for. She suddenly changed gear, from a slow, easy beat to a clip of the wings that gave her a power push with each quick thrust as she climbed up. The Swift was rapidly pulling away, a great gap between them. Still the old Hobby climbed, till she was some 200 feet higher. Then she turned down in a shallow-angled stoop, her speed increased still more by her wing-beats. She turned the pace on and the gap that had been several hundred yards began to close at a fantastic rate. It was like a racehorse, flat out, coming up on a lumbering old carthorse. Now, in just the same way, the old Hobby came up on the Swift. This time there was no side-slipping, no dodging out of the way. She simply put out one foot and took him with no trouble whatsoever. Her children had had a demonstration that was perfect. There was no doubt in my mind that a Hobby was the fastest British bird.'

THE PEREGRINE FALCON

British Isles population (2002): 1,500 pairs (increasing)

I am watching a Peregrine Falcon preening. It is perched on the edge of a nest platform high up on the spire of Norwich Cathedral. Down below I can see a portion of the Cathedral Close and, beyond that, playing fields, tennis courts, the prison on the hill in the distance and the inner ring road below it which follows the river Wensum round to Norwich railway station. It is a female Peregrine, always known as the 'falcon'. She is a third larger than the male which is always referred to as the 'tiercel', hence tierce, a third. Watching the falcon I can see the wind ruffle her breast feathers and the glint in her eye as she watches a pigeon pass overhead.

It is the falcon's eyes that compel attention – large and with a brown iris. If scaled up in proportion, our eyes would be as big as grapefruits. The size of a falcon's eye and an area on the retina known as the 'fovea', which is crammed with rods and cones, gives them eyesight that is eight times more acute than ours. The falcon scratches the feathers behind her bill and immediately a grey film, the nictitating membrane, closes over the eye to protect it from the needle-sharp tips of her talons. The eyelids are yellow and the feathered area below the eye is black, helping to minimize glare, and this marking continues down either side of the face to form the characteristic pirate's moustache. The yellow, waxy cere, containing the *nares* or nostrils, stretches round and above the slate-blue, black-tipped bill. A tooth and notch in the bill enables the falcon, if necessary, to administer the *coup de grâce* to its prey on the ground.

The Peregrine's plumage shades from dark grey at the head through blue-grey on the back to a paler blue at the rump. The tail feathers have dark bars and a pale tip. The back and wing coverts have transverse bars with straw-coloured edges and the primaries are dark at the tips with faint transverse barring along their length.

The falcon busies herself preening her breast feathers, pulling them through her bill and adjusting them just so. The feathers are white, decorated with tiny black streaks over the crop region, leading down through black spots, crescents and arrowheads to strong horizontal barring on the lower breast, flanks and thighs. Underneath these feathers is pure down that provides better insulation against cold or heat. She raises her right foot and picks at a bit of dry skin on one of her toes. Her legs are short and she has big, powerful feet armed with razor-sharp talons. There is an oil gland at the base of her tail and she busies herself anointing her head so that she can rub it over her plumage to weatherproof it.

Finally, the falcon pulls her primaries through her bill, facing forward to align the barbules on the leading edge and leaning over her back to align those on the trailing edge. The primaries, the secondaries and the tail feathers have stiff quills. They are the feathers that drive and steer the Peregrine through the air at high speed and enable it to catch its prey. The falcon leans forward, raises her tail and squirts a stream of cream-coloured faeces onto the belfry below. She fluffs up her feathers, rousing, leans forward and drops off the nest platform to dive down over the Cathedral green and away into the distance.

The Peregrine Falcon is described by Leslie Brown in his *New Naturalist* book *British Birds of Prey*, published in 1976, as 'the world's most successful bird. It is a matchless flier and a spectacular predator, killing almost all its prey in flight with a stoop of dazzling velocity and accuracy.' The speed at which a Peregrine stoops has been variously estimated from over 100 miles per hour to a staggering 275 miles per hour, although there have always been arguments over the reliability of these estimates.

To settle this argument, Leo Dickinson, a cameraman and sky-diver, teamed up with Lloyd Buck, a bird-trainer for the film and television industry. Lloyd trained three falcons, Lucy, Sage and Willow, to follow a lure, a yellow bean-bag, weighing just over 1lb. Lloyd started by flying them from a tethered balloon. At first they were easily distracted by other birds flying in the neighbourhood. They also had to cope with carrying a tiny accelerometer strapped to their backs, which measured the G-forces recorded during the flight. After a while, they were stooping and catching the lure before it hit the ground with no problem at all. Leo and Lloyd discovered a bridge over a 500-foot deep ravine in Italy that was ideal for their purposes. They realized that if the falcon was held back slightly after the lure was dropped, it had to fly really hard to catch the lure before it hit the ground. Timing was everything. Was the camera ready? Was the falcon ready? Lloyd looked at her anxiously – was she keen? "Wait! ... Wait!" The falcon squirted a jet of faeces down into the ravine below. "Ready!" The falcon roused, fluffed up her feathers. She was prepared to go. "Set!" The cameras starting turning. "Go!" The lure was dropped and the falcon cast off. Realizing she needed greater speed, the falcon started pumping her wings to catch up with the lure. This first time she didn't make it, but over several days the delay in releasing the falcon was varied. On one flight, the accelerometer showed that one of the falcons had pulled 6G (six times the force of gravity) and reached a speed of just under 200 miles per hour in less than two seconds. It was no wonder that the Peregrine was the falconer's favourite bird.

One of the best Peregrines I ever saw that was trained to fly at game belonged to Tony Huston. He was married to Margot, sister of the present Marquess of Cholmondeley, owner of Houghton Hall in Norfolk. I went hawking with him several times during the 1980s, both at Houghton and just outside Burnham Market in Norfolk. I can remember one peerless day in October when we were on Beacon Hill and Tony's pointer, Nelson, was working out in front seeking out a covey of partridge. Suddenly Nelson came to a point, rigid as though cast in bronze. Tony removed the hood, leash and jesses from the falcon, let her rouse and cast her off into the wind. Up and up she went, working hard, ringing up into the sky, Tony keeping an eye on her all the time as we quickly made our way round to a position upwind of the covey of partridges. By now the falcon was 600–700 hundred feet up, a mere dot in the sky. Tony watched and as she turned towards him downwind he shouted at Nelson to put the covey up and they shot up in a 'bomb-burst'. The falcon wheeled, closed her wings and stooped vertically, the air rushing through her primaries sounding like tearing linen, before levelling out and knocking one of the partridges out of the air. Feathers blowing in the wind were all that remained to remind us of such a lightning strike.

The origins of falconry are probably to be found at the end of the last Ice Age, suggests Gordon Robinson in his excellent book *The Sinews of Falconry* published in 2003: 'Ice-age Man had begun the laborious task of domesticating wild animals; wolves and jackals (from which all dogs are descended), sheep, cattle, goats, pigs and horses.' Man then would certainly have seen Peregrines and would have been in awe of their sky-scything stoop as they killed their prey. He would have found that the Peregrine's tractable temperament allowed it to be readily trained to provide a variety of food for hungry mouths. Falconry developed and spread along three separate lines: the trade routes from China, from the Indus valley (what is now Pakistan) and from the Middle East. It was at Khorsabad in Persia that a bas-relief of a falconer holding a hawk was discovered, dating from over 3,000 years ago.

The slow-moving caravan trains trading into Europe gradually brought with them the art of falconry, the practice of which was established in England by Anglo-Saxon times. The falconer would have been on horseback flying his falcons from the fist if he was after cranes, kites or rooks. For all other quarry the falcon was trained to 'wait on', circling high overhead, 500 feet up, waiting for partridge or duck to be flushed out by dogs. Whichever method was used, the initial training involved carrying the falcon to get it used to everyday sights and sounds, a process known as 'manning', and 'breaking it to the hood'. The hood was made of leather and there was a knack, only achieved by practice, in popping it onto the falcon's head and pulling the leather braces shut with one's teeth.

It would be the falconer's task to know which falcons were keen and the order in which they should be flown. Judging whether a falcon was fit to fly was not as exact a science as it is today. Now falcons are weighed every day, their behaviour noted in a daybook and their rations altered accordingly. Previously the falconer felt the big pectoral muscles and took a judgement on whether the bird was fat or lean. But there was one golden rule that still applies: 'don't try to fly your falcon 'till it has roused, shaken its feathers, and done a shit!'

The Bayeux tapestry created after the Norman conquest of the Saxons depicted King Harold carrying a hawk on his fist. Falconry received a big boost from the returning Crusaders, since they brought with them expertise gleaned from Middle Eastern falconers. One of the Crusaders was the Holy Roman Emperor Frederick II. He published the first book on falconry in 1250 AD. From then on, for the next 400 years, falconry flourished on a par with hunting and fishing. The population of Peregrine Falcons in Britain in thirteenth century has been estimated to have been about 2,000 pairs. In the thirteenth century there is the first written evidence of a particular eyrie (nest site), on Lundy Island in the Bristol Channel from which Henry III bestowed falcons 'to his beloved cleric Aid de Eston'. It was common practice for landowners of estates on which Peregrines bred to have to supply eyasses, birds taken from the nest, as a form of rent. Falconry reached its peak during the reigns of the Tudors. It was a sport for aristocrats, for those who could afford to employ falconers and build mews where their birds were housed.

Falconry continued to flourish under successive kings. It faltered under Cromwell's Commonwealth and was driven underground for a time, but kept going. Cromwell himself was a keen falconer and even found time to stop at some fields just outside Aylesbury to fly his falcons after his great victory at Worcester. In Antonia Fraser's biography of Cromwell published in 1973, she tells us that a Puritan satirist aimed a vitriolic dart at him: 'Do you not hawk? Why mayn't we have a play?'

Falconers up until the eighteenth century called their Peregrine Falcons either 'Blue Hawks (when referring to a bird in adult plumage) or 'Red Hawks' (when referring to one in its first-year that has not yet moulted). In 1250 AD, Albertus trapped a migrant Peregrine and called it Falco Peregrinus. In 1678 John Ray adopted the name and Anglicized it as Peregrine Falcon. In 1735 Carl Linnaeus devised a simple method of classifying species in the natural world and in 1771 the Peregrine became formally known as *Falco peregrinus* (*Falco* after its sickle-shaped bill and *peregrinus* meaning wanderer).

It was the invention of the shotgun and the Enclosure Acts at the end of the eighteenth century that saw an end to falconry as a means of putting food on the table. However, the killer blow was delivered by the passing of the Game Act of 1831, which legalized the role of gamekeepers and protected game birds reared for shooting. A relentless onslaught ensued against the Peregrine; it was easy, with the much-improved shotgun, to pick them off at their traditional nesting sites. Eventually there was public revulsion at the unremitting slaughter of birds of prey, and in 1880 the Wild Birds Protection Act was passed, giving them protection during the breeding season. Another 74 years were to elapse before all the British birds of prey, apart from the Sparrowhawk, were at last granted year-round protection by the Bird Preservation Act of 1954.

In 1954 my prospects were on the up and up, too. I had made my first film, which had been shown in the cinemas and now I knew what I wanted to do as a career. I read everything I could about Peregrines, re-read Henry Williamson's book *The Peregrine's Saga*, published in 1923, and plunged into Francis Heatherley's *The Peregrine Falcon at the Eyrie*. Dr Heatherley was a heart specialist at the Manchester Hospital. He was a keen bird-watcher whose hobby was photography, and combined these two passions to produce this extraordinary book, the first detailed study of a pair of breeding Peregrine Falcons in the wild. He watched them for three years and took excellent photographs of the adults and their four young. It was published by *Country Life* in 1913. In his foreword he has a swipe at egg collectors who ruined his second season's watching: 'This book is dedicated to all egg collectors in the hope that some day they will realize that the shell is not the most important part of a bird's egg.'

Dr Heatherley begins his book by stating that he hoped '... my narrative may raise new friends for the Peregrine Falcon and other rare birds.' On 7 April 1912 he tells us that there was one egg. On 11 April a full clutch of four and on 16 May when he went into the hide for the first time, there were four chicks: 'The falcon flew off as we approached the eyrie, and she immediately started calling the alarm as she circled overhead. Her harsh cry seemed to me more like "*aitch, aitch, aitch*" than the "*kek, kek, kek*" in the books. The young formed a round heap, like a pancake raised in the middle. Already it was possible to distinguish two males by their smaller size; these were in the centre of the heap and underneath. The down on the chicks was thin, so that they looked a pinkish-white.'

The birds were watched for 13 days and nights, mostly by Dr Heatherley but relieved from time to time by six other trusted observers. Dr Heatherley liked his creature comforts; he had a mattress, a Jaeger sleeping bag with three blankets, pillows, sandwiches wrapped in greaseproof paper and thermoses of tea. The hide was lashed to the rocks by rope hawsers and was only five feet away from the nest ledge. He wrote, 'After 15 minutes the tiercel arrived with a mangled thrush. The young immediately came to life and squatted in a ring as he held the quarry under his talons and tore bits out of it with his beak: they whimpered and each, convulsing, raised its open beak in the hope of being chosen for the red morsel he held lightly in the tip of his beak.'

Normally, at this stage the falcon would brood the young until they were 14 days old, but she was always uneasy at the closeness of the hide and of the camera shutter. The tiercel was much more trusting: '... and feeling that the chance of photographing the tiercel at a distance of five feet was not an everyday occurrence, I rapidly exposed my last seven plates on him.' The photographs are magnificent and I particularly admire the one of the tiercel perched on a rock. He's looking directly at the camera, ready for flight – tailed fanned out and wings arching over his back. It's a masterpiece.

On 24 May one of the watchers recorded, 'At 4.50 a.m. the falcon is calling the long, drawn-out, gull-like food cry, to which he replies with the same cry and flies out to meet her. She transfers the quarry from her talons to his in the air. He brings it in, a Song Thrush, an adult, and quite intact, head and all.' Thrushes, Blackbirds and Puffins were the main prey brought into the eyrie. The falcon seems to have been a bit of a termagant, as the watcher continues: 'Then she broke her gloomy silence, and seemed to give him a bit of her mind. She was evidently in a towering rage. She hissed and clucked as he yelped and yapped. At one time she stood there like a fury, spitting and snarling at him. She took half a step forward as if for two pins she would kill him where he stood.' The watcher adds, 'If some may think this all rather far-fetched I recommend them to watch such wild birds at close quarters. I do not mean the broken-spirit wretches one sees in zoos.'

Dr Heatherley and his band of watchers kept detailed notes of behaviour and the food brought in. On 27 May, early in the morning, one of the watchers heard a shot fired and was concerned that the falcon had been killed. When Dr Heatherley took over he realized with alarm that the young had not been fed for six hours: 'At 1.30 the tiercel arrives with a whole unplucked Puffin. The chicks were simply ravenous, and pressed on him so that he was driven with his back to the wall.' Through 28 and 29 May there was a grim famine, with no food brought in at all.

On the 30 May at 6.30 a.m. the falcon brought in a bird: 'This long disappearance of the falcon gave rise to a great deal of discussion. We could not of course tell whether the falcon that turned up after the interval was the original or another pressed into service. I am rather inclined to the view that it was a fresh bird, owing to the bold way in which she came into the eyrie.'

By 6 June the young were wing-flapping and on 12 June Dr Heatherley recorded 'The young were scampering around and only one was left in the nest. I had nothing to do but listen to the old birds luring them farther and farther away to be fed.'

Dr Heatherley modestly concludes his story with this plea: 'Modern bird photography and nature study are, however, lifting the veil. In all this I wish it to be distinctly understood that I am simply a bird-lover with some knowledge of photography. What little experience I have of the official ornithologist makes me anxious not to be confounded by him, as I think the present mania for egg-collecting and bird-collecting deplorable, considering the difficulties it places in the way of study when so much remains to be learned of living birds.' It is a very thought-provoking book, which made an everlasting impression on me. I longed to see a Peregrine Falcon.

In the meantime I was busy making films. I had made five films for the BBC, one of which, *The Vanishing Hedgerows*, had won a prestigious prize at the 1973 Monte Carlo Festival, and another had been short-listed for a BAFTA. Then, in 1974, I read a book, *In the Shadow of the Falcon*, by Ewan Clarkson, which was to re-ignite my passion for Peregrines. The book told in quite simple terms of the roller-coaster fortunes of the Peregrine over the years, with particular emphasis on the organochlorine crisis that had so badly affected most birds of prey, but in particular the population of the Peregrine, which had been decimated.

I called Christopher Parsons, Head of the BBC Natural History Unit in Bristol and we met with Ewan Clarkson and also with a representative from the RSPB's Public Relations Department. Involving the RSPB was vital as we would need their co-operation in finding a suitable nest for filming. I started writing the script, and as this was to be the first major film on the Peregrine, I knew we must include a sequence on the vital work being carried out at Cornell University in the States on the captive breeding of Peregrines for reintroduction into the wild. Peregrines in the States had been affected even more severely by pesticides than those in Europe.

First we had to find a nest site that would allow us to get close-up shots of the parent birds as they reared their young. I had asked Maurice Tibbles to be my cameraman – he was originally a photographer at the *Daily Mirror* but left to concentrate on wildlife filming. By the time I met him, he had made several films in the *Private Lives* series for the BBC, including a highly acclaimed one on the Cuckoo. In April we travelled to Scotland to look for a nest site that would be viable for filming.

Roy Dennis, the Highlands Officer for the RSPB, was to be our mentor. He met us at Inverness Airport and off we went looking for a suitable site. Roy's reputation was formidable: he had worked for four years at Loch Garten as an assistant warden monitoring the return of the Osprey as a breeding bird, and then went to Fair Isle to run the bird observatory for seven years before being appointed the RSPB's Highlands Officer. Now he was responsible not only for the return of the Osprey but also for Peregrines, Golden Eagles and other rare birds found in the Highlands.

For days we scoured the Scottish Highlands for the perfect site. There were lots of glimpses of far-away Peregrines but no suitable nest ledges. Just when we were about to give up, Roy was contacted by John Lister-Kaye, a local naturalist, who knew of a site that might do. It was in Glen Affric near Cannich and the ledge had once been a Golden Eagle's eyrie.

As Roy, Maurice and I topped the hill overlooking the site, I was rewarded by my first good view of a Peregrine as the falcon circled slowly overhead, scolding us with her "*kek-kek-kek*" alarm call. Through my binoculars I could pick out the black horizontal markings on her chest and on her slowly beating wings. After a couple of circuits she landed on a rock above and to the right of the nest site where, she continue to harangue us.

Unfortunately, we could now see that there was no natural ledge nearby on which a hide could be placed. It would therefore have to be lowered into position and suspended using wire cables. BBC Bristol's design department produced some excellent Styrofoam cladding which, when painted, blended in naturally with the cliff.

The hide was lowered into position and secured. Roy told us that if the birds did not accept the hide within the next four hours it was to be cut down – end of film. Maurice took the first watch, watching from a look-out point on a hill overlooking the nest. His face as I took over from him two hours later told the story. The eyasses, Peregrine chicks, were huddled together at the back of the ledge and he had not seen either the falcon or tiercel. I settled down to wait and watch. Nothing happened during the first hour. Time was ticking away as I scanned the sky for either of the adult birds. There was about 20 minutes of the second hour remaining when the tiercel flew past the nest site and dropped some prey on the plucking rock. Shortly afterwards the falcon appeared, picked up the prey and flew towards the nest. The eyasses rushed forward, but she pulled out at the last minute. She tried another approach, again sheared off. Finally, on her third attempt, she flew right in, landed on the ledge and started to feed the eyasses. As soon as I was sure that the falcon was not spooked by the hide, I rushed back to Maurice yelling to him that everything was alright. For the first time in days his perpetual 'Eeyore' expression slipped and he looked happy.

The relationship between cameraman and director when filming wildlife is unique, my job essentially being to see that he had everything he needed to do his job. Either Roy or I saw Maurice into the hide and at the end of the day I would ferry the cans of film back to Inverness and make sure that the van from Denham Laboratories picked them up from London airport for processing.

Filming went well. The weather was excellent, the falcon was very tolerant and Maurice shot some excellent footage. The falcon was on or around the nest for the first fortnight, with the tiercel responsible for bringing in food. The falcon piled food into the four chicks and in the first fortnight they grew very quickly. They were getting up to eight feeds a day. Their original pure white down disappeared, to be replaced by a greyer down from which their flight and tail feathers were now appearing.

When he went down to ring the young Peregrines, Roy, who was appearing at intervals throughout the film, noticed the latest prey brought to the nest and commented, "Today, looking into the nest, I can see that it's not been a very good day for homing pigeons. There's probably been a race from Thurso over the Highlands and the tiercel has caught some of the stragglers going south."

Peregrine Falcons and carrier or racing pigeons have always sparked controversy. During the Second World War, Peregrines were outlawed because it was feared they might intercept important messages from downed airmen waiting to be rescued at sea. The Air Ministry ordered their destruction, and in a sinister move the British Museum of Natural History sought the co-operation of egg collectors in carrying out this work. After the war the population quickly recovered.

Twenty years later, it was ironic that the pigeon-racing fraternity in Wales, who for some time had claimed that Peregrines had been taking more and more of their best birds, should have been the spur that instigated a study. In 1960 they petitioned the Home Office, seeking an order to destroy Peregrines. The Home Office contacted the Nature Conservancy, which in turn asked the British Trust for Ornithology to organize a survey. Dr Derek Ratcliffe from the then Nature Conservancy was put in charge and the survey was launched at the end of 1960. The results were startling, showing that the occupation of breeding territories, particularly in the south of England and Wales, was down about 50%. Only the Highland region in Scotland was unaffected.

At this time, incidents of bird deaths were being reported in the Press. In the spring of each year large numbers of birds were found dead, particularly in East Anglia. In one area of 593 hectares, which included areas of woodland, it was estimated that 5,688 Wood Pigeons, 118 Stock Doves, 59 Rooks and 89 Pheasants died. In 1961 the mystery was solved: cereal crops were being dressed with the organochlorine pesticides dieldrin and aldrin as protection against wheat bulb fly. Pigeons, the main prey of Peregrines, fed on the newly drilled wheat and in no time at all had ingested a lethal dose of the pesticide. A Peregrine feeding on a pigeon containing dieldrin or aldrin would not die straight away, it was much more insidious than that. Gradually, over time, as the Peregrine ate more and more affected prey, substantial quantities of pesticide built up in its body. This had two effects: first, it affected the bird's breeding performance and secondly, in certain cases, it caused death.

This is Dick Treleaven's account from his book *Peregrine* published in 1977: 'May 28th 1961. She mounted in the wind on outstretched wings and climbed to approximately 150 feet – then crumpled in the air, going into what I can only describe as a flat spin, revolving like a top, completely out of control. She drifted inland and fell into a field of corn. I ran over and picked her up – she was still panting hard, her eyes opening and shutting – a sign of inevitable doom known to everyone who has kept a hawk. A sticky, brownish liquid dripped from her beak. I kept vigil with the falcon until midnight. I rushed down first thing in the morning. She was dead. The dead falcon arrived at Cambridge and was later transferred to another organization, where, through an unfortunate misunderstanding outside my control, it ended up in a dustbin without any analysis having been done. As far as I am aware, this was the first occasion that the corpse of a Peregrine had been found since the link with toxic chemicals had been under scrutiny. It might have provided an invaluable basis for research on the effects of toxic residues on the food chain. A great opportunity was missed.'

Derek Ratcliffe was keen to unravel the mystery of why the reproductive capacity of Peregrines was being compromised. In 1951 five out of ten eyries that he visited held broken eggs. On 10 April he saw a falcon pecking at something in its nest. He climbed up to the site and saw that it was one of her own eggs that she had been eating. During the next five or six years other observers commented on broken eggs and of the falcon eating broken eggs. Since this phenomenon had become common after the introduction of pesticides, was this the link?

As a first step, Dr Ratcliffe started weighing eggs laid during the pesticide crisis and comparing them with eggs collected during the 1930s. There was an average difference of 0·69 grammes. This was a big step forward. Now he needed to check the thickness of the shell over the same period. This process was what we filmed Dr Ratcliffe re-enacting.

Using a micrometer, he demonstrated that up until 1947 there was a constant shell thickness and that thereafter it diminished by 20%. The same decrease in shell thickness was found in other birds of prey, particularly in Sparrowhawks, Merlins and Golden Eagles. Further research showed that the pigeon 'fancy', as far back as 1946, had been recommending using DDT, the first organochlorine pesticide to be developed, on homing pigeons to control parasites. This fact and the Peregrine's predilection for pigeons, homing or wild, was the final link in the chain.

To summarize, in 1946–7 when DDT was first introduced, the Peregrine population was at 90% of the pre-war level, estimated at 900 pairs. In 1955, when dieldrin was first marketed, the population was up to 95%. The crash started in 1957 and bottomed out in 1961 when a voluntary ban on the use of dieldrin and aldrin as dressing for spring-sown cereals, was implemented. The recovery in the Peregrine population started in 1964 and continued spectacularly, year by year.

Back at the eyrie we were filming in Glen Affric, the young Peregrines were fully feathered and engrossed in getting their feathers into working order, seeking out the last tufts of down and nipping out any parasites that may have come in with prey. There was plenty of wing-flapping to build up their big pectoral muscles and they spent whole periods just looking out from the nest site learning the geography of the glen, ready for their first flight. By 22 June two of the young had flown and the two remaining youngsters were quite capable of feeding themselves from a grouse that the falcon had brought in.

Earlier in the year, in April, I had gone to film the work of Tom Cade at Cornell University in the States, where the Peregrine population had been particularly badly affected. The aim of Tom's Peregrine Fund was to improve the husbandry required to breed Peregrine Falcons in captivity and to then reintroduce the resulting offspring back out into the wild in North America.

A hawk barn had been built comprising 36 aviaries each with separate breeding compartments. A corridor with one-way glass windows allowed each pair of birds to be viewed and they were also linked by an audio-system to a central control point so that courtship vocalizations could be monitored. When a clutch of eggs was laid, they were removed and placed in an incubator and turned six times a day. On hatching, the point where the chick was attached to the yolk sac was swabbed with antibiotics to prevent infection. To get the chicks to feed, Jim Weaver, the person in charge of the captive Peregrine Falcon breeding programme, imitated the "*chup-chup*" of the parent bird. This makes them gape so that they can then easily be fed with forceps. They were soon self-feeding and at two-and-a-half weeks old were reintroduced to their parents. In 1974 three pairs had reared 21 young and two others two young – a grand total of 23 young.

Some of those young were kept for breeding but the majority were destined to be returned to the wild. While we were filming there in 1975, Tom Cade wanted to reintroduce some captive bred birds at a traditional Peregrine nest site at nearby Taughannock Falls in New York State, last used in 1946. The original nest ledge had eroded away so an artificial site was created and three young Peregrines were placed in it to imprint on the site before they could fly. They were fed remotely down a chute so that they did not get conditioned to humans. When eventually they flew, transmitters on their legs enabled Tom's researchers to check where they were. The reintroduction was a great success and between 1977 and 1997 The Peregrine Fund reintroduced 3,300 captive-bred Peregrines back into the wild. They stopped then because their objective had been fulfilled.

At the end of June, back at Glen Affric, the nest was empty; all the young had flown. There were a few clumsy landings in the heather but day by day the young Peregrine's flying expertise improved. They were soon soaring with ease over the glen. One day the falcon flew in with a Carrion Crow and dropped it to test their skill in catching prey in the air. The four youngsters played 'pass the parcel' with it until one of them missed a catch and it fell into the heather. The parent birds could relax at last.

I made two further films on Peregrine Falcons, both of which were shot in Cornwall. In one of them Dick Treleaven told me about the first kill he had seen: "It was 10 June 1955 in the middle of the afternoon. The two adult Peregrines were airborne again, patrolling the cliff-face. Five minutes later I see a large party of feral pigeons flying along the coast and turn inland up the valley instead of continuing their journey north along the coastline. A moment later they caught sight of the falcon; they made a hurried U-turn and came back down the valley again, then swung low over my head, travelling parallel to the cliff-face. The tiercel reappeared from out of the sun in a stoop, with wings partially open and elbows well forward, streaked straight over me and into the middle of the flock, struck one pigeon hard on the back, bound to it amidst a cloud of feathers and lifted it out of the flock. It was all over in seconds and I could hardly believe my eyes. I made a note that the tiercel was slightly below the pigeons when he struck. The whole of the action took place at very close quarters; the feathers drifted lazily over my head and I stood up and caught two or three in my hand. I kept them in my birding cap for a couple of years as a lucky charm."

Dick also had this to say about the future of the Peregrine: "I think we've always got to be on our guard about the effect of new pesticides. Down here in Cornwall we do definitely have lower clutch sizes. It could be a density problem, it could be something else. Our recovery rate here is on a par with the west of Scotland. Inland sites are much better, coastal birds are always the first to suffer. We must always be on our guard."

Persecution of the Peregrine is still rife: poisoned bait is still being put out by pigeon fanciers to kill falcons, and on the grouse moors in the Peak District, the Pennines and the eastern Highlands in Scotland there is still wanton destruction of Peregrines. The adults returning to roost at their traditional eyries are particularly vulnerable to anyone with a night-sight and a rifle. When I think of this, I am always reminded of the phrase from the poem *A Sparrowhawk's Lament – Timor mortis conturbat me*.

The British population of breeding pairs of Peregrine Falcons in the British Isles in 2012 was probably over 1,500 pairs. In addition, there will be non-breeding birds, juveniles from the previous season, and unmated adults – perhaps another 300 birds, at least. As the population has increased, Peregrines have adapted to nesting in different locations – pylons, radio masts, bridges, tall buildings and churches.

In Henry Stevenson's book *The Birds of Norfolk*, published sometime prior to 1923, I found a reference to Peregrine Falcons and Norwich Cathedral: 'At the beginning of the nineteenth century a Mr Kittle noticed a Peregrine, which arrived at the cathedral by the middle of September, and left it about the first week of March, and continued to do so for eight successive years; he also remembered that it was generally to be seen near the top of the spire, and invariably on that side which by sailors is called the leeward, from which it used to fly at pigeons.' Mr Kittle went on to say that more recently a female that frequented the same spot was shot while chasing a pigeon on one of the bridges.

By coincidence, just before Christmas 2009, pupils at Norwich School, which is right next to the cathedral, spotted a pair of Peregrines and the news filtered through to me. I immediately contacted Nigel Middleton, the Hawk and Owl Trust's Conservation Officer for East Anglia and as a first step we agreed that I should ring the Bishop of Norwich, The Right Reverend Graham James, to let him know. I asked him if he would give us his blessing to put a platform for the Peregrines on the spire. He was enthusiastic and suggested I contact Phil Thomas, the Estates Manager. At the same time we formed a small committee to push the project forward. As well as Nigel and myself, this committee included Dave Gittens, who agreed to design the nest platform and organize cameras, Phil Littler, our ringer, and Stuart Horth, Chief Fire Officer of the Norfolk Fire Brigade, who would take care of safety issues as the platform was positioned about a third of the way up the spire. All this was going to cost money and Peter Cooper, chairman of our fund raising committee, worked hard twisting arms on the 'old boys' network. Firms and individuals were incredibly generous and we soon had the funds available to purchase two cameras and the materials for the nest platform itself. On 15 November 2010, John Fisher, biology master at Norwich School, reported seeing both tiercel and falcon present. The following are notes of progress from my journal:

'18/2/11. 10.00. To Norwich for installation of nest platform. Great teamwork carrying and pushing platform up to south-east window four days earlier so that it could then be painted in position. Tiercel seen on second brocket from top of spire by golden cockerel weather vane. Nigel said that the falcon had killed earlier. Gravel poured in and cameras fitted into position, one giving side view, other a 'top shot'. A freezing cold day.'

David Gittens reported that the cameras were working perfectly. He and Peter Grant, head of building works, had worked miracles putting up aerials (it was line of sight) from the platform to the roof of the library and then linking them by cable to the cathedral computer. For five days nothing happened, but then there was exciting news:

'25/2/11. My wife Liza shouted to me, "Peregrine's on the box!" Excellent news. It was the tiercel perched on the edge of the box, looking a bit nervous. He then hopped down into the box and inspected the gravel, looked around. The tiercel looks up and calls to the falcon

perched on a brocket above him. Shuffles around the box, checking it out. He calls to the falcon again and jumps to perch on edge of box. Stayed 31 minutes altogether.'

'26/2/11. Heavy rain overnight. Tiercel in residence. Very wet falcon arrives at 08.19. Comes back again at 08.47 and does some nest-scraping in gravel.'

'2/3/11. 09.55. Tiercel brings in a kill. His submissive behaviour, bowing and scraping, is part of the mating ritual.'

The pair had now bonded and established a routine. The tiercel guarded the nest platform at night and there was an excellent shot of him sleeping, his head under his wing. Then they would both fly off before dawn, the street lighting allowing them to hunt while it was still dark.

On 23 March disaster struck:

'23/3/11. 09.59. I was standing next to Richard Kemp, one of the top Anglia Survival wildlife cameramen, who was filming flying shots of the resident falcons. Suddenly there was a crescendo of screaming from the spire. Through my binoculars I could see a large juvenile falcon strafing the nest platform. The side camera showed the tiercel ducking each time the interloper made a pass. On one pass the falcon perched for a moment on the platform. The resident falcon was driven away and the tiercel joined the interloper and off they flew, soaring east, away into the distance.'

The tiercel was overwhelmed by the juvenile falcon. They went through a courtship ritual, mated, and on 24 April, against all expectations, she laid an egg.

'24/4/11. 07.21. Falcon drops down into box at 07.34. Very upright position, legs well apart, head high. Holds this position. Egg-laying imminent, I think. 08.13 egg is laid. Falcon shuffles around, covers egg. 10.13 flies off leaving egg exposed, wonderful burnt-sienna brown.'

By 29 May, as we were past our estimated hatching date, I had emailed Jemima Parry-Jones, world authority on birds of prey, for advice. She replied, 'I think you'll find that 33 days is the usual time for Peregrines, but they have been known to go for a little longer. As this is a very young bird and inexperienced, and only laid one egg, there is a high chance that it is not going to hatch. That is very normal for inexperienced birds of all species.' Sadly, that is exactly what did happen. On 6 June, about ten days after the latest expected hatching date, just before 1 a.m. the falcon broke open the egg to reveal the chick; it was dead.

Six months later I was again watching the Norwich Cathedral Peregrines on their nest platform. They went through their bonding display and were facing each other diagonally across the platform and bowing submissively to each other while calling *"chupp-chupp-chupp"* and an almost chick-like *"weep-weep-weep"*. Jemima Parry-Jones tells me that the female is a four-year-old bird, not last year's juvenile. They mated and I was sure everything was going to be fine. The following are extracts from my journal that year:

'20/3/12. 15.58. Tiercel arrives, looks a bit apprehensive. Falcon flies in. Ritual bowing. Falcon up onto perch, "kekking" away. Suddenly an intruder, another falcon, flies in and lands on the near perch for a nano-second. There is a burst of "kekk-kekking" from the resident falcon. The intruder skedaddles.'

'22/3/12. Last night at 22.15 the falcon was rather lethargic. Hadn't eaten the Blackbird that the tiercel had brought in. Should be good news in the morning. And so it was. First egg laid at 04.38. By the infra-red light the egg looks white, not chestnut-brown.'

By 30 March the falcon had laid her complete clutch of four eggs. I marvel at how, when the falcon takes over, she closes her talons to avoid damaging the eggs. The eggs are turned every 15 minutes or so and incubation takes from 28 to 33 days. The weather that summer was vile – but fair weather or foul the eggs had to be kept warm as they developed. The falcon often tucked her head under her wing for a catnap at night – brooding is so boring – and occasionally picked up a bit of bone and juggled with it.

'30/4/12. 14.08. Falcon incubating. Tiercel arrives and they change over. As he settles down to brood he clucks encouragement to the chick struggling to chip itself out of the egg. He cocks his head to watch the falcon fly overhead.'

'2/5/12. 08.05. Liza rang, "You've got a baby!" Anna, a life-long friend and devoted Peregrine watcher had phoned her with the news. At 08.20 Dave Gittens rang and confirmed it. I watched the falcon pull out the eggshell and crunch into the shell, sucking up any tasty fragments of albumen in the process. The still-wet chick was hidden behind her soft breast feathers.'

The tiercel and falcon take it in turns to brood the white, downy chick. The chick needs feeding and the falcon tells the tiercel to get out of the nursery and go hunting. For the next four weeks he will be the main food provider. Later in the day a second egg hatched. The tiercel brings in food, neatly plucked. Jan Smith, a Hawk and Owl Trust volunteer in charge of the marquee and volunteers on Cathedral Green, says that there is terrific interest in the newly hatched chicks. Volunteers answer questions and help visitors to get good views of the falcons through the telescopes provided.

'4/5/12. 13.40. Falcon eating eggshell. Third egg hatched. Tiercel made three kills this morning, one was stolen by a Herring Gull. 17.25. Change-over. Tiercel covering chicks only partially. Falcon brings in a kill and feeds chicks. She utters a "chup-chup" call to make them gape, then pops in a morsel of flesh.'

Twenty-four hours a day the adults are on duty, safeguarding the chicks, keeping them warm and fed. The remaining egg is not going to hatch; it's probably not fertile. The tiercel brings in a kill and is allowed to feed the chicks. Their original white down has been replaced by a mushroom-coloured down. The first signs of proper plumage are showing.

'18/5/12. A freezing cold afternoon with chill wind blowing. The falcon is trying to cover the chicks. One of them slips out behind and wanders off over the nest platform. The falcon sees what has happened, turns and follows the chick to the corner of the nest platform. She picks it up by the scruff of its neck, drags it back to the other chicks and resumes brooding.'

On 19 May, when the chicks are 21 days old, Phil Littler removes them from the nest platform so that they can be ringed. Each of them has a thin metal band attached to one of their legs; on it is a unique number and an address to be contacted if the bird is found. The unhatched egg is removed and sent away for analysis.

'26/5/12. 09.05. The chicks very active on the platform. They are wing-flapping and walking about. The two eldest have primaries beginning to show well. The youngest chick

has a deformed beak – the lower mandible is out of true on the left-hand side. 14.52.
Chicks were being fed by the falcon when an aircraft flew over. Both chicks and the adult
saw it and uttered their "kek-kek" alarm calls.'

I have been away in Scotland for a week watching Golden and White-tailed Eagles and
on the way back phone to ask after the Peregrines. I'm told the youngest chick, the one
with the deformed beak, is not likely to survive.

During my absence the other chicks have progressed well and are beginning to look like
Peregrines. Unlike the adults, with their slate-blue back feathers, their plumage is brown.
Their breast feathers are a very pale buff with dark brown vertical streaks and the tail feathers
have straw-coloured tips. The chicks have not got rid of all their down and their feathers are
still growing and have yet to harden off. It is vital that the chicks are not deprived of food
now; if they are, their feathers will show hunger traces, areas of weakness, and might break.

'10/6/12. 08.57. Smallest chick died yesterday evening. A dog barks below. The two eyasses
(unfledged chicks) peer down. Flies buzzing everywhere. The eyasses doze. A band plays
nearby and an ambulance wails along the inner ring road.'

'12/6/12. 04.45. Another intense, frenzied period of wing-flapping. The eldest eyass is
a tiercel, the other a falcon. So frenzied is the wing-flapping that the two eyasses for a
moment mesh together. The tiercel disentangles itself, steps back onto the ledge and, oops!

he's airborne. One of the adults shadows him as he makes his first flight. He makes a perfect landing on the belfry. 12.48. The eyass falcon, after more wing-flapping, was perched on the ledge. She started scratching and slipped. She ended up in the Bishop's garden to receive a rowdy reception from a family of Jays.'

In a matter of days the eyass tiercel was able to fly up and perch on the top crocket just under the Golden Cockerel weather vane. Andy Thompson, a Hawk and Owl Trust volunteer, records some stunning photographs of the two eyasses playing a game of aerial tag, honing their flying skills. They will be dependent upon their parents for another six weeks or so and then they will go off to seek their own territory. I watch the two adults return to their nest platform, bowing to each other, reinforcing the bond between them. It is a happy conclusion to a successful breeding season.

The Peregrine, whose scything stoop from the sky quickens the heart and gladdens the eye, is an intricate part of our life. At the top of the food chain, it is a prime indicator of our environment's health. The Peregrine Falcon is the Koh-i-noor diamond amongst our British birds of prey. We destroy it at our peril.

CONCLUSION

Bruce and I have come to the end of our quest to assess the state of the 15 birds of prey breeding in Britain. We now understand why the male Sparrowhawk of the fifteenth century, the musket, was right to be frightened of death, as encapsulated in the phrase in the poem *A Sparrowhawk's Lament, Timor mortis conturbat me.*

Although birds of prey have many physical qualities that we admire – the keenest eyesight, powerful talons and flesh-rending bills, thrilling hunting techniques, including the ability to stoop at 200 miles per hour to kill their prey – their pitch at the top of the food-chain is a fragile one. It is a finely balanced existence and they are very vulnerable.

We have nothing but admiration for all those working with birds of prey: scientists, conservationists and bird-watchers and, particularly, the writers, poets, artists, wildlife filmmakers and TV presenters who have done so much to change the public perception of these wonderful birds. There are some heartening stories: the Osprey is increasing, the Red Kite is expanding its range and the White-tailed Eagle is now firmly re-established. The Marsh Harrier is doing very well, the Montagu's Harrier shows a slight increase and the Goshawk is slowly spreading out from its strongholds. The Common Buzzard is now the most frequently seen bird of prey, the Golden Eagle is stable, the Hobby is steadily increasing and the Peregrine Falcon now breeds in every county in the British Isles.

On the other hand, it was sad to learn that some of our birds of prey are not faring at all well. The Sparrowhawk and the Merlin are in decline and the Kestrel is no longer our commonest bird of prey. Illegal persecution in pursuit of game preservation has affected the Red Kite, Goshawk, Golden Eagle and Peregrine Falcon. Disturbingly, indiscriminate and illegal killing continues and in 2013 the Hen Harrier virtually became extinct as a breeding bird in England. That is a disgrace.

Nearly 50 years ago I made a conservation film for the Jersey Wildlife Preservation Trust. The final scene was dramatic. Gerald Durrell was seated behind a desk, lit by a single candle. On the desk beside him were two downy bird of prey chicks. "Every year", he said, "we spend millions of pounds on man-made things and on beautiful buildings, monuments, libraries and art galleries to house books and works of art. But in a way, isn't the animal world God's art gallery, aren't the animals God's works of art? You can recreate an art gallery, but you can't recreate an animal species once it has been destroyed, and to exterminate an animal species is as easy as snuffing out a candle." Gerry's finger is poised over the candle flame. As he snuffed it out, the chicks disappeared into darkness.

FURTHER READING

Birkhead, Tim. 2008. *The Wisdom of Birds*. Bloomsbury.

Brown, Leslie. 1976. *British Birds of Prey*. New Naturalist Series No 60. Collins.

Brown, Leslie & **Amadon**, Dean. 1968. *Eagles, Hawks, Falcons of the World*. Country Life.

Buxton, Anthony. 1932. *Sporting Interludes in Geneva*. Country Life.

Carter, Ian. 2001. *The Red Kite*. Arlequin Press.

Clarke, Roger. 1996. *Montagu's Harrier*. Arlequin Press.

Clarkson, Ewan. 1974. *In the Shadow of the Falcon*. Hutchinson.

Chapman, Anthony. 1999. *The Hobby*. Arlequin Press.

Cocker, Mark & **Mabey**, Richard. 2005. *Birds Britannica*. Chatto & Windus.

Dare, P.J. 1998. A Buzzard population on Dartmoor, *Devon Birds* 1955-93.

Dennis, Roy, 1996. *Golden Eagles*. Colin Baxter.

Dennis, Roy. 2008. *A Life of Ospreys*. Whittles Publishing.

Gordon, Seton. 2003. *Days with the Golden Eagles*. Whittles Publishing.

Greenoak, Francesca. 1981. *All the Birds of the Air*. Penguin Books.

Gurney, J.H. 1921. *Early Annals of Ornithology*. Witherby.

Heatherley, Francis. 1913. *The Peregrine Falcon at the Eyrie*. George Newnes.

Hines, Barry. 1968. *A Kestrel for a Knave*. Michael Joseph.

Hosking, Eric & **Newberry**, Cyril. 1944. *Birds of the Day*. Collins.

Jameson, Conor. 2013. *Looking for the Goshawk*. A&C Black

Jonsson, Lars. 1992. *Birds of Europe*. Christopher Helm.

Kenward, Robert. 2006. *The Goshawk* T. & A.D. Poyser.

Lack, David. 1954. *The Natural Regulation of Animal Numbers*. Oxford at Clarendon Press.

Lockwood, W.B. 1993. *The Oxford Dictionary of British Bird Names*. Oxford University Press.

Love, John A. 2013. *The Saga of the Sea Eagle*. Whittles Publishing.

Lovegrove, Roger. 2007. *Silent Fields*. Oxford University Press.

Mabey, Richard. 2005. *Nature Cure*. Chatto & Windus.

Munsterberg, Peggy. 1980. *The Penguin Book of Bird Poetry*. Penguin Books.

Mynott, Jeremy. 2009. *Birdscapes*. Princeton University Press.

Moore, N.W. 1957. The past and present status of the Buzzard in the British Isles. *British Birds*.

Newton, Ian. 1986. *The Sparrowhawk* T. & A.D. Poyser.

Nicholas, W.W. 1939. *The Sparrowhawk's Eyrie*. Country Life.

Orchell, Jack, 1992. *Forest Merlins in Scotland*. The Hawk and Owl Trust.

Ogilivie, Malcolm & **Winter**, Stuart. 1989. *Best Days with British Birds*. British Birds.

Pearson, Bruce & **Burton**, Robert. 1991. *Birdscape*. Harper Collins.

Pearson, Bruce. 1991. *An Artist on Migration*. Harper Collins.

Prytherch, Robin. 2013. The breeding biology of the Common Buzzard. *British Birds*.

Rackham, Oliver. 1986. *The History of the Countryside*. Phoenix Press.

Ratcliffe, Derek, 1980. *The Peregrine*. T. & A.D. Poyser.

Robinson, Gordon. 2003. *The Sinews of Falconry*. Self-published.

Treleaven, R.B. 1977. *Peregrine*. Headland Publications.

Tubbs, Colin R. 1974. *The Buzzard*. David & Charles.

Watson, Donald. 1977. *The Hen Harrier*. T. & A.D. Poyser.

Watson, Jeff. 2010. *The Golden Eagle*. T. & A.D. Poyser

White, Gilbert. 1789. *The Natural History of Selborne*. B. White and Sons.

White, T.H. 2007. *The Goshawk*. Jonathan Cape.

Yalden, Derek & **Albarella**, Umberto. 2009. *The History of Birds*. Oxford University Press.

ACKNOWLEDGEMENTS

To paraphrase T.S. Eliot, 'It's the journey not the arrival that matters.' Writing A *Sparrowhawk's Lament* has been a long journey and I want to remember all those who have supported me: Bruce Pearson, who has been at my side throughout the journey producing the exquisite black-and-white field sketches that accompany the text; Sarah Whittley who, when I was at my wit's end, pointed me in the right direction; Richard Mabey and Mark Cocker who kindly read what I had written and gave me constructive advice; Ian Newton who told me what aspects of a Sparrowhawk's life I should study; Dave Culley for introducing me to his web-site, Sparrowhawk Island; Eddie and Tina Anderson, who, ably abetted by Mick Carroll, were my ideal travelling companions; and, finally, Ian Carter and Stephen Moss who volunteered to check the accuracy of what I'd written.

I interviewed a wide variety of experts for each of the birds of prey: Ian Newton, Dave Culley and Chris Packham for the Sparrowhawk; Roy Dennis and Tim MacKrill on the Osprey, Roy Dennis on the Golden Eagle; Roy Dennis, Lloyd Buck and Jemima Parry-Jones about the Peregrine Falcon; Steve Roberts, Bob Bijlsma, Andy Page, Chris Packham, John Harwood and Robert Baker for the Honey Buzzard; the late Barbara Handley, Peter Davis, Ian Carter, Karl Ivens, Steve Thornton and Derek Holman about the Red Kite; John Love and Dave Sexton for the White-tailed Eagle; John Buxton, Nigel Middleton and Andrew Bloomfield on the Marsh Harrier; Stephen Murphy, Richard Saunders, Jude Lane, Andy Dobson, Anthony Milbank, Chris Packham and George Winn Darley about the Hen Harrier; Bob Image, Andrew Bloomfield, David Lyles and James McCallum for the Montagu's Harrier; Robert Kenward, the Marchant brothers, Garry and Mike, and Noel Cunningham-Reid on the Goshawk; Peter Dare and Robin Prytherch for the Common Buzzard; John Videler, Phil Littler, Jason Fathers, Colin Shawyer and Nigel Lewis on the Kestrel; John Knight, Jack Orchell and Wilf Norman about the Merlin; and Simon Clark, Chris Sperring, Simon Dudhill and Martin Hayward-Smith for the Hobby.

I would also like to remember the late John Buxton, Roger Clarke, Dick Treleaven and Derek Ratcliffe. I was very lucky to meet and work with them.

At the Hawk and Owl Trust's reserve in Norfolk I talked with Nigel Middleton, Leanne Thomas, David Smith, Tim Smith, Geoff Clark, Eric Adnams, Derek Jennings, Graham Blanchfield and Vic Gerrard. At their reserve at Fylingdales Moor in North Yorkshire I met Fred Strickland Constable, John Edwards, John McEachan, Brian Walker, Tanya Eyre, Chris Hansell and David Hutton.

The Norwich Cathedral Peregrine Falcon project created great interest. Specifically I'd like to thank Phil Thomas, Henry Freeland, Peter Grant, Richard Vincent, Stuart Horth, Carrie Kerry, Jan Smith, Andy Thompson, Lin Murray, John Fisher and Benjie Wilcock amongst others for making it such a success. Gordon Brown, our vet, carried out post-mortems on the two eyass Peregrine Falcons that died in 2013.

Carole Showell, the librarian at the British Trust for Ornithology was especially helpful in unearthing papers and books that I requested. Mike Toms, Peter Lack, Graham Appleton and Simon Gillings all came up with the information I needed.

I would like to thank Lord Coke for giving me access to the Holkham Hall library, and Suzanne Reynolds, the curator, for very patiently sorting out the books I requested. Clare Castle at the Cambridge University zoology department's library also sought out reference books for which I asked.

The RSPB at Sandy and in Scotland were constant in their support. In particular I thank Jeff Knott, Mark Eaton, Helen Mason, Graham Madge Brian Reid and Lucy Tozer. Mark Percival at the RSPB film unit gave me access to the many first class birds of prey films they have produced. Madeleine Westwood and Mike Pinhorn searched for titles or photographs that I needed to view.

Stephen Moss, the original producer of the BBC TV series *Springwatch,* arranged for me to have access to the series which I felt had done so much to modify the public's perception of birds of prey for the better. Alan Baker, in charge of the archive, was briskly efficient as were Joanne Stevens and Catherine Cruikshank.

As a result I was able to contact the many wildlife cameramen, who had spent days and nights in difficult conditions, capturing stunning images of our birds of prey. Simon King, John Aitchison, Manny Hinge, Hugh Miles, Mike Richards, Rick Price, Mike Potts, Stephen de Vere, Richard Kemp, Ian McCarthy and Hugh Maynard all had fascinating stories to tell me. Peter Dobson and Nigel Bean described the development of CCTV cameras that allow close-up shots to be taken of birds of prey at their nest sites.

I particularly want to thank David Harsent for unravelling the religious implications of Gerard Manley Hopkins's poem *The Windhover* and for writing the elegant requiem in memory of the juvenile Hen Harrier known as *Bowland Beth.*

I cannot list all those who have helped me but these must be named: Dave Anderson, Phil Atkinson/BTO, Mark Avery, Simon Barnes, Rebecca Barnham, Steve Bennington, Tim Birkhead, Jeremy Brettingham Smith, Jonathan Brown, Nick Brown, David Chandler, Robin Chittenden, David Cholmondeley, Janis Clarke, David Clayden, Richard Cobham, Silvia Combe, David Connell, Peter Cooper, Andy Davis, Nick Dixon, Helga Dowie, Ed Drewitt, Lee Durrell, John Fanshawe, Anna Farlow, Jan Faull, Richard Fegen, Jane Fenton, John Flowerdew, Stephen Frank, Jonathan Elphick, Brian Etheridge, Robert Gillmor, Thom Goddard, Danny Green, Ian Grindy, Phil Gunning, Barbara Hall, Gina Harding, Bill Hesketh, Phil Holms, David Hosking, Caroline Hunt, Margot Huston, Tony Huston, Susan Jameson, Sophie Jewry, Alex Laver, Simon Lester, Richard Marriott, Bernie Marsham, Derwent May, Sally May, Anna McEvoy, Harriet Mead, Anthony Milbank, Steve Mills, Giles Morris, Bill Murphy, Lyn Murray, Jeremy Mynott, Malcolm Ogilvie, Dave Ovenden, Andrew Parkinson, Steve Petty, Graham Rebecca, Jayne Redpath, Mike Richardson, Douglas Russell, Norman Sills, Ashley Smith, David Smith, Gary Smith, Marjorie Stabler, Jo Stewart Smith, Jane Turnbull, Roger Upton, Lee Walker, Mark Watson, Matthew 'Chalky' White, Geoff Williamson, Richard and Ann Williamson, Peter Wilson and David Withers.

I owe a great deal to Judy Cox who copy edited my text, conforming it to the Princeton University Press 'bible', and also to Jayne Savage who transcribed the many interviews I recorded. At Princeton University Press I am grateful to Robert Kirk and David Campbell, and at **WILD***Guides* to designer Robert Still and copy editor Jessica Gotham. Working with my editor from **WILD***Guides*, Andy Swash, and his wife Gill, has been a great experience. Their kindness, good humour and close attention to detail, which they convey in a very relaxed fashion, has propelled the project forward from a gleam in my eye to the finished book.

And, finally, I want to thank my friends and family. During my research trips up and down the country they have looked after our home, walked the dogs and fed the chickens, and made sure the fox didn't get them at night. They were always curious about what I was doing and wanting to know when the book would be completed. I owe them a huge debt of gratitude and I hope that their faith in me has been repaid when they read the book.